FROMMER'S
A SHOPPER'S GUIDE TO
BEST BUYS IN
ENGLAND, SCOTLAND & WALES

FROMMER'S
A SHOPPER'S GUIDE TO
BEST BUYS IN
ENGLAND, SCOTLAND & WALES

by Vicki and Dick Johns

1986-87 Edition

Published by Frommer/Pasmantier Publishers
A Division of Simon & Schuster, Inc.
1230 Avenue of the Americas
New York, New York 10020

ISBN 0-671-55625-8

Manufactured in the United States of America

Design by Stanley S. Drate/Folio Graphics Co. Inc.

Although every effort was made to ensure the accuracy of price information appearing in this book, it should be kept in mind that prices can and do fluctuate in the course of time.

CONTENTS

INTRODUCTION

This book will save you money! The *Shopper's Guide to Best Buys in England, Scotland and Wales* lists hundreds of exciting, sometimes unusual places to shop for uniquely British merchandise. It is a must for every visitor to Great Britain who would like precise information on where to shop. It is also very useful for the resident who would like to discover new bargains throughout the country. *Even if you are not visiting Great Britain, you can still use this Guide!* Many famous British products can be ordered by mail. Even after the shipping and duty expenses, you can save up to 50% and more on the U.S. retail price of many items.

The *Guide* is easy to use, with maps and detailed information on department stores, boutiques, factory outlets, craft centers, and those fascinating out-of-the-way speciality shops that will truly turn your shopping into an adventure. We have concentrated on the most frequently purchased and the most famous British products.

The *Guide* is especially useful for budget-minded shoppers who are looking for special bargains. We have listed many factory outlet shops which sell famous products direct to the public at large savings. Many of these factories also have tours of their facilities. What a fun way to shop, meet the people, and learn about the country at the same time!

We also list some very expensive and exclusive shops, including a diamond outlet in London. Even if you don't buy anything, you'll enjoy browsing.

This is the first and only comprehensive guide to the great bargains in Great Britain's factory outlets and other shops. It is also the first and only comprehensive guide to factories which allow tours of their facilities.

There's something for everyone!

HOW TO USE THE SHOPPER'S GUIDE

You can find what you are looking for in three ways:

(1) Towns are listed alphabetically in the *Guide*. If you know the name of the towns along your itinerary, merely look up the names to find the best buys in town.

(2) If you want to shop for a particular item (i.e. fine bone china) look in the Product Index. All the towns and outlets which sell that item are listed.

(3) If you want to visit a particular company (i.e. Wedgwood) look in the Company Index to find where it is located.

It's as easy as 1, 2, 3!

TYPES OF SHOPS

We have listed the following types of shops in the *Shopper's Guide:*

(1) FACTORY OUTLETS. A factory outlet is a store which sells first and second quality items directly to the public, usually at a large savings. Outlets may or may not be located at the factory site.

Seconds or *irregulars* are items with small flaws which are often not very noticeable. For example, a crystal stemware second might only have a small bubble that will only affect its appearance. Many of England's world-renowned companies have such strict quality control standards that even their irregular merchandise is extremely fine. Many of the crystal and china companies sell only seconds. If so, we have noted this.

The merchandise offered at factory outlets may vary daily. If you see what you want, buy it. Next time you go back, the chances are it will be gone. Remember during Christmas and the tourist season, the merchandise turnover is very rapid.

(2) FACTORY SHOWROOMS. Many manufacturers have showrooms at their factories. These showrooms sell products direct to the public, usually at a large savings. Both first and second quality items may be sold.

(3) RETAIL STORES. We have included stores which have uniquely British products, or those which are otherwise interesting. They often do not have bargain prices, but they make for an exciting visit.

(4) CRAFT WORKSHOPS. These are small one-or-two-person shops where items are handmade by the owners. Don't expect fancy surroundings—some shops are in the owner's home. Do expect unique, handcrafted goods with a personal touch.

(5) CRAFT CENTERS. Craft centers sell products made by groups of local artisans. A visit to a craft center is a good way to see a number of craft items at one location. Most craft centers have craftspeople creating their products as you watch.

(6) **MARKETS.** Each town has its own market day, with local products being sold. We have listed some of the most popular markets, as well as those and some that are well-known for particular items.

SPECIAL NOTES

(1) The shops and outlets listed in this guide did not pay to be included.

(2) Every effort has been made to ensure the accuracy of the information in this book. However, changes in information and prices do occur. We encourage you before traveling any long distance to confirm the information. The prices listed are not binding and may change at any time.

(3) If you would like to see a shop or factory added to this book, please fill out the following form and send it to us. We will be sure to consider it for our next edition. If you find that any of the information we have listed is incomplete or inaccurate, we would appreciate it if you would send us the correct information. It will help us to keep the book current. Thanks!

To: Vicki and Dick Johns
     Frommer/Pasmantier Publishers
     1230 Ave of the Americas
     New York, NY 10020

Please note the following new/additional information for the *Shopper's Guide to England, Scotland and Wales.*

Name of Company: _____

Address: _____

Telephone: _____

Hours: _____

Currency: _____

Products: _____

_____

_____

_____

_____

_____

_____

Tours: _____

_____

_____

_____

Mail Orders: _____

_____

_____

Sender's Name: _____

Address: _____

_____

THE $25-A-DAY TRAVEL CLUB—HOW TO SAVE MONEY ON ALL YOUR TRAVELS

In this book we'll be looking at how to get your money's worth while shopping in Great Britain, but there is a "device" for saving money and determining value on *all* your trips. It's the popular, international $25-a-Day Travel Club, now in its 23rd successful year of operation. The Club was formed at the urging of numerous readers of the $$$-a-Day and Dollarwise Guides, who felt that such an organization could provide continuing travel information and a sense of community to value-minded travelers in parts of the world. And so it does!

In keeping with the budget concept, the annual membership fee is low and is immediately exceeded by the value of your benefits. Upon receipt of $18 (U.S. residents), or $20 U.S. by check drawn on a U.S. bank or via international postal money order in U.S. funds (Canadian, Mexican, and other foreign residents) to cover one year's membership, we will send all new members the following items.

(1) *Any two* of the following books
Please designate in your letter which two you wish to receive:

Europe on $25 a Day
Australia on $25 a Day
England on $35 a Day
Greece including Istanbul and Turkey's Aegean Coast on $25 a Day
Hawaii on $35 a Day
Ireland on $25 a Day
India on $15 & $25 a Day
Israel on $30 & $35 a Day
Mexico on $20 a Day
New York on $45 a Day
New Zealand on $25 a Day
Scandinavia on $35 a Day
Scotland and Wales on $35 a Day
South America on $25 a Day
Spain and Morocco (plus the Canary Is.) on $35 a Day
Washington, D.C. on $40 a Day

Dollarwise Guide to Austria and Hungary
Dollarwise Guide to Bermuda & The Bahamas
Dollarwise Guide to Canada
Dollarwise Guide to the Caribbean (including Bermuda and the Bahamas)
Dollarwise Guide to Egypt
Dollarwise Guide to England and Scotland
Dollarwise Guide to France

Dollarwise Guide to Germany
Dollarwise Guide to Italy
Dollarwise Guide to Japan and Hong Kong
Dollarwise Guide to Portugal (plus Madeira and the Azores)
Dollarwise Guide to Switzerland and Liechtenstein
Dollarwise Guide to California and Las Vegas
Dollarwise Guide to Florida
Dollarwise Guide to New England
Dollarwise Guide to the Northwest
Dollarwise Guide to the Southeast and New Orleans
Dollarwise Guide to the Southwest

(Dollarwise Guides discuss accommodations and facilities in all price ranges, with emphasis on the medium-priced.)

A Guide for the Disabled Traveler
(A guide to the best destinations for wheelchair travelers and other disabled vacationers in Europe, the United States, and Canada by an experienced wheelchair traveler. Includes detailed information about accommodations, restaurants, sights, transportation, and their accessibility.)

Shopper's Guide to the Best Buys in England, Scotland and Wales
(Describes in detail hundreds of places to shop—department stores, factory outlets, street markets, and craft centers—for great quality British bargains.)

Bed & Breakfast—North America
(This guide contains a directory of over 150 organizations that offer bed & breakfast referrals and reservations throughout North America. The scenic attractions, businesses, and major schools and universities near the homes of each are also listed.)

Dollarwise Guide to Cruises
(This complete guide covers all the basics of cruising—ports of call, costs, fly-cruise package bargains, cabin selection booking, embarkation and debarkation and describes in detail over 60 or so ships cruising in Alaska, the Caribbean, Mexico, Hawaii, Panama, Canada, and the United States.)

Dollarwise Guide to Skiing USA—East
(Rates and describes the many resorts in Massachusetts, Vermont, New Hampshire, Connecticut, Maine, Quebec, New York, Pennsylvania, plus new areas in North Carolina, the Virginias, and Maryland. Includes detailed information about lodging, dining, and non-skier activities.)

Dollarwise Guide to Skiing USA—West
(All the diverse ski resorts of the West—in California, Colorado, Idaho, New Mexico, Montana, Oregon, and Wyoming—are fully described and rated. Lodging, dining, and non-skier activities are also included.)

Frommer's Travel Diary and Record Book
(A 72-page diary for personal travel notes plus a section for such vital data as passport and traveler's checks numbers, itinerary, postcard list, special people and places to visit, and a reference section with temperature and conversion charts, and world maps with distance zones.)

How to Beat the High Cost of Travel
(This practical guide details how to save money on absolutely all travel items—accommodations, transportation, dining, sightseeing, shopping, taxes, and ore. Includes special budget information for seniors, students, singles, and families.)

Marilyn Wood's Wonderful Weekends
(This very selective guide covers the best mini-vacation destinations within a 175-mile radius of New York City. It describes special country inns and other accommodations, restaurants, picnic spots, sights, and activities—all the information needed for a two- or three-day stay.)

Museums in New York
(A complete guide to all the museums, historic houses, gardens, zoos, and more in the five boroughs. Illustrated with over 200 photographs.)

Swap and Go—Home Exchanging Made Easy
(Two veteran home exchangers explain in detail all the money-saving benefits of a home exchange, and then describe precisely how to do it. Also includes information on home rentals and many tips on low-cost travel.)

The Fast 'n' Easy Phrase Book
(The four most useful languages—French, German, Spanish, and Italian—all in one convenient, easy-to-use phrase guide.)

The New York Urban Athlete
(The ultimate guide to all the sport facilities in New York City for jocks and novices.)

Where to Stay USA
(By the Council on International Educational Exchange, this extraordinary guide is the first to list accommodations in all 50 states that cost anywhere from $3 to $25 per night.)

(2) A one-year subscription to *The Wonderful World of Budget Travel*

This quarterly eight-page tabloid newspaper keeps you up to date on fast-breaking developments in low-cost travel in all parts of the world bringing you the latest money-saving information—the kind of information you'd have to pay $25 a year to obtain elsewhere. This consumer-conscious publication also features columns of special interest to readers: **Hospitality Exchange** (members all over the world who are willing to provide hospitality to other members as they pass through their home cities); **Share-a-Trip** (offers and requests from members for travel companions who can share costs and help avoid the burdensome single supplement); and **Readers Ask . . . Readers Reply** (travel questions from members to which other members reply with authentic firsthand information).

(3) A copy of *Arthur Frommer's Guide to New York*

This is a pocket-size guide to hotels, restaurants, nightspots, and sightseeing attractions in all price ranges throughout the New York area.

(4) Your personal membership card

Membership entitles you to purchase through the Club all Arthur Frommer publications for a third to a half off their regular retail prices during the term of your membership.

So why not join this hardy band of international budgeteers and participate in its exchange of travel information and hospitality? Simply send your name and address, together with your annual membership fee of $18 (U.S. residents) or $20 U.S. (Canadian, Mexican, and other foreign residents), by check drawn on a U.S. bank or via international postal money order in U.S. funds to: $25-A-Day Travel Club, Inc., Frommer/Pasmantier Publishers, 1230 Avenue of the Americas, New York, NY 10020. And please remember to specify which *two* of the books in section (1) above you wish to receive in your initial package of members' benefits. Or, if you prefer, use the last page of this book, simply checking off the two books you select and enclosing $18 or $20 in U.S. currency.

Once you are a member, there is no obligation to buy additional books. No books will be mailed to you without your specific order.

PLANNING YOUR TRIP

INFORMATION SOURCES

The British Tourist Authority (B.T.A.) offers the visitor a vast number of booklets, brochures, maps and general information. They have national overseas offices to help make your trip more enjoyable.

B.T.A.
40 West 57th Street
New York, New York 10019
Tel. 212/581-4700

B.T.A.
875 North Michigan Avenue
Chicago, Illinois 60602
Tel. 312/787-0490

B.T.A.
612 S. Flower Street
Los Angeles, California 90017
Tel. 213/623-8196

B.T.A.
Plaza of the Americas
North Tower
Suite 750, Lock Box 346
Dallas, Texas 75201
Tel. 214/720-4040

In Great Britain, most towns have a Tourist Information Center. They are usually found near the major attractions or in town halls, kiosks, council offices or central libraries.

WHAT WILL THE TRIP COST?

It is sometimes difficult to estimate the cost of an overseas vacation. The following should help you determine your expenses in advance.

If you are taking a package tour of Great Britain, you will already know the basic cost, and will only have to budget for extra meals, incidentals, and of course shopping.

(1) ACCOMMODATIONS: Many British homeowners rent out rooms on a bed and breakfast basis for about £7 to £10 per person. These accommodations are not fancy, but they are always clean. Bathrooms are usually down the hall.

Guest houses are similar to pensions in other parts of Europe. They have from two to ten rooms that cost from £7 to £20 per person per night. Breakfast is usually included in the cost. Bathrooms may be connected to some rooms, or may be down the hall.

Hotels in Great Britain come in all varieties and price ranges, from about £10 to £70 per person. Meals are extra. There are several well-known hotel chains such as Holiday Inn, Best Western, Hilton, Trusthouse Forte, and others.

(2) MEALS: In bed and breakfasts and guest house arrangements, breakfast is usually included at no extra cost. A continental breakfast will typically cost about £1. A full English breakfast will cost around £3.

Lunches at fast-food places will cost about £1. Lunch at a typical restaurant or pub will range from £2.50 to £4. Bar lunches in hotels cost about the same.

Dinners can of course be expensive, but a good meal in an average restaurant can be enjoyed for about £5 to £8.

(3) TRANSPORTATION: Car rentals vary from about £75 per week for a small two-person car; up to about £300 per week for a 12-person van. Remember that gas is about £3.50 per gallon.

If you're traveling by train, get a Britrail pass from your travel agent. These are good for various periods of unlimited train travel. For example, the passes cost about $110 for one week, or $250 for one month. Other bargain fares are also available.

(4) ENTRANCE FEES: Most museums, castles, estate houses, and other attractions charge an entrance fee. If you plan ahead, you can estimate the cost by multiplying the number of attractions you want to visit by about $2. An Open to View ticket, which can be purchased from British Travel Authority offices for about $25, allows you to visit over 500 castles, country houses, and stately homes.

(5) INCIDENTALS: Miscellaneous costs add up quickly. These may include maps, postage, postcards, books, tips, laundry, snacks, and so forth. Include $5 to $10 a day for these items.

(6) SHOPPING: One of the enjoyable aspects of foreign travel is searching for treasures to take back as mementos of your trip as well as buying gifts for everyone at home. And as you will see from the rest of this book, there are some great bargains in Great Britain. Your shopping budget will be limited only by the amount of money you have available for spending. But don't be surprised if you spend more than your limit. It is especially easy with the help of our "plastic money" cards.

Note that London prices for everything are about 10% to 20% higher than in the countryside, although many times the retail prices are still a savings over those in the United States.

We strongly suggest that you read good travel guide books while planning your trip. They will have specific suggestions and information on other budgeting matters which you will find useful.

Helpful Hints

BANKING HOURS AND HOLIDAYS

Generally, banking hours in England and Wales are from 9:30 a.m. to 3:00 p.m. Monday through Friday. In Scotland, banking hours are from 9:30 a.m. to 3:30 p.m. with a lunch break from 12:30 to 1:30.

Banking Holidays are usually: Christmas Day, Boxing Day (December 26), New Year's Day, Good Friday, Easter Monday, May Day (beginning of May), and Spring holiday (end of May).

BUSINESS HOURS

Most businesses are open Monday through Saturday 9:00 to 5:00. In small towns, shops will usually close at 1:00 p.m. one day a week. You will note however that many places are open seven days a week during the heavy tourist season, which is mid-May through mid-September. Larger stores are usually open until 7:00 p.m. or 8:00 p.m. two days a week.

We have included the hours of each store and outlet for your convenience.

CHAIN STORES

A number of stores which we have included have outlets throughout Great Britain. Instead of describing the store innumerable times, we have provided one store description and a list of all of the store locations at the end of the book.

CREDIT CARDS

All credit cards are not honored at all establishments abroad. If you prefer to carry as little cash as possible, it is a good idea to carry several different credit cards on your trip.

Remember please that the exchange rate on the day of the purchase with a credit card is not applicable. On international credit card purchases, the exchange rate is determined on the day which your credit card company processes your bill.

A list of the credit cards which have wide international use follows:

American Express
P. O. Box 39
Church Street Station
New York, New York 10008
Toll-free 800/528-4800

Diners Club
P. O. Box 17326
Denver, Colorado 80217
Toll-free 800/525-9135

MasterCard International
888 Seventh Avenue
New York, New York 10019
212/974-5785
If you will call this number, MasterCard International will refer you to a bank in your area which will issue you a credit card application.

Visa
P. O. Box 8999
San Francisco, CA 94128
415/570-3200

Most financial institutions (banks, savings and loans, credit unions) issue either MasterCard or Visa credit cards. Please call your bank and check the yearly fee and the finance charges.

Please note that MasterCard (formerly Master Charge) is sometimes called Access in England and EuroCard in Europe. In Great Britain Barclays Bank issues its own Visa card, which is known as Barclaycard.

Many of the shops or factories listed in this book state that they accept "all credit cards." In fact, they may not be fully aware of the wide range of credit cards available, so do not be surprised if they refuse to accept some cards.

CUSTOMS AND DUTY

If you plan on shopping overseas, it is necessary to be familiar with the customs and duty regulations of the United States.

Before you leave the U.S., it is wise to register with U.S. Customs any foreign-made article or any article of value you are taking with you, or to take with you a proof of prior possession (e.g. sales slip). Otherwise a duty may be levied on these items when you return from overseas. All firearms should be registered whether made in the U.S. or abroad.

Be sure to have a prescription or written statement from your personal physician that any medicine is being used under a doctor's direction. Carry your drugs in their original containers.

When you return to the U.S., you must declare, at the price paid, everything you've acquired abroad, including gifts given to you and articles worn or used. If you fail to declare or understate values, penalties can be severe. Ask for a receipt for each purchase. It will simplify everything.

Upon arrival back in the U.S., you must pay required duty on items you bring with you in U.S. currency, with a personal check, a government check, a money order, or a traveler's check.

DUTY-FREE EXEMPTIONS

A. You may bring up to $400 (retail value) worth of articles acquired abroad back to the U.S. duty free *if:*

● The articles are for personal use or gifts
● The articles accompany you
● You have been out of the country at least 48 hours
● You have not claimed the exemption within the preceding 30 days

You may include in this duty-free exemption:

● 100 cigars (those of Cuban origin are prohibited) and 200 cigarettes
● 1 liter (33.8 fl. oz.) of wine, beer or liquor if you are 21 years of age or over. (Most states also have restrictions on the amount of liquor and tobacco which may be brought in.)

B. The next $1000 in items is dutiable at a flat 10% rate. Families living in one household and returning together may combine their purchases on a joint declaration and multiply their exemptions accordingly.

C. Gifts from abroad can be received in the U.S. free of duty and tax if the same person does not receive more than $50 in gift shipments in one day. Gifts intended for more than one person may be placed in the same package if the gifts are individually wrapped and labeled both inside and out as to recipient, and if the value of each person's gift does not exceed $50. Mark the package UNSOLICITED GIFT and indicate contents and retail value. The U.S. Postal Service collects duty on improperly marked consolidated packages and individual gifts worth more than $50. Duty cannot be prepaid. On your return to the U.S., you do not declare gifts you have shipped.

D. If you exceed the $1400 or the combined family allowances, a duty will be charged on the rest of the items according to the Tariff Schedules of the United States. The average tourist purchase is dutiable at about 12%. The book which lists the various tariffs can be found at most local libraries.

If you take out of, or bring into, the U.S. more than $5000 in currency or negotiable instruments, you must file a report (Customs Form 4790) with U.S. Customs.

Articles purchased in duty-free shops in foreign countries are subject to U.S. Customs duty and restrictions, but may be included in your personal exemption.

If you mail home personal belongings which you took with you from the U.S., mark AMERICAN GOODS RETURNED on the shipping carton.

Following these rules will make your shopping and your trip go more smoothly.

DUTY-FREE SHOPS

Do not expect any great savings in duty-free shops which are often found at airports. Even though they do not pay a duty on their items, their markup is often higher than an average store. So shop carefully, know your products and prices before purchasing at these shops!

LONG-DISTANCE PHONE CALLS

It is a common practice for overseas hotels to add a very high surcharge onto your international phone calls. Originally, the fee was to cover the hotel's cost of providing phone service. Now, however, many hotels charge a high fee and make a profit on the calls. The surcharge may be from 100% to 400% of the actual cost of the call. When you check out of the hotel you receive the bill, and it can be a real whopper! (AT&T notes one $18 overseas call to Chicago that had a $62 surcharge added to the bill.) The charge varies from hotel to hotel.

Always ask the hotel management about its policy. If the hotel staff is not helpful, or if they do not know the charge (sometimes even the staff will not be told what the charge is), then there are several ways to assure a reasonable charge:

- **Call collect.** The call will be billed to the number you call, at the rate used in that area. Many times, U.S. long-distance rates are cheaper than overseas rates. Also, the hotel surcharge will be less.
- **Use your telephone calling card**—the call will be billed to your home phone, and the surcharge will be lower.
- Call from a post office, railway station, airport, or other public phone. There will be no surcharge. (And if you call collect the rate may be lower.)
- Call your party in the U.S., give them your number, and have them call you back. A short call like this will be relatively inexpensive, even if it has a 100% surcharge.

AT&T is negotiating with tourist boards and hotel organizations to try to limit these surcharges. Some hotels have agreed to specific limits, such as $10 per call. This program is called TELEPLAN. Unfortunately, very few hotels have TELEPLAN. Some that do are:

> **Comfort Hotels**—100% surcharge, but not more than $6 per call dialed direct, or $10 per call dialed by the hotel operator. Collect calls or calling card calls have a flat charge of only $2 per call.
> **Hilton Hotels**—100% surcharge, with the same maximums as above, but $6 on collect or calling card calls.
> **Marriott Hotels**—100% surcharge, but not more than $9.50 per day; $5 on collect or calling card calls.

MAIL ORDERS

Mail order sales began in Great Britain many years before the U.S. It is therefore a highly developed and very organized way to shop if you are unable to actually visit England, Scotland, and Wales. We have noted those companies which will take mail orders. You may have to write first for an order form and/or a catalog. Instructions as to the amount of postage, insurance, delivery time, and often the duty will usually accompany the forms. Air mail letters from the States take an average of a week. Surface mail takes six to seven weeks.

Catalogs are very expensive to produce. Please only order those catalogs in which you are truly interested.

When shopping for crystal and china by mail, you must supply the pattern name or number and the piece description or number. If you visit a department store that carries the pattern you want to purchase, ask for a pamphlet that has the information you'll need for future orders. Often you can obtain the information you need by simply looking at the shelves of crystal and china which are displayed for shoppers.

Most companies which deal in international mail order sales allow you to return items for either a credit or cash. Many companies also guarantee your satisfaction. The items must usually be returned to the company within 14 days with the customer paying the freight. Often the company will ask that you send a note explaining the reason for the return. Remember that to get most items back to Great Britain in two weeks, you will more than likely have to air mail them. It is safer to make sure you want what you are buying. Many companies have size and measurement charts, which should help reduce the number of returned items, if instructions are followed and read in advance.

MAPS

Many of the outlets listed in this book are in small, out-of-the way towns and villages. It is great fun to visit these places, plus this is an excellent way to see parts of Great Britain that the average tourist misses. You should, however, purchase a detailed road map or atlas to assist in finding the best routes to and from these towns.

We have however provided maps to the stores and outlets that may be difficult to find. In smaller towns there are usually only one or two main streets, and shops can be easily located.

For London there is an excellent free map printed by London Transport entitled *London—Bus, Tube and Street Map and Tourist Information*. A must for all of those who visit London.

MONEY MATTERS

The Pound Sterling. The currency in Great Britain is the pound sterling. The pound is divided into 100 units which are called pence. Paper money is printed in the following denominations: £1, £5, £10, and £20 notes. The coins are 50 pence, 20 pence, 10 pence, 5 pence (all silver) and 2 pence, 1 pence and ½ pence which are bronze. The 50 pence and the 20 pence coins are both seven-sided. Pence is usually written as 10p, or 50p.

Exchange Rates. The rate of exchange for £1 was about $1.25 at the time of printing. Please check the rate of exchange at the time of your departure, as the rate changes daily. The current rate of exchange is available at an international bank or in the business section of your newspaper.

You will always get your best rate of exchange at a bank. It is worth checking rates of exchange at several banks if you plan on cashing a great deal of money at one time, as they can vary from bank to bank.

If you need British currency and the banks are closed, you can also exchange your money at the desk of your hotel, at the larger travel agents, in the exchange offices of the larger department stores, or at one of the innumerable *bureaux de change* you will see on the street.

Note that there are transaction fees on exchange rates. The fee is either a flat rate or a percentage of the amount you're exchanging—depending on the institution. If the fee is a flat rate it's obviously more economical to exchange $100 at one time than to exchange several smaller amounts.

Try to make an accurate guess as to the amount of money which you will need. If you must sell your pounds back to the bank to convert them into U.S. dollars, you will lose money

Money In and Money Out. You will be glad to know that you may take as much currency as you would like into Great Britain. You are not restricted as to the amount of Sterling you may take out either. (Many countries have restrictions on money coming in and out.) However, if you take more than $5000 out of or into the United States, you must report this to U.S. Customs on Form 4790.

POST OFFICE HOURS

In Great Britain, most post offices are open Monday through Friday from 9:00 a.m. to 5:30 p.m. and on Saturdays from 9:00 a.m. to 12:30 p.m.

SALES

The largest sales of the year are held in January and July. We have nothing in the U.S. that begins to compare with this excitement. Be sure to leave all children and extra belongings at home. Carry a shoulderbag, or put your wallet in your coat pocket. Arrive early, wait in line, and be ready to make quick decisions. The best merchandise at the best prices is snapped up immediately. Make a list of your wants and needs and plan on fighting the crowds. Bargains are abundant, prices are exceptionally low, and people wait all year for these sales.

SENIOR CITIZEN AND STUDENT DISCOUNTS

Senior citizen discounts are usually available only to the holders of a British pension book. Some student discounts are available with a valid student identification.

SHIPPING

Many stores or factories will ship your purchases home for you. Be sure to take advantage of this. They have shipped before, and they will be familiar with all of the necessary packing material to help your package arrive home safely. Even if you want to hand carry your product, let them pack it for you. The extra charge is worth it!

Many factories will also recommend people whom they hire to ship for them. You may want to take your products to them for shipping. Be sure to fully insure *all* of your merchandise through any shipper. Keep a list of all of the items you ship and the date. Don't wait till you get home—you may have forgotten what you shipped, when, and where.

Air mail postage is extremely expensive, but if you are in a hurry it's well worth it. Air mail to the U.S. takes an average of seven to nine days. Surface mail is also expensive (when compared to rates in the United States). Your things are carried by boat back to the U.S. It takes between four and eight weeks to get your merchandise, which seems like forever when you are waiting.

I would suggest that if you plan on mailing things home, take your own scissors, wide shipping tape, string and shipping labels! Pack your things in your hotel room or your rented car—not at the post office. Clothing is easy to ship. (In all we ended up shipping 15 boxes home.) Boxes are found at grocery stores, but it is tricky to find them with lids. Address the boxes with your *home* return address. Read all of the information under CUSTOMS AND DUTY and DUTY FREE REGULATIONS. It will explain all of the how-tos and details.

When you mail goods from Great Britain, you will be asked to show your passport and to fill out a form declaring what is inside your package and its value. It is quite a process, so be sure to plan on at least an hour if you have six or seven boxes. The post office will allow you to tie your boxes with string, which I do recommend. Most of our boxes came back looking like they had been put through a crusher machine. We did mail some china home in cardboard boxes inside of our extra clothes and new sweaters. All arrived home safely. Sacks and newspapers also are great for cushioning. My sisters had large quantities of crystal and china mailed directly from the factory, and every piece arrived safely.

Both of my sisters also carried several boxes home on the plane and were charged an extra baggage fee, which was less than postage would have been. You might check with your airline to see what their extra baggage policy is before leaving. Some airlines will only allow a certain number of pounds per person and no excess baggage, while others will allow you to pay for extra weight. Of course, carrying boxes around can be very expensive if you are tipping someone to carry your luggage.

There are pros and cons both ways. You have to decide what is best for you.

Shipping furniture is very specialized, and all merchandise must be crated. Most antique dealers are familiar with this procedure and can help with all the details. Remember to insure your purchase. Many department stores in the U.S. purchase antiques in Great Britain and crate them home via ship.

In the back of the book is a chart entitled PURCHASES IN GREAT BRITAIN. It will help you keep an accurate record of purchases and shipping dates.

Breakage is not a pleasant thought, but realistically, something may be broken. All of the companies which mail your goods home have instructions on what to do if your items are broken. Save all boxes, receipts, and shipping labels and follow their procedures. All of these companies ship their items fully insured against breakage.

Claims for breakage through independent carriers involve a different procedure, and you should be sure to ask for instructions and details from each shipper.

Items which you mail through the British post office cannot be insured. You are therefore taking a risk. We do not recommend sending fragile items through the postal system.

SIZES, METRIC CONVERSIONS
WOMEN'S SIZES
Dresses, Suits, Separates

	Misses and Women								Junior Miss				
AMERICAN	6	8	10	12	14	16	18	20	9	11	13	15	17
BRITISH	5	8	9	10	12	14	15	18	30	31	32	33	35
CONTINENTAL	34	36	38	40	42	44	46	48	35	36	38	40	42

Stockings

AMERICAN AND BRITISH	8	9	10
CONTINENTAL	1	2	4

MEN'S SIZES

Suits and Coats

AMERICAN AND BRITISH	36	38	40	42	44	46
CONTINENTAL	46	48	50	52	54	56

Shirts

AMERICAN AND BRITISH	14	15	16	17
CONTINENTAL	36	38	41	43

METRIC CONVERSIONS

1 meter = 39.37 inches
1 kilogram (kilo) = 2.2 pounds
500 grams = 1.1 pounds

TAX (VALUE ADDED TAX)

The European Value Added Tax (VAT) is similar to the American sales tax. In Britain it is presently 15% of the price of an item. If you are visiting from abroad, some shops will not charge the VAT if your purchase is shipped directly home. Other shops will give you a form to fill out for a refund. The form must be validated at the customs office as you leave Great Britain. You then send the form back to the store, which will refund your 15%. Naturally, this is a lot of trouble for the store, so they may require a minimum purchase.

TOURS

When factory tours are available we have noted this, along with the necessary instructions. Please note that at many of the large, famous factories, tours are booked six to eight months in advance, and reservations are taken on a first come, first serve basis. Request the necessary forms from the factories, fill them out completely, and be sure to put three alternate dates down for your visit. This will help everyone avoid disappointment, flared tempers, or embarrassment. Often the companies will send pamphlets with information on their tours, hours, shopping, etc. This is most helpful when planning your itinerary.

TRAVELER'S CHECKS

The simplest and safest way to carry money when abroad is to use traveler's checks. They will be replaced if lost or stolen—cash will not!

If possible, obtain traveler's checks in pounds sterling before you leave on your trip. They are much easier to cash in the United Kingdom than traveler's checks in dollars.

It is best to get smaller denominations since many small businesses cannot make change for large amounts. Traveler's checks usually get a better rate of exchange than cash.

Be sure to keep the check numbers listed in two different places, and mark each check off as it is used. While making this list, you might want to put down your passport number and all charge card numbers as well. Such a list will save a lot of headaches if your wallet or luggage is stolen or lost. Unfortunately, I am speaking from experience. In Paris all of our luggage and checks were stolen from our car in the middle of the day.

If your checks are lost or stolen, it will be easier to cope if this happens Monday through Friday. The headquarters for the various companies which sell traveler's checks are usually closed on the weekends.

The major companies issuing traveler's checks in the U.S. are: American Express, Bank of America, Citicorp, MasterCard, Thomas Cook, and Visa. All of the checks from these companies are recognized in Great Britain. It might be worth calling each to find if there is a charge for the checks and what, if any, that charge is. If you are traveling for a month, it would be necessary to take a large sum of money with you. The savings you might experience with a few phone calls could add up. For a toll-free number on each company, call 800-555-1212.

Do not leave wallets, purses, luggage, jewelry, etc. for even a moment. The crime rate overseas is comparable to that in the U.S., so take extra precautions. Replacing passports, reissuing traveler's checks, and filling out police forms, which are necessary for collecting insurance, can take precious days away from your vacation as well as cause frustration and anger. Preventive measures are best.

TRADITIONALLY FAMOUS BRITISH PRODUCTS

ANTIQUES

For centuries antiques have been crated and shipped out of Great Britain, so that it's hard to believe that there's anything left to buy, but indeed there is. Antique stores abound throughout the country in major cities and small towns and villages, where the greatest buys will often be found. Besides antique stores, street markets are great places to ferret out smaller antique pieces, and so, too, are jumble sales (similar to our garage sales), which are often held in small towns at local schools or church or town halls. Auction houses are also found in most major cities, and attending an auction can be an exciting experience where you may be lucky enough to pick up some particularly treasured item at a reasonable price. Be sure you know the rules before bidding. Local newspapers are another good source for locating antiques for sale, if you have the time and the patience to scan the classifieds.

Educate yourself as much as possible about the particular antiques or collectibles that interest you so that you can compare British and American prices and also so that you can identify the genuine antique from the new reproduction that has been made to look antique. If you aren't comfortable with your expertise, then it's best to stick to reputable dealers who guarantee the authenticity of their merchandise.

In general, right now, prices for English antiques are far lower (as much as 50%) in the United Kingdom than they are here in the United States, even when you add the cost of shipping. Some stores will crate and ship items home for you, or more likely, will use a special antiques shipping service like Michael Davis. Be sure that the agreed shipping price includes delivery of the item to your door, not just to the dock, and also check to see if you will be charged any duty or if you need a certificate of authentication guaranteeing that the item is over 100 years old and therefore not subject to duty.

Currently, the hottest furniture market seems to be for Victorian pieces, which until 20 or so years ago were scorned and therefore quite low-priced. Recently, prices for Victorian furniture have shot up while, of course, the prime 18th-century classic designs by such famous cabinetmakers as Chippendale, Hepplewhite, and Sheraton, if they can be found at all, sell for even more astronomically high prices. Smaller objects—like inkwells, horse brasses, snuff boxes, canes, watercolors, and commemorative pottery—can be found for much more reasonable prices and have the added advantage of being easy to transport. Regardless of what you choose, you'll find plenty of antique hunting grounds throughout England and Scotland, and you can spend many delightful hours looking through "one man's junk" in search of your own particular treasure.

CHINA, POTTERY AND PORCELAIN

Before discussing the fine quality china that's available in Britain, let's first define some terms that will help you in your shopping.

Earthenware—low-fire pottery, usually red or tan in color, that is porous after the first firing and therefore must be glazed before it can be used domestically.

Stoneware—high-fire ware with slight or no porosity, it's half-way between hard porcelain and earthenware. The chief difference between stoneware and porcelain is the color, which ranges from yellowish buff to dark brown and is derived from iron or other impurities in the clay mix.

Porcelain—a mixture of kaolin (an extremely pure clay that is pure white when fired), feldspar, and flint, which can be fired at extremely high temperatures. Hard-paste porcelain refers to a true porcelain that is fired above 2420 degrees Fahrenheit to produce a hard, non-porous, vitreous body that is white and translucent and rings when struck. Strength and whiteness are increased by ageing the paste. Soft-paste is a relative term when applied to porcelain, the standard of hardness being that of Chinese porcelain.

China—a generic term now applied to table ware of all kinds from delicate porcelain cups to rough earthenware mugs.

Bone China—made from a porcelain paste to which bone ash has been added to increase translucency. A British innovation.

Pottery—general term for clayware.

The story of English china, at least from the mid-1700s on, is largely devoted to the quest to imitate hard-paste Chinese porcelain and also to bridge the gap between delicate porcelain and coarse earthenware and stoneware.

Around 1730 John Astbury, a Staffordshire potter, successfully incorporated crushed calcined flints to create a stronger earthenware clay mixture that could be fired at higher temperatures and thus produce a whiter, hard, non-porous body that could be salt-glazed to give a clear, reasonably smooth surface. This improved earthenware was soon imitated throughout the potteries, but the greatest and most celebrated of all 18th-century experimenters was Josiah Wedgwood (1730–1795), who developed a whole range of improved high-fire earthenwares and fine stonewares, which for ornamental purposes required no glaze. The most famous of these were his black basaltes and also his jasperware, which he stained using seven colors—dark blue, lavender, sage and olive green, black, bluish pink, and, rarely, yellow—before embossing it with white jasper reliefs.

Strangely, Josiah Wedgwood never tried to make true porcelain, but other potters did. From the 1740s on, they strove to imitate Chinese porcelain, but with little success, because the really prime, pure ingredients of kaolin clay and feldspar were not available. They therefore mixed white clay and a glass-like substance together. This mixture was fused with lime and chalk, but it could only be fired at a low temperature to produce soft-paste porcelain that was fragile. These soft-paste porcelains were produced at such famous factories as Bow, Chelsea, Derby, and Liverpool in the mid-18th century.

Only Plymouth, Bristol, and New Hall made true hard-paste porcelain when the necessary ingredients—china clay and china stone—were obtainable from Cornwall. These ingredients were fused with lime and potash and could be fired at very high temperatures, but the porcelain so produced was still not satisfactory. Still, the search for the mix that would produce true hard-paste porcelain did lead to the development of bone china. Bone ash was added to the ingredients outlined above, and this produced a lighter white substance that was more receptive to bright colors than either hard-or soft-paste porcelain; it was also more durable and less costly than the earlier soft-paste porcelains. Since 1793, when it was first marketed by Josiah Spode, bone china has remained the most famous and best loved of all the fine English chinas. Among the many famous names associated with its production are Spode, Minton, Coalport, Derby, Worcester, Wedgwood, and Doulton.

Numerous other developments, of course, followed the introduction of bone china: vividly colored Japan-patterned ware in the late 18th century; lustre wares in the early 19th century; English majolica by Minton in 1851; transfer printed plates and other ware; willow pattern, and many other designs and innovations that are still available in the showrooms today.

Earthenware figures, developed in the second half of the 18th century, have also been a staple favorite. Their popularity increased steadily along with the refinements in technique of earthenware manufacture, that progressed from figures with cloudy streaks of color to those using a whole range of brighter colors that could endure the heat required to fire the glaze. The Woods of Burslem made some of the finest figures from the mid-18th century to mid-19th century. Thereafter the quality of workmanship declined to the familiar, cruder flat-back figure group for the mantelpiece that was developed at the height of the Victorian era. Today, Royal Doulton (so named in 1902) still produces much loved and much collected figurines that range from London street characters like the Old Balloon Seller to Kate Greenaway children, from Beswick animal figures to the Bunnykins nursery series. The company even manufactures a series of Williamsburg characters. There are usually about 200 figurines in current production.

Some of the finest china factories in the world are found in Britain, and you shouldn't miss the chance to see the craftsmen at work. Prices are far below the retail prices in the United States, and the savings at all of the factories are also substantial, while seconds offer even greater discounts. The selection is also broader. Some of the famous manufacturers, all in the Stoke-on-Trent area, that are listed in this guide are: Caversall China Co.; Coalport-Fenton; Crown-Staffordshire in Fenton; Healacraft China in Longton; Royal Grafton, also in Longton; Royal Winton; Spode; and Josiah Wedgwood & Sons in Barlaston.

Visit their showrooms and choose among the marvelous selections of fine bone china, earthenware, and stoneware, and know that whatever you choose, you'll be purchasing those very fine elements of design, color, pattern, and workmanship that we have discussed above.

Besides those well-known factories manufacturing famous bone china and fine stonewares, you'll also discover many individual potters, some quite famous, who will welcome you into their studios where you can watch them preparing the clay for the wheel, kneading and working it to remove the air bubbles (which could cause the vessel to explode during the firing), placing and centering it on the wheel, and using their fingers and thumbs to shape and smooth out the clay. When the piece is fully formed, it is taken off the wheel, turned upside down, and trimmed of excess clay. Handles, spouts, and other decorations are added, and the piece is fired just enough to harden the clay, which is then glazed either by dipping, brushing, or spraying. Finally, the pieces are stacked in the kiln and fired at appropriate temperatures.

Some of the more famous English pottery manufacturers mentioned later in the book include Denby in Derby, Henry Watson's in Wattisfield, Poole in Dorset, and Prinknash in Cranham.

CRYSTAL, GLASS

From the 15th century to the 18th century Venice dominated the European glass industry, producing the famous colorless or single-colored glass, a product that stressed the plasticity of the medium rather than its brilliance. In the 18th and early 19th century Britain took the lead by developing "lead" glass, which lent itself to embellishment with cut decoration and which continues to win the hearts of so many customers around the globe.

The lead glass developed by Ravenscroft around 1675 had a much greater refractive power than earlier glass and was also heavier and darker. These properties led the English to design shapes that differed from Venetian and earlier glass—solid instead of hollow-stemmed glasses for example, plus a great number of new articles such as candlesticks, salt cellars, sweetmeat glasses, oil lamps, milk jugs for the tea table, and so on. The cut-glass decoration mania seems to have emerged as a response to a tax of 9s 4d per hundredweight (112 pounds) imposed in 1745 on the material used to make any item. Obviously, manufacturers looked for ways to increase the number of objects that they could manufacture from one pot of metal and so they discontinued such extravagances as the folded foot on wine glasses and the ornamented stems. As a compensation they decided to decorate the bowl with engraving or cutting. From 1760 on cutting increased and the range of motifs broadened—pyramids, diamonds, circles, flowers. Later, after the turn of the century all manner of ingenious decorations appeared, which may account for John Ruskin's dismissal of all cut glass as "barbarous." Whatever Ruskin's opinion, cut glass (or what we call crystal) is still prized today and certainly, when you see how effectively it is employed on lighting appliances, from the simplest of candlesticks to the most elaborate of chandeliers, you can understand why. For a glimpse of its brilliance, stop at the Victoria and Albert museum to view the chandelier, made around 1820, that contains as many as 4500 separate pieces, or visit Bath to see an earlier example that still hangs majestically in the Assembly Rooms.

For shoppers today Thomas Webb and others continue to manufacture this shimmering glass. Although this book doesn't include Ireland, as taxes increased, many glass manufacturers went to Ireland, where glass was not taxed, and established such famous names as Waterford, Cork, Dublin, and Belfast. Keep that in mind, if you should be crossing the Irish Sea. Then, too, you'll find plenty of the Irish variety in the English and Scottish showrooms where you'll have the selection of a lifetime at incredible savings. Among the many manufacturers listed are:

Caithness Glass—Oban, Perth, and Wick, Scotland
Cumbria Crystal Ltd.—Ulverston, England
Dartington Glass Ltd.—Great Torrington, England
Edinburgh Crystal—Penicuik, Scotland
Nazeing Glass Works Ltd.—Broxbourne, England
Regency Crystal Ltd.—Halesowen, England
Royal Brierly Crystal—Brierly Hill, England
Stuart Strathearn Ltd.—Crieff, Scotland
Thomas Webb Crystal—Amblecote, England
Tudor Crystal—Stourbridge, England
Wedgwood Crystal—King's Lynn, England

While you're visiting the factories take the opportunity to watch the craftsmen at work, gathering a ball of molten glass onto the end of a long hollow tube, rotating, swinging, and tilting it to create the bowl of the vessel, then adding the stem and the foot before taking it to the annealing chamber for controlled gradual cooling. By holding the glass against the edge of a revolving wheel, geometric patterns are cut into the glass. The crystal is then dipped into an acid bath, which gives it an instantaneous and lasting brilliance.

ENGRAVINGS, PRINTS AND WATERCOLORS

Britain's social and political history has been recorded by hundreds of artists and authors whose books are often filled with engravings, watercolors, and other illustrations. Many of these famous prints have been reproduced for collectors or have been torn out of books and are sold individually at specialized antiquarian bookstores or print stores throughout the country. Unless you're a real print maven and know how to identify an original print from a reproduction, and really know the ins and outs of the current print market, you'll probably do best to buy simply what appeals to you without too much thought about its authenticity or essential value, unless, of course, the price doesn't warrant such whimsicality.

In the specialized stores you'll find all manner of prints, etchings, engravings, lithographs, and reproductions to search through—political cartoons and caricatures à la Hogarth; sporting life etchings by Thomas Rowlandson; early posters and ads from trade catalogs; illustrations and drawings by Aubrey Beardsley, William Blake, and Sir John Tenniel; botanical, ornithological, and animal prints and much, much more that will charm and engage your curiosity. Bring one of these home and it will always remind you of your visit.

Despite the booming art market in the United States, most American collectors and art buyers have shown little interest in watercolors so that the market is still virtually a British monopoly. Perhaps there's good reason, for the British do seem to have a deep fondness for the medium and so, too, have many of their artists, especially the great landscapists of the 18th and 19th centuries—Thomas Girtin, Joseph M. W. Turner, John Constable, Alexander and John Robert Cozens, John Sell Cotman, and even contemporaries like Reginald Marsh.

The most distinctive quality of watercolor is its transparency and the role that the paper—white or tinted—plays as it shines through in the composition. This allows artists to create a whole range of delicately luminous effects especially well-suited to the depiction of water, light, sky, and the subtle and varied plays of light that the changeable British climate produces daily from dawn to dusk. Among connoisseurs the English watercolor style refers to a pure mode of painting that eschews such techniques as scrubbing with a damp cloth to produce a soft blur suggestive of an airy atmospheric quality, rubbing with a tissue that enables the artist to define shapes in a landscape such as clouds, or cutting, scraping, hatching, and stippling the way the great inventive Turner did to create his effects.

Many charming 19th-century watercolors of varying quality and condition can be found in antique stores and galleries throughout Britain along with a great number of fine contemporary landscapes and other paintings. Remember, if you do purchase a watercolor, that over time direct sunlight causes the colors to fade, so if you don't want to keep it in the dark but you are buying it as a possible investment, you may want to re-think your choice.

HATS

For centuries hats have been worn as symbols of respect, indicating a man's station in life, his financial worth, his caste, his breeding, and his worth to the community. Today, of course, times have changed greatly, and hats are now worn primarily for pleasure, for protection, for warmth, and for fashion.

A true haberdasher can help a gentleman choose a hat that will frame his face, have a flattering effect on his appearance, and help disguise his facial flaws. The simple act of creasing a hat in a certain way, for example, can enhance certain facial features.

Certain hats are especially associated with the British. The tall silk hat, created by haberdasher John Heatherington in his Charing Cross shop, first appeared in 1798 in England. An instant success, it almost caused a riot, and he was accused of breaching the peace by wearing "a tall structure having a shining luster calculated to frighten timid people." In London today visitors will still see the top hat being worn, mainly at royal or formal occasions like banquets and weddings. Today it is no longer made of silk, but it is still almost entirely hand-made of cotton cloth, hatter's plush, and shellac, and it remains the most elegant hat a man can wear.

The hat we know as the derby became popular in England around 1850 when a hatter named William Bowler (hence the English name for it) designed the derby as a hard-crowned hat with a stiff protective brim for steeplechase riders. He hoped it would prevent head injuries, and it is still worn today by both men and women in horseback riding and jumping competitions. The modern version is made of felt, a tough material that can be shaped without sewing.

Hats still remain very popular with the English and the Scots. Resembling the French beret, the Scottish tam-o-shanter is a woolen cap with a tight head band and a flat circular crown, but it sports an extra flourish—a pompon in the center. Then, of course, there's the symbol of the British workingman, the peaked cap, which has now become a dashing fashion statement in itself whether made of tweed or a plain wool. The British remain among the best hat makers in the world and continue to make most hats by hand. Visitors will find hats in all styles, colors, shapes, and prices—all of them making for a fetching, long-lasting, and useful souvenir.

KNITS AND WOOLENS

The British Isles is probably most famous for its high-quality woolens. Many American retail store buyers and woolen garment manufacturers make regular bi-annual visits to the mills in northern England and Scotland to purchase their magnificent fabrics or gar-ments.

Hand-knitted items are often made by cottage industry workers—women working at home who sell their finished goods to local stores. Three traditional and most sought-after sweater styles are Aran, Fair Isle, and Shetland, which were traditionally handmade of top-quality wool in those Scottish and Irish islands. When purchasing such a sweater or garment, do check the label to see whether it is indeed handknit and of prime quality rather than machine loomed. Don't rely on the price to tell you.

APPROXIMATE YARDAGE NEEDED
FOR SEWING WITH WOOL

	FABRIC 29″ WIDE	FABRIC 56″ WIDE
LADIES		
Skirt	1¾ yds.	⅞ yds.
Suit	5–6 yds.	2½–3 yds.
Coat	5 yds.	2½ yds.
Dress with sleeves	4½ yds.	2¼ yds.
Sleeveless dress		
A-line skirt	4 yds.	2 yds.
GENTLEMEN		
Jacket	5 yds.	2¾ yds.
Suit	8 yds.	5 yds.
Coat	8 yds.	4 yds.

Scottish cashmere sweaters are also much prized and can be purchased at a fraction of their American prices. Cashmere, which is combed from the under-fleece of the Kashmir goat that inhabits the Himalayas in India, China, and Tibet, is valued for its warmth, which it delivers without sacrificing softness and lightness. Lambswool generally comes from lambs in Australia that are sheared when young to ensure that the fleece is soft enough for the manufacture of elegant knitwear. Cashmere and Shetland (lambswool) sweaters and other garments are excellent buys.

A pleasant time can be spent watching the wool manufacturing at the many small or large mills around the country, often located in picturesque villages and housed in 200-year-old buildings. The wool used in weaving is graded according to fineness, softness, elasticity, shrinkage, etc. The most frequently used method of evaluating wool, the Bradford system, grades wool according to the fineness of the fiber. The constant againt which all the wool is measured for fineness is a thread of yarn 560 yards long, which represents one count. Wool is graded from 40 counts (which is the most coarse) to 80 counts (which is the very finest). The three basic ways of weaving the fabric—satin, plain, and twill—are supplemented by all kinds of designs, like herringbone, for example.

Some of the famous woolen manufacturers mentioned in the guide are:

Brynkir Woolen Mill Ltd.—Gwynedd, Wales
James Pringle—Edinburgh, Scotland
Linton Tweeds Ltd.—Carlisle, England
Peter Anderson Ltd.—Galashiels, Scotland
Robert Noble—Peebles, Scotland
St. Georges Woollen Mills Ltd.—Isle of Man, England
The Cambrian Factory—Llanwrtyd, Wales
Trefriw Woollen Mills Ltd.—Trefriw, Wales

LEATHER AND SHEEPSKIN PRODUCTS

Although the Italians are the pre-eminent leather workers and designers, the British are also known for the production of sturdy, long-lasting leather products like their strong, serviceable briefcases that are made from saddle leather and guaranteed to last a lifetime or handmade shoes of similar fine quality.

Sheepskin products are also worth buying in Britain for the savings can range from 25% to 50% off American prices. Good shearling coats are great buys and so, too, are sheepskin boots, which are hard to find in the United States. Sheepskin slippers for men, women, and children are also attractive, warm, affordable items to look for.

RAINGEAR

The raincoat was, in fact, invented by a Scottish chemist, Charles Macintosh, who developed a waterproof fabric in 1823, and the Brits still refer to their beloved macintoshes or "macks" for short. Later Thomas Burberry improved the quality of the cloth and today his name is synonymous with the high-fashion raincoat or trench coat that has become the *de rigueur* uniform for most well-dressed upwardly mobile men and women, particularly in the United States. The famous trench coat (a modified version of a raincoat still worn by many British schoolchildren as part of their uniform) with its leather-covered buckles at the waist and cuffs is certainly a bargain in Britain at today's exchange rates, and moreover you'll find a much greater choice of colors and styles here in the Burberry stores. Department stores also carry a vast selection of raincoats, many of which have warm, zip-out linings. They're versatile and great for the traveler.

Besides the macintosh the well-dressed English man or woman requires a sturdy "brolly"—umbrella to you—to help keep dry during the proverbial British showers and drizzles.

Although the imports from Hong Kong and other cheap flimsy umbrellas are ubiquitous, a true handmade umbrella with a solid wooden handle, sturdy spokes, and strongly handsewn material can still be found and is a glory to behold and to wield. The price will be high, but it will be worth it.

SILVER

In the 18th century the British produced more fine silver than any other country and the craft had its greatest flowering thanks to such famous artisans as Paul de Lamere, Matthew Boulton, Paul Storr, and the Batemans. The fact that the sterling standard established in 1719 continues to this day attests to this as much as anything else.

The British had established a sterling standard as early as 1300 and begun the practice of assaying and hallmarking later in the century. If the object was up to sterling standard, a mark was stamped on it, and this is still done today by the London and provincial Goldsmiths Companies.

When shopping for silver, look for the hallmarks on the base of the object. There are many books available documenting the hallmarks of English and American silver. Briefly, the assay mark tells you where it was assayed. A lion passant (walking) was the sign of the London assay; a ship sailing from behind a castle signifies Bristol. Other marks indicate the silversmith's name (usually simply his initials); the warden's name from the goldsmith's company responsible for the assay is usually expressed by a single letter of the alphabet; a final mark—a reigning monarch's head—indicated that duty had been paid. This last was introduced in 1784 and discontinued in 1890—hence there are four possibilities: George III, George IV, William IV, and Victoria. A higher standard of silver known as the Britannia standard was introduced at the end of the 17th century but was used only until 1739. It was indicated by Britannia—the august lady holding oval shield and trident. Obviously, if you find such a piece, treasure it!

Naturally, 18th-century silver is much prized by collectors, and more than likely it's either in a museum or priced completely out of range for most, but if you browse in the markets of London, you may well find some small handsome silver pieces. Some will be sterling quality; most will be silver-plated. Don't confuse silver plate with Sheffield plate. The earliest Sheffield plate was created by a process accidentally discovered in 1742 by Thomas Boulsover, who fused silver and copper together. The sheets of silver were hand-rolled onto copperware and these objects are high-priced, although less sought after by collectors. This early Sheffield plate can be identified by examining the edge of a piece to determine whether a fingernail can catch the edge of the sheet of silver. From 1838 on electroplating was introduced and today's silver plate is still produced by electrolysis. EPNS or EPWM stamped on the underside of a piece of silver signify respectively electroplated nickel silver or electroplated white metal.

Today the craft as handcraft is almost non-existent, but remember, even today's machine-made silverware may have value in time. Still, there's plenty of good quality sterling if you look around. The place to start is at the London Silver Vaults at 53-54 Chancery Lane, a complex of over 30 shops where you can gaze at such treasures as a rare Queen Anne chocolate box for $54,000 or purchase new silver or silver plate items like coasters or photograph frames for reasonable prices.

TAILORING

England, especially London's Savile Row, is synonymous with the art of fine custom tailoring. The British wool and wool worsted fabrics are considered the finest in the world. (Woolen yarns are spun from shorter fibers directly after carding and have a soft fuzzy texture; worsted yarns are made only from the best—finest and longest—fibers which, after the carding process, are combed until all the fibers lie parallel.) If you're a lover of tweeds, then select the fine durable Harris tweed that is woven only around Stornoway on the island of Harris in the Outer Hebrides.

If you can afford it and have the time to undergo a number of fittings, then by all means think about purchasing a custom tailored suit or jacket. It will last forever, and the people in the know will notice.

To the trained eye there is a large difference between a ready-to-wear suit and a custom-tailored suit. The differences lie in 1) the application of the interfacing; 2) the handling of the collar and the facings; 3) the appearance of the buttonholes and pockets; and 4) the finishing details. We hope that the following hints will help you in your shopping.

Look for the following details. Where you find several layers of fabric at cuffs and hems, for instance, the edges should remain thin and lie absolutely flat. The seams of the suit should be tacked slightly to the underside of the garment. The coat should conform to body shape without bagging or being taut. The collar should not lie flat across the back, but should curve slightly, hugging the neck. The lapels should be gently curved and spring back into place when lifted up. The fold of the lapel should lie close to the chest and not gap. The shoulders should be square and crisp, not drooping, and the sleeves should be gently eased into the armhole with virtually no puckering. Much of this shaping is accomplished with hand sewing that will help a coat hold its shape. To observe the hand sewing on your suit, look under the collar where the stitches are usually visible. Also check the inside of the armhole where the lining is often finely sewn into place by hand. The stitches should be small and even. Handfinished buttonholes were once a sign of quality and still are, although ready-to-wear manufacturers now try to imitate this detail.

A true indication of a quality custom-tailored suit is the manner in which the edge of the suit is finished. The best coats are hand sewn about a quarter of an inch from the edge, usually around the collar, down the lapels, and often part way around the bottom of the coat, using two strands of silk thread in an almost invisible backstitch. You may have to use your fingers to try to separate the fabric, in which case you'll know an experienced tailor has been at work.

Some of the more famous English tailors include Hardy Amies, Hawkes, and Kilgour French, & Stanbury, the last at 33 Savile Row. If you can't afford a suit, try a custom-tailored shirt from Turnbull & Asser, another peculiarly English institution that will reward you with a very finely crafted shirt that will last for years.

TOBACCO AND PIPES

Many people, when they think of an Englishman, conjure up an image of a country squire, attired in tweeds, cravat at his throat, sturdy Oxfords or brogues on his feet, deerstalker or cap on his head, Labrador at his side, and a distinguished-looking briar pipe in his hand.

The elegant tobacco shops that still exist in London and other towns testify to the English penchant for tobacco and pipes, especially the briar (made from thorny plants) for its cool, flavorsome smoke. The tobacconists' windows and counters display an amazing variety of aromatic tobaccos blended to perfection, along with all the smoking paraphernalia, from the common items to unique antique sterling silver cigarette cases. For the smoker, a delightful stop.

SOME FINAL THOUGHTS

Although the English are not famous for their cuisine, certain foodstuffs are worth seeking out: King of British cheese, Stilton, for example, that has been aged with a healthy dose of port; jellies and preserves from Tiptree; fragrant blends of teas from the illustrious Mr. Twining or Jackson's of Piccadilly; single malt whiskies like Glenn Fiddich or Glenn Grant; all of which and much more can be found exquisitely arrayed at Fortnum and Mason or Harrod's Food Hall.

ENGLAND

WELCOME TO ENGLAND

To visit England is to glimpse into the past. All that you have dreamed it would be is true!

Winding cobblestone streets lined with timbered Tudor inns are found throughout the countryside. Museums filled with centuries of art and history are in every city. Stone churches with colorful stained glass windows and huge cathedrals offer visitors a glimpse into her fascinating past. Buildings which have been in existence for hundreds of years stand on every corner and are still in use. England's magnificent gardens and parks—both formal and ruggedly natural—are filled with flowers, vines, bushes, and century-old trees. Castles and palaces once the homes of world rulers are now open for your visit. They are beautifully restored with many original antiques and furnishings. Street markets abound and offer a festive side of British life that should not be missed.

Many consider England's theater to be the most exciting in the world! Dynamic new plays, operas, and ballets constantly open and feature some of the most talented performers anywhere. In summer, outdoor bands play in city squares, and sidewalk cafes are filled with sightseers watching the passersby. Pubs and taverns, a traditional part of British life, are especially fun to visit.

England's friendly people are always willing to make your trip a pleasant experience. The entire country welcomes visitors. Signs are posted with maps and information is free for the asking. Tours and buses are color coded. Travel info and books are readily available.

Once you have visited England, you will start counting the days until you can return to one of the most exciting and scenic countries in the world!

SHOPPING IN ENGLAND

Welcome to one of the best shopping centers in the world. Anything your heart desires, in any style, color or price, is available in England. Specialty shops are abundant: purse shops, tobacco shops, china stores, silver vaults, and much more. Department stores seem to be at every corner. Some of the world's best antiques can be found in England. The world's largest furniture store, as well as one of the largest bookstores and the largest department store, are all to be found in London.

Many people claim that inflation and the recent recession have put an end to bargains in England, but shopping bargains are everywhere, and we intend to help you find them to make your vacation more exciting.

The number of stores, outlets, and factories throughout the country may seem overwhelming at first glance. But remember that England is easy to tour. No town is farther than 100 miles from the coast. From London to the northernmost tip of Scotland is only 665 miles. Many of the best factories and stores are concentrated in certain areas. We have included maps whenever possible to provide directions.

When shopping, be sure to first look for British-made items, as those will be the best buys. Imported items will have a duty added to the cost of the item, but the cost may still be less than in the U.S.

England's quality manufactured products are exported all over the world, and very often the demand far exceeds the supply.

Fine bone china, porcelain, and pottery from England have been famous for centuries. The history of this industry was radically changed by many of the manufacturing processes created in Stoke-on-Trent with its perfect clay, excellent transportation system, abundant coal, and creative craftsmen.

If you want real savings, visit the pottery factories direct, most of which are still located in Stoke-on-Trent. Be sure to bring style numbers and pattern designs if you are hoping to add to your sets of dinnerware—it's easy to be overwhelmed with the choices and forget which things you wanted.

The English hand-blown lead crystal industry is also one of the largest in the world, producing a vast selection of well priced, exquisitely designed, durable vases, decanters, glasses, and hundreds of other pieces.

Custom made as well as much of the ready-to-wear apparel for men and women is exceptionally well-tailored. The selection of fine woolens, cashmere, and tweeds is incredible. London's trendy designers and boutiques, thriving since the early 60s, have continued to amaze the world fashion industry with daring new designs. Raincoats, leather goods, and hats are among the traditional British-made clothing products.

Also look for hand-wrought willow baskets, jewelry in antique and contemporary settings, antiques, etchings, silver, rare books—and hundreds of other treasures. Where to find it? Craft centers, street markets (there are 100 in London alone), numerous auction houses (not just for the wealthy with most items priced under £100) "jumble sales" (comparable to yard sales in the U.S.), and newspaper ads will provide happy hunting grounds. Last visit, for instance, I picked up a newspaper only to find my dream castle for sale. If it is not for sale in England, it probably cannot be found.

I can almost guarantee that once you start shopping, whatever amount of money you brought will not be enough to take advantage of all the wonderful buys you'll encounter—the only answer is a return trip.

Enjoy the shopping in England.

ENGLAND
Outlets in Northern England

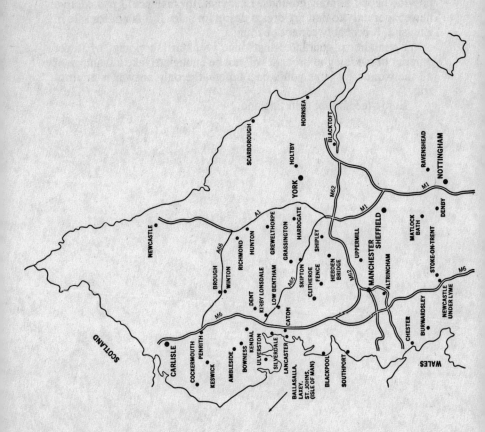

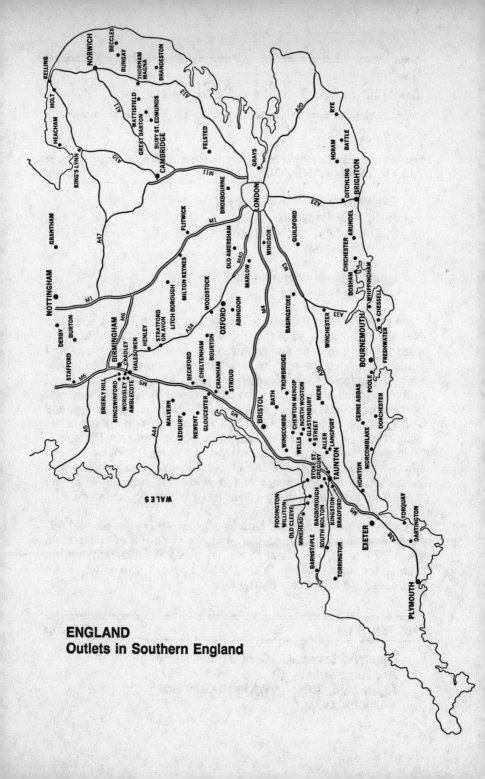

ENGLAND
Outlets in Southern England

Best buys in england

ALLER, NEAR LANGPORT   *Pottery*

The Pottery (craft workshop)
Aller, Near Langport
Somerset TA10 OQN, England
Tel. 0458-250244

HOURS: Monday–Saturday "dawn to dusk"
CREDIT CARDS: None

PRODUCTS: The Pottery is owned and run by Bryan and Julia Newman, who make all of the stoneware pottery by hand. They produce a variety of oven and tableware, decorative plates, vases, and some ceramic sculpture. The tableware is microwave, oven, dishwasher, and freezer safe. A coffee set with six mugs is £34.50. An oil and vinegar bottle is £3.35, a two-pound casserole is £6.10, a general purpose bowl is £1.90, and a small teapot is £6.90. Jugs, mugs, and vases range in price from £1.80 to £17.45 depending on the size of the pice. They have an annual sale three weeks prior to Christmas. Visitors are welcome to watch the work in progress. The clay (a blend of clays from Cornwall and Dorset) is made up on the premises. The glazes produce a wide range of soft colors and surfaces. They are made from natural materials such as feldspar, whiting, and wood ash.

LOCATION: Aller is a small farming village "of 280 people and 903 cows" in southwest England, just two miles northwest of Langport on the A372 road. This is about 15 miles due east of Taunton. There is a sign on the main road which says "Aller Pottery." The pottery has a nice courtyard and is very pleasant.

ALTRINCHAM   *Clothing*

Lakeland Sheepskin Centre (retail store)
29 George Street
Altrincham, Cheshire WA14 1RJ, England
Tel. 0619-289224

HOURS: Monday–Saturday 9:00–5:30
CREDIT CARDS: Access, American Express, Diners Club, Visa

PRODUCTS: Excellent, excellent, excellent! Get your credit cards ready and watch your budget fly out the window. Sweaters in all price ranges are available for men and women. Many of the colors and styles are unique to this shop. Quality cotton and woolen skirts in prints and solid colors with coordinated blouses were also being sold. The sheepskin coats (both short and long) were superbly styled and unique. And then come the leather and suede skirts, blazers, and jackets, where you may lose control of your wallet. The Lakeland Sheepskin Centre seems to have the perfect formula for style.

A cream blouse in polyester/viscose twill fabric was £15.99. A lovely sweater in a wool/cotton blend with drop shoulders for a man or a woman was only £19.99. An Aran sweater in virgin wool was £32.50. A fully lined ivory leather jacket, gently gathered from the yoke, was £259, with a fully-lined matching skirt for £185—together a stunning outfit that will never go out of style! A men's fully lined taupe leather jacket with top stitching was £139. An elegant ladies' leather blazer was £159—a perfect addition to any wardrobe.

The Cumberland sheepskin coat for men is a classic—leather-bound for longer life with inside zipper pockets. The coat length is 34″ and the price £229 for sizes 36 to 44. The Bedale sheepskin coat for women is 31″ long and £179 for sizes 10 to 18. My favorite was the Copenhagen full-length sheepskin coat 45″ long for £399.

Herdwick ties in pure new wool are about £3.50 while Herdwick his-and-her-tweed caps are from £6.99 in sizes 6¾ to 7⅜. Skirt lengths of Herdwick wool are £12.99 each; Aran knitting wool on a 35-ounce cone is £8.75, and eight real horn buttons are £6.50. (All prices include the VAT.) The VAT refund will be sent to you on all orders over £10.

MAIL ORDERS: Lakeland has a mail order color brochure with full mailing instructions. If you are unsure of your U.K. size, give the size you would normally wear at home and your measurements in centimeters. They will convert the measurements for you.

LOCATION: Altrincham is a suburb to the southwest of Manchester on the A56 in west-central England. The shop is situated on George Street in the main shopping precinct. It is one block south and west of the Altrincham Railway Station.

AMBLECOTE, NEAR STOURBRIDGE   *Crystal*

Thomas Webb Crystal (factory/showroom)
Dennis Hall, King William Street
Amblecote, Stourbridge, West Midlands DY8 4EZ, England
Tel. 0384-392521

HOURS: Shop: Monday–Friday 9:30–4:30; Saturday 9:30–1:00
(Closed on Bank Holidays)
Museum: Monday–Friday 9:30–4:30 (Closed on Bank
Holidays)
CREDIT CARDS: Access, Visa

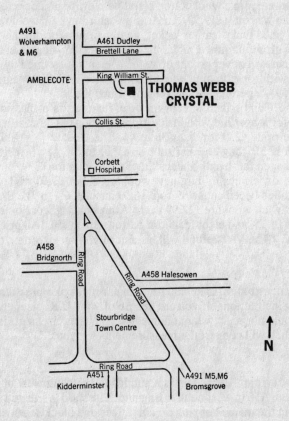

PRODUCTS: Thomas Webb Crystal has been manufactured since 1855. There is a good selection of first and second quality decanters, bowls, glasses, goblets, vases, compotes, candlesticks, and other items in a nicely displayed showroom. A coffee shop serves light refreshments. (Unfortunately we are unable to release prices from Thomas Webb.)

Thomas Webb Crystal was awarded a certificate of distinction in the "Come to Britain Trophy" competition organized by the British Tourist Authority.

TOURS: Factory tours are available Monday through Friday at 10:15, 11:00, 11:45, 2:15, and 3:00. Children under eight are not allowed to tour the factory. There is a charge of 50 pence for adults and 25 pence for children. Groups of 10 or more people must book tours in advance.

LOCATION: Amblecote is near Birmingham in central England. The town is one mile north of Stourbridge on the A491 to Wolverhampton. Stourbridge is just west of Birmingham. See the map above.

AMBLECOTE, NEAR STOURBRIDGE   *Crystal*

Webb Corbett Royal Doulton Crystal (factory outlet)
Coalbourne Hill
Amblecote, Near Stourbridge, West Midlands DY8 4HF,
   England
Tel. 03843-295281

HOURS: Monday–Friday 10:00–5:00; Saturday 10:00–1:00
CREDIT CARDS: Access, American Express, Diners Club, Visa

PRODUCTS: Seconds, discontinued or experimental lines are sold at reduced prices at this shop. There are three small rooms of crystal glasses, bowls, bells, vases, pitchers, and candlesticks. There are some unusual shapes which we did not see at other outlets. These products have a wide price range. Most of the items were priced under £30 but I am not at liberty to disclose specific prices.

TOURS: Tours are given at 10:00 and 11:15, and include demonstrations of glass blowing, cutting, and polishing. All the stages of glass manufacturing are explained by a trained guide. Tours must be booked in advance. The cost, which includes lunch, is £5 per person.

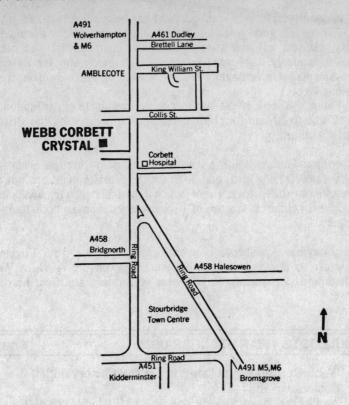

LOCATION: Amblecote is in central England about 10 miles west of Birmingham, and about one mile north of Stourbridge on the A491. See the map below.

AMBLESIDE   *Hand-Blown Glass*

Adrian Sankey Glass
Rothay Road
Ambleside, Cumbria LA22 0EE, England
Tel. 0966-33039

HOURS: Open daily 9:00–5:30; closed Monday, closed in January.
CREDIT CARDS: Access, American Express, Visa

PRODUCTS: In this small workshop visitors will find a range of functional and decorative lead crystal glassware. The two young craftsmen have a distinctive collection of richly colored glass.

Visitors can watch the molten material being worked into finished pieces. The glass is blown in the traditional manner and all work is hand finished. Each piece is individually colored by a complicated technique that results in a diversity of colors. On the base of the piece is the "pontil mark," which is the sign of handmade glass.

Birds, candlesticks, bowls, bud vases, large flower vases, cased paperweights, ruby glass and art deco brass lamps are created at Adrian Sankey Glass. A posy vase is £3.95, a bowl £9.95, a ruby paperweight £11.50, a large opal vase £18.50 and an art deco lamp £52.50.

Fun to watch, enjoyable to shop and all visitors very welcome.

LOCATION: Ambleside is in the center of the Lake District in northwest England on the A591. See the map below.

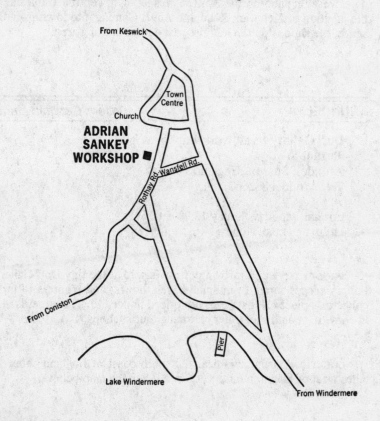

AMBLESIDE   *Clothing*

Lakeland Sheepskin Centre (retail store)
100, Lake Road
Ambleside, Cumbria LA22 ODE, England
Tel. 0966-32364

HOURS: April to November: Monday–Saturday 9:00–6:00; Sunday 10:30–6:00. Mid-November to March: Monday–Saturday 9:00–5:30

See the write-up under ALTRINCHAM.

LOCATION: Ambleside is in the center of the Lake District in northwest England on the A591. The shop is in central Ambleside at the junction of Kelswick Road and A591. Coming into town from the south, the shop is on the left just past a large parking area.

ARUNDEL   *Pottery, Ceramic Murals*

Duff Gallery (craft workshop)
Tarrant St.
Arundel, Sussex, England
Tel. Arundel 882600

HOURS: Monday–Friday 10:00–5:00
CREDIT CARDS: None

PRODUCTS: Hand-thrown pottery is sold at the tiny Duff Gallery. Pottery pieces range from small vases, bowls, and planters to large collector's pieces. Most items are priced under £20. The street is also lined with a number of other charming tourist shops.

LOCATION: Arundel is near the south coast of England about 18 miles west of Brighton on the A27 road. See the map below.

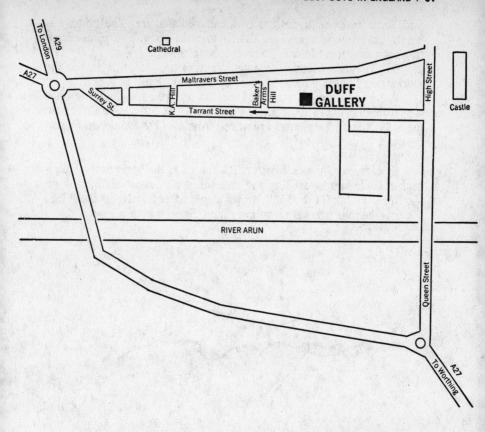

BAGBOROUGH   *Pottery*

Quantock Design Ltd. (factory/showroom)
The Quantock Pottery
Bagborough, Taunton, Somerset TA4 3EF, England
Tel. 0823-433057

HOURS: Monday–Friday 9:00–5:00; Saturday by appointment
    only.
CREDIT CARDS: Access, Visa

PRODUCTS: Quantock Pottery carries a range of handmade domestic and decorative stoneware pottery such as casseroles, vases,

and lamp bases with designs of local wild flowers. The pottery is mostly in browns and beiges similar to terra cotta. The pieces have flowers and other designs, and are quite unusual. Very nicely displayed. They have some seconds. Visitors are welcome to see the workshop. The showroom also has other craft items.

A King Arthur doorstop is £16.95, a chicken and duck four-pint casserole dish is £16.75, a butter dish sells for £6.50, a large Briar rose jug is £9.20, and lamp bases are priced from £7.75 to £25 depending on the size.

LOCATION: Quantock Pottery is situated in the heart of the Quantock Hills in southwest England nine miles northwest of Taunton on the A358. Watch for the small brown signs. After turning off the A358, the road becomes a narrow country lane. See the map below.

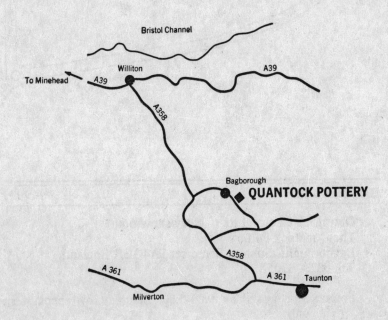

BALLASALLA, ISLE OF MAN   *Porcelain*

Shebeg Gallery (workshop)
Ballasalla, Isle of Man, England
Tel. 0624-823497

HOURS: Monday–Friday 9:00–5:30; Saturday–Sunday 10:30–
12:30 and 2:00–5:00. Closed for 14 days beginning December 25th.
CREDIT CARDS: None

PRODUCTS: In this workshop visitors will find figurines in matt
and glazed porcelain which has been fired to 1300° C. The subjects
have been drawn from rural life in Britain with people and animals as
the main subjects. Mr. Harper has specialized in pedigree cattle (15
breeds), which are totally hand painted and minutely detailed. The
Aberdeen Angus bull was truly a work of art! Cats, dogs, sheep,
lambs, ducks, and horses are also available. Prices quoted include the
VAT plus shipping and insurance in the United Kingdom. Overseas
prices must be requested. A four-inch shepherd and dog is £16.90. A
small two-inch matt porcelain lamb is £3.90. An eight-inch goat on a
rock is £42. All of the cattle sculpture, which are on a ceramic plinth
with polished wood base, are £81.
Over 11 years of work have gone into the cattle porcelain designs.
They are not sold in any shops, only directly to the public. Only 25
cattle figures can be created each week so plan on at least one month
for the creation to be completed.
If you have an animal with particular markings, please send a
clear photograph of front, rear, and both sides, to help them create a
distinct likeness.
A price list of the figures plus shipping costs will be sent upon
request. Payment in full must accompany each order. A full refund is
given if a customer is not satisfied.

LOCATION: The Isle of Man is off the northwest coast of England.
Ballasalla is in the south of the Isle of Man, about a mile north of
Castletown. From Douglas take the A5 south to Ballasalla, about eight
miles. Turn right onto the A34 for Ballamodha. The Gallery is 300
yards on the left after a right turn onto the A4. Parking is on the
premises.

BARNSTAPLE   *Pottery*

C.H. Brannam Ltd. (factory outlet)
Litchdon Potteries
Litchdon Street
Barnstaple, Devon EX32 8NE, England
Tel. 0271-43035 or 76853

HOURS: Shop: Monday–Friday 9:00–1:00 and 2:00–5:00
Factory: 6:00–2:00
CREDIT CARDS: Barclaycard

PRODUCTS: Litchdon Potteries specializes in pot covers, planters, patio pots, wall pots, and bulb bowls. Clay flower pots and saucers in all sizes are sold. Some pottery kitchenware is sold as well as some Italian terra cotta planters. Seconds are available. Special sales are held July 23rd to August 5th.

Litchdon Potteries is the only British clay pot manufacturing plant in operation today.

Pottery making in Barnstaple can be traced back to the early sixteenth century.

In 1879, there were two potteries in the city. With a few men and some basic machinery, C.H. Brannam Ltd. was created. During this period, horses dragged rollers to prepare the clay. The retail shop was on the ground floor of the owner's home. Today the firm, employing 60 people covers an acre adjoining the original site. Their present production consists of glazed pottery, traditional items, such as pitchers and bread pans, large terra cotta garden vases, and millions of flower pots annually.

The local Fremington Clay, plus glazes and other materials, are supplied to small potteries, studios, and art schools throughout England. The clay field is three miles away from the factory. After the clay is dug out, it must be placed outside to age for 12 months before it may be used. The factory uses about 30 tons of clay per week.

Lumps of clay are fed into four pot-making machines on three floors of the factory. Spinning steel dies press out the pots, which are then transported to a drying room where they dry for 24 hours.

The pots are then placed in kilns capable of holding 4000 small pots or 350 of the largest pots. It takes five full days to complete the entire firing process.

The pottery comes in two color combinations—dark brown or oatmeal glaze over terra cotta. A ten-inch bread crock is £14.99, a wine cooler £2.99, a baking dish £4.77, an air-tight storage jar £3.44, and a six-pint casserole dish is £7.84. All of the glazes used are certified as complying with British and American standards of lead and cadmium release.

The pottery selection is vast and the prices exceptionally reasonable.

TOURS: Tours are given at 10:15, 11:00, and 11:45 and last about 40 minutes. Groups are asked to make arrangements in advance with a minimum of 15 people in a group.

LOCATION: Barnstaple is in the far southwest of England near the west coast. It is due west of Taunton about 50 miles on the A361 road. The factory and shop are located directly behind the Imperial Hotel on Litchdon Street just off the square and clock tower.

BARNSTAPLE   *Sheepskin and Leather Goods*

Messrs. S. Sanders and Son, Ltd. (factory/retail shop)
Pilton Bridge
Barnstaple, North Devon, EX32 7AA England
Tel. 0271-42335 and 45481

HOURS: Monday–Friday 8:00–5:00; Saturdays during summer months 9:30–12:00
CREDIT CARDS Access, Barclaycard, Visa

PRODUCTS: This sheepskin tannery has been on the same site for over 200 years. They sell men's and women's sheepskin coats, natural shape sheepskin rugs, hides and hide rugs, leather goods, wool scarves, toys, car seat covers, gloves, mitts, and handbags. Sheepskin rugs range in price from £17 to £24. Men's and women's gloves range from £8.90 to £12.80. Women's sheepskin coats range from £120 to £178, and men's from £180 to £195. There are usually two seasonal sales held during autumn and January. They will ship goods abroad.

MAIL ORDER: They do offer a mail order service.

TOURS: The 30-minute tour is offered to groups of 20. Arrangements must be made in advance.

LOCATION: Barnstaple is in the far southwest of England near the west coast. It is due west of Taunton about 50 miles on the A361 road. Go through the center of town, past the Imperial Hotel, and the clock tower in the roundabout. Turn north onto the A39 toward Lynton. This will become Pilton Causeway. The shop will be on your right just before Pilton Park on your left.

BASINGSTOKE   *Craft Items*

Viables Centre (craft centre)
Harrow Way (Old A30)
Basingstoke, Hampshire RG22 4BJ, England
Tel. 0256-3634

HOURS: Tuesday–Friday 1:00–4:00; Saturday–Sunday 2:00–5:00
CREDIT CARDS: None

PRODUCTS: Visitors will find a community of craftspeople in a rural setting of old farm buildings. Each craftsperson has a workshop of his own. Represented crafts include silver items, jewelry, pottery, furniture, leatherwork, screen-printed fabrics, metal engravings, soft toys, wood turning, and bronze castings.

Pottery vases begin at £2.50, silver charms begin at £3.50, and soft toys begin at £5. A very talented artist creates bronze castings which can cost up to £5000 per piece.

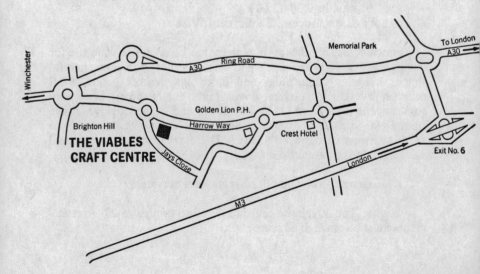

On weekends a tea shop is open for visitors. During the May Day Bank Holiday weekend a large craft fair is held. Large rooms are available catering to groups.

LOCATION: Basingstoke is 30 miles southeast of London on the M3. Take exit number 6, then take the A30 south. See the map on the preceding page.

BATH   *Clothing*

Lakeland Sheepskin Centre (retail store)
5 Union Street
Bath, Avon, BA1 1RP England
Tel. 0225-66313

HOURS: Monday–Saturday 9:00–5:30

See the writeup under ALTRINCHAM.

LOCATION: Bath is in the southwest, about 12 miles southeast of Bristol on the A4 road. The shop is in the center of Bath's pedestrian shopping area. It is on Union Street half a block north of the Tourist Information Centre, or about one block north of the Roman Baths.

BATH   *China, Crystal, Figurines*

Reject China Shop
34 Stall Street
Bath, Avon BA1 1QG, England
Tel. 95-50870

HOURS: Monday–Saturday 9:00–6:00

See the description for this same company under LONDON.

LOCATION: Bath is in the southwest, about 12 miles southeast of Bristol on the A4 road. The Reject China Shop is in the center of town, just across the street (west) from the Roman Baths. See the map below.

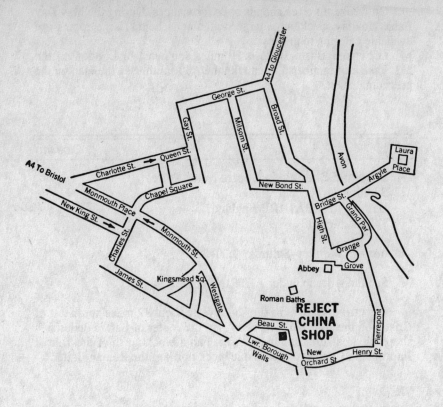

BATH   *Kitchen Shop*

Scoops (retail store)
26 Milsom Street
Bath, Avon BA1 1DG, England
Tel. 0225-66066

HOURS: Monday–Saturday 9:30–6:00; June–July: Sunday 12:00–
6:00

See the write-up under STRATFORD-UPON-AVON.

LOCATION: Bath is in the southwest, about 12 miles southeast of
Bristol on the A4 road. See the map.

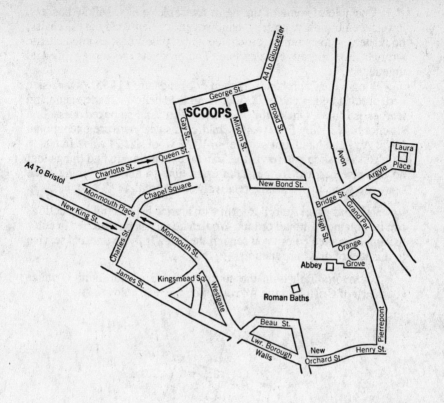

BATH *Handmade Crafts*

Wellow Crafts (craft centre)
Kingsmead Square
Bath, Avon BA1 1RP, England
Tel. 0225-64358

HOURS: Monday–Saturday 9:30–5:30
CREDIT CARDS: American Express, Barclaycard, MasterCard

PRODUCTS: Wellow Crafts is a small retail shop which represents about 180 local craftspeople. About 30 different types of crafts are represented and a daily demonstration takes place in the shop. Wellow Crafts has received writeups in *Harper's, Vogue, Time,* and *The Daily Telegraph.*

A sample of some of the items available: quilts, willow baskets, jewelry, embroidery, pottery, handwoven woolens, tea cosys, chairs, bookshelves, toy animals, crocheted items, pillow cases, caned chairs, wrought iron, jigsaw puzzles, etc. The products are top quality and unique.

Winnie the Pooh handscreened bookends are £14.95. A king-size ecru crochet bedspread is £225. A handmade bellows, made of elm and leather, is £40.50. One of the best buys was a hand-smocked dress for a six-month-old baby for £14.40. Children's sweaters were exceptional buys. An Aran hand knit sweater in 100% wool size 24 was £16.60.

This is a shop where visitors can take their time to find things that no one else carries. It does take extra time to find everything since there are so many items in a relatively small area.

MAIL ORDERS: An order form with a price list and full instructions can be obtained for mail orders. Woolen items will be matched in color to sample woolen colors you send in the mail. Truly an unusual service in this day of mass production.

LOCATION: Bath is in the southwest of England about 12 miles southeast of Bristol on the A4 road. See the map below.

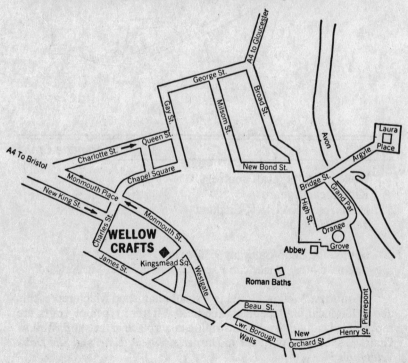

BATTLE   *Suede Clothing*

Lilian Forshaw
"Potters"
Darwell Hill, Netherfield
Battle, East Sussex TN33 9QL, England
Tel. 042482 300

HOURS: By appointment only on Tuesday and Thursday
CREDIT CARDS: Access, Visa

PRODUCTS: Lilian Forshaw has created a company which makes high quality beautifully finished garments in very soft lambskin suede. All garments are fully lined. Ninety-nine percent of her business is done by mail order. Sample garments are, however, at the shop (in her home) and can be seen by appointment. You pick the color and style of the garment and each one is custom made. It takes about four weeks to complete a garment. It is then mailed to you.

If you are not totally satisfied, your money will be refunded in full if you return the garment in perfect condition within 14 days. Prices begin at £84.50 and go up to £153.50.

This is a small company which fashions top quality styles and is only for the serious shopper, not just for browsers.

"Preston" is a neatly styled blouson suit with sleeves gathered into small cuffs. It is belted with a suede covered one-inch wide elastic with an oval suede buckle. The top is available in plain or perforated suede in sizes 10 to 30, at a cost of £135.50 for sizes 10 to 14. (Prices increase according to your size.) The fully lined matching six-gore skirt "Hurst" has a narrower center front panel. It is a gentle A line, very flattering for the larger lady, available in sizes 10 to 30. The cost is £99.75.

MAIL ORDER: Lilian welcomes mail orders. She will send an instruction sheet for measurements, sizes, and a well-illustrated brochure with swatches of the beautiful skins she uses. There is a $2 charge for the brochure. It would be best to plan on two months for the manufacturing and shipping of the garment.

LOCATION: Battle is near the southeast coast about six miles northwest of Hastings on the B2100. Her cottage is named Potters and is on the B2096 four miles to the west of Battle on the road to Heathfield just above the crossroads of Darwell Hole. It is on the right, opposite Doctors Farm. During the summer, the house is not easily seen as it is on the edge of a bush woodland near the lovely old village of Brightling.

BECCLES   *Dried Flowers*

Winter Flora
Hall Farm
Weston, Beccles, Suffolk NR34 8TT, England
Tel. 0502-713346

HOURS: Monday–Friday 9:00–5:00; weekends by appointment
CREDIT CARDS: None

PRODUCTS: Winter Flora is a manufacturer of dried floral arrangements in a large variety of sizes, shapes, and colors. Almost all of the flowers and grasses are grown on their own 30-acre farms in Broome and Weston. Most of the seeds are sown under glass in March and planted in the fields in May. Flower picking begins in July and ends in October. August is the peak harvesting and drying month when the barns and drying rooms are a spectacular mixture of colors and aromas.

The unloading of the mass of pinks, blues, mauves, corals, and autumn shades is wonderful to watch as the trailer loads of flowers are driven to the barns and hung for drying. Flowers, grasses, and preserved foliage make each of their arrangements colorful and unique. Posies and loose bunches of flowers are available from £1. Seconds are also available at reasonable prices. Prepackaged arrangements of flowers and grasses in boxes are sold for £4.90 to £5.60. They supply over 800 shops in the United Kingdom.

TOURS: It is best to visit in autumn and winter. Large groups can only be accommodated in October and November by appointment. Tours last about an hour.

LOCATION: Beccles is in the east of England, about 18 miles southeast of Norwich on the A146 road.

BECKFORD, NEAR TEWKESBURY   *Silk Items*

Beckford Silk (factory/showroom)
The Old Vicarage
Beckford, Near Tewkesbury, Gloucestershire GL20 7AD,
England
Tel. 0386-881507

HOURS: Monday–Friday 9:00–1:00 and 2:00–6:00; Saturday 2:00–
5:00
CREDIT CARDS: None

PRODUCTS: Beckford Silk was started in 1975 in the converted
coach house of the Old Vicarage. James and Marthe Gardner print silk
and sell mainly scarves and silk ties. It is a small quaint shop with silk

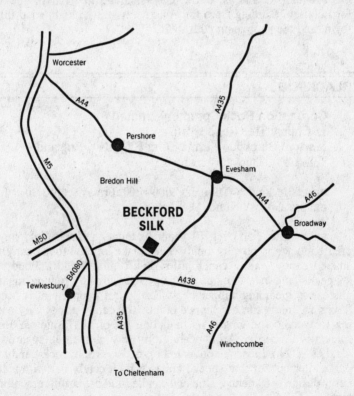

designs and colors of exceptional quality. Prices are 30% to 40% above manufacturer's prices, which is about 50% of what one would expect in a retail outlet. Silk scarves vary from £5 to £11.50 with the average scarf selling for £8.50. Silk ties are £6.50, handkerchiefs £2.75, evening bags £11.50, and dresses are £75. Some second quality items are always available.

TOURS: Groups are limited to 10 people. The printing usually takes place Monday through Friday from 9:00–12:00 and from 2:00– 6:00. The silk must also be steamed, color separated and washed. A brochure given to purchasing customers explains all of these processes.

LOCATION: Beckford is in west England about 15 miles south of Worcester, just east of Tewkesbury across the M5 Motorway. See the map. Beckford Silk is at the Old Vicarage in front of the Beckford church. Coming from the A435, stay on the main road through town, and the shop is on your right.

BLACKPOOL   *Rock Candy*

Coronation Rock Company Limited
11 Cherry Tree Road North
Marton, Blackpool, Lancashire FY4 4NY, England
Tel. 0253-62366

HOURS: Monday–Thursday 9:00–4:00; Friday 9:00–3:30
CREDIT CARDS: None

PRODUCTS: For over 50 years Coronation Rock Company has created rock and novelty candy. They make lettered rock candy, fruit-shaped candy, candy canes, after dinner mints, and molded candy shapes. The candy is made over open gas fires by boiling sugar and glucose in gleaming copper pans. Real oil of peppermint is used for flavoring. Items can be shipped home. The candy prices vary according to weight and length. A miniature jar of old-fashioned English sweets is 79 pence. An appealing tiny tray with three sugared fruit candies is 79 pence. A souvenir box of Blackpool rock candy is 69 pence, perfect for that special child. A rock candy bar with a strawberry design is 69 pence. Unusual candies and delightful remembrance gifts.

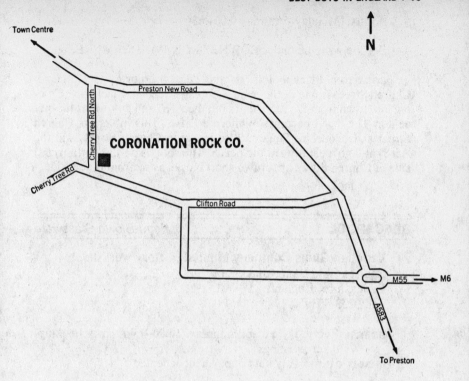

TOURS: A viewing gallery allows visitors to view the manufacturing area without entering it. Tours can be given to groups of up to 25, with a tour lasting about 45 minutes. Arrangements for group tours must be made in advance.

LOCATION: Blackpool is in northern England on the western seacoast. The Coronation Rock Co. is on the east side of town near the M55 motorway. See the map.

BLACKPOOL   *Clothing*

Lakeland Sheepskin Centre (retail store)
68 Church Street
Blackpool, Lancashire FY1 1HP, England
Tel. 0253-27432

HOURS: Monday–Saturday 9:00–5:30

See the write-up under BOWNESS-ON-WINDERMERE.

LOCATION: Blackpool is on the coast of northwest England. Church Street is one of the main shopping streets in Blackpool. Coming into town from the M55, exit onto the A583 and go toward the city center. The A583 becomes Whitegate Drive. This intersects Church Street at Devonshire Square. Turn left onto Church Street (still the A583) and go west toward the beach. The shop is on the north (right) side of Church Street about two short blocks away from the seaside.

BLACKPOOL   *Hand-Blown Glassware*

Venetian Glass Company Limited (factory/workshop)
Squires Gate Lane, Blackpool
Lancashire, England
Tel. 0253-403950

HOURS: Every day except Saturday, 10:00–4:40; party bookings taken evenings
CREDIT CARDS: Any kind of payment accepted

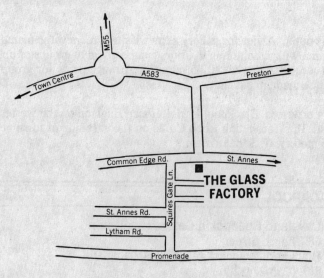

PRODUCTS: Venetian Glass Company's skilled glassblowers create animals, figurines, and all kinds of glassware. They have a special seconds shop in the factory. Items can be shipped anywhere.

TOURS: Fifteen-minute tours are given throughout the day. Advance booking is advised for parties over 30.

LOCATION: Blackpool is on the northwest coast of England. See the map below.

BLACKTOFT, NEAR GOOLE   *Pottery*

Jerry Harper Handthrown Pottery (workshop)
Staddlethorpe Lane
Blacktoft Near Goole, N. Humberside DN14 7XT, England
Tel. Howden 41082

HOURS: Monday–Friday 9:00–5:00; most Sundays 11:00–5:00
CREDIT CARDS: None

PRODUCTS: Jerry Harper creates handmade stoneware embossed with the Yorkshire rose. He sells goblets, vases, plates, pitchers, mugs, and tankards. All of his stoneware was very inexpensive. Goblets and mugs were priced from £1.80, beakers (a glass with a wide mouth) £1.80, plates from £1.60, pitchers between £1.60 and £5.50, and tankards from £3.20. Seconds are available. Glazes are usually two-toned in beiges, browns, or blues.

TOURS: Tours are given which last 20 to 40 minutes. There is a charge of £5.50 per tour for groups of up to 50 people. Arrangements for tours must be made in advance.

LOCATION: Blacktoft is in north-central England six miles due east of Goole, which is about 30 miles east of Leeds on the M62. Traveling on the M62, go east past Goole 10 miles to exit 38. Turn back toward Newport on the B1230. Go three miles to Gilberdyke. Then go south three miles on an unnumbered road to Blacktoft.

BOSHAM   *Craft Items*

Bosham Walk Craft Centre
Bosham, West Sussex PO18 8HX, England
Tel. 0943-579475

HOURS: Monday–Sunday 10:00–5:30; November 1–March 31;
    closed at 5:00 on weekdays
CREDIT CARDS: Access, Barclaycard

PRODUCTS: Bosham Walk is in one of the oldest and best known
villages in Sussex. Bosham Walk brings together more than a dozen
small craft shops under one roof. The inside of the building is arranged
as an old Sussex street scene, and contains old ship timbers, oak
beams, and rustic wooden porches.

The shops offer a selection of items including jewelry, engraved
glass, portraits, lanterns, and macrame. There is also a bookshop,
boutique, clock restorer, weaver, art gallery, and an antique tool collector's shop. The shops will ship items overseas.

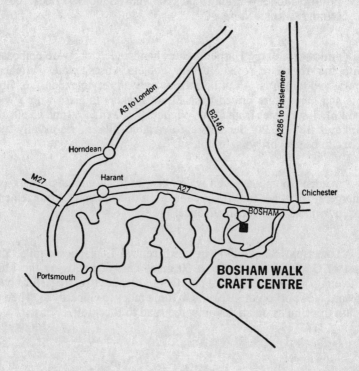

Marine watercolors and oil paintings are priced from £48, original brass and copper lamps from £22, antique clocks from £50, antique tools from £10, English pewter items from £6, bronze sculpture from £120, hand-knit wool sweaters from £28, and porcelain sculptures from £7.

LOCATION: Bosham is on the south coast three miles west of Chichester, and 17 miles east of Portsmouth, one mile south of the A27 coast road. Follow the signs to the Quay. The Craft Centre will be on your right. See the map below.

BOURNEMOUTH   *Kitchen Shop*

Scoops (retail store)
48 Westover Road
Bournemouth, Hampshire BH1 2DA, England
Tel. 0202-25366

HOURS: Monday–Saturday 9:30–6:00; June–July: Sunday 12:00–6:00

See the write-up under STRATFORD-UPON-AVON.

LOCATION: Bournemouth is on the south-central coast of England, just west of the Isle of Wight.

BOURTON-ON-THE-WATER   *Pottery*

Bourton Pottery (craft workshop)
Clayton Row
Bourton-on-the-Water, Gloucestershire, GL54 2DN, England
Tel. None

HOURS: Monday–Saturday 8:30–5:30; Sunday in summer 11:00–5:00
CREDIT CARDS: Access, Visa

PRODUCTS: This small pottery workshop has a very good selection of well made, functional, and decorative pottery pieces. They

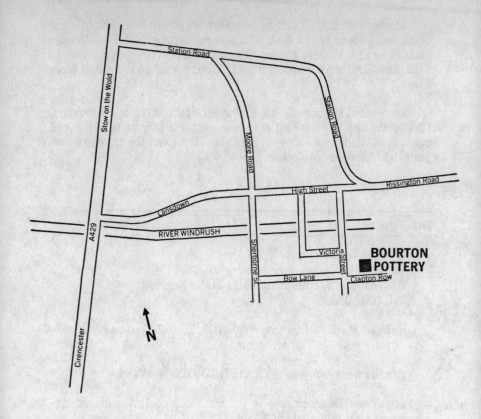

tend to specialize in items under £5. Vases, cups, bowls, mugs, plates, and pitchers are just a few of the many items that they sell. A great place for small gifts! The pottery workshop is behind the display room so visitors may watch the items being made. Some seconds are available.

LOCATION: Bourton-on-the-Water is in the Cotswold Hills area to the northwest of London (about 20 miles due east of Gloucester). The town is about halfway between Oxford on the east and Cheltenham on the west, five miles north of the A40 road on the A429. It is one of my favorite villages in all of England. Picture-perfect stone houses with beautiful English gardens are beside a tiny stream filled with ducks. Tiny bridges, quaint gift shops, excellent restaurants, and no traffic make this a perfect retreat for visitors. Americans should take lessons from the British on how to slow down. See the map above.

BOURTON-ON-THE-WATER   *Perfumes*

The Cotswold Perfumery Ltd. (factory shop)
Victoria Street
Bourton-on-the-Water, Gloucestershire GL54 2BU, England
Tel. 0451-20698

HOURS: Monday–Sunday 9:00–5:00. (Opened later in the summer). Closed Christmas Day, Boxing Day, New Year's Day

CREDIT CARDS: American Express, MasterCard, Visa

PRODUCTS: The Cotswold Perfumery was founded in 1963. Today they produce ten perfumes, each fragrance unique but all essentially British. Each fragrance is available in the form of cologne, bath oil, or bubble bath. Visitors may sample each perfume. The fragrances are blended on the premises from over 800 aromatic ingredients from all over the world. They have a nice selection of handblown perfume

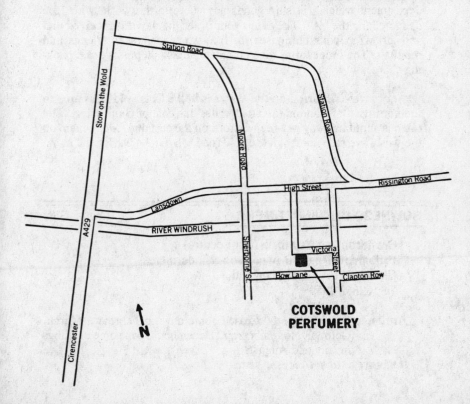

bottles. They also have a catalog with a variety of elegant products and perfumes and hold an annual sale in January.

Any three mini bottles of cologne sell for £2.25, while a six-bottle mini collection is £3.95. After-shave lotion for men is £3.20 for 48 milliliters. Most of the bath oils are £3.45 for 48 milliliters while most perfumes cost £6.95 for 7 milliliters. Prices are very reasonable and the aroma inside of this factory makes it a very worthwhile stop.

TOURS: A self-guided tour may be taken which shows the history of perfume making. Per Fumum is an Exhibition of Perfumery with a lovely perfume garden to stroll through at your leisure. Visitors will find an experience which includes "smell-vision," which is an audio-visual and fragrance show in a specially constructed theater. A perfume quiz tests the accuracy of your nose against the experts. A reproduction of an early perfume lab allows the visitor to step back in time. Learn how essential oils are extracted from plants and blended as well as how perfumes are classified.

MAIL ORDERS: The Cotswold Perfumery does have a mail order department which will ship goods anywhere in the world with 15% deducted for the VAT. They ship your order the day it is received and will gift wrap your purchases for free when mailing to friends and relatives. The order forms give complete details on postage and packing charges.

LOCATION: Bourton-on-the-Water is in the Cotswold Hills area to the northwest of London (about 20 miles due east of Gloucester). The town is about halfway between Oxford on the east and Cheltenham on the west, five miles north of the A40 road, on the A429. See the map.

BOWNESS-ON-WINDERMERE *Crafts, Gifts*

Craftsmen of Cumbria (craft centre)
Fallbarrow Road, Bowness-on-Windermere
Cumbria, LA23DH, England
Tel. 09662-2959

HOURS: Daily 9:30–6:00 Closed some days in February, March, October, November, and December. Open some evenings in July and August.
CREDIT CARDS: Access, Visa

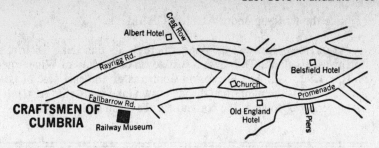

PRODUCTS: Craftsmen of Cumbria is a large craft centre set in an eighteenth-century building. They sell a variety of craft items such as jewelry, leather, pottery, lapidary, woodwork, glass engraving, and crystal, plus a selection of craft-oriented gifts. At times craftspeople are working on their items in the center. Due to the vast selection of items at this shop, we have chosen to give price ranges. Silver jewelry ranges from £1 to £20, leather goods are priced from 1 to £20, pottery ranges from £3 to £30, and lapidary is priced from 10 pence to £100. There is a seasonal sale in September or October. They will ship goods.

TOURS: Touring is on a casual basis (not guided). For groups over 10, please telephone in advance.

LOCATION: Bowness-on-Windermere is in the northwest Lake District of England just south of Windermere on the A592. See the map.

BOWNESS-ON-WINDERMERE　　*Leather Clothing, Sweaters*

Lakeland Sheepskin Centre (retail store)
Crag Brow House
Lake Road
Bowness-on-Windermere, Cumbria LA23 3BT, England
Tel. 09662-4466

HOURS: March–October: Monday–Saturday 9:00–6:00; Sunday
10:30–6:00
Except mid–July through August: Monday–Saturday
9:00–9:30; Sunday 10:30–9:30
November–February: Monday–Saturday 9:00–5:30; Sunday 10:30–5:30

See the write-up under ALTRINCHAM.

LOCATION: Bowness-on-Windermere is in the Lake District in northwest England. The town is just south of the city of Windermere on the A592 road. The Sheepskin Centre is on the east side of Lake Road, which is the main road through town (and is also the A592). It is in the center of town at the corner of Lake Road and Helm Road.

BOWNESS-ON-WINDERMERE   *Horn Products*

The Horn Shop (retail factory outlet)
3 Crag Brow
Bowness-on-Windermere, Cumbria LA23 3BX, England
Tel. Windermere 4519

HOURS: Monday–Saturday 9:00–6:00
            Summer: Monday–Saturday 9:30–8:00; Sunday 1:00–9:00
CREDIT CARDS: Access

PRODUCTS: At this shop you will find various products hand made from sheep, goat, and cattle horn. This is one of the oldest crafts in the world. The horn is cut, shaped, and polished. The Horn Shop makes over 180 different horn items such as combs, ships, buttons, cutlery, walking sticks, spoons, and powder horns. The workmanship is excellent and prices are reasonable. A large ladle in real horn sold for £10. A classic graduated horn necklace was priced between £9 and £20. A set of six staghorn-handled steak knives was about £48. Elegant horn spoons and scoops for all purposes were from £2 to £5. For creative sewers there are elegant staghorn buttons from 40 to 50 pence each.

LOCATION: Bowness-on-Windermere is in the northwest of England in the famous Lake District. It is just south of the town of Windermere on the A592. The shop is on the east side of the main road, being the A592, in the center of town.

BOWNESS-ON-WINDERMERE   *Woolen Items*

Windermere Woolens (retail store)
Glebe Road
Bowness-on-Windermere, Cumbria LA23 3HB, England

HOURS: Monday–Saturday 9:00–5:30; Monday–Sunday (Easter until October) 8:30–5:30

See the write-up for Moffat Woollens Limited in the town of MOFFAT, SCOTLAND.

LOCATION: Bowness-on-Windermere is in the Lake District in the northwest of England just south of Windermere on the A592. The shop is on the lake shore in the Aquatics Centre. From the steamer pier, go south and take the first right turn onto Glebe Road. The Tourist Information office is on the corner. Windermere Woollens is 150 yards down the road. There are two Scottish flags flying from the company's flagpole.

BRADFORD-ON-TONE   *Alcoholic Cider*

R. J. Sheppy and Son
Three Bridges
Bradford-on-Tone, Taunton, Somerset TA4 1ER, England
Tel. 082-346-233

HOURS: Easter to Christmas: 8:30 to dusk from Monday–Saturday; Sunday 12:00–2:00
January to Easter: Monday–Saturday only 8:30–6:00
CREDIT CARDS: None

PRODUCTS: R. J. Sheppy and Son started producing cider commercially in 1925. Somerset is known as Cider Country and due to the climate and suitable soil, some of the best cider apple orchards in the country are located here. In the past each orchard usually processed its own brand of cider in an old stone mill using a heavy wooden screw press and oat straw to bind the apple pulp together.

Today, of course, a high-powered apple mill and hydraulic press with nylon cloth is used to extract and filter the juice, which is then put into large barrels and vats to ferment and mature into cider.

Many of the small, rural cider farms now sell their apples to large commercialized cider producers. R.J. Sheppy & Son is one of the few old-fashioned farms left. The farm has a total of 42 acres of apple orchards. Over the years, they have won over 200 awards for their quality cider.

The Farm Shop sells cider, mugs, shortbread, cheese, and other foods. Their prices are competitive with other cider producers.

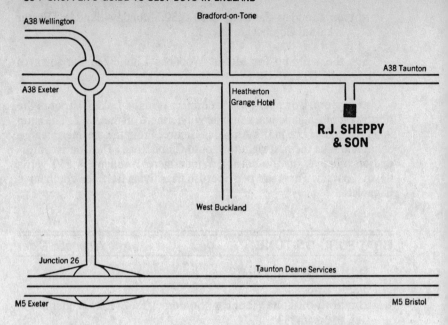

TOURS: Guided tours which take up to two hours are available. Tours include a visit to the orchards, cellars, press room, farm/cider museum (with slides of cider-making), and cider tasting. The charge is £1.25 per person. Ploughman's lunches can usually be booked in advance at an extra charge.

LOCATION: Sheppy's is in the southwest, roughly midway between Wellington and Taunton on the A38. This is about 1½ miles from the M5 junction 26. See the map.

BRANDESTON   *Wine*

Brandeston Priory Vineyards
Brandeston, Woodbridge, Suffolk 1P13 7AU, England
Tel. 072-882-462

HOURS: May 1–October 1: daily 10:00–5:00
CREDIT CARDS: Access, Barclaycard

PRODUCTS: Visitors will find vineyards where wine is bottled and sold. Prices begin at £3.62 a bottle. A small shop offers a selection of wine, crafts, and souvenirs.

TOURS: Daily tours which last up to an hour are given. Groups of any size are welcome as long as arrangements are made in advance.

LOCATION: Brandeston is near the east coast. From Ipswich take the A12 north about 13 miles and turn north onto the B1116. At the town of Hacheston turn left onto an unmarked road to Easton. Then go northwest to Kettleburg, then Brandeston.

BRIERLEY HILL   *Crystal*

Royal Brierley Crystal (factory/outlet)
North Street, Brierley Hill
West Midlands DY5 3SJ, England
Tel. 0384-70161

HOURS: Factory Shop: Monday–Saturday 9:00–4:30; Tea Shop/ Restaurant: Monday–Friday 9:00–4:00; Saturday 9:00– 2:00
Both shops and a crystal museum are open on Sundays from May through September.
CREDIT CARDS: Access, American Express, Visa

PRODUCTS: Royal Brierley Crystal manufactures full lead crystal with a minimum of 30% lead oxide which gives it extra brilliance. Each piece is mouth-blown and hand decorated. Royal Brierley Crystal is allegedly the only company in the world to have the Royal Warrant to supply crystal to her Majesty the Queen.

The variety is extensive—bowls, vases, pitchers, wine goblets, champagne glasses, sherry glasses, decanters, jugs, etc. Some of the crystal is frosted. In the shop you will find second quality items, rejects and discontinued lines. Their quality is superb! Highly recommended!

Over 200 years of experience are behind Royal Brierley Crystal. Prices are excellent. A honey pot which Winnie the Pooh would have been proud to own is £10. Small wine glasses are £5 and large wine glasses are £5.50 each. A square spirit decanter which would enhance any bar is £38. A quart jug is £20. These prices are a reduction of at least 100% on retail prices. Their major sales are held in February and July. They will package items for shipment, but you must mail the packages yourself.

TOURS: Factory tours which last about 1½ hours are given for groups of up to 50 people. The tour includes visits to different departments: mixing of raw materials, furnaces, glassblowing, processing departments, cutting and decorating. It is essential that arrangements for group tours be made in advance. Written requests will be accepted beginning each October 1st for tours during the following spring. Please specify three alternate dates. If you phone in your reservations, please call between 11:00 and 1:00. Morning tours begin at 11:00 Monday through Friday. Afternoon tours start at 1:00 Monday through Thursday. The charge is 50 pence per person—only 16 years and older.

Should you wish to visit the Honeyborne Museum situated on the grounds, a separate application must be sent to the curator. Viewing time for groups is noon, and the tour lasts about 30 minutes. Admission charge is 15 pence per person.

If you are interested in staying in the area, they provide a list of hotels and restaurants.

LOCATION: Brierley Hill is just west of Birmingham, about nine miles due south of Wolverhampton. See the map.

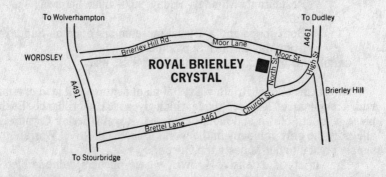

BRIGHTON   *Craft Items*

Barclaycraft Craft Gallery
7 East Street
Brighton, Sussex BN1 1HP, England
Tel. Brighton 0273-21694

HOURS: Monday–Saturday 10:15–1:00 and 2:00–5:30
CREDIT CARDS: Access, American Express, Diners Club, Visa

PRODUCTS: Barclaycraft Craft Gallery is a small shop which specializes in exclusive ceramics, jewelry, glass, wood, and contemporary original prints. Some of the finest individual work of British studio craftsmen and women is sold here. Between four and six special exhibitions are held each year. Barclaycraft Craft Gallery is the only gallery south of London to be recommended by the British Crafts Council in their *Selected List of Craft Shops and Galleries in England and Wales.* Prices range from £5 for a small vase to £500 for a collector's quality pottery bowl. Most items are priced between £20 and £100. Shipping can be arranged. The VAT is refundable to customers returning overseas.

LOCATION: Brighton is on the south coast of England about 33 miles south of London on the A23. The Craft Gallery is just behind the Tourist Information Centre near the Royal Pavilion. See the map below.

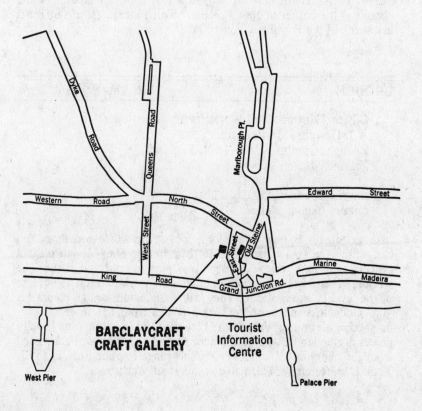

BRIGHTON   *Clothing*

Lakeland Sheepskin Centre (retail store)
161 North Street
Brighton, Sussex BN1 1VF, England
Tel. 0273-202421

HOURS: Monday–Saturday 9:00–5:30

See the write-up under ALTRINCHAM.

LOCATION: Brighton is on the south coast of England about 33 miles
south of London on the A23. Coming into town on the A23 (Preston
Road, then London Road), go toward the city centre and the Royal
Pavilion. Just before reaching the Pavilion, turn right onto Church
Street. Then take the first left onto New Road. Go one block, and the
shop is at the corner of New Road and North Street. (North Street is
just south of the Royal Pavilion.)

BROUGH   *Jewelry Craft Items*

Clifford House Craft Workshop
A.J. Designs, Market Street
Brough, Cumbria CA17 4AX, England
Tel. 09304-296

HOURS: Monday–Sunday 9:00–6:00
CREDIT CARDS: None

PRODUCTS: Exquisite jewelry is sold at this small workshop. You
can watch the two women create their items. They design elegant
bracelets, spoons, rings, earrings, and pins in gold and silver. The
sterling silver thimbles are works of art. The workmanship and design
of the jewelry are fantastic! They will also custom design pieces for
you. Collectors' silver thimbles are priced from £21 to £35, hand-
finished pewter pieces vary from £12 to £35, and many creative jewelry
pieces are under £75. Hand-knit mohair and silk cardigans are priced
from £36. Very creative pottery animals range in price from £1 to £7.
Various craft items are also sold at this small workshop.

LOCATION: Brough is in north central England about 20 miles southeast of Penrith on the A66 road (about 30 miles due west of Darlington). Upon entering town from the A66, turn left at the roundabout. The shop is half a block on the right side of the street.

BROXBOURNE   *Crystal*

Nazeing Glass Works Ltd. (factory/showroom)
Nazeing New Road
Broxbourne, Hertfordshire EN10 6SU, England
Tel. Hoddesdon 464485

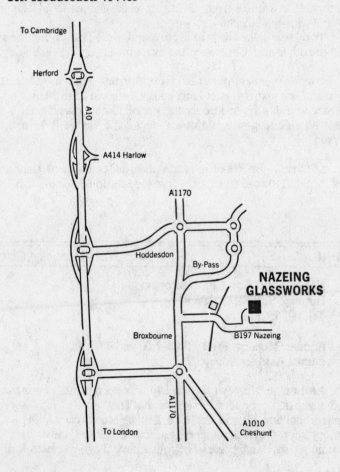

HOURS: Monday–Thursday 9:00–4:00; Friday 9:00–3:30; Saturday 9:30–1:00

CREDIT CARDS: None

PRODUCTS: Nazeing Glass Works was started in 1928 in a farmhouse. A family built a small glass furnace in a goat shed on the banks of the River Lee. Today the company has become the largest producer of handmade stem glasses in the Commonwealth. Craftsworkers have been hired from ten foreign countries—due to a shortage of skilled English glassblowers. It often takes five full years of training to become a master glassblower.

At this factory visitors will find 27½% lead crystal glasses, decanters, vases, ashtrays, bells, fruit bowls, etc. First and second quality pieces, including pub and restaurant glassware, are carried at the factory. Prices range from £3 for six plain glasses to £45 for a lead crystal whisky decanter.

Two large sales are held each year. One is held during the spring and the other near Christmas, the exact dates varying each year.

TOURS: Factory tours are given Monday through Friday at 1:45 p.m. and last approximately one hour. Groups of 15 to 30 may take the factory tour, but no one under the age of 15 may participate. Visitors must be able to go up and down steps. The charge is 35 pence per person.

LOCATION: Broxbourne is about 10 miles north of London just east of the A10 road (the exit before Hoddesdon). See the map.

BUNGAY   *Sheepskin Products*

Nursey and Son Ltd. (factory outlet)
Bungay, Suffolk, England
Tel. 0986, 2821

HOURS: Monday–Friday 9:00–1:00 and 2:00–5:00

CREDIT CARDS: None.

PRODUCTS: Nursey and Son Ltd. has been manufacturing leather and sheepskin products for 190 years. They are the only sheepskin coat production firm in the elite British Menswear Guild. At their factory shop they sell slippers, moccasins, gloves, mitts, hats, rugs, footmuffs, toy lambs, etc. They also have a wide selection of very fashionable coats for men and women in a wide range of colors. The factory does carry seconds. A color brochure is available explaining the care and maintenance of your new sheepskin coat. Nursey and Son Ltd. will ship your purchases home.

LOCATION: Bungay is in eastern England, 15 miles southeast of Norwich, just a few miles west of Beccles.

BURTON-ON-TRENT   *Brewery*

Bass Museum
Bass Brewing (Burton) Limited
137 High Street
Burton-on-Trent DE14 1JZ, England
Tel. 0283-45301

HOURS: Museum: Monday–Friday 11:00–4:30
Brewery Tours: Monday–Friday 10:00–12:30 and 2:00–4:45. Tours are also available at 7:15 p.m. and 9:45 p.m.
CREDIT CARDS: None

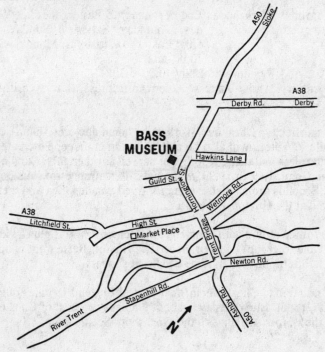

PRODUCTS: In 1777 William Bass founded the brewing company that became famous for its ales and beers. The museum is open to the public. Tours of the brewery can also be arranged. Refreshments can be arranged along with a 30-minute sampling of the ales. A maximum of 30 persons can tour at one time. Be sure to ask for a very informative brochure entitled *The Brewing Process.* For adults there is a charge of £1 and for school children (over 13 years and under 18 years) 60 pence. Please request a form from the above address. All arrangements must be made in advance.

LOCATION: Burton-on-Trent is in central England about 30 miles northeast of Birmingham. The town is at the intersection of the A50 (from Leicester to Stoke-on-Trent) and the A38 (Birmingham to Derby). See the map.

BURWARDSLEY, NEAR CHESTER   *Candles*

Cheshire Candle Workshops Limited
Burwardsley, Near Chester CH3 9PF, England
Tel. 0829-70401

HOURS: Workshops: End of January to Easter: Tuesday, Wednesday, Thursday, Saturday, Sunday 10:00–5:00; Easter to Christmas: Monday–Sunday 10:00–5:00
Restaurant: Daily 10:00–4:30
CREDIT CARDS: Access, American Express, Barclaycard, Diners Club, Visa

PRODUCTS: Cheshire Workshops manufactures hand-sculpted candles. Visitors will also be able to watch craftspeople create handcrafted glass and rustic wood signs as well as other gifts. Candle prices range from £1.69 to £9.99, while glass items range from 98 pence to £10. Seconds are available in handcarved candles. Tea and meals are served at the Hayloft Restaurant.

TOURS: Tours with candlemaking demonstrations plus a video are available to groups of 15 or more. The Hayloft Restaurant is open for lunch, afternoon tea, and late candle-lit suppers.

LOCATION: Chester is in west-central England 15 miles due south of Liverpool. Burwardsley is about 9 miles southeast of Chester. Follow the yellow AA signs to the Workshop. See the map.

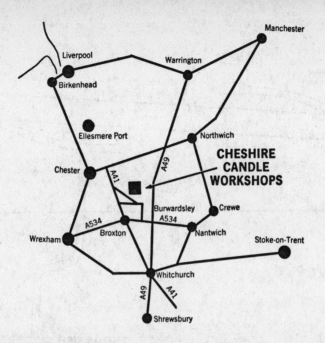

BURY ST. EDMUNDS   *Embroidery Kits*

The Danish Embroidery Centre (retail shop)
Windsor Wood House
Little Saxham
Bury St. Edmunds, Suffolk 1P29 5LA, England
Tel 0284-810999

HOURS: Tuesday–Saturday 10:00–4:30
CREDIT CARDS: None

PRODUCTS: The Danish Embroidery Centre sells elaborately detailed cross–stitched embroidery kits. They also feature retail embroidery catalogs for Eva Rosenstand and Clara Waever embroideries.
Pictures, bellpulls, calendars, tablecloths, placemats, napkins, clocks,
bookmarks, and mobiles are just a few of the items they carry. Hoops,
rings, backings, hangers, and other needlework tools are also carried
to help complete your project. Gifts, silk flowers, and books are also
sold. A cross stitch map of Great Britain is £18, a cushion designed by
Jane Rainbow is £15.50, a daisychain necklace is £18 and a detailed

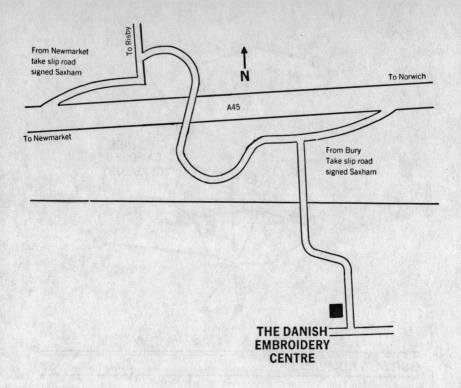

cross stitch design of English birds is £27.60. An enjoyable place to visit if you enjoy needlework.

MAIL ORDER: The catalogs mentioned above are printed in Danish, English, and German. The company encourages overseas orders and has a detailed sheet on mailing instructions and postage. They guarantee their quality or goods may be returned in 21 days and the money, less postage, will be refunded. The VAT will be deducted from the cost of overseas orders. Overseas customers should send sterling and a statement whether they wish air or sea mail. Members of the Embroidery Club receive a 10% discount. Ask for details.

LOCATION: Bury St. Edmunds is in eastern England about 28 miles east of Cambridge on the A45 road. See the map.

CAMBRIDGE   *China, Crystal, Cutlery, Giftware*

Barretts (retail store and mail order company)
2 St. Mary's Passage
Cambridge CB2 3PQ, England
Tel. 0223-66711

HOURS: Monday–Saturday 9:00–5:00
CREDIT CARDS: MasterCard, Visa

PRODUCTS: Barretts, founded in 1782, sells china, earthenware, and crystal. Barretts carries only the finest quality merchandise from world-renowned manufacturers such as Wedgwood, Royal Doulton, Minton, Spode, Coalport, Royal Worcester, Aynsley, Royal Crown, Derby, Waterford, Stuart, Edinburgh, Galway, Webb Corbett, Thomas Webb, Denby, Midwinter, Hornsea, Worcester, etc. Nonstock patterns and pieces can be ordered. If you are short on time, Barretts is an excellent place to do all of your shopping. They are organized and most helpful.

Barretts will send you lists of their merchandise with the prices in pounds converted into dollars. (The prices fluctuate due to the rate of exchange.) All export customers are given 20% off of normal retail prices. Computed at an exchange rate of £1 equaling $1.17, the following prices were great values for any visitor. A Waterford Lismore goblet was $16.80. A Royal Doulton Carlyle place setting was $58.45. The Royal Worcester popular Evesham place setting was $34.44. (At our department store in Salt Lake City a Lismore goblet was $33.50 and an Evesham place setting was $82.) Shipping and duty were not included in the above prices, but the savings would still be incredible.

MAIL ORDERS: Barretts specializes in worldwide mail order sales. "In general our mail order customers from the U.S. and Canada can save 33% (*after* mailing and duty have been paid) over prices in retail stores in the U.S.A." Exact mailing costs depend entirely on what is ordered. If you will send a list of what you want to purchase, Barretts will send a price quote which will include mailing and insurance. For military customers stationed in Britain, Barretts will be happy to mail your items through the APO system.

LOCATION: Cambridge is about 54 miles north of London on the M11 motorway. The shop is a few yards away from the world-famous Kings College Chapel just off Market Square.

CAMBRIDGE   *China, Crystal*

Etcetera China Shops (retail store)
17 Rose Crescent
Cambridge CB5 8HR, England
Tel. 0223-350001

HOURS: Monday–Saturday 9:00–5:30
CREDIT CARDS: MasterCard, Visa

PRODUCTS: This firm is a high-volume retailer of quality English fine bone china and crystal. They carry many famous brands at substantial savings: a Minton china five-piece place setting in the Grasmere pattern was £40 (the U.S. price would be near $155); a Waterford crystal goblet for $13.50 would cost $33 in the States. Savings on U.S. prices were from 45% to 75%! Some of the brands they sell include Aynsley, Coalport, Doulton, Minton, Royal Doulton, Waterford, and Wedgwood. The Doulton figurine of the Old Balloon Seller was £60. This sells in the U.S. for $185.
Purchases will be shipped home. Irregular pieces are also sold.

MAIL ORDER: A mail order division is located at Britannia House, 19/21 Godesdone Road, Cambridge CB5 8HR.

LOCATION: Cambridge is about 54 miles north of London on the M11 motorway. The shop is just 100 yards from the Market Square in the center of town.

CAMBRIDGE   *Glassware*

Midsummer Glassmakers of Cambridge (craft centre)
Auckland Road
Cambridge, CB5 8DW, England
Tel. 0223-316464

HOURS: Shop: Tuesday–Saturday (Bank Holiday Mondays) 10:00–5:00; Workshops: Tuesday–Friday (Bank Holiday Mondays) 10:00–12:30 and 1:30–4:30
CREDIT CARDS: Access

PRODUCTS: Dillon Clarke, a graduate of the Royal College of Art, designs all of the glass pieces including tableware such as tankards, decanters, jugs, wine glasses, and candlesticks, paperweights, animals, blown vases, and sculptural pieces which sometimes feature enamels and silver details. Wine glasses are priced at £10, colored vases at £10, and small items such as paperweights and animals are priced at £7. They consistently stock a selection of seconds with reductions of up to 50%. They hold a Midsummer Sale for two weeks following Midsummer's Day, and a January sale the first three weeks in January. They will ship goods on request.

TOURS: Visitors may visit the workshop and watch the glassmakers at work. Group size is limited to 40.

LOCATION: Cambridge is about 54 miles north of London on the M11 motorway. See the map.

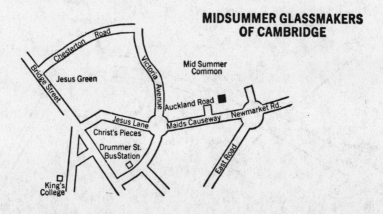

MIDSUMMER GLASSMAKERS OF CAMBRIDGE

CARLISLE   *Couture Fabrics, Knitwear, Blankets*

Linton Tweeds Limited (factory/showroom)
Shaddon Mills–Shaddongate
Carlisle, Cumbria CA2 5TZ, England
Tel. 0228-27569

HOURS: Monday–Friday 10:00–4:00; Saturday 10:00–12:00
CREDIT CARDS: Access, American Express, MasterCard

PRODUCTS: Linton Tweeds is a small mill that manufactures ladies' couturier quality tweeds which are sold all over the world. The mill was founded in 1919 and has been selling fine fabrics since then to top fashion designers including Yves Saint Laurent, Dior, Nina Ricci, Givenchy and Courreges. Local, Australian, and New Zealand wools are used. Pure wool is the basic raw material for Linton Tweeds fabric, but they also use luxury hair fibers such as alpaca and mohair. More recently, some synthetic fibers have also been used. The quality of their woven goods is outstanding! The mill shop sells various fabrics, depending upon what's available. There is also a large selection of wool thread and yarn. Most of the fabrics were £8 to £20 per yard.

TOURS: A tour (taken in groups of 12 to 15) of the mill lasts about an hour.

LOCATION: Carlisle is in the northwest corner of England, very near the Scottish border. See the map below.

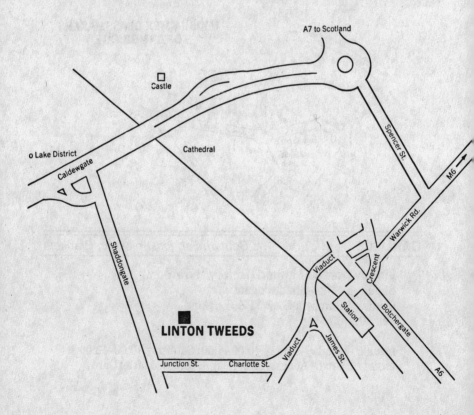

CATON, NEAR LANCASTER   *Pottery*

The Lunesdale Pottery (craft workshop)
Farrier's Yard
Caton Near Lancaster, England
Tel. 0524-770284

HOURS: "Open most times but telephone in advance"
CREDIT CARDS: None

PRODUCTS: Barry and Audrey Gregon have a small pottery workshop. Barry's work includes unusual contemporary stoneware pieces
made from natural textured clays with granite glazes. Audrey's sculpture tends to be abstract; her other specialties are lamp bases, planters, and bird and animal miniatures. Her larger sheep pieces are
charming. An intriguing pottery bowl was £48 while most of the miniatures were under £12.

LOCATION: Caton is in the northwest, about four miles northeast
of Lancaster on the A683 road. The pottery is on the right behind some
other buildings. Watch for the small sign.

CERNE ABBAS   *Wrought Iron*

Cerne Valley Forge (factory showroom)
Mill Lane
Cerne Abbas, Dorset DT2 7LA, England
Tel. Cerne Abbas 298

HOURS: Monday–Friday 9:00–5:00; Saturday 10:00–5:00; closed
       for lunch 1:00–2:00
CREDIT CARDS: None

PRODUCTS: For centuries, Cerne Abbas was a thriving country
town, having grown up around its famous Benedictine abbey. This
town contains memories of many famous people. Queen Elizabeth I
and Queen Victoria both patronized its boot and glove industry. Sir
Walter Raleigh was tried and acquitted for "making treasonable utter-
ances" at the Nag's Head Inn, now a private house.

The figure of a giant man—180 feet high—carved into the chalk hillside overlooks the village. It is estimated that he is 3000 years old.

Of many enterprises originally prospering in this area, only Cerne Valley Forge, which has produced hand-forged ironwork since 1789, remains. Products now for sale include fireplace screens and hearth accessories, wall lamps, lanterns, garden furniture, and small items for plants and patios. Fireplace screens are priced from £26.50 to £49, fire baskets from £25 to £71.95, and fireside accessories, such as pokers and tongs range from £2.75 to £15.25. They will ship abroad on request.

MAIL ORDER: Cerne Valley Forge has a mail order department.

TOURS: Visitors are welcome to look around the forge and watch the blacksmiths at work at any time. A phone call prior to a visit would be appreciated.

LOCATION: Cerne Abbas is in the southwest of England about seven miles north of Dorchester on the A352 road.

CHELTENHAM   *Kitchen Shop*

Scoops (retail store)
Rotunda Terrace
Montpellier Street
Cheltenham, Gloucestershire GL50 1SS, England
Tel. 0242-41271

HOURS: Monday–Saturday 9:30–6:00; June–July: Sunday 12:00–6:00

See the write-up under STRATFORD-UPON-AVON.

LOCATION: Cheltenham is in western England, about eight miles east of Gloucester on the A40. This is also about 37 miles west of Oxford on the A40.

CHESSELL, NEAR YARMOUTH, ISLE OF WIGHT   *Porcelain*

Chessell Pottery (factory outlet)
Chessell, Near Yarmouth, Isle of Wight PO41 OVE, England
Tel. 0983-78-248

HOURS: Studios: Monday–Friday 9:00–4:00
Exhibition Showroom: Monday–Friday 9:00–5:30
Admission: Adults 15 pence; children 5 pence.
Weekends from May to September the showroom is open
from 10:00–5:00. No charge for admission during this
time.

CREDIT CARDS: Access, Diners Club, Visa

PRODUCTS: Chessell Pottery was started in 1978 by John and
Sheila Francis, both graduates of the Royal College of Art in London.
At Chessell Pottery visitors will find unique one-of-a-kind porcelain
pieces with water gardens as the central theme and tiny elaborate
flower details. The items are mostly decorative such as vases, candleholders, and table lamps.

Porcelain clay is used to create the products, and small bits of
oxide are added to give color. The items are all decorated while the
pottery is still damp.

The quoted prices include the VAT. A small vase is £4.85. An
unusual bonsai tree with butterflies will be about £25.30. A round table
top, guaranteed to be the only one in your neighborhood, will cost £69.
A plain small swan is £4.60. For the workmanship and detail involved,
the prices are very reasonable.

MAIL ORDER: Chessell Pottery is equipped to ship items abroad.
They also have a very attractive black-and-white brochure.

LOCATION: The Isle of Wight is off the south coast, just south of
Portsmouth. Chessell is a village on the west side of the Isle of Wight.
From Newport take the B3401 west toward Fresh Water and Totland.
The pottery is at the turnoff toward Brook.

CHESTER   *Wool Clothing, Scottish Crafts*

Clan Royal (retail store)
Paddock Row, Grosvenor Centre
Chester, Cheshire, England
Tel. 0244-26510

HOURS: Monday–Friday 9:00–5:30

See the write-up under EDINBURGH, SCOTLAND.

LOCATION: Chester is in west central England 15 miles due south
of Liverpool. It is on the border of Wales. Grosvenor Centre is a
shopping arcade off Grosvenor Street in the center of town. This is just
north of the castle.

CHESTER   *Clothing*

Lakeland Sheepskin Centre (retail store)
31 Bridge Street Row
Chester, Cheshire CH1 1NW, England
Tel. 0244-31978

HOURS: Monday–Saturday 9:00–5:30

See the write-up under ALTRINCHAM.

LOCATION: Chester is in west central England 15 miles due south
of Liverpool. The store is in the center of town on the ancient "Rows"
on Bridge Street. This is about two miles south of the cathedral.

CHEWTON MENDIP   *Cheese*

Chewton Cheese Dairy
Priory Farm, Chewton Mendip
Bath, Somerset BA3 4NT, England
Tel. 076121-666

HOURS: Monday–Friday 8:30–5:00; Saturday 9:00–5:00, Sunday 9:00–1:00. In January, February, and March they close at 4:00.

CREDIT CARDS: None

PRODUCTS: Fresh dairy produce is sold at Chewton Cheese Dairy. All of the items come from their own farms. Cheese, butter, cream, eggs, homemade pies, scones, and cakes make this an enticing shop.

The company is especially known for their handmade cheddar cheese, which is made into *truckles*. They will be happy to mail the cheese anywhere in the world. A six-pound truckle of cheese is £9.80 with additional postage to the States at £7.10.

TOURS: Tours of the cheese dairy are given daily at 9:00 and 12:30. Admission is 50 pence per person. A guide is provided for booked parties of 15 to 50 people. Duration is approximately one hour. You can observe buttermaking by hand two days a week at the Farm Shop. All coaches must make advance arrangements.

LOCATION: Chewton Mendip is in the southwest, about 15 miles south of Bristol. Take the A37 from Bristol about 13 miles, then turn onto the A39. See the map below.

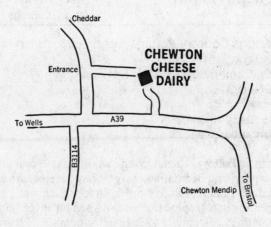

CHICHESTER   *Clothing*

Lakeland Sheepskin Centre (retail store)
83 East Street
Chichester, Sussex PO19 1HA, England
Tel. 0243-773170

HOURS: Monday–Saturday 9:00–5:30

See the write-up under ALTRINCHAM.

LOCATION: Chichester is on the south coast of England about 13 miles east of Portsmouth on the A27. Coming from the west, enter town on the A259. This will become West Street, then East Street. East Street is a busy shopping area, and is also a pedestrians only street. The shop is about halfway down the street on the right. Coming from the east, enter town on the A285. At the roundabout with the A259 go west onto East Street. The shop is on the left just inside the pedestrians only part of East Street.

CLIFTON, NEAR PENRITH   *Pottery, Handwoven Rugs and Cushions, Paintings*

Wetheriggs Country Pottery (factory showroom)
Clifton Dykes
Penrith, Cumbria CA10 2DH, England
Tel. 0768-62946

HOURS: Daily 10:00–5:30
CREDIT CARDS: None

PRODUCTS: Pottery, handwoven wool rugs, cushions, commemorative pots, and decorative charges (large plates) are a specialty at this outlet. Each month from April to October, there are exhibitions of paintings and photography. Coffee mugs sell for £1.65, jugs £2.25 to £18, handwoven rugs from £25 to £50, and handmade tiles are £5 each. Seconds are available. Customer purchases and special orders can be shipped. The rugs are of superior quality in Jacob and Herdwick as well as hand dyed wools. I fell in love with the weaver's work and went home with three works of art. Highly recommended for wool rugs!

TOURS: Group tours can be made by arrangement. The tour lasts about one hour and can be given for groups of up to 30. Casual visitors can buy a guide book which has a map to help them find their way around. There is a Beehive Kiln Museum with a social and historical display of pottery and tools. The "blunger" and the steam house may be visited where the machines are found that once mixed the clay. You may also see the pits where clay was put to dry in the sun. The potters and weavers are often at the shop and always ready to answer questions. Admission for adults is 75 pence, and children are free. There is a tearoom where it is possible to buy homemade scones, cakes, sandwiches, and snack meals. We had lunch at the shop and the food was excellent. This was one of my favorite shops and museums. Very well done and extremely informative.

LOCATION: Penrith is in the northwest corner of England, 19 miles south of Carlisle on the M6 motorway. From Penrith, take the A6 south. Watch for the left turn to Cliburn. Follow the signs to the pottery. See the map.

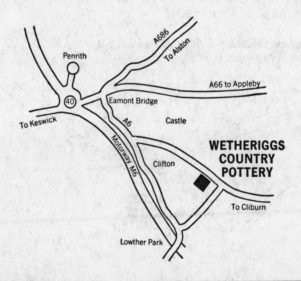

COCKERMOUTH   *Woolen Products*

The Sheepskin Warehouse Shop
Norham House
Cockermouth, Cumbria CA13 9JS, England
Tel. 0900-826233

HOURS: Monday–Saturday 9:00–5:30

See the description for this same shop under KIRBY LONS-
DALE.

LOCATION: Cockermouth is in the northwest, just north of the
Lake District. It is about 30 miles west of Penrith on the A66 road. The
shop is on the main street, opposite Wordsworth House (the home of
William Wordsworth).

CRADLEY, NEAR HALESOWEN   *Crystal*

Regency Crystal Limited (factory/showroom)
Unit 2, Maypole Fields
Cradley, Near Halesowen,
West Midlands B63 20B, England
Tel. Cradley Heath 68348

HOURS: Monday–Friday 9:00–4:30; Saturday 10:00–1:00
CREDIT CARDS: None

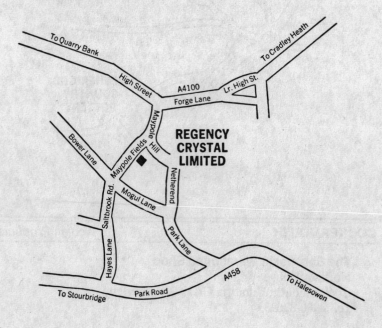

PRODUCTS: Regency Crystal manufactures full lead crystal which is mouth blown and hand cut. They make a full range of crystal glassware, bowls, and vases. The company also makes crystal ashtrays, biscuit barrels, candlesticks, punch sets, rose bowls, goblets, and liqueur glasses. They'll fill out forms for a VAT refund.

The small factory showroom normally sells second quality crystal, but first quality items can also be ordered. Informal tours of the factory are available.

The following are showroom prices and include the VAT. A Kensington eight-ounce brandy glass is £5.86, a liqueur glass £3.10, a tall champagne £6.33, and a matching brandy decanter £27.60. Kensington matching pieces include over 36 different items. A biscuit barrel is £15.64, short candlesticks £7.47 each, a honey pot £6.90, a punch bowl £69 and a nine-inch fruit bowl £27.60. For the paperweight collector there are 38 different sports figures for sale at £7 to £10.50 each. The most expensive item available the day I visited was £69.

LOCATION: The town of Halesowen is in central England on the western outskirts of Birmingham. Take the A458 northwest out of Halesowen, and see the map below.

CRANHAM *Pottery*

Prinknash Pottery (factory/showroom)
Prinknash Abbey
Cranham, Gloucester GL4 8EX, England
Tel. 0452-812239

HOURS: Factory hours: Monday–Saturday 10:30–5:00 (closed for lunch 12:30–1:30)
Showroom hours: Monday–Saturday 9:00–6:00, Sunday 9:30–6:00
Tearoom hours: Daily 9:00–5:30
CREDIT CARDS: Access and Visa

PRODUCTS: Prinknash Pottery is on the grounds of the Prinknash Abbey, which was designed and built as a Benedictine monastic community. A Benedictine abbey has to be economically viable, and the monks work at farming, gardening, making pottery, incense, vestments, stained glass, ironwork, and other crafts. The Pottery is by far the largest of these industries. Originally, the monks produced all the

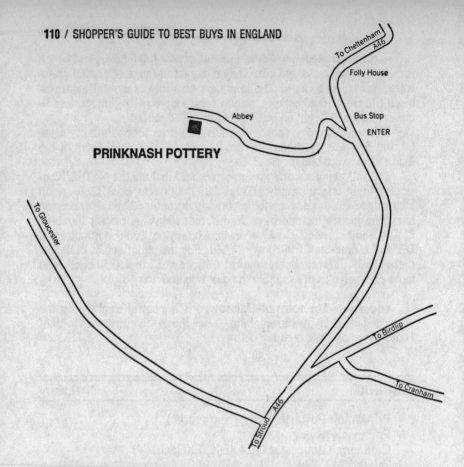

pottery. As demand for the pottery grew, outside workers joined the members of the community at the potter's wheel until the present building was opened in 1974.

A visit to Prinknash Pottery is unique, for the Benedictine community welcomes visitors to the abbey church and the monastery walled garden, which offers relaxation in a tranquil atmosphere and a breathtaking view of the Vale of Gloucester.

All types of glazed pottery are produced, including plates, thimbles, bowls, jugs, vases, tankards, candleholders, goblets, planters, trays, boxes, ginger jars, and much more. Many items are gift boxed. Especially notable are the famous pewter glaze and bronze glaze items. All the prices at the Pottery are regular retail prices. Prices are, however, very reasonable. Items begin at £1.55 and go up to £23. For example, in the pewter and bronze glazes: vases £1.55 to £4.75; jugs £1.55 to £9.65; coffee sets £29; candleholders £1.65 to £2.05. More typical white finish items with 24 carat hand-gilded gold bands are: ginger jars £4.15 to £8.95; lidded jars £4.75 to £11.15; vases £4.75 to £8.95; and candleholders £4.45. There are numerous patterns and decorative motifs. Many items are hand-gilded with 24-carat gold bands. In addition to traditional stoneware items, there are unusual plates with stained-glass decorations. There is also fine ivory or black finish earthenware with delicate floral decorations. There is a series of plates, cups, and saucers with British wildlife paintings, plus a series of items in a rich burgundy glaze.

TOURS: Guides are available to conduct visitors on a tour of the Pottery Viewing Gallery. About 20% of the items are exported all over the world. There is a charge of 30 pence per adult, and 10 pence per child for the tour.

LOCATION: Prinknash Pottery is in south central England near Cranham, about four miles southeast of Gloucester. Entrance is from the A46 road, which runs parallel to the M5 motorway. See the map.

DARTINGTON   *Tweed Fabric Woolen Clothing*

Dartington Hall Tweed Mill and Shop
Plymouth Road, Shinners Bridge
Dartington, Totnes, South Devon TQ9 6JE, England
Tel. 0803-864388

HOURS: Mill: Monday–Thursday 9:00–12:30 and 1:30–5:00; Friday 9:00–12:30 and 1:30–4:00
Shop: Monday–Thursday 9:00–5:15; Friday 9:00–5:00; Saturday 10:00–5:00
CREDIT CARDS: Access, Visa

PRODUCTS: The Dartington Hall Tweed Mill produces tweed fabric from raw wool. Self-guided tours are allowed through the mill, and the tweed can be purchased at the shop. Tweeds are priced from £8 to £20. Sweaters begin at £14.99 while skirts begin at £15.99. The shop also sells 100% pure new wool ladies' and men's outerwear (knitwear, skirts, coats, etc.). They have low factory door prices for high-quality products.

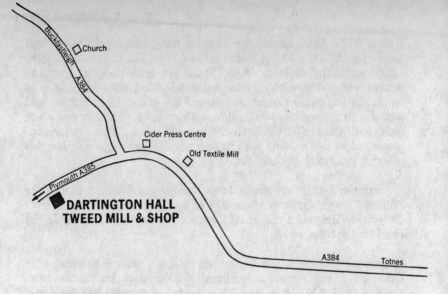

While in Totnes, you may also want to visit the Dartington Cider Press Centre, at the same location as the Tweed Mill. There is a craft centre, shops, gallery, exhibitions, and a restaurant. It is open Monday–Saturday 9:30–5:30.

LOCATION: Dartington is in the far southwest of England near the south coast. It is just west of Totnes on the A384 road. From Exeter, take the A38 south about 20 miles to Ashburton. Go about two miles further and turn east onto the A384 road. Dartington Hall is about 3½ miles on the left, just before you reach Skinner's Bridge. This is about nine miles west of Paignton. See the map.

DENBY   *Stoneware, Pottery*

Denby Tableware
Denby Pottery (factory/showroom)
Denby, Derbyshire DE5 8NX, England
Tel. 0773-43641

HOURS: Factory: Monday–Thursday afternoons
Showroom: Monday–Friday 10:00–4:00; Saturday 9:00–4:00
CREDIT CARDS: None

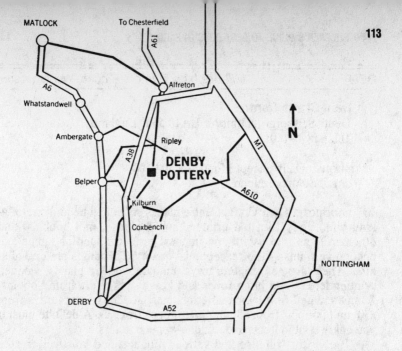

PRODUCTS: Denby Pottery has produced stoneware since 1809. The shop at the factory sells a variety of oven-to-table items at discounted prices. These include cups, plates, serving pieces, casseroles, bowls, vases, mugs, candleholders, lamps, and much more. The quality and patterns are excellent. Designs range from rustic browns to delicate flowers with a cream-colored glaze. There are also giftware items, and a set of children's tableware.

For specific prices and a more comprehensive product description, see MATLOCK BATH Denby Seconds Shop.

TOURS: Tours of the factory are conducted each afternoon Monday through Thursday except on factory holidays. Tours take 40 minutes, and begin at 1:30 and 2:15. The charge is 50 pence for adults, and 25 pence for children and senior citizens. Wheelchairs cannot be accommodated due to the number of stairs.

Parties of up to six people, or casual visitors, can be accepted without prior arrangements. However, booking in advance is advisable. Groups up to 48 persons are accepted, but prior booking is essential.

LOCATION: Denby is in central England about eight miles north of Derby on the B6179 road. Derby is about eight miles west of Nottingham. See the map. The factory is on the east side of the B6179.

DENT   *Mill Bobbins, Printers Blocks, Woolen Items*

Dent Crafts Centre
Dent, Sedbergh, Cumbria LA10 5SY, England
Tel. 05875-400

HOURS: Daily except Monday 9:30–5:00
CREDIT CARDS: None

PRODUCTS: Dent Crafts Centre makes some unique and one-of-a-kind gifts. They turn old printers' wood blocks, mill bobbins, and other artifacts into useful and unusual products such as lamps and decorative trains—all of exceptional quality. The lamps are one-of-a-kind. They also sell printers trays, antique wooden planes, wooden printing letters and jump ropes and key chains made from bobbins. Lamps created from wooden letters start at £28, printers trays from £30, mill bobbins from £3, and jump ropes from £3. A definite must if you enjoy bobbin items and antique wooden letters.

The visitor will also find various products and knitwear created from Shetland and local wools. Also available at Dent Crafts Centre are pottery items, turned wood, soft toys, furniture, ironwork, and other wares. Product prices range from £1 to £50. They will be happy to ship your items abroad.

LOCATION: Dent is in the northwest, near Sedbergh, which is about 25 miles northeast of Lancaster (or about 10 miles east of Kendal). On the M6 motorway, take exit No. 37 onto the A684, and go east to Sedbergh. Then take an unnumbered road from the center of Sedbergh to the southeast toward Dent. The craft center is about three miles, halfway between Sedbergh and Dent.

DERBY   *Crystal*

Derwent Crystal Ltd. (factory outlet)
Little Bridge Street
Friargate, Derby, Derbyshire England
Tel. 0332-360186

HOURS: Monday–Saturday 9:00–5:00
CREDIT CARDS: Barclaycard, Visa

DERWENT CRYSTAL LTD.

PRODUCTS: Derwent Crystal Ltd. manufactures handblown full lead crystal. They are a small company making various tableware glasses and crystal decanters. Engraving and sand blasting are a specialty. Prices vary from £6 for a small vase to £20 for a piece of stemware.

TOURS: Tours are given Monday through Saturday between 10:00 and 4:00. A maximum group size should be between 20 and 30 people.

LOCATION: Derby is in central England about 10 miles west of Nottingham on the A52. See the map.

DERBY   *China, Giftware*

Royal Crown Derby (factory outlet)
Osmaston Road
Derby, Derbyshire DE3 8J2, England
Tel. 0332-47051

HOURS: Monday–Friday 9:00–12:30 and 1:30–4:00
CREDIT CARDS: None

PRODUCTS: Royal Crown Derby creates beautiful china tableware and giftware. There are innumerable patterns, styles, and colors. Seconds are sometimes available.

TOURS: Tours are given Monday through Friday at 10:30 and 1:45. The tour lasts two hours and is £1 per person. Groups of up to 30 are accepted and arrangements must be made in advance. A free museum is open on weekdays from 9:00–12:30 and 1:30–5:00.

LOCATION: Derby is in central England about 10 miles west of Nottingham on the A52. Royal Crown Derby is in the southeast part of town, about halfway out of town on the south side of Osmaston Road. This is also the A514.

DITCHLING   *Pottery Crafts, Watercolors*

The Craftsman Gallery
8 High Street
Ditchling, East Sussex BN6 8TA, England
Tel. 07918-5246

HOURS: Monday–Saturday 10:00–5:00; Wednesday 10:00–1:00. Closed for lunch, 1:00–2:00.
CREDIT CARDS: None

PRODUCTS: The Craftsman Gallery is a tiny pottery workshop and craft gallery in the ancient village of Ditchling, which lies at the foot of the South Downs.
Jill Pryke, a potter, trained at Wimbledon School of Art and taught pottery. She now produces tableware and decorated pots. Her work is earthenware, characterized by a soft green glaze. She will accept commissions, including those with lettering for commemorative work.
The Gallery also stocks Sussex-made craftwork, including batiks, copperware, engravings, metalwork, wall hangings, and weaving. Watercolors of Sussex landscapes by Doris Kirlew are also available. Pottery lanterns are priced between £10 to £15, pill boxes in wood £2, corn dollies £1.25 to £5, silk scarves £9, framed etchings from £15 and framed watercolors from £75–95.

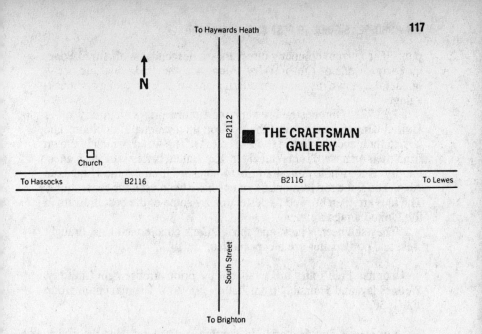

TOURS: Special visits to the pottery workshop attached to the gallery are available by prior arrangement either during gallery hours or by appointment. Maximum number for tour groups is 15.

LOCATION: Ditchling is in the south of England, five miles north of Brighton near the coast on the B2116. See the map.

DORCHESTER   *Beer, Wines, Spirits*

Dorchester Brewery (brewery)
P. O. Box No. 2
Dorchester, Dorset DT1 1QT, England
Tel. 0305-64801

HOURS: Monday–Friday 9:00–5:30
CREDIT CARDS: None

PRODUCTS: Charles Eldridge and his wife established the predecessor of this establishment, the Green Dragon Brewery, in 1837. The present brewery was built in 1880, and this company now owns 200 pubs. The current company directors are descendants of Alfred Pope, an early owner of the brewery. Alongside the traditional ale brewhouse, they have installed a modern plant for lager brewing and packaging.

In 1972, Dorchester brewery won more prizes than any other United Kingdom brewery at the London International Exhibition. The key to their success lies in the ingredients. The water, which is drawn from their own well, is crystal clear. The malted barley is of the highest quality. Only whole-cone traditional hops are used for the Huntsman Ales. The same top fermenting yeasts have been used for generations. The ales are then brewed to perfection by some of the best brewers in the United Kingdom.

They sell beer, wines, and spirits. Cask conditioned ales, draught ales, and bottled ales are all specialties.

TOURS: Free tours are available by prior arrangement Tuesday, Wednesday, and Thursday from 2:30 to 5:00 p.m. The maximum group size is 30.

LOCATION: Dorchester is in southwest England near the coast, about 25 miles west of Bournemouth on the A35 road.

FELSTED   *Wines*

Felstar Estate Wines
The Vineyards
Crick's Green
Felsted, Essex CM6 3JT, England
Tel. 0245-361-504

HOURS: May–October 10:00–4:00
CREDIT CARDS: None

PRODUCTS: J.G. and I.M. Barrett raise grapes at their vineyards so they can sell delicious wines. The wines range in price from £3.40 to £4.25 according to the variety and vintage.

TOURS: Vineyard visits, which are given for £1.50 per person, include a tasting of two different wines. The tours are given from May to October. Groups are welcomed at a price of £1.25 per person. It is necessary to book groups in advance.

LOCATION: Felsted is in eastern England. From London take the M11 about 20 miles north of Bishop's Stortford, then take the A120 east about 13 miles. Turn right on the B1417 and go about two miles south to Felsted.

FENCE, NEAR BURNLEY   *Slate*

Slate Age (Fence) Ltd. (factory showroom)
Fence Gate, Fence
Burnley, Lancashire BB12 9EG, England
Tel. 0282-66952

HOURS: Monday–Saturday 8:00–4:00
CREDIT CARDS: None

PRODUCTS: This company manufactures and sells gifts made from green or black slate such as clocks, pen sets, lamps, and letter openers. They also sell fireplace parts in slate and sandstone cut to the buyer's specifications, and house signs made to order. The slate used is from the Ordovician geological period and is over 450 million years old. Their quality is excellent!
A table clock with brass Roman numerals was £19.50. An attractive double candleholder was £4.05 while a charming note pad and pen desk set was £4.35. An unusual lamp base in the shape of slate books was priced very reasonably at £16.30. They will ship items to other parts of the world.

TOURS: Tours last 30 minutes. There is a group limit of 10 and they request advance notice.

LOCATION: Burnley is in west-central England about 20 miles due north of Manchester. This is also about 18 miles due east of Preston. The village of Fence is about 2½ miles north of Burnley. This is about halfway between Nelson and Padiham on the A6068.

FIDDINGTON, NR. BRIDGWATER   *Pottery*

Whitnell Pottery (workshop/showroom)
Fiddington, Bridgwater
Somerset TA5 1JE, England
Tel. 0278-732663

HOURS: Open every day 9:00–6:00
CREDIT CARDS: None

PRODUCTS: This small pottery has been run by John Harlow since 1972. He makes domestic fine stoneware, porcelain, and some press-molded flatware. Most items are hand thrown. Some of the glazes are borax-feldspar based, and others use local rock such as shale, limestone, sandstone, and gritstone. A partial list of items includes ashtrays, biscuit barrels, bowls, breadcrocks, casseroles, cheese bells, coffee sets, egg cups, goblets, honey pots, jugs, lamp bases, mugs, oil and vinegar sets, pie dishes, plates, salt and pepper sets, soup sets, spice jars, teapots, vases, watering cans, and wine sets. Commissions are also accepted for individual pieces such as commemorative items and dinner services.

TOURS: Group visits, with a maximum of 15 persons, can be arranged by appointment only, for a flat fee of £10. The tour, with demonstrations, lasts about an hour. There are no restroom facilities!

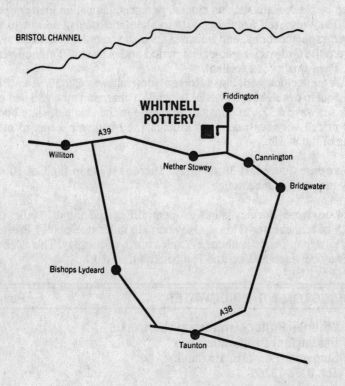

LOCATION: Whitnell Pottery is in the southwest of England, west of Bridgwater, between Cannington and Nether Stowey. Take the A39 road west out of Bridgwater and pass through Cannington. Turn right at the road to Fiddington, where there will be a "Pottery" sign. Drive down the narrow lane about six tenths of a mile; turn left at the pottery sign, and follow the even narrower lane about four tenths of a mile to the pottery. The pottery is situated in buildings dating from about 1650. These roads are only for the adventurous traveler with a small car. See the map.

FLITWICK   *Crystal, Stoneware*

DEMA Glass Limited (factory outlet)
Maulden Road
Flitwick, Bedford MK45 5NS, England
Tel. 0525-712174

HOURS: Monday–Friday 9:30–3:30
CREDIT CARDS: None

PRODUCTS: This small outlet has second-quality handcut Thomas Webb crystal and Denby oven-to-tableware products. These are very high quality products, and the second-quality items sell for up to 60% off the recommended retail price. The crystal is elegant and includes all types of stemware, vases, decanters, lamps, punch sets, candleholders, sugar and cream sets, bells, and perfume bottles. The stoneware, made by Denby, is oven, microwave, freezer, and dishwasher safe. The tableware items include everyday patterns to more formal patterns of dishes, tureens, pitchers, tea sets, and other items. Denby also makes ceramic lamps, vases, ashtrays, planters, bowls, and mugs.

LOCATION: Flitwick is about 30 miles north of London just east of the M1 motorway.

If approaching from the south: Leave the M1 at junction 12, and take the A5120 toward Bedford. Proceed along this road until reaching the bridge in Flitwick, then turn right down Kings Road. Then see the map below.

If approaching from the north: Leave the M1 at junction 13, and proceed easterly ⅒ mile to the signpost for Ridgemont and Ampthill. Turn right and proceed about 1½ miles. At the junction for the A418 road, turn left and proceed along this road for three miles. Turn right

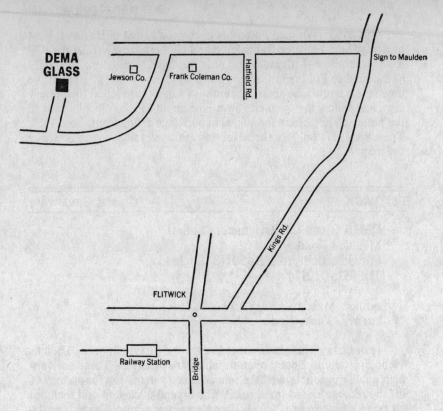

down a minor road marked for Steppingly and Flitwick. After 2½ miles the road terminates at the bridge marked on the detailed map below. Turn left and immediately right down King's Road. Then see the map.

FRESHWATER, ISLE OF WIGHT   *Glass*

Alum Bay Glass Ltd. Glassmakers (workshop)
London House, Queens Road
Freshwater, Isle of Wight P040 9EP, England
Tel. 0983-753473

HOURS: Monday–Friday 9:30–1:00 and 2:00–5:00, Easter to September every day 9:30–5:00
CREDIT CARDS: American Express, Diners Club, MasterCard, Visa

PRODUCTS: Alum Bay glass makes handmade decorative colored glass. The glass, which is similar to the glass made in Venice, is made in two tank furnaces fired with propane. The furnaces run all day every day to insure a constant supply of fine metal. The unique colors are added by the glassmaker as the piece is made. The colored glass added is of a lower melting point so that the colors will flow when mixed. The glassware is free blown with no molds. Each piece is therefore unique. Ten colors are available.

Vases, paperweights, perfume bottles, glass fruit, and jewelry are sold. The designs and colors are all very unusual. Miniature pieces begin at £2.40, paperweights £9.40, vases £8.60, jugs £13.80 and small bottles with stoppers £18.

TOURS: From a balcony visitors can watch the glass being blown. For large groups, arrangements must be made in advance.

MAIL ORDER: Alum Bay glass has a very sophisticated color brochure with an order sheet explaining all details. Overseas prices, including shipping, will be sent on request.

LOCATION: The Isle of Wight is off the south coast, just south of Portsmouth. Freshwater is a small village at the west end of the Isle of Wight. It is about one mile east of Totland. From Totland, go west on the B3322 and where it stops at the cliff edge, park in the car park right by the workshop and showroom.

GLASTONBURY   *Sheepskin Products*

Avalon Basket & Sheepskin Shop (A. Hembrow & Son)
Wells Road
Glastonbury, Somerset BA6 9AG, England
Tel. 0458-31760

Also: Avalon Sheepskin Shop
7 Market Place
Glastonbury, Somerset BA6 9AG, England
Tel. 0458-31720

HOURS: Monday–Saturday 9:00–5:30
CREDIT CARDS: Access, American Express, Barclaycard, Diners Club, MasterCard, Visa

PRODUCTS: Sheepskin products from three other companies (Morland's, Baily's and Draper's) are sold at this store as well as some products which Avalon itself manufactures. You can see the work through a glass window.

Hats, mittens, gloves, coats, jackets, and vests are carried. A special clearance rack offers special bargains. Suede and leather coats and jackets were offered at very reasonable prices.

Some boots, purses, and shoes were carried but they were not manufactured on the premises.

A few handmade willow baskets were available but most of the baskets being sold were Oriental imports.

LOCATION: Glastonbury is in the southwest of England about 22 miles northeast of Taunton on the A361. The Avalon shop is on the north side of town on the A39 road. The second shop, on Market Place, is in the center of town.

GLASTONBURY   *Sheepskin Garments, Footwear, Rugs*

Baily's of Glastonbury (factory/showroom)
Morlands Factory Shop
Glastonbury, Somerset BA6 9YB, England
Factory Tel. 0458-32131
Showroom Tel. 0458-32222 ext. 284

HOURS: Monday–Saturday 9:00–5:00
CREDIT CARDS: Access, American Express, Diners Club, Visa

PRODUCTS: Baily's is a processor of sheepskins, manufacturing high quality sheepskin garments, footwear, rugs, and other items. The factory shop carries a very extensive variety of over 600 sheepskin garments for both men and women in many styles and shades. There is also a large stock of sheepskin slippers, ankle boots, full-length fashion boots, plus hats, mitts, gloves, rugs, and other items. This company purports to be the largest single producer of these items in the UK. They will give you a form to obtain a refund of the VAT. Very highly recommended! Excellent quality! They carry first- and second-quality items. Be sure to ask if you do not see your size. They have more items downstairs.

A women's pair of luxury reversed suede sheepskin boots with a turn-down top was £49.99. The top stitching and detail of the boot was as handsome as the colors—gray suede, nut suede, dark brown, or holly. If you could even find this type of boot in the U.S., the cost would be at least $150. A men's pair of eight-inch-sheepskin-lined brown suede boots with a rubber sole and zipper side were £44.99 per pair. Men's and women's slippers in countless styles were priced from £15.99 to £27.99.

The boots were so beautifully made that I sent home four pair. My feet stay toasty warm all winter, and I am ordering more to match outfits.

TOURS: Factory tours for small parties can sometimes be arranged, with three to four weeks notice generally being required.

LOCATION: Glastonbury is in southwest England, about 22 miles northeast of Taunton on the A361. The factory shop is just south of town on the main A361 (A39) road, midway between Glastonbury and the town of Street. There is a sign leading you to the factory and to the car park.

GLASTONBURY   *Sheepskin Coats, Boots, Slippers*

R. J. Draper & Company Ltd. (factory/showroom)
Chilkwell Street
Glastonbury, Somerset BA6 8YA, England
Tel. 0458-31118

HOURS: Monday–Saturday 9:30–5:30
CREDIT CARDS: None

PRODUCTS: For almost 50 years the craftsmen of R. J. Draper and Company have been turning the finest sheepskins into coats, boots, slippers, rugs, gloves, and mittens. Factory showroom prices for sheepskin coats run from £129 to £239. They feature a full range of styles in beautiful suede skins with matching collars and cuffs. They also have some men's and women's boots and slippers. Prices are generally about 20% below normal retail prices.

TOURS: Tours for groups of 20 or more people can be arranged in advance by calling the factory.

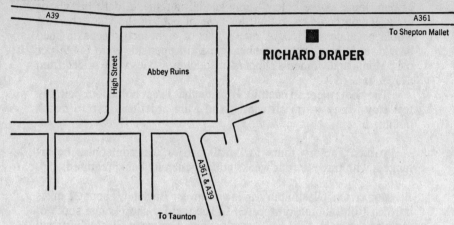

LOCATION: Glastonbury is in southwest England, about 22 miles northeast of Taunton on the A361. The factory shop is below the Tor (the famous cone-shaped hill and tower) on Chilkwell Street, which is also the A361 road to Shepton Mallet. See the map.

GLASTONBURY   *Glass Engraving, Painted Signs, Local Crafts*

Workface (craft centre)
Market Place
Glastonbury, Somerset BA6 9HL, England
Tel. 0458-33917

HOURS: Monday–Saturday 9:00–5:00
CREDIT CARDS: None

PRODUCTS: This craft centre has been recently organized by the Facility for Art and Craft Enterprise Ltd. (FACE). The purpose is to train up to 200 young people in arts and crafts by placing them with host businesses in the area and to promote and stimulate arts and crafts businesses.

Craft products from all over the West Country are sold. Studio/ shops run by local artisans are open to the public. Prices on products range from £5 for a vase, up to £1000 for a bronze sculpture. Special seasonal sales are held at Christmas and midsummer.

TOURS: Groups of up to 30 people at a time are welcome.

LOCATION: Glastonbury is in the southwest of England, about 22 miles northeast of Taunton on the A361. The Market Place is located in the center of town.

GRANTHAM   *Bronze Sculpture*

Minerva Fine Arts of London Limited (factory outlet)
"The Old Malthouse," Springfield Road
Grantham, Lincolnshire NG31 6AA, England
Tel. 0476-76484

HOURS: Monday–Friday 9:00–5:00
CREDIT CARDS: None

PRODUCTS: Minerva Fine Arts of London manufactures cold cast resin bronze reproductions of original sculptures by well-known artists.

The traditional method of casting metals was smelting. In the modern method utilized by this company, pure powdered bronze is mixed with a chemical bonding agent to form a liquid which is layered and poured into a mold to form a shell which hardens by chemical reaction. The outer bronze shell is then filled to give the sculpture weight and strength. This technique allows every detail of the artist's work to be reproduced without distortion.

Each sculpture is cast, polished, patinated, and sealed by hand. Subjects portrayed often include animals such as horses, dogs, birds, and other forest creatures. Horses range in price from £100–£300. Dogs are £20 and up. They will ship goods elsewhere.

MAIL ORDER: They will accept mail orders.

LOCATION: Grantham is in east central England about 24 miles east of Nottingham on the A52 road.

GRAYS   *Clocks*

Smallcombe Clocks (factory showroom)
Gee House
Globe Industrial Estate, Rectory Road
Grays, Essex RM17 6ST, England
Tel. 0375-77181

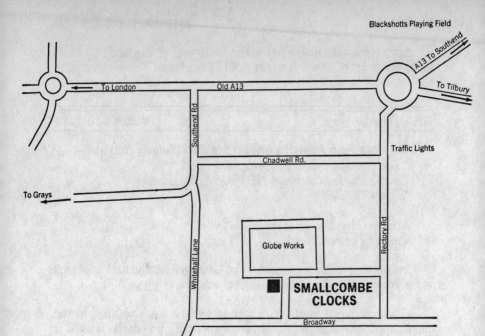

HOURS: Monday–Friday 9:00–5:00
CREDIT CARDS: Access, Barclaycard, Visa

PRODUCTS: At this factory showroom, visitors will find grand-father clocks with chain and weight-driven Westminster movements in mahogany, yew, oak and walnut veneers, and solid wood. China/strike wall clocks (regulators), strike pendulum wall clocks, English dial clocks, pine clocks, wooden marine-style barometers and mantel clocks are also manufactured here. English, French, German, and Japanese movements are used to ensure top quality. A wall regulator was priced at £235. Pine wall clocks were about £26.80 each. Marine style clocks with barometers were from £17.40 to £67.25, depending on the type of wood, the detail of the workmanship, and the amount of brass. For those of you with unlimited funds, the Regent grandfather clock is truly a wonderful must for £2488. Visitors will find clocks sold here that fit anyone's budget. The clocks are beautifully finished.

Most of the year, factory seconds are available. A factory sale is also held each year, although the dates vary.

MAIL ORDERS: Mail orders will be accepted.

LOCATION: Grays is in southeast England, about 24 miles due east of the center of London on the A13 road. The city is on the north side of the River Thames. See the map.

GREAT BARTON, NEAR BURY ST. EDMUNDS   *Craft Items*

Craft At The Suffolk Barn
Great Barton Near
Bury-St.-Edmunds, Suffolk IP31 2SD, England
Tel. Great Barton 317

HOURS: March–December: Wednesday–Friday 10:00–6:00; Saturday–Sunday 10:00–6:00. Bank Holidays 2:00–6:00.
CREDIT CARDS: None

PRODUCTS: Inside this 200-year-old Suffolk Barn you'll find handmade crafts from the East Anglian Region. Candles, glass animals, puzzle mugs, chopping boards, floral arrangements, pub games, and embroidery pictures are only a few of the many craft items sold. A medieval Suffolk puzzle mug is £5.50, an old English pub game £6, maize dolls £4.25, spinning tops £1.60, herb planters £5, a child's wheelbarrow £8.50, and framed old Suffolk prints cost from £8.50. Many of the items are unique small gifts priced well under £15. Light refreshments are served, all of which are baked on the premises.

LOCATION: Bury-St.-Edmunds is in eastern England about 28 miles east of Cambridge on the A45 road. From Bury-St.-Edmunds take the A143 northeast about two miles. Turn left on Fornham Road. The shop is about three quarters of a mile on the right.

GREAT TORRINGTON   *Crystal*

Dartington Glass Ltd. (factory/showroom)
School Lane, Great Torrington, North Devon EX38 7AN, England
Tel. 08052-2321

HOURS: Factory: Monday–Friday 8:30–5:00
Factory Shop: Monday–Friday 9:00–5:00; Saturday and holidays 10:00–4:00

During summer months, opening times are sometimes altered without notice. Before traveling, please phone 08052-3797.

CREDIT CARDS: Access, Barclaycard

PRODUCTS: Dartington Glass makes elegant hand-blown 24% lead crystal glassware. They make a large variety of items such as wine glasses, tumblers, beer glasses, pitchers, vases, decanters, goblets, ashtrays, buckets, bowls, candleholders, and much more. Many of them have simple, flowing lines with beautifully proportioned handles and accents.

Silica sand, red lead, potash, soda ash, and other chemicals are carefully blended, and placed in the furnace. At 1100° to 1400° centigrade, melting takes 10 hours or so.

The glassblowers work in teams of seven or eight men. Red hot glass on the end of the blowpipe is shaped in a basic mold. More glass is added to the item as it passes on to other members of the team, and the item is perfected in several stages. The blower's tools today are basically the same as those used hundreds of years ago.

The finished piece is then slowly cooled to room temperature over a four-hour period by passing through the annealing tunnel. Finishing is done by diamond cutters, sandblasting, special washing, and polishing.

The Glass Shop at the factory has "B" quality glassware from the entire range of Dartington products. Sample prices include: a delicate cream and sugar at £6.75, an elegant punch bowl for £13.25 (this would cost $60 in the States), a pair of Irish coffee goblets £5.75, a Regency crystal bowl £7.75, a pair of claret glasses with simple but bold lines £7.45, and a solid, superbly crafted ship's decanter £14.95, which would be $50 in the U.S. if you could find one. These are some of the best buys we have seen anywhere in the world!

This company was founded in 1967 by the Dartington Hall Trustees as part of a plan to encourage rural reconstruction in North Devon. The company drew its expertise from the long-established Swedish glass industry. That connection is still strong, with about 20 members of the staff being from Sweden.

TOURS: Factory tours are given every 15 minutes Monday through Friday between 9:30 and 10:30, and again between 12:00 and 3:30. There is a nominal charge. Large groups should be booked in advance.

LOCATION: Great Torrington is in the far southwest of England, about 20 miles due south of Barnstaple. For the location of the Dartington factory within Torrington, see the map. Watch for the sign at the Parish church. Turn into School Lane, then take the second left.

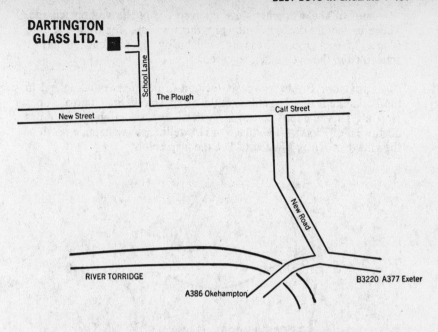

DARTINGTON GLASS LTD.
School Lane
The Plough
New Street
Calf Street
New Road
RIVER TORRIDGE
A386 Okehampton
B3220 A377 Exeter

GREWELTHORPE *Clothing, Crafts, Looms*

Grewelthorpe Handweavers Ltd. (factory showroom)
Grewelthorpe
Ripon, York HG4 3BW, England
Tel. 076 583-209

HOURS: Daily 10:00–6:00
CREDIT CARDS: Access, Eurocard, Visa

PRODUCTS: This shop was converted from an old cowshed on this farm property. The weaving studio was formerly the farm's hay barn. The first new building on the property, the woodworking workshop was custom built for the manufacture of looms and weaving equipment.

They sell a variety of gifts and crafts, as well as tweed coats and accessories.

The only real specialty, however, are the handmade looms. Looms range from £65 to £565. The looms are made of kiln-dried elm, which is sealed and hand waxed. The looms, designed by Malcolm McDougall who has been weaving 20 years, have been designed to make weaving faster. They will ship items overseas.

TOURS: The workshops are open to the public without charge. There are lecture demonstration programs available for groups of 25 to 60 at £12.50 per group. These are available by appointment and may be scheduled in the evenings if required.

LOCATION: Grewelthorpe is located in north-central England in the Yorkshire Dales, ten miles southwest of Thirsk, the home of James Herriot. This is about 40 miles north of Leeds and about six miles northwest of Ripon. The village of Grewelthorpe is one mile north of the village of Kirby Malzeard. See the map below.

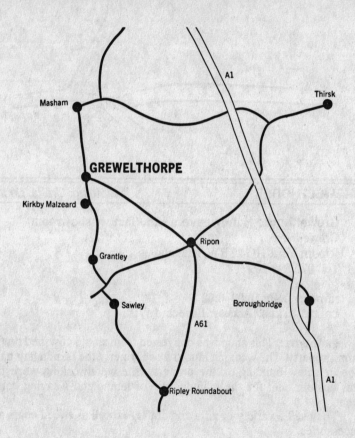

GUILDFORD   *Clothing*

Lakeland Sheepskin Centre (retail store)
93/95 High Street
Guildford, Surrey GU1 3AA, England
Tel. 04836-3426

HOURS: Monday–Saturday 9:00–5:30

See the write-up under ALTRINCHAM.

LOCATION: Guildford is about 10 miles southwest of London on
the A3. Coming from London, take the exit onto the A320 going south.
At the roundabout, take the second left onto the A320 (Stoke Road).
Proceed south, going under the railroad, past York Street, and onto
Chertsey Street (still on the A320). Proceed to the intersection with
High Street and turn right. The store is about a block down on your
right, next to the Angel Hotel.

HALIFAX   *Craft Centre*

Calderdale Piece Hall
Halifax, West Yorkshire HX1 1RE, England
Tel. 68725 (call locally)

HOURS: Monday–Saturday 9:00–5:00
CREDIT CARDS: Each store different.

PRODUCTS: Piece Hall was built in 1770. It was named Piece Hall
because of the lengths of cloth which were once sold from the original
315 merchants' rooms. At this time the weaving of cloth was a cottage
industry, the items being completed in people's cottages. Buyers were
unable to travel to each village to look at the merchandise, so the
pieces of cloth were brought to centers such as Halifax by individual
weavers or by manufacturers. The cloth was then sold to buyers from
all over Europe.
  Piece Hall has been totally restored with all of its arched and
colonnaded galleries that surround a massive cobbled quadrangle. The
merchants rooms now contain craft and antique shops, an Industrial
Textile Museum, an Art Gallery, and on Friday and Saturday a colorful
open air market. Enjoyable to visit if you are in the area.

LOCATION: Halifax is in north central England, about 12 miles southwest of Leeds on the A646. See the map below.

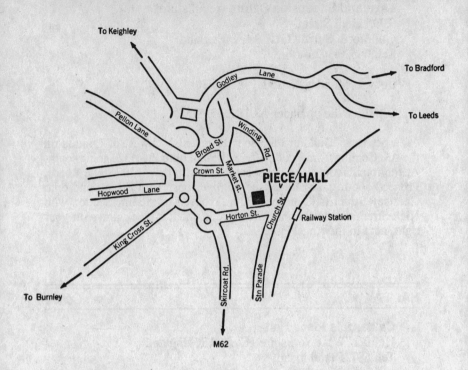

HARROGATE   *Wool Clothing, Scottish Crafts*

Clan Royal (retail store)
29 Station Square
Harrogate, England
Tel. 0423-58508

HOURS: Monday–Saturday 9:00–5:30

See the write-up under EDINBURGH, SCOTLAND.

LOCATION: Harrogate is in north central England about 15 miles north of Leeds on the A61.

HEACHAM   *Lavender*

Norfolk Lavender Limited (factory showroom)
Caley Mill, Heacham
King's Lynn, Norfolk PE31 7JE, England
Tel. 0485-70384

HOURS: Monday–Friday 9:00–4:00, October to the end of May;
daily 9:30–6:00, end of May to the end of September.
Cottage Tearoom open daily from the end of May to the
end of September.
CREDIT CARDS: Access, Barclaycard

PRODUCTS: Established in 1932, this family business has almost
100 acres of lavender in production. They are the largest growers and
distillers of lavender in Britain. Their headquarters, Caley Mill, was
built of local sandstone in about 1800. The old miller's cottage has
been converted into an attractive tearoom.

They sell lavender products manufactured from lavender oil produced by their company. Their products include items such as sachets,
perfume talc, solid cologne lavender sticks, dried lavender flowers,
soaps, bubble bath, bath cubes, and hand and body lotion. A perfume
spray costs £2.30, hand and body lotion sells for £1.60, and a Victorian
sachet is priced at 90 pence. They will ship to other parts of the world.

MAIL ORDER: Details of the mail order service they operate are
available on request. Lavender plants and rooted cuttings of named
varieties are sent by mail in spring and autumn.

TOURS: Frequent tours of the gardens and lavender distillery (not
factory) are given daily during July, August, and September. The
length of the tour is 45 minutes.

The lavender harvest takes place during July and August. There
are guided tours for booked coach parties at 11:00, 12:00, 2:00, and
3:30. The approximate length of these tours is 1½ hours. Refreshments
are available in conjunction with the tours.

LOCATION: Heacham is located on the east coast, about 10 miles
north of King's Lynn on the A149 road. This is about 55 miles north of
Cambridge, on the east side of the bay known as The Wash. See the
map next page.

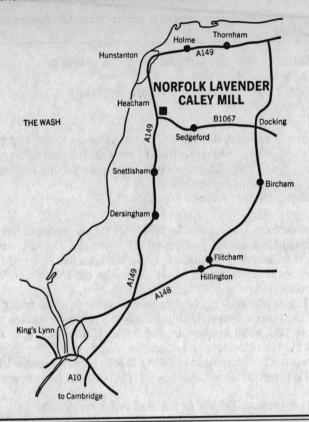

HEBDEN BRIDGE

Clogs, Leather Products

F. Walkley Clogs, Ltd. (factory showroom)
Clog Mill
Hebden Bridge, West Yorkshire HX7 9NH, England
Tel. 0422-842061

HOURS: Monday–Friday 9:00–4:30; Saturday and Sunday 9:00–5:00
Open in the evenings for guided tours booked in advance.
CREDIT CARDS: None

PRODUCTS: This is the largest clog manufacturer in the United Kingdom. Housed in a 100-year-old mill, they sell all types of clogs (including a chocolate clog in their restaurant)! There are over 2500 pairs of all styles of clogs in stock. Wooden, brass, and copper clogs are sold for souvenirs, as are hand-painted clog soles made by local artists. They also sell leather goods such as belts, hairslides, and key rings. Prices are mill shop prices and thus lower than regular retail. They will try to oblige shipping abroad.

TOURS: Visitors are able to watch the clogs being made when the shop is open. The guided tour is £15 for tours booked in advance mornings, afternoons or evenings (except Saturday and Sunday afternoons). The tour lasts 45 minutes and covers the entire clogmaking process. Group size is limited to between 20 to 50 people. Coffee is provided free after the tour. Walkley's restaurant caters to all types of meals from snacks to full à la carte service. They are licensed to sell wines and spirits.

LOCATION: Hebden Bridge is in central England about 20 miles north of Manchester, or about 10 miles west of Bradford on the A646. See the map below. The shop is about a mile toward Halifax on the A646 road, on the right.

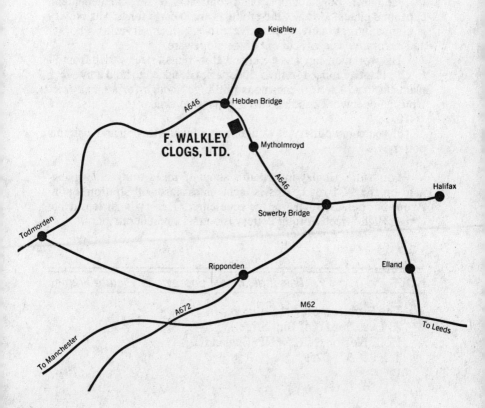

HENLEY-IN-ARDEN   *Pottery*

Torquil Pottery (workshop/showroom)
81 High Street
Henley-in-Arden, Solihull
West Midlands B95 5AT, England
Tel. 05642-2174

HOURS: Tuesday–Saturday 9:00–6:00
CREDIT CARDS: None

PRODUCTS: Torquil Pottery is located in a half-timbered black and white building which was originally a coaching inn. Reg Moon lives and works here producing a wide range of stoneware and porcelain pottery pieces each entirely worked by hand. His stoneware glazes, being made of local wood ash, are unique.

He makes bowls, lamps, plant containers, vases, candleholders, cups, and plates. Many of the products are in earth tones. His pottery is unique in that many pieces have circles, which serves as a border and decorative accent, cut out of the stoneware.

His workmanship was excellent. Bowls in all sizes varied from £7 to £20. Planters ranged from £5.50 for a pot designed to hold a five-inch plant up to £28 for an enormous pot large enough for a small tree. Unusual openwork candleholders, somewhat similar to goblets, were £6.50.

If you enjoy pottery, it would be worthwhile to stop and visit this pottery.

LOCATION: Henley-in-Arden is about 15 miles south of Birmingham on the A34 road. This is eight miles north of Stratford-upon-Avon, on the A34 road. As the road enters Henley-in-Arden, it becomes High Street. Torquil Pottery is on this street at number 81.

HOLT   *Paintings, Maps, Engravings, Picture Frames*

The Picturecraft Art Gallery
23 Lees Yard (Off Bull Street)
Holt, Norfolk NR25 6HP, England
Tel. 026-371-3259

HOURS: Monday–Saturday 9:00–1:00 and 2:00–6:00. Early closing on Thursday.
CREDIT CARDS: Barclaycard

PRODUCTS: Near the town center visitors will find a spacious gallery where professional artists display their work on a no commission system. This allows visitors to purchase items directly from the artist.

Inside of this building is a very comprehensive picture framing service with a large selection of mats and frames.

LOCATION: Holt is in eastern England. It is about 20 miles northwest of Norwich on the B1149 or about 33 miles northeast of King's Lynn on the A148.

HOLTBY NEAR YORK   *Sculpture, Pottery*

The Studios
Sally Arnup, Sculpture
Mick Arnup, Pottery
Holtby near York Y01 311A, England
Tel. 0904-489377

HOURS: Monday–Sunday 10:00–6:00
CREDIT CARDS: None

PRODUCTS: Sally Arnup creates bird and animal bronzes. Her pieces are unique and bold. Prices range from £100 for smaller pieces to £8000 for almost lifelike pieces. Her work has been exhibited at the Royal Academy, Royal Scottish Academy, Royal Society of British Arts, the Society of Portrait Sculptors, and the Paris Salon. Many of her bronze pieces are limited to editions of 10. Her husband throws pottery priced from £1 for small vases to £80 for large decorative bowls. He works in the same study with her. During June, many of Sally's items are exhibited at the York Festival.

They will ship items abroad for visitors.

LOCATION: Holtby is in northeast England, five miles northeast of York on the A166.

HONITON   *Pottery*

Honiton Pottery Ltd. (factory/showroom)
30–32 The High Street
Honiton, Devon EX14 8PU, England
Tel. 0404-2106

HOURS: Monday–Thursday 9:00–12:00 and 2:00–4:30; Friday
9:00–12:00 and 2:00–4:00
CREDIT CARDS: None

PRODUCTS: Honiton Pottery, established in 1880, makes a variety
of hand-painted vases, decorative items, table lamps and shades,
tableware, kitchen items, and cookware. A selection of first-grade
pottery is available, but the shop mostly sells second-quality items. A
section of the showroom also has artists' materials and craft kits for
experts and beginners.

TOURS: Visitors are welcome to take a self-guided tour of the
factory to see the craftspeople at work. A very helpful souvenir guide
gives descriptions of each process.

LOCATION: Honiton is in the far southwest, about 17 miles northeast of Exeter on the A30 road.

HORAM   *Wines, Ciders*

Merrydown Wine PLC (manufacturer/factory outlet)
Horam Manor, Horam
Heathfield, East Sussex TN21 OJA, England
Tel. 04353-2401

HOURS: Monday–Saturday 8:45–7:30; Sunday 12:00–2:00
CREDIT CARDS: Access, Diners Club, Visa

PRODUCTS: Merrydown was founded in 1946, and the first 400
gallons of Vintage Cider were produced in Jack Ward's garage on a
200-year-old press borrowed from a local farmer. A year later the
brothers bought the ruin of seventeenth-century Horam Manor. Mer-

rydown is now the fourth largest cider producer in the United Kingdom.

They sell wines, spirits, beers, and ciders. Merrydown cider litres are priced at £1.35 per bottle, mead is £2.45 per bottle, Country Wines are £2.45, and 1066 Elderflower wine is £2.84. A wide selection of wines are available: red currant, elderberry, honey, gooseberry, and wheat, raisin and apple.

TOURS: Tours of the winery are conducted from April 24th until the end of October, Tuesday through Friday at 10:00, 11:15, 2:00, and 3:00, and Saturdays by prior arrangement at 10:00, 11:15, and 2:00. The cost for adults is £1 and for children 12 to 18, it is 50 pence.

For group tours of up to 40 people, it is essential that reservations be made well in advance. A deposit of £10 is required for each party at the time of confirming reservations.

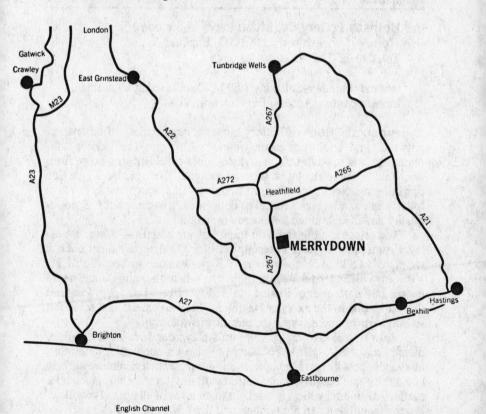

The tour includes an audiovisual presentation showing the history of Merrydown and cidermaking, and sampling of the products. As certain parts of the tour are in the open, visitors are reminded to wear clothing suitable to protect them against any inclement weather.

The tour of the winery is not suitable for elderly or infirm visitors due to certain obstacles and factory traffic. Due to government regulations, children under the age of 12, school parties, and dogs cannot be accommodated.

LOCATION: Horam is near the southeast coast of England about 10 miles north of Eastbourne on the A22, then the A267. See the map.

HORNSEA   *Pottery*

Hornsea Pottery Co. Ltd. (factory/showroom)
Hornsea, Yorkshire HU18 1UD, England
Tel. 040-12-2161/4211

HOURS: Monday–Saturday 10:00–5:00. Closed at Christmas.
CREDIT CARDS: Access, Barclaycard, Visa

PRODUCTS: Hornsea Pottery makes a large variety of tableware, giftware, and cookware pottery items. All items are freezer-safe, oven-safe, microwave-safe, and dishwasher-safe. Patterns range from very traditional to the latest modern designs. There is also a nice line of gift items: clocks, ceramic art people, wall plaques, trinket boxes, toiletry sets, and a beautiful set of collector Christmas plates. Second-quality and discontinued items are also sold.

The prices are the same on the following patterns—Fleur, Tapestry, Bronte, and Saffron. A teacup sells for £1.40, a tea saucer is £1, a tea plate is £1.15, a dinner plate is £2.35, and an oatmeal bowl is £1.95. Visitors will find baskets for their use when shopping since many people buy a number of items at these low prices. Bus tours frequent this outlet due to the excellent facilities. They do have a vast selection so don't worry about trying to beat the crowds.

Visitors will also find a children's playground, cafe, tea garden, picnic area, and a gift shop. There is also an enchanting miniature model village with terraced houses and shops set in a miniature harbor, and a fairy-tale country scene dotted with tiny farms, churches, and a castle. This model village is a delight to children of all ages. The village is open from Easter to September, and there is a nominal charge.

TOURS: Tours of the factory commence at 10:00 a.m. daily, and last about 25 minutes. Tours are in groups of 12 people. Groups of 12 or over must book in advance.

LOCATION: Hornsea is on the central east coast of England about 10 miles north of Kingston upon Hull, or 30 miles due east of York. As you enter town on the B1244 you will pass by the Hornsea Mere, a large lake. After passing the lake bear right (south) on the main road. This is the B1242 toward Withernsea. The name of the road changes from West Gate, to Market Place, to South Gate. At the intersection with Hull Road, keep going straight south onto Rolston Road. The entrance to Hornsea Pottery is on Rolston Road about one-half mile further south, on the right.

HUNTON, NEAR BEDALE *Signs, Clocks, Barometers*

Robin Watson Signs (factory outlet)
Robins Return, Hunton,
Bedale, North Yorkshire DL8 1QU, England
Tel. 0677-50388

HOURS: Monday–Friday 9:00–5:00
CREDIT CARDS: Access, Barclaycard, Visa

PRODUCTS: This firm sells signs for homes and offices. They also sell ship clocks and barometers in solid brass, and traditional school-style clocks in mahogany or pine. An interesting item is the personalized birthday clock indicating your child's name, weight, and date of birth. They also sell hand-painted and hand-carved portraits of dogs. (Customers wishing to purchase these should bring a photograph of their dog with them.)
They will ship for you. It is possible to order personalized items such as signs, clocks, or portraits at the factory, and they will ship them to the States upon completion. Sign prices range from $15 to $150, clock prices range from $18 to $75, birthday clocks are $20, and portraits are $60.

TOURS: Tours for groups of up to 30 people can be accommodated. Buffet snacks and beer may be arranged if one week's prior notice is given.

LOCATION: Hunton is in northeast England, just west of Bedale on the A684. Bedale is about 30 miles northwest of York, just west of the A1 road (about 6½ miles west of Northallerton). From Bedale, take the A684 road west toward Leyburn. After passing through Patrick Brompton, take the second right turn to Hunton (about one mile). At the "T," turn left. Then turn right beside the white "New Inn" pub.

ISLE OF MAN

See BALLASALLA
    LAXEY
    ST. JOHNS

ISLE OF WIGHT

See CHESSELL
    FRESHWATER
    WHIPPINGHAM
    VENTNOR

KELLING   *Pictures, Maps, Engravings, Craft Items*

The Picturecraft Art Gallery
The Old Reading Room
Coast Road, Kelling
Holt, Norfolk NR25 7EL, England
Tel. 026-370-528

HOURS: Monday–Sunday 10:00–5:00. Closed all day Thursday.
CREDIT CARDS: Barclaycard

PRODUCTS: Inside the old village reading room visitors will find a collection of paintings, signed limited-edition prints, antique maps, and engravings as well as a selection of locally made craftware. Prices on maps, engravings, and prints in England are far more reasonable than in the United States. The range of techniques, styles, subjects, and colors will astound the newcomer. Definitely worth looking into while visiting!

LOCATION: Kelling is near the east coast of England about eight miles west of Cromer on the A149. Cromer is 23 miles north of Norwich on the A140. The shop is clearly situated on main A149 road.

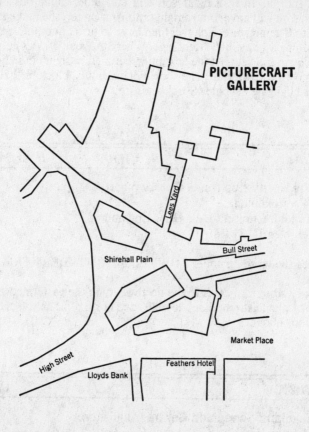

KENDAL   *Clothing*

Lakeland Sheepskin Centre (retail store)
24, Stricklandgate
Kendal, Cumbria LA9 4ND, England
Tel. 0539-20718

HOURS: Monday–Saturday 9:00–5:30

See the write-up under ALTRINCHAM.

LOCATION: Kendal is in the northwest, on the eastern edge of the famous Lake District (about 20 miles due north of Lancaster). From the M6 motorway, take exit 37 west about five miles on the A684 to town. As you enter Kendal you will encounter numerous one-way streets. You will have to turn right onto Ann Street, then take the next left onto Stramongate. You will then have to turn left onto New Road. After doing so stay in the right lane. Where the road divides go straight onto Lowther Street. At the next intersection turn right onto Highgate. This is by the Town Hall. The shop will be about a block further on the left, as Highgate becomes Stricklandgate.

KENDAL   *Horn Products*

The Horn Shop (retail factory outlet)
94 Stricklandgate
Kendal, Cumbria LA9 4RL, England
Tel. Kendal 31018

See the write-up under BOWNESS-ON-WINDERMERE.

LOCATION: Kendal is in the northwest, on the eastern edge of the famous Lake District (about 20 miles due north of Lancaster). See the directions above.

KESWICK   *Clothing*

Lakeland Sheepskin Centre (retail store)
11 Lake Road
Keswick, Cumbria CA12 5BS, England
Tel. 0596-72961

See the write-up under ALTRINCHAM.

LOCATION: Keswick is in the northwest, to the north of the famous Lake District about 18 miles west of Penrith on the A66 road. From the A66, exit at the roundabout intersection with the A591 and go to the town center. You will come to a "T," and turn left onto High Hill. This becomes Main Street. At the town square bear right. The shop will be on your left just after you leave the square.

KING'S LYNN   *Crystal*

Wedgwood Crystal Limited (factory/showroom)
Oldmedow Road, Hardwick Industrial Estate
King's Lynn, Norfolk PE30 4JT, England
Tel. 0553-65111

HOURS: Factory: Monday–Friday 9:00–5:00
            Showroom: Monday–Friday 9:00–5:00; Saturday 9:00–
            4:00
CREDIT CARDS: Access, Barclaycard

PRODUCTS: Wedgwood Crystal makes 24% lead crystal products
of superior quality. They have a large variety of pieces such as vases,
candleholders, decanters, bowls, goblets, champagne glasses, paperweights, animal giftware, miniatures, bells, and much more. Wedgwood is famous the world over for their designs and quality. Prices at
this factory shop start at about £4 and go up to £20 for first-quality
items. There are special sales in November and December.

TOURS: Regular tours are offered Monday to Friday from 9:30 to
2:00. There is a nominal charge. Annual holidays may affect the
schedule. All bus tours must make arrangements in advance.

LOCATION: King's Lynn is in eastern England about 45 miles
north of Cambridge on the A10 road. The Wedgwood factory is on the
southern edge of town. There is a large roundabout where the A10,
A47, and A149 roads meet. Take the roundabout exit toward town on
the A149. Then immediately turn right onto either Scania Way or
Hansa Road. Both lead to Oldmedow Road. Turn right onto Oldmedow Road, and the factory is a short way down on the right.

KINGSTON ST. MARY, NR. TAUNTON   *Woolen Products*

Church Farm Weavers
Kingston St. Mary
Taunton, Somerset, TA 28, England
Tel. 082345-267

HOURS: Tuesday–Saturday 2:00–6:00, or by appointment
CREDIT CARDS: None

PRODUCTS: Of the many hundreds of villages we visited in England, Kingston St. Mary remains my most vivid memory. The tiny village is much the same as it must have been hundreds of years ago, with stone houses that look as if they belong in a movie setting. Each home had a lovely garden with a painter's palette of budding flowers, and ancient trees inhabited each courtyard. Century-old gravestones surrounded a beautifully restored tiny church. If I could recommend one perfect setting in all of England, this tiny village would win.

At this quaint shop, visitors will find a weaving workshop, which is open to the public. John Lennon and Talbot Porter can often be seen working on their looms. A large amount of their work consists of commissions from churches for vestments and altar fontals.

Church Farm Weavers sells handwoven cloth and woolen products. Rugs, tweeds, wall hangings, stoles, blankets, and ecclesiastical ware are created from plant-dyed handspun wool. Rugs range from £16 to £100. An average rug 33" × 56" will cost about £45.

An excellent price for a quality product. Handwoven ties are £4.50 each. Head scarves vary between £7.50 and £12.50 depending upon the scarf size and the amount of handspun wool used. Beautiful handwoven stoles which would complement any outfit are priced from £20 to £35 each. For handwoven tweed fabric, visitors can expect to pay £9 to £12 per yard. I have never seen handwoven tweed fabric for sale in the States at any price. They will ship items for you. High quality items!

TOURS: Lectures and demonstrations for groups of up to 20 can be arranged in the mornings or evenings at a cost of £12.

LOCATION: Taunton is in the southwest, about 35 miles southeast of Bristol on the M5 motorway. The Church Farm Weavers is in the town of Kingston St. Mary, which is three miles north of Taunton. From the Taunton Railroad Station, take the Kingston Road North about three miles. Upon entering Kingston, turn right onto Church Street. The shop is beside the renowned thirteenth-century church in one of the most picturesque settings in England.

KINGSWINFORD   *Engraving Studio*

Simon J. Gidden Engraving Studio
Broadfield House Glass Museum
Barnett Lane

Kingswinford, Brierly Hill, West Midlands DY6 9QA,
  England
Tel. 294653

HOURS: Wednesday–Friday 2:00–5:00; Saturday 10:00–1:00 and
  2:00–5:00; Sunday 2:00–5:00.
  Closed Monday and Tuesday. Open Bank Holiday Mon-
  days; closed Christmas Day, Boxing Day, and New
  Year's Day.
CREDIT CARDS: None

PRODUCTS: The Broadfield House Glass Museum contains glass
from the Roman period to present, with a special emphasis on glass
and crystal from Stourbridge during the nineteenth century. The
museum is outstanding and was the winner of the Best Small Museum
Award in 1981.
  A small workshop studio is found at the museum, where Simon J.
Gidden demonstrates the technique of copper wheel glass engraving to
visitors. Each piece of crystal is cut by hand and many pieces are one-
of-a-kind. Names and dates can be added to any items, whether or not
the crystal was purchased from Mr. Gidden.

TOURS: Tours of the museum are given regularly. Admission
charges for individuals are 40 pence to 75 pence; for individuals in
groups of 15 or more, 20 pence to 40 pence. Groups are welcome
outside of normal museum hours if arrangements are made in advance.

LOCATION: Kingswinford is in central England about 12 miles due
west of downtown Birmingham. This is three miles north of Stourbridge on the A491 road. Watch for the signs on the A491, which will
direct you to Barnett Lane.

KIRBY LONSDALE   *Woolen Products*

The Sheepskin Warehouse Shop
Market Square
Kirby Lonsdale, Via Carnforth LA6 2AN, England
Tel. 0468-71390

HOURS: Monday–Saturday 9:00–5:30; Sunday 1:00–5:30
CREDIT CARDS: Access, Barclaycard

PRODUCTS: Mark Birkbeck & Co. owns the Sheepskin Warehouse Shops, which are direct outlets for many of the sheepskin products which they manufacture. Products available include elegant sheepskin men's and women's jackets, short and long coats, mittens, gloves, slippers, and moccasins. Children's tweed or sheepskin coats are available in all sizes. The styles and colors are superb! Of course sheepskin rugs are abundant. Stylish men's and women's leather coats and jackets are also sold in a wide variety of colors.

Sheepskin coats begin at £100, lambskin gloves from £12, lambswool slippers from £7, leather blousons from £69.90 and wool sweaters from £9.95.

Recently the store has started selling a variety of quality woolen sweaters, which they purchase from other suppliers.

LOCATION: Kirby Lonsdale is in the northwest, about 13 miles northeast of Lancaster on the A683 road. The shop is on the market square in the center of town.

LANCASTER   *Pottery*

Hornsea Pottery Co. Ltd. (factory/showroom)
Wryesdale Road
Lancaster, Lancashire LA1 3LA, England
Tel 0524-68444

HOURS: Monday–Saturday 10:00–5:00. Closed at Christmas.
CREDIT CARDS: Access, American Express, Barclaycard, Diners Club, Visa

PRODUCTS: Hornsea Pottery makes a large variety of tableware, giftware, and cookware pottery items. All pieces are of excellent quality, and are freezer-safe, oven-safe, microwave-safe, and dishwasher-safe. Patterns include traditional to contemporary designs. Typical prices are: teacup £1.40, tea saucer £1, tea plate £1.15, dinner plate £2.35, oatmeal bowl £1.65, and cream jug £1.95. There is also a line of very nice gift items: clocks, ceramic art people, wall plaques, trinket boxes, toiletry sets, and a beautiful set of collector Christmas plates. Second-quality items may be purchased at the factory showroom.

Other amenities include a children's playground, a gift shop where you may buy the exclusive range of Granny Bentley Food Products, a café, tea garden, picnic area, and children's farmyard. There is also a Rare Breeds Survival Unit, where 19 acres of grassland have been fenced off to preserve animals that were in danger of extinction. Pathways meander through this picturesque environment, offering the visitor the opportunity to look and learn about rare breeds. Among the unusual farm animals and birds to be seen are White Park and Highland cattle, Herdwick sheep, Golden Guernsey goats, and Bronze turkeys. A nominal charge is made to enter this area, which is open from Easter through September. The entire complex is set in 42 acres of landscaped parkland.

TOURS: Tours of the factory begin at 10:00 a.m. daily and last 25 minutes. Tours are in groups of 12 people. Larger groups must book in advance.

LOCATION: Lancaster is in the northwest of England, on the coast just off the M6 motorway. The pottery is about six miles from the motorway exits No. 33 or 34. There are numerous signs to follow from either motorway exit or from the city center. If coming from the south, take the motorway exit No. 33 and go north on the A6 toward Lancaster. At the roundabout you will see a Hornsea Pottery sign directing you to take the third turn out of the roundabout. This will be St. Oswald Street. Then turn right onto Bowerham Road. Then take the sixth left onto Coulston Road. (If you miss this turn watch for the sign directing you to turn left onto Newlands Road. It's longer, but the signs will get you there.) The factory is down Coulston Road on your right.

LANGPORT   *Antique Pine Furniture*

Herald House
North Street
Langport, Somerset TA10 9RQ, England
Tel. 0458-250587

HOURS: Monday–Saturday 9:30–6:00
CREDIT CARDS: Access, Eurocard, MasterCard

PRODUCTS: Maggie Ribbons has an antique store which specializes in antique stripped pine and country furniture. Much of her furniture is shipped to the most exclusive department stores in the States. (Unfortunately I cannot mention their names.) She has chosen to specialize in larger pieces such as cupboards, dressers, bookcases, tables and blanket boxes. All of the pieces which I saw were beautifully restored, which can greatly enhance the value of a piece. I could have easily furnished my entire home in a matter of minutes since I adore this type of furniture.

An Irish buffet seven feet long from the 1800s was a steal at £400. An Irish bookcase with shelves above, closing doors with glass and drawers from about 1820 was £450. An elegant Irish food cupboard dated 1800 was £520. Two blanket boxes three feet long circa 1860 were £50 each.

The owner will help you make arrangements for shipment back to the States.

LOCATION: Langport is in the southwest of England, a few miles east of Taunton on the A378 road. The A378 becomes North Street. If you are entering town from the direction of Taunton, the shop will be on your left.

LAXEY, ISLE OF MAN   *Wool Products*

St. Georges Woollen Mills Ltd. (factory/shop)
St. George's Mills
Laxey
Isle of Man, England
Tel. 0624-781395

HOURS: Monday–Friday (showrooms and handloom unit) 10:00–5:30; Saturday (showroom only) 10:00–5:30
CREDIT CARDS: Credit cards welcome.

PRODUCTS: The Manx Woolen Mill was founded in 1881. Visitors can watch the Manx tweeds and tartans being woven. A large variety of woolen items are available such as travel rugs, sport jackets, ties, socks, hats, skirts, kilts, coats, capes, knitwear, scarves, skirt lengths, bags, purses, knitting wools, lambskin and sheepskin products.

Ladies Manx tartan kilts begin at £31.95. Sweaters begin at £15.95, scarves at $3.75, ties at £4.50, and purses from £11.95. Knitting wool is only 35 pence per ounce.

LOCATION: The Isle of Man is off the northwest coast of England. Laxey is on the east coast of the Isle of Man. From Douglas, the capital of the Isle of Man, go seven miles north on the A2. Turn right down Church Hill after passing Laxey Glen Gardens on the left. The mill is about 200 yards down the road.

LEDBURY   *Pottery, Wood, Glass, Crafts*

Collection Craft Gallery (craft centre)
13 The Southend
Ledbury, Herefordshire HR8 2EY, England
Tel. 0531-3581

HOURS: Monday–Friday 9:00–1:00, 1:45–5:30; Saturday 10:00–
5:30
CREDIT CARDS: None

PRODUCTS: Collection Craft Gallery opened in 1980 after the renovation of the eighteenth-century building in which it is housed.

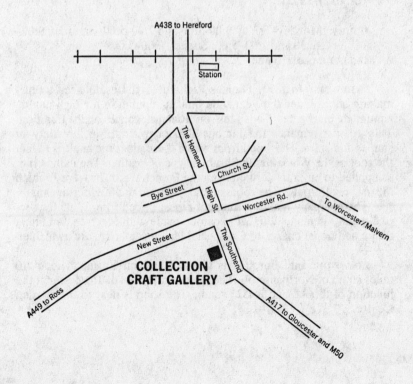

This gallery stocks work by over 50 craftspeople and features mainly pottery, wood, and glass. They also sell leather, baskets, brass boxes and paperweights, greeting cards, and ceramic bowls and boxes made in their own workshop. Top quality merchandise is well displayed.

Three major exhibitions are held each year during the spring, summer, and autumn. The exhibition lasts two full weeks.

LOCATION: Ledbury is in western England, due east of Hereford about 14½ miles on the A438. See the map.

LITCHBOROUGH   *Briar Pipes*

Richard Martin (factory/showroom)
18 Farthingstone Road
Litchborough, Towcester
Northamptonshire NN12 8JE, England
Tel. 0327-830212

HOURS: Monday–Friday 9:00–1:00 and 2:00–5:00; Saturday 9:00–
        12:30 and 2:00–5:00; Sunday 2:00–5:00
CREDIT CARDS: None

PRODUCTS: In 1890, Thomas Richard Martin established a pipe-making shop. Over the years, he built a reputation for high-quality handmade briar pipes. Today his son, Richard, carries on the tradition. This company makes the famous Blakemar Briars in a variety of shapes and sizes. The wood from which these pipes are made is in fact the root of the White Heath Shrub, a type of heather. The name briar, as applied to pipes, is derived from the French word "bruyere," which means "heath root." The root is imported from the Mediterranean.

The company makes a range of pipes, priced from £2.95 for second-quality items to £30. Most can be made with Meerschaum lining for an additional charge of £2. Special handmade briars are available.

LOCATION: Litchborough is in south central England, about 10 miles south of Northampton. The town is just west of Towcester at the junction of the A5 and A4525 roads. The shop is next to the Garden Centre.

LONDON

London, the largest city in Europe, offers the best shopping in the world. It also contains an immense variety of people and lifestyles and is an exciting place to wander around.

The aura of history is everywhere, though it is sometimes crowded by the hustle and bustle of the present. Be sure to take the time to visit the numerous fascinating historical sights and buildings. (A good plan is to take a half-day bus tour of the city, then to go back to the sights you'd like to see in detail.)

London's streets are always busy and full of rushing traffic. Because of this, it's easiest to get around by bus, underground subway, or taxi. Driving your own car can be a bit traumatic until you get used to driving on the "wrong" (left) side of the road. The double-decker buses are both picturesque and fun to ride. We've found, by the way, that the taxi drivers drive more safely and are more courteous than in most other large cities.

In fact, Londoners in general are very helpful and friendly—they are accustomed to visitors from all over the world. It is fun just to sit and watch the crowds; you'll see some amazing and outlandish characters, as well as some typically British types sporting top hats (and in the law courts, powdered wigs). With 12 million visitors a year, London has tourists everywhere—each one with a map and a camera.

A very pleasant aspect of London is the surprising number of trees, green areas, and parks in the city. Many private homes also have small garden plots with flowers and shrubs that brighten the streetscape.

Greater London with all its suburbs covers an area of about 700 square miles. The tourist, however, will only be interested in a small area in the center of town, and that is where the best shopping is, too. Although central London's streets twist and turn, and the names change every few blocks, it is relatively easy to find your way around. We highly recommend, however, that you obtain a copy of the British Tourist Authority map of central London. It contains all the major sights and shows the location of all the underground stations. Best of all, it also indicates the primary shopping streets by color coding,

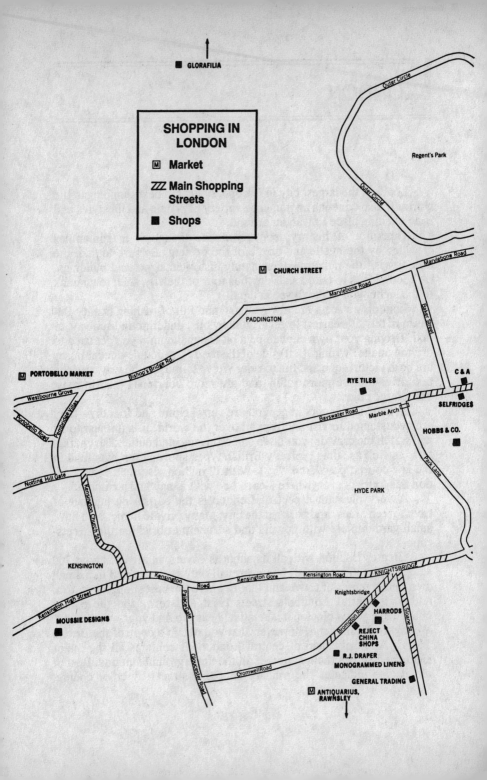

SHOPPING IN
LONDON

Ⓜ Market

ⵣⵣⵣ Main Shopping
Streets

■ Shops

Ⓜ GLORAFILIA

Regent's Park

Outer Circle

Outer Circle

Marylebone Road

Ⓜ CHURCH STREET

Marylebone Road

Baker Street

PADDINGTON

Ⓜ PORTOBELLO MARKET

Bishop's Bridge Rd

RYE TILES

C & A

Westbourne Grove

SELFRIDGES

Bayswater Road

Marble Arch

Portobello Road

Pembridge Villas

HOBBS & CO.

Park Lane

Notting Hill Gate

Kensington Church St

HYDE PARK

KENSINGTON

Kensington Road

Kensington Gore

Kensington Road

KNIGHTSBRIDGE

Kensington High Street

Palace Gate

Knightsbridge

HARRODS

Sloane St.

MOUSSIE DESIGNS

Brompton Road

REJECT
CHINA
SHOPS

Gloucester Road

R.J. DRAPER

MONOGRAMMED LINENS

Cromwell Road

GENERAL TRADING

Ⓜ ANTIQUARIUS,
RAWNSLEY

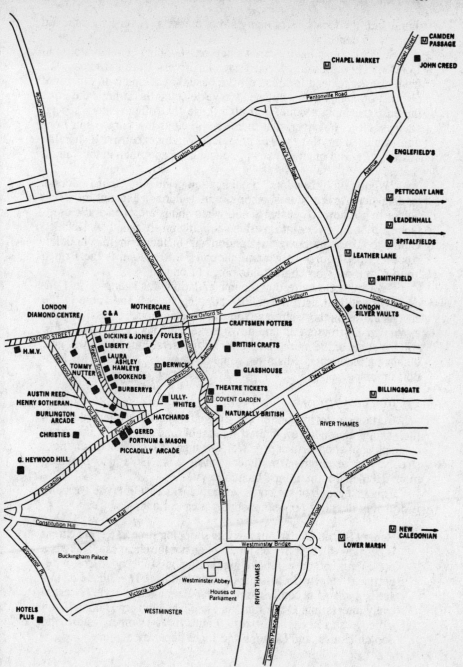

Ⓜ CAMDEN LOCK

Ⓜ CAMDEN PASSAGE

JOHN CREED

Ⓜ CHAPEL MARKET

ENGLEFIELD'S

Ⓜ PETTICOAT LANE →

Ⓜ LEADENHALL →

Ⓜ SPITALFIELDS

Ⓜ LEATHER LANE

Ⓜ SMITHFIELD

LONDON SILVER VAULTS

CRAFTSMEN POTTERS

LONDON DIAMOND CENTRE

C & A   MOTHERCARE

OXFORD STREET   New Oxford St

H.M.V.

DICKINS & JONES   FOYLES

BRITISH CRAFTS

LIBERTY

LAURA ASHLEY
HAMLEYS
BOOKENDS

Ⓜ BERWICK

GLASSHOUSE

TOMMY NUTTER

BURBERRYS

THEATRE TICKETS

LILLY-WHITES

COVENT GARDEN

AUSTIN REED
HENRY SOTHERAN
BURLINGTON ARCADE

HATCHARDS

NATURALLY BRITISH

BILLINGSGATE

CHRISTIES

GERED
FORTNUM & MASON
PICCADILLY ARCADE

RIVER THAMES

G. HEYWOOD HILL

Piccadilly

Constitution Hill   The Mall

Ⓜ NEW CALEDONIAN →

Ⓜ LOWER MARSH

Buckingham Palace

Westminster Bridge

Westminster Abbey
Houses of Parliament

RIVER THAMES

Victoria Street

HOTELS PLUS

WESTMINSTER

along with the locations of many street markets. A very valuable aid for only 35 pence.

Several books have been written on shopping at retail stores in London. These books try to list each and every store in the city. We have chosen instead to focus on the best shops—some of which are also factories or factory outlets. We've selected the largest, the most famous, the most unique, and also those that offer visitors special savings. Note, however, that there are precious few bargains in London. Almost everything will be at least 20% more expensive than in the countryside. But many items will be much cheaper than in the United States.

"What's on in London," a publication printed by 80 of London's leading department stores, shops, and galleries, explains in detail where to go, how to get there, and when shops are open and closed. Once a month, a very informative shopping insert called "A Detailed Guide to Your Shopping in London" is included in this booklet. Another good source of general shopping information is the British Tourist Authority brochure "Shopping in London."

Set forth below are our recommendations for shopping in London. We will first list the leading shopping streets, and some of the special stores on those streets. You can spend as much or as little time as you wish browsing up and down these fabulous streets. Next, we will list some of the more popular street markets. Finally, we will give details on recommended stores, some of which are a "must" for London shopping.

SHOPPING STREETS

Certain streets in London are known for the variety and quality of their shops. If you have a limited amount of time and would like to see a sampling of good British products, we suggest you stroll down these streets. (For exceptional individual stores, we have also provided more detailed information, which follows.)

This first group of streets is several blocks east of Hyde Park and is probably the most popular shopping area in London.

Regent Street. One of our favorite shopping streets, Regent Street is perhaps the best in London, though not the cheapest. There is a good range of stores, including the famous Liberty & Co., a department store with top quality merchandise. The façade of this store, built in a combination Tudor-Renaissance style, is especially interesting. Other famous establishments are Hamley's toy store, Austin Reed men's store, Laura Ashley women's store, the Scotch House, and Dickens and Jones department store.

Oxford Street. This has long been known as "the" shopping street in London due to the large number of department stores, including Marks & Spencer, Selfridges, C & A, Debenhams, D. H. Evans, and Bourne & Hollingsworth. There are also many small shops and boutiques. The street, usually filled with shopping crowds, is busiest between Oxford Circus and Marble Arch.

Bond Street. New Bond and Old Bond Streets are famous for their expensive, elite products. Chauffeur-driven limousines visit these shops with names such as Loewe, Chanel, Gucci, and Yves Saint Laurent. The window displays are elegant, even if you don't want to buy. The famous auction house of Sotheby's is on New Bond Street. Old Bond Street is especially known for its art and jewelry shops.

Burlington Arcade. This covered shopping arcade has a skylight over the shop owner's mahogany-bordered curved windows. As you glance down the row of exclusive and expensive shops, you know you are in London for sure. Nowhere else in the world could offer such charm and class. The Arcade is just east of Old Bond Street, off Piccadilly.

Piccadilly Arcade. Directly across Piccadilly Street from the Burlington Arcade, this short, covered shopping mall has shop signs made of wrought iron. Expensive and charming.

Piccadilly Street. The famous Fortum & Mason store is in the middle of Piccadilly. Along with numerous airline offices and travel centers, there are many small and interesting shops.

Jermyn Street. Just south of Piccadilly is Jermyn Street, especially known for its custom shirt shops. There are also several antique dealers and other fashion stores.

Charing Cross Road. Foyles bookstore is on this street, along with a number of other bookstores. Otherwise, we were not impressed with the numerous small, somewhat junky stores.

Another group of popular shopping streets is just to the south of Hyde Park:

Knightsbridge. Fashionable clothing stores abound on Knightsbridge. Also, at the corner of Knightsbridge and Brompton Road is the Scotch House, which is full of quality products from Scotland (but they are not cheap).

Brompton Road. The justly famous Harrods department store takes up a full block on Brompton Road. A visit to Harrods is a must for every shopper. There are also a number of small shops with quality merchandise, so stroll down the street to see the neighboring stores as well.

Beauchamp Place. About halfway down Brompton Road, Beauchamp Place is a small street with numerous specialty shops. On the corner you will find the Reject China Shops, which carry an extensive range of fine crystal and china.

Sloane Street. Around the corner from Brompton Road is Sloane Street. Though it's achieved some renown as a shopping street, we were not impressed. There are some cute shops, but this street is probably not worth going out of your way for.

The following streets are in the west end of Hyde Park, in the well-to-do residential area known as Kensington (as in Kensington Palace).

Kensington Church Street. Many antique stores line this street. Prices are not cheap, but it's worthwhile just browsing among all the beautiful antiques. There are also a number of fashionable clothing stores and other shops.

Kensington High Street. The Antique Hypermarket is full of expensive antiques. Across the street, the Kensington Market also contains some antiques as well as clothing and other items. Marks & Spencer has a department store at the entrance to the High Street Kensington underground station. Numerous other small shops are also worth visiting.

MARKETS

In London there are over 100 markets. Many of them hark back to the colorful days of Charles Dickens and have remained unchanged for years. We have chosen to list the markets that visitors might enjoy the most.

The markets are colorful, noisy, crowded, and sometimes dirty. Dress casually. Plan on bargaining at most of the markets, as it is expected. The markets are usually crowded with tourists and with the

British themselves, so travel as lightly as possible. A camera would be fun, but do not expect glamor!

Note that to find these markets, we highly recommend obtaining a free copy of the London Transport's bus, tube, and street map, available all over town in hotels, tourist attractions, bus or underground stations, and Tourist Information Centres. The map shows all of central London's main streets with the locations of the markets and the underground routes. Of all the publications on London, this small, handy free map is one of the most useful.

Camden Passage—357 Upper Street, Islington N 1. In the northeast of London, a block north of the Angel underground station, off Upper Street on the right. Tel. 01-359-0190. Monday through Saturday 10:30–5:30. On Wednesdays and Saturdays an open-air market. Stalls and tiny shops are found all along the street. Antiques are the main focus, but the visitor will also find many other treasures. You will also find about 20 boutiques at this market.

Petticoat Lane—Middlesex Street, E 1. In the East End part of town, one-fourth mile east of the Liverpool Street underground station; or one-eighth mile north of the Aldgate station. On Sunday from 9:00–2:00 visitors can hear the Cockney-Jewish barkers (vendors) offering their items for sale. You will find mostly new items such as kitchenware, glassware, cutlery, and crockery. The prices at Petticoat Lane are cheap. Be sure to arrive early to avoid the throngs of people.

Portobello Market—177 Portobello Road, W 11. At the west end of town, half a mile northwest of the Notting Hill Gate underground station; or one-fourth mile southeast of the Ladbroke Grove station. Tel. 01-431-2875. On Portobello Road off Westbourne Park Road, W 11, this market has existed since Victorian times. The general market is open Monday through Saturday from 7:00–6:00 (Thursday till noon only). The real activity is on Friday and Saturday when over 300 stalls suddenly appear. Shop owners peddle anything the visitor might want to buy: porcelain, jewelry, antique dolls, and used clothing. Be careful, as sometimes prices are extremely high due to the heavy tourist trade.

The London Silver Vaults—Chancery Lane WC 2. In the east part of town, a block south of the Chancery Lane underground station. Tel. 01-242-3844. The London Silver Vaults opened in 1882. Today they contain one of the largest collections of sterling and other silver items in the world. There are 68 member stores that belong to the group. The underground vaults have an entrance from the Southampton Buildings. They are also located above ground on Chancery Lane. Monday through Friday they are open 9:30–5:30, and on Saturday 9:30–12:30. Silver items of every size, shape, and price are offered for sale.

Other London street markets are listed below, but we do not necessarily recommend them. Some that we visited were very dirty. Others contained a good variety of merchandise, but there were no bargains. If you are adventurous, however, and would like to see some interesting sights, you may want to visit a few of these street markets. The hours of the markets may vary. For exact times, call the London Tourist Information Center; all of their numbers are listed in the phone book.

Antiquarius (also called the Chelsea Antique Market), in the southeast part of town on King's Road, SW 3. An antique market of over 100 stalls filled with china, jewelry, books, and mostly non-furniture antiques. The closest underground station is at Sloane Square. Then go southwest down King's Road almost half a mile. The market is between Shawfield Street and Flood Street on the left.

Berwick Street and Rupert Street, Soho, W 1. One-fourth mile north of the Piccadilly Circus underground station. This market in the heart of Soho specializes in fruits, vegetables, and other foods. It is in an area of rather seamy night clubs and porno shops.

Billingsgate, EC 3. This is a wholesale fish market from which restaurants and stores buy their fish. Active mostly in the very early mornings (5:30 a.m.), it is a block south of the Monument underground station, on the banks of the Thames River, about one-fourth mile west of the Tower of London.

Camden Lock, NW 1. This market is in the north of town, one-fourth mile north of the Camden Town underground station. Located near an actual canal lock, it is touted as being in an "attractive" setting. We were very disappointed. Mostly junk and souvenir items, with a few local craft goods.

Chapel Market, White Conduit Street, Islington, N 1. This is in the northwest, one-fourth mile northwest of the Angel underground station. Clothing, odds and ends, and fresh food.

Church Street, NW 8. This is in the north of town, just west of Regent's Park, one-fourth mile north of the Edgware Road underground station. It is a general market with some furniture. There is also a variety of antiques, especially in Alfie's Antique Market on Church Street.

Covent Garden, W 1. We found this to be a pleasant general market. It is now called the "Jubilee Market," and is located at the site of the old, famous flower, vegetable, and fruit market. It spills out into several side streets and is a fun place to browse. It is just outside, and south of, the Covent Garden underground station (half a mile east of Piccadilly Circus).

Leadenhall, EC 3. This Victorian covered market contains mostly fresh food and plants. It is in the East End, one-fourth mile north of the Monument underground station, or one-fourth mile east of the Bank station.

Leather Lane, EC 1. A lunchtime market held during the week, one-fourth mile north of the Chancery Lane underground station, or west of the Farringdon station.

Lower Marsh, Lambeth, SE 1. This is a lunchtime market just south of Waterloo Station, on the south side of the River Thames. (Just east of Westminster Abbey.)

New Caledonian (Bermondsey), Tower Bridge Road, SE 1. This antique market is held on Fridays only. Come early for the best buys. It is in the southeast, on the south side of the River Thames, about half a mile south of the London Bridge underground station.

Smithfield, EC 1. This is a wholesale meat market and distribution point for the city's meat. Activity starts about 6:00 a.m. It is in the east of town, just west of the Barbican underground station.

Spitalfields, E 1. A wholesale fruit, vegetable, and flower market, located in the East End area one-fourth mile northeast of the Liverpool Street station, or one-fourth mile north of the Aldgate East station.

LONDON   *Clothing*

Austin Reed (retail shop)
103 Regent Street
London W1, England
Tel. 01-734-6789

HOURS: Monday–Saturday 9:30–5:30
CREDIT CARDS: All major credit cards.

PRODUCTS: Austin Reed was established in 1911. If your husband happens to be a non-shopper, this one store can offer him everything under one roof. Prices are very reasonable. The Cue Shop is for the newest men's fashions. The English Country Shop offers the conservative dresser many choices. And the Harry Hall room is full of riding wear and sportswear. One entire floor is full of suits. Another floor is lined with sport coats on the top rack and slacks to match below. Of course accessories are also sold: shirts, hats, ties, scarves, coats—five floors in all.

A very smart-looking reversible zipper navy jacket was £45. A "Cool Wool" two-piece gray suit, great for the summer months, was £120. A striped pure wool town suit was an outstanding buy at £135. A sports coat in silk and wool with a very tailored check was £97. Shirts in every color and style with a vast selection of collar shapes started at £14.95. Most shirts come in a choice of sleeve lengths.

Visitors will receive excellent help from the staff who, of course, are trained to coordinate clothing.

Designer collections are also available for women. While your husband is shopping, take some time to find a fun dress that no one else will have. A pure silk cream dress in a fashionable 1920s look was £125. A pure cotton dress with pleats and a sash was very smart-looking at £65. A three-piece silk suit was beautifully tailored and very fashionable. The jacket was £85, the skirt £65, and the matching camisole £35. A matching hat and bag could be purchased to complete the outfit.

For a list of other Austin-Reed stores, see Chain Stores at the front of the book.

LONDON   *Books*

Bookends (Bargain Books) Ltd.
172 Regent Street
London W1, England
Tel. 01-734-5887

HOURS: Monday–Saturday 10:00–6:30; Thursday 10:00–8:00;
Sunday 11:30–6:00
CREDIT CARDS: None

PRODUCTS: In this small and well organized bookstore, visitors
will find book remainders offered at a substantial savings, often 30% to
50%. The books are all organized by category. The company purchases publisher's extras and some dated material and passes the savings to the customer. We purchased a book normally £1.50 for 50
pence.

LONDON   *Clothing*

Burberry's Ltd. (retail store)   Also at:
18 Haymarket   161 Regent
London SW1, England   Street
Tel. 01-930-3343   London W1,
                                          England
                                          Tel. 01-734-4060

HOURS: Monday–Saturday 9:00–5:30; Thursday till 7:00
CREDIT CARDS: All major credit cards

PRODUCTS: Burberry's is the creator of the famous Burberry raincoat. At this shop visitors will find top quality, tailored men's,
women's, and children's clothing. Raincoats, sweaters, blazers, jackets, skirts, and shirts are sold with the Burberry label, which sym-
bolizes expensive merchandise that never goes out of style. Good
service, excellent workmanship, and nice displays will make the
visitor feel at home when shopping.

LONDON   *Department Store*

C & A
376 Oxford Street
London W1, England
Tel. 01-629-7272

HOURS: Monday–Saturday 9:30–6:00; Thursday till 8:00
CREDIT CARDS: Access, Visa

PRODUCTS: C & A is a department store chain that cuts all frills and believes in bringing the best value to customers. The store offers mostly clothing and accessories. Due to its heavy buying power, many items are offered at exceptional values. Men's three-piece wool suits started at £70. Rows of colorful sweaters, an excellent buy at prices from £14, filled the display tables. There were hordes of people the day we visited, so we asked if a sale was in progress. The answer, "Not really, every day looks like this." There are several C & A stores in London, and 87 other stores throughout Great Britain.

LONDON   *Art*

Christie's Contemporary Art
8 Dover Street
London W1X 3PJ, England
Tel. 01-499-6701

HOURS: Monday–Friday 9:30–5:30; Saturday 10:00–1:00
CREDIT CARDS: American Express, Diners Club, MasterCard, Visa

PRODUCTS: Christie's Contemporary Art was formed in 1972. Europe's "leading publisher of lithographs, etchings, and other graphics," they are a subsidiary of Christie's International, which owns the famous 216-year-old auction house, Christie's.
Each year over 150 new images are offered in eight mailings. Included are works of such well-known artists as Henry Moore, Joan Miró, and David Hockney, as well as many new artists that they are introducing to the world.

Prices started at £35, while the masterprints ranged in price from £500 to £8000.

These original lithographs are not reproductions of paintings but original works of art conceived and created by artists who are using their chosen medium to produce effects that could not be achieved in any other way. As such they have the same investment potential as paintings, drawings, or watercolors.

The plates are cancelled on completion of the limited edition, and each print is then signed in pencil by the artist and numbered. With each work you receive biographical information about the artist, details of how the prints are made, and a Certificate of Authenticity from Christie's Contemporary Art.

MAIL ORDER: Christie's has full mail-order service with a beautiful color brochure explaining all details. The items are shipped to your home fully insured either framed or unframed. If you are not satisfied with any of the prints, they may be returned within 45 days of receipt for a full refund.

LOCATION: Dover Street is two streets west of Old Bond Street, just north of Piccadilly Street.

LONDON   *Clothing, Fabric, Items for Home*

Dickins & Jones
Regent Street
London W1A 1DB England
Tel. 01-734-7070

HOURS: Monday–Wednesday 9:30–6:00; Thursday 9:30–7:00; Friday 9:30–6:00; Saturday 9:00–6:00
CREDIT CARDS: Access, American Express, Barclaycard, Diners Club

PRODUCTS: Dickins & Jones, a very exclusive department store owned by Harrods Ltd., has a complete range of women's fashions, including such classic British names as Aquascutum, Burberry, and Alexon. British designers such as Roland Klein, Janice Wainwright, Emanuel, and Baccarat are also represented. A full range of European designer clothing is carried—Escada, Maxmara, Mondi, and Louis

Feraud. An extensive range of fashion, accessories, and fabrics from Britain and the continent are well displayed and enticing for the visitor.

The men's department includes designs by Christian Dior, Jaeger, and Pringle. They are famous for their Designer and Dress Collections by Gaston Jaunet, Lutz Teutloff, and Frank Userday. Parigi has also designed a new collection for them called Parigi Sport.

A red silk, pleated, dropped-waist dress by Parigi from the Designer Room was £115. A black exotic evening dress by Jean Varon was £252. A man's tweed sports coat by Jaeger was £115, and a Christian Dior shirt was £21.95.

An extensive collection of decorative items for the home includes china, crystal and linens.

Seconds on some items are carried during their two sale periods of January and July. They will be happy to ship items for you.

LONDON   *Pewter*

Englefield's (retail shop)
Reflection House, Cheshire Street
London E2 6EP England
Tel. 01-739-3616

HOURS: Monday–Friday 10:00–4:00
CREDIT CARDS: None

PRODUCTS: The Worshipful Company of Pewterers was empowered in 1534 to inspect and make pewter throughout the United Kingdom, and the Crown and Rose mark was chosen to certify the quality of London pewter. On completion of an apprenticeship, craftsmen were received into the company and granted the right to strike their own touchmark together with the London mark. Englefield's, founded in 1700, is now the last remaining London pewterer and holds the right to use the Crown and Rose as a trademark.

Crown and Rose pewter is entirely lead free, containing 94% tin, 4% antimony, and 2% copper. It is, after gold, silver, and platinum, the most valuable metal in common use. Unlike silver, it can be displayed in the open without the need for constant polishing.

The pewter goods sold by this company include traditional beer tankards, wine flagons, goblets, vases, candlesticks, tea and coffee services, bowls, boxes, bells, and other tableware. Many of their pieces are made from authentic and original molds of the 1700s and

1800s, and these items are called "Britain's Heritage." Over 100 designs are sold, and the quality of work is outstanding.

Tankards ranged from £25.45 to £28.50, goblets from £16.15 to £30, vases from £34.50 to £72. Christening spoons were £6.40 each.

LONDON   *Gourmet Food*

Fortnum & Mason PLC
181 Piccadilly
London W1A 1ER, London
Tel. 01-734-8040

HOURS: Monday–Friday 9:00–5:30; Saturday 9:00–5:00
CREDIT CARDS: American Express, Carte Blanche, Diners Club, JCB, Visa

PRODUCTS: The name of Fortnum & Mason is synonymous with gourmet food. Brandy butter, caviar, Akbar blend coffee, cherry mincemeat with walnuts, Christmas pudding, ginger cake, minted apple chutney, smoked salmon, almond marzipan, and handmade chocolates are but a few of the hundreds of scrumptious delicacies sold at this store. Of course numerous wines, sherrys, cognac, and other liquors are available, as well as exquisite blends of teas and coffees from all over the world. This firm is especially known for its hampers, or wicker baskets, full of gourmet food and drink.

Fortnum & Mason began as a small grocery stall in 1707 on the same site as the present building. They built a distinguished clientele by providing delicacies from the Far East and elsewhere, and they have a long and distinguished history of service to the royalty.

The large clock above the store has become a London landmark. Every hour, two doors on the side open, and four-foot-tall figures of Mr. Fortnum and Mr. Mason appear. As the clock chimes, they move forward and bow to each other. An eighteenth-century tune is played on 17 bells, and the figures return to their pavilions.

Fortnum & Mason now also sells gift items, including cooking ware, crystal glasses, desk sets, decorative accent pieces, games, picture frames, dolls, perfume, silver dishes, and many other top quality items. They also sell high fashion clothing for men and women.

Prices are not cheap, but all items are of excellent quality. The gourmet foods are quite unusual and well worth the price.

The firm will provide the paperwork for the VAT refund on purchases over £50.

The Soda Fountain restaurant in the store is open from 9:30 a.m. to 11:15 p.m., and is a very popular pre- and post-theatre supper spot. (The entrance is on Jermyn Street.)

MAIL ORDER: An excellent full color catalog is available, and everything can be ordered by mail. In fact, the company is well known for shipping orders all over the world.

LONDON   *Books*

Foyles
113–119 Charing Cross Road
London WC2, England
Tel. 01-437-5660

HOURS: Monday–Saturday 9:00–6:00; Thursday 9:00–7:00
CREDIT CARDS: None

PRODUCTS: Foyles, a favorite with us, is one of the largest bookstores in the world. The books are divided by subject category into travel, science fiction, mystery, advertising, geography, political science, etc. Be sure to ask for their free directory, which lists all of the book classifications alphabetically and their location. We counted 249 categories—what fun! The choices are totally mind-boggling. (Prices of books are the same or less than in the States.) They sell book remainders in the basement and used books on all subjects as well as new books. We found the travel section to be the most complete of any store we have ever visited. Our clerk said that people from all over the world come here to buy books that are unavailable in their own countries. The staff is most helpful. Highly recommended if you are a book buff!

Note that several of the staff members speak foreign languages and will be happy to assist you in your language.

MAIL ORDER: The mail order department will be happy to attend to your orders or requests. Please phone 01-439-8501.

LONDON   *Bone China, Crystal*

Gered (retail store)
173/174 Piccadilly
London W1V OPD, England
Tel. 01-734-7262

HOURS: Monday–Saturday 9:00–5:00
CREDIT CARDS: American Express, Diners Club, MasterCard, Visa

PRODUCTS: Gered is a division of Josiah Wedgwood and Sons. They stock the following makes of English china: Wedgwood, Coalport, Adams, Masons, Royal Doulton, Minton, Royal Crown Derby, Royal Worcester, and Spode. The elegant Stuart crystal is also sold here. The choice and selection is immense. The displays are very well done and it is a pleasure to shop here. If you are unable to go to the factory outlets due to lack of time, this is an excellent one-stop-shop for your china purchases. Gered is most helpful and extremely organized—a pleasure to deal with.

Visitors will be pleasantly surprised at the reasonable prices found at Gered. A five-piece place setting of Wedgwood's "Black Colonnade" was £57, and of Wedgwood's "Wild Strawberry" was £38. A five-piece place setting of Wedgwood's Queen's Ware "Volendam" was £18.50 and of Wedgwood's "Potpourri" was £22. A five-piece place setting of Spode's "Blue Colonel" was £74, while the elegant "Fleur De Lys, Gold" was £110. A five-piece place setting of Royal Doulton bone china "Belmont" was £92, and "Harlow" was £55.

All Wedgwood Group products are declared for duty purposes at retail value. The Stateside duty on Wedgwood and Coalport Bone China is approximately £12.80 on every £100 spent. The Stateside duty on Queen's Ware, Ironstone, Oven Ware, and Jasper is about £8.50 on every £100 spent. Highly recommended for tourists on a tight schedule!

MAIL ORDER: Gered has a mail order department. If you will request the specific pattern you want, they will be happy to mail you a catalog and a price list free of charge. Delivery usually takes five to seven weeks. After paying postage and insurance and U.S. duty, English china is still up to 50% cheaper when bought direct from Gered than if purchased in the States.

LONDON	*Books*

G. Heywood Hill Ltd.
10 Curzon Street
London W1Y 7FJ, England
Tel. 01-629-0647

HOURS: Monday–Friday 9:00–5:30; Saturday 9:00–12:30
CREDIT CARDS: None

PRODUCTS: This shop, specializing in fine bindings and printing, sells old and new books. There is a large selection of old children's books, and also of gardening and architecture books. They will search for requested second-hand books and are happy to insure and ship purchases for customers. Their mail order service is fast and reliable.

LOCATION: Curzon Street is at the east end of Hyde Park near the Stanhope Gate. This is a long block north of Piccadilly.

LONDON	*Tapestry Kits*

Glorafilia
The Old Mill House
The Ridgeway, Mill Hill Village
London NW7 4EB, England
Tel. 01-906-0212/3

HOURS: Monday–Friday 10:00–5:00; Saturday 10:00–4:00 September to May; Saturday 10:00–1:00 June to August
CREDIT CARDS: Access, Barclaycard

PRODUCTS: Glorafilia is located in an eighteenth-century building in the middle of an English village. They sell tapestry kits that they manufacture themselves, as well as old embroideries and accessories in connection with needlework. Most of the kits use wool or pearl cotton yarn. The designs are all original and the kits are varied for use by the beginner as well as the advanced needlepointer. A Victorian rose, wool, chair seat kit is £42, a wool four-season embroidery picture kit is £17.95, and a cottage wool tea cosy kit is £19.50. Top quality products! A sale is usually held the first two weeks in April.

MAIL ORDERS: Glorafilia has a beautiful full color catalog with complete instructions on how to order from abroad.

LOCATION: This shop is in the northwest suburbs of London, about 2 miles out from the North Circular Road near the M1 motorway. See the map below.

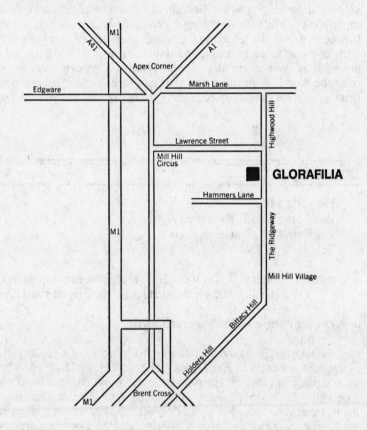

LONDON   *Toys*

Hamley's of Regent Street Ltd.
188 Regent Street
London W1, England
Tel. 01-734-3161

HOURS: Monday–Saturday 9:00–5:30; Thursday till 8:00
CREDIT CARDS: Access, American Express, Visa

PRODUCTS: Hamley's is "the world's biggest toy shop and a whole lot more." Its large picture windows are enchantingly decorated and would entice any toy lover into the store. Upon entering, the visitor cannot help noticing the train that goes above the escalator, and the groups of children who congregate at the counters. This six-story toy store, one of the largest in the world, is organized into toy subjects such as models, teddy bears, and trains. Visitors will find unique and unusual, as well as standard, toys. Hamley's imports toys from all over the world. A fun place to visit and to buy. You will see people leaving with sacks of toys even though Christmas is months away.

LONDON   *Department Store*

Harrods Ltd.
Brompton Road, Knightsbridge
London SW1, England
Tel. 01-730-1234

HOURS: Monday–Friday 9:00–5:00; except Wednesday 9:30–7:00; Saturday 9:00–6:00 (open longer during sales and Christmas)
CREDIT CARDS: All major credit cards

PRODUCTS: Harrods, founded in 1835, began as a grocery store. Today it is in a class by itself, a city within a city, and the second most visited place in London. Harrods has acres of selling space and a staff that varies between 4000 and 6000 members. The store has its own bank, funeral service, beauty parlor, catering department, decorating staff, grocery store, and even a full-time doctor. Doormen dressed in green surround the building, which has 80 large display windows. Throngs of people speaking languages from all over the world enter all day long. About 25,000 shoppers pass through the doors each day.

Harrods is for everyone. Before visiting, we had the misconception that Harrods was only for the very wealthy. But there is a vast price range on all of their merchandise from cheese to pianos to clothing and shoes. You simply pick those items that fit your pocketbook.

Every department is filled with so many choices that it becomes difficult to make up your mind. Nowhere else will you again have the choice and selection of products imported from all over the world that is available at Harrods.

Harrods has three rooms that are like movie settings. The first is the tiled meat department, which has fresh meat and salamis hanging from the ceiling. Fresh flowers are on each table. Butchers are dressed in white and are busy attending to customers' special needs. The second room is the marbled and tiled room filled with cheeses, breads, fruit, and wines. Floral displays are made of bread on the walls above the baskets. The third room is the "fish market," which is tiled from floor to ceiling. Fresh fish is bought daily, and in the corner is a fresh fish display that is changed each morning—magnificent and well worth a picture!

The huge cosmetics department has marble columns. The shoe department offers leather, lizard, plastic, and suede. The women's clothing goes from mod to designer gowns. Fur coats, sweaters, purses, and accessories each have complete departments. China and crystal fill room after room. Furniture, pianos, antiques, paintings, and appliances take up floors. A travel agency, theater booking department, antique prints, new and used books, and a lending library are found within Harrods' walls. Seven restaurants offer the shopper a chance to eat and to relax. It goes on and on.

Words cannot do justice to Harrods. Plan on spending several hours just to browse through all of the departments. You will need to allow yourself even more time for shopping. Harrods will mail your purchases and will refund the VAT to visitors.

Exciting, noisy, colorful, complete, and very London. An absolute must for every visitor!

If we were on a very tight schedule, we would pick Harrods as the one place to stop and shop in London. We cannot think of a single British product (popular with tourists) that they do not stock.

LONDON *Books*

Hatchards (retail store)
187 Piccadilly
London W1V 9DA, England
Tel. 01-439-9921

HOURS: Monday–Friday 9:30–5:30; Saturday 9:00–5:00. The store is closed on Good Friday and Easter Saturday, on Bank Holidays and on December 25 and 26.
CREDIT CARDS: None

PRODUCTS: Hatchards is one of London's oldest bookstores, established in 1797. Hatchards has distinctive black-and-gold paintwork and bow-fronted windows. It is only a stone's throw from Fortnum's and almost directly opposite the Royal Academy. There are four floors of books covering a wide range of subjects. They are especially well known for their gardening and extensive art department as well as a comprehensive travel section. Browse forever and buy books that could never be found in the States.

MAIL ORDER: Hatchards of Piccadilly operates an excellent mail order service that sends books all over the world.

LONDON   *Books, Maps, Engravings*

Henry Sotheran Ltd. (retail shop)
2, 3, 4, and 5 Sackville Street, Piccadilly
London W1X 2DP, England
Tel. 01-734-1150 or 01-734-0308

HOURS: Monday–Friday 9:00–5:30
CREDIT CARDS: Access, American Express, Diners Club, Visa

PRODUCTS: Sotheran's is one of London's oldest and most famous bookstores, founded in York in 1761. They sell rare books, antique maps and prints, engravings, and new books. They will find any book for you anywhere in the world. They specialize in buying and selling prints, especially English hand-colored engravings, mainly from the nineteenth century. A good selection of old engraved maps as well as English watercolors and drawings by book illustrators are also available for puchase. *The Second World War* by Sir Winston Churchill includes six volumes in black cloth with the dust jackets (1948–1954) and cost only £28. *Shirley* by Charlotte Brontë includes three volumes from 1849. The books are half red morocco with gilt paneled spines and were £485. They offer some publishers' remainders at a 50% savings. A book sale is held from January 14th to February 3rd.

MAIL ORDER: Henry Sotheran Ltd. has a very complete mail order service for their rare, new, and used books, maps, engravings, watercolors, prints, and periodicals. They have over 200 years of expertise.

LOCATION: Sackville Street runs north from Piccadilly, just west of Piccadilly Circus.

LONDON   *Records, Tapes*

H. M. V. (Record Shops) Ltd.
363 Oxford Street
London W1R 2BJ, England
Tel. 01-629-1240

HOURS: Monday–Saturday 9:30–6:30; Thursday till 8:00; Tuesday 10:00–6:00
CREDIT CARDS: All major credit cards

PRODUCTS: Visitors will find four floors of records and tapes. Classical, jazz, popular, rock 'n' roll, Western, and instrumental recordings are abundant. Upon entry, one may feel the need to be 18 or under due to the flashy first-floor entrance, but a complete selection of all kinds of music is available. Prices for albums and tapes are approximately the same as in the States.

If you enjoy a certain type of music, such as guitar, be sure to visit as there are vast numbers of performers under each category and they are from all over the world.

LONDON   *Gourmet Food*

Hobbs & Co.
29 South Audley Street
London W1, England
Tel. 01-409-1058

HOURS: Monday–Saturday 10:00–7:00
CREDIT CARDS: Access, American Express, Barclaycard

PRODUCTS: This shop specializes in gourmet foods from all over Europe, which includes pâté de foies gras, mint jelly, duck pâté, mixed fruit chutney, Italian antipasto, venison sausages, and numerous other items.

Fresh produce and baked goods are also sold. There is also a large variety of herbs and spices. The wines range from reasonably priced to very, very expensive. In fact, the shop is known for its high prices—which reflect the unusual, exclusive merchandise. The hampers, or wicker baskets, full of goodies were very reasonable and ranged from £16 to £250.

Hobbs & Co. opened in Covent Garden in October 1979 and moved in November 1981 to a new shop at 29 South Audley Street. All products stocked at the shop have been carefully selected and scrutinized, as the owner believes in selling "nothing but the best"—be it Seville orange marmalade or 1948 Lafite Rothschild.

Romilly Hobbs, the founder-director, has personally visited each locality to see for herself the sources of all products and to ensure that they are the best available. All suppliers are specialists in their individual products. Meticulous attention together with distinctive labeling and packaging present a unique service.

In 1984 they expanded their operation with the acquisition of John Baily & Son, the poulterers of Mount Street. They have also opened their own kitchens, to satisfy the catering needs of their clients.

All items can be packed and shipped upon payment of an extra charge.

MAIL ORDER: A mail order catalog is available for ordering food hampers.

LOCATION: Audley Street is about two blocks east of Hyde Park, and runs along the side of Grosvenor Square (the site of the Roosevelt Memorial). The shop is 25 yards south of the square.

LONDON   *Accommodation and Sightseeing*

Hotels Plus
Gatwick Airport Tel. (0293) 34851
Victoria Station Tel. 828-4646

Concordia Head Office
Terminal House
52 Grosvenor Gardens Victoria
London SW1 WOAU, England
Tel. 01-730-3467

Hotels Plus is a central booking agency. They book B&Bs, hotels, theaters, concerts, sightseeing tours, sports events, flowers, package tours, and telex services. Near Gatwick Airport, Hotels Plus can often get discounts on top quality hotels, depending upon the occupancy rate of the hotel. For this service people pay £2.50 per transaction. (There is no savings on the other bookings. It simply saves time to be able to do it all at one place.)

LONDON (ISLINGTON) *Antique Pine Furniture*

John Creed Antiques Ltd.
Camden Passage
London N1, England
Tel. 01-226-8867

HOURS: Monday–Saturday 10:00–5:30
CREDIT CARDS: Access, American Express

PRODUCTS: Refurbished antique pine furniture for reasonable prices—even unusual and authentic pieces that are difficult to find, are available at this quality antique store. When we were there, they had just sold a roomful to a leading American department store. They will crate and ship pieces home, although you should be aware that shipping may take a while and is expensive.

LOCATION: Camden Passage is in the northern suburb of Islington, about one-fourth mile north of the Angel underground station.

LONDON *Clothing, Fabric*

Laura Ashley
208/210 Regent Street
London W1, England
Tel. 01-734-5824

HOURS: Monday–Saturday 9:30–6:00; Thursday till 7:00
CREDIT CARDS: Access, Visa

PRODUCTS: Even before I knew it was Laura Ashley, the display windows drew me into this shop, beautifully finished in oak. On one wall are the famous Laura Ashley fabrics, wallpaper, border prints, and matching decorative accessories. The other walls are lined with cotton blouses, skirts, dresses, jackets, sweaters, and gowns—all at prices far lower than in the U.S. From the crowd inside buying, the British also feel these items are a good price. We had to stand in line to try clothes on and to pay. Definitely worth a visit if you like Laura Ashley clothing. They will give a VAT refund but you must remember to ask.

A navy-and-white cotton dress was a good buy at £34.95. A stunning linen jacket and skirt would be a good buy for the working woman. The jacket was £49.95 and the skirt was £21.95.

Country Furnishing Cottons were £5.95 per meter, great for a crisp new look. Wallpaper was £3.95 to £5.95 per roll, a great savings when compared to Stateside prices. Large octagonal lamp bases were £22.95 each. Printed tiles in various designs were £22.50 per pack.

Note that this is one of a large chain of stores. For the locations of the others, see the list of chain stores in the front of the book.

LONDON *Department Store*

Liberty & Co. Ltd. (retail shop)
Regent Street
London W1R 6AH, England
Tel. 01-734-1234

HOURS: Monday–Saturday 9:30–6:00; Thursday till 7:00
CREDIT CARDS: All major credit cards

PRODUCTS: In 1894, Arthur Liberty founded Liberty & Company. From the beginning he imported fabrics from the East, handwoven silks from India, cashmeres from China, and crepes and satins from Japan. The textures and the colors of the fabrics were more elegant than anything available to Europe at the time. However, it was found that once the cloth was made into garments, many of them did not hold up under England's wet climate.

Arthur Liberty began convincing British manufacturers to reproduce the fabric combining ancient techniques and modern machinery. The weaving processes were eventually modified to create new types of fabric with vivid colors, textures, and durability. Within 20 years the English textile industry was greatly changed.

Liberty fabrics became famous throughout the world and a wholesale fabric business was created in addition to the retail store. Through the years, Liberty has acquired a number of smaller fabric companies to expand its special look. Many of the new designs on fabrics are commissioned from freelance designers and colored by the Liberty design studios. Each year during the spring and autumn new colors and fabrics are introduced to complement the classic fabrics, some of which date back to 1880. The fabrics today are machine printed using copper rollers or silk screen printing methods.

Some fabrics currently produced by Liberty include silk twill, chintz, Varuna wool (a lightweight wool challis), Jubilee (a mixture of 82% cotton and 18% wool), cotton poplin, and Tyrian silk (a plain woven lightweight silk).

The retail shop is a beautifully timbered building, one of my favorites in London. Inside, visitors will find a courtyard with a skylight, wooden balconies and bold wooden beams. The store is simply elegant. The displays are clever and at times we wanted to pinch the clerks to see if they were real. They reminded us of mannequins and seemed to blend right in with the atmosphere.

The fabric and linen department of course is exceptional, and the number of choices is somewhat overwhelming. Decorators are available to help if you are unsure of your choice.

At Liberty & Co. you will also find regular department store merchandise such as wool sweaters, skirts, accessories, blazers, etc. Do not expect any special prices but do expect quality and service.

A peacock feather silk scarf was £27.50, a bean-bag frog from £2.95, Varuna wool (printed) £5.45 per meter, plain Varuna wool £8.95 per meter, and Tana Lawn (a fine Egyptian cotton) for £5.45 per meter if printed and £4.25 per meter if plain. Ready-to-sew wool skirts (many from Liberty fabrics) ranged from £10.95 to £29.95.

Be sure to bring your camera to Liberty & Co. Ltd. You could never find a more charming building in all of England!

LONDON   *Sportswear*

Lillywhites Ltd.
Piccadilly Circus
London SW1Y 4QF, England
Tel. 01-930-3181

HOURS: Monday–Saturday 9:30–6:00
CREDIT CARDS: Access, American Express, Carte Blanche, Diners Club, JCB, THF Gold Card, Visa

PRODUCTS: The name of Lillywhites has been synonymous with sport—sports equipment, clothing, footwear, and leisurewear—for more than 100 years, making it the longest established retail organization of its kind in the world.

Founded by James Lillywhite, a cricketer of considerable repute, the first Lillywhites shop opened in 1863 in the Haymarket of London. The game of croquet was new to Britain, and badminton had only just been invented. Interest in athletics was spreading, and soccer and rugby football were becoming popular. Lillywhites became renowned as the most knowledgeable retailer in that specialized market. When Lillywhites outgrew the Haymarket premises and moved to Piccadilly Circus in 1925, the store already catered to 34 different sports.

In 1934, Lillywhites received the grant of the Royal Warrant as Shoemakers to King George VI. The distinction was followed by an award of the Royal Warrant as Outfitters to the Queen in 1955. The business has supplied equipment and clothing for the Olympic Games, expeditions, and numerous sporting bodies.

Lillywhites of Piccadilly Circus offers over 30 sports departments on six floors and over 30,000 square feet is devoted to sport and leisure clothing, including the latest designer ranges, sporting equipment, and footwear. Expert, trained staff are available in every department, dispensing professional advice.

The ground floor, recently extended by 2000 square feet, is devoted to a large collection of American sports, soccer, and rugby football.

Special services offered by Lillywhites include racket stringing, a ski workshop for an all-year-round ski service, and a new two-hour express ski service. A fully equipped gymnasium on the first floor offers an opportunity to test the latest equipment. Recently Lillywhites introduced a revolutionary electronic indoor golf simulator, the ideal way to perfect the game, try out new equipment, and practice new techniques.

MAIL ORDER: An International Department handles all international mail orders.

LONDON   *Children's Items, Mothers' Items*

Mothercare Limited (retail store, mail order)
174–176 Oxford Street
London W1, England
Tel. 01-629-6621

HOURS: Monday–Saturday 9:00–5:00
CREDIT CARDS: Access, Eurocard, MasterCard, Mothercare Card, Visa

PRODUCTS: In the United Kingdom there are over 212 Mothercare stores; in the U.S. there are over 137 stores. This London store is very neat and colorful, with everything for the mother-to-be, the mother, the infant, and children in general. Maternity clothes, nightgowns, strollers, baby furniture, toys, socks, diapers, linens, playpens, swings, car seats, and innumerable other items are sold. It is great fun to compare merchandise in Britain with that in the U.S. The British have a number of new products we have yet to discover, especially in the area of safety. (Over half of the accidents in homes involve children under 5.)

The clothing for children is well made, colorful, stylish, and wonderfully well priced. A fully baby layette with over 30 pieces included was only £52.36. A lovely christening robe with a voile hat was £8.50. The baby furniture, made in all colors, is well designed and reasonably priced. Stuffed toys are guaranteed to be safe, and many are much more reasonably priced than in the States. There are baby carriers in all colors and styles. Definitely a must to visit!

For a list of the other Mothercare stores in the United Kingdom, see the Chain Stores section at the front of this book.

MAIL ORDER: Mothercare has a full-color catalog from which you can order by mail. (There is a slight charge for the catalog; the price will vary with the season.) Full details of how to order and how to pay are found on the order form. (Some bulky things cannot be shipped overseas, but those items are so marked.) Exchanges are accepted if the merchandise is returned within two weeks of receipt. The delivery time is six to ten weeks, and the shipping charge for surface mail is 25 pence per British pound. Mothercare has an extensive mail order exporting department that is well organized and capable of answering all questions.

LONDON	Sweaters

Moussie Designs Ltd.
1 Pembroke Villas
London W8 6PG, England
Tel. 01-937-6033

HOURS: Monday–Saturday 10:00–6:00
CREDIT CARDS: Access, American Express, Visa

PRODUCTS: At this shop visitors will find all hand-knitted sweaters for adults and children. A unique assortment of sweaters patterned with hearts, rabbits, snowmen, reindeer and bobbies were £95 each. Some exclusive beaded evening sweaters cost £150. Exquisite lace blouses with antique lace inserts were priced from £69 to £99. Edwardian nighties from the days of kings and queens began at £69. Lace collars for blouses, dresses, and sweaters started at £14.

A winter sale is held in January and a summer sale in August. The VAT refund is offered to Americans who will be returning to the States. Moussie Designs Ltd. will be happy to ship your purchases home for you. (Surprise! The owner's name just happens to be Moussie.)

LOCATION: Pembroke Villas runs south from Kensington High Street near the west end of Hyde Park. It is just south of Holland Park, and one street west of Earl's Court Road.

LONDON	British Products

Naturally British
13 New Row, Covent Garden
London WC 1, England

HOURS: Monday–Saturday 9:00–5:00
CREDIT CARDS: Major credit cards

PRODUCTS: All the merchandise here is made in Britain. Many skillfully handmade wooden items are displayed. Pottery is abundant in all colors, glazes, and styles. Sweaters of all weights, yarns, and colors are sold; most have been knitted by hand. Soft items as well as toys are available. It is a fun place to visit for a special gift.

LOCATION: New Row is one short block to the east of Leicester Square (about one-fourth mile east of Piccadilly Circus).

LONDON   *Pottery*

Rawnsley Academy Limited (factory outlet)
13 Radnor Walk, Chelsea
London SW3 4BP, England
Tel. 01-352-1366

HOURS: Monday–Friday 9:30–6:00; most Saturdays 10:00–2:00
CREDIT CARDS: None

PRODUCTS: A nice selection of handmade and hand-decorated earthenware pottery is sold here. Prices ranged from £4 for a small vase to £20 for a decorative plate. Second-quality items are offered at a 50% savings. Each piece of pottery is an "edition of one" and is initialed with the artist's name. Many of the pieces are in blue or brown tones covered with animals or flowers.

TOUR: The public is welcome to watch the products being made. A special demonstration of throwing pots, in which the visitor may participate, costs £1 per person. The instructions take about 15 minutes with a maximum group size of 12. Arrangements for groups must be made in advance.

Rawnsley Academy Limited will pack and ship purchases home.

LOCATION: Radnor Walk runs south from King's Road in Chelsea. The factory is located about 20 yards off King's Road. This is in the southwest part of downtown London, about half a mile southwest of the Sloane Square underground station.

| **LONDON** | *China, Crystal, Figurines* |

Reject China Shops
33–35 & 56–57 Beauchamp Place,
  Knightsbridge
London SW3, England

Also at:
134 Regent Street
London W1R 5FA,
England

Tel. 01-581-0733 (same number for both stores)

HOURS: Monday–Saturday 9:00–5:00; Sunday 10:00–6:00
CREDIT CARDS: Access, Barclaycard, Visa, American Express,
Diners Club, Carte Blanche

PRODUCTS: The Reject China Shops sell china, crystal, giftware,
and figurines from well-known manufacturers. Reject China Shops
love American business and they are totally prepared to handle customer requests. I will therefore list every company whose products
they carry: Aynsley, Adams, Belleek, Beswick, Burgess & Leigh,
Coalport, Caverswall, Cristal de Paris, Crown Staffordshire, Denby,
Elizabethan, Enoch Wedgwood, Herend, Hummel, Hornsea, Johnson Brothers, Lenos, Limoges—Haviland, Limoges—Bernardaud,
Lladro, Masons Ironstone, Metropolitan Glass, Midwinter, Myott
Meakin, Portmeirion, Paragon, Palissy, Poole Pottery, Richard Ginori,
Royal Albert, Royal Grafton, Royal Worcester, Spode, Thomas China,
Thomas Webb, Villeroy & Boch, and Vista Allegre. Crystal manufac-
turers they carry are Atlantis, Baccarat, Edinburgh, Lalique, Or-
refors, Royal Doulton, St. Louis, Stuart, Tudor, Tyrone, and Waterford.

Most of the stock is first quality, the same as one would buy in a
department store. All items are available as single pieces, in place
settings, or in complete sets with all serving pieces.

The following are *export prices* of some of the most popular lines.
They do *not* include shipping, insurance, or duty. Coalport's Country-
ware—10″ plate £5.90, 8″ plate £3.40, 6″ plate £2, teacup and saucer
£4.70, and five-piece setting £16; Spode's Christmas Tree—10″ plate
£4.50, 7½″ plate £3.40, 6″ plate £2.90, teacup and saucer £5.50, five-
piece setting £16.30, and teapot £16.80; Royal Worcester's Evesham—
10″ plate £5.50, 8″ plate £3.85, 6″ plate £2.75, teacup and saucer £6.55,
and five-piece setting £18.60; and Edinburgh Crystal's Thistle Suite—
white wine £18.40, tall champagne £22.70, goblet £22.70, and wine
decanter £101.70.

The Reject China Shops are a must, and highly recommended for the visitor who is on an organized tour or who has no extra time to visit each and every china factory. All of the best names are displayed under one roof, and thanks to the store's high-volume purchasing power, they do have good prices. The selection is almost overwhelming.

All of their shops are well organized and prices are easily visible. They are always ready for the masses of visitors that come each year. Don't miss these shops!

MAIL ORDER: A beautifully color-photographed catalog entitled "Reject China Shops" illustrates clearly their bone china tableware, earthenware, stoneware, porcelain tableware, pottery tableware, crystal, Hummels, figurines, and various serving pieces. You simply write down the name of the manufacturer, the pattern, and the piece, and a quotation will be sent to you.

The store insures, dispatches, and ships any size order to arrive safely at your front door anywhere in the world. Payment can be made by credit card or an International Money Order in sterling. Shipping charges will be clearly shown on your estimate. If breakages occur, just send a photograph and the store will process.

As we go to press, we've received letters advising us of problems involving overseas shipments from the Reject China Shops. Since they ship hundreds of orders each year, this may not be a significant problem; however, readers should be aware of possible difficulties.

LOCATION: Beauchamp Place runs south from Brompton Road, which is just south of Hyde Park.

LONDON   *Sheepskin Products*

R.J. Draper & Company Ltd.
121 Sydney Street
London SW3 6NR, England
Tel. 01-351-3527

HOURS: Monday–Saturday 9:30–5:30

See the listing under GLASTONBURY.

LONDON	*Ceramic Tiles*

Rye Tiles Ceramic Consultants Ltd. (showroom)
12 Connaught Street
London W2 2AF, England
Tel. 01-723-7278

HOURS: Monday–Friday 9:00–5:00
CREDIT CARDS: None

PRODUCTS: Rye Tiles offers quality tile with an emphasis on color and design for walls, floors, and fireplaces. The hand-painted Bodiam tiles come plain or with birds and flowers. They are shaded in subtle colors and the designs are exquisite. A series of eighteenth-century designs with flowers, birds, and boats has charming soft colors on either Rye or Bristol white-glazed tiles.

Over 90 border tiles are available in a wide range of colors and designs. Tailored plaids, conservative stripes, bold art deco, and geometric patterns are also sold in all colors and variations.

The quality and detail of their workmanship is excellent! However, since the tiles are handmade, variations in shades do occur. Therefore when purchasing tiles, make sure to order enough to cover a complete area, as a color variation may occur in the next batch ordered.

Hand-painted tiles for walls, floor and fireplace were £2.80 to £3.10 per tile. Enamel printed wall tiles 4″ in diameter with one color were £36 per square yard. The glazed and floor tiles are divided into Group A and Group B colors. Group A tiles were £29 to £35 per square yard. Group B tiles, which contain most of the colored tiles, varied from £31 to £33 per square yard.

If you would like a custom home with a special look, be sure to visit this shop. Many of their tile designs have been selected by the Design Centre of London.

LOCATION: Connaught Street is just north of Hyde Park and just west of Edgeware Road. It runs west from Edgeware Road, starting about two blocks from the Marble Arch.

LONDON   *Department Store*

Selfridges Ltd.
400 Oxford Street
London W1A 1AB, England
Tel. 01-629-1234

HOURS: Monday–Saturday 9:00–5:30; except Thursday 9:30–7:00
CREDIT CARDS: All major credit cards

PRODUCTS: Selfridges brings the best products for the best prices
to their customers. This well-stocked store has seven floors full of
merchandise neatly displayed by sizes, styles, and colors. Their merchandise is oriented toward the average income wage earner so prices
are affordable. The store's mass buying power enables them to keep
prices down.
   "We sell about everything from pins to fur coats, and saucepans to
fine quality furniture and china." Selfridges holds a three-week summer sale, which begins June 28th, and a three-week winter sale, from
December 27th. Normally only seconds are carried in the sale. They
will ship purchases to all parts of the world.

MAIL ORDER: Selfridges operates a mail order department to deal
with customer inquiries, but do not issue a regular catalogue.

LONDON   *Theater Tickets*

   In a very popular ticket booth on Leicester Square in London,
you will find lines of people waiting for theater tickets. Each afternoon
tickets for the theater held that evening are sold at half the normal
price for a 70p booking fee. (They do not have a phone number.)

LONDON   *Pottery*

The British Crafts Centre
43 Earlham Street, Covent Garden
London WC2H 9LD, England
Tel. 01-836-6993

HOURS: Monday–Friday 10:00–5:30; Saturday 1:00–5:00; Thursday open till 7:00

CREDIT CARDS: MasterCard, Visa

PRODUCTS: The British Crafts Centre is a small permanent exhibition by eight potters who have been working and/or teaching for the past 20 years. Four of the eight are throwers, and the other four are hand builders. Each potter is famous in his or her unique right, and each piece is truly unique. (Special exhibitions are held here and items other than pottery are displayed.) This shop is more for the collector than the casual shopper. Prices varied from £3.45 to £1,000. Stainless steel firetools ranged from £17 to £52. A tapestry woven rug was £500. An unusual stoneware dish, which would be a striking addition to any collector's display, was £250. They will ship your purchases.

LOCATION: Corner of Neal and Earlham Streets, just north of the Covent Garden underground station.

LONDON   *Pottery*

The Craftsmen Potters Association (craft centre)
William Blake House
Marshall Street
London W1V 1FD, England
Tel. 01-437-7605

HOURS: Monday–Friday 10:00–5:30; Saturday 10:30–5:00

CREDIT CARDS: Access, American Express, Diners Club, Visa

PRODUCTS: The pottery here ranges from functional to decorative pieces. Sculptural ceramics in stoneware and porcelain are also sold. Pottery tools and a library of books on pottery are also carried. This pottery is in the more expensive range. Vases are priced from £25 to £80, mugs from £2, plates from £9, teapots from £41, and jugs from £47. Many of the pieces at this shop are bold and striking works of art, more for collectors than for casual shoppers. During the months of January and August, a 10% discount is given on all goods.

LOCATION: Marshall Street is three short blocks east of Regent Street—one block east of Carnaby Street. This is about halfway between the Piccadilly Circus and Oxford Circus underground stations.

LONDON	*Department Store*

The General Trading Company (retail store)
144 Sloane Street
Sloane Square
London SW1X 9BL, England
Tel. 01-730-0411

HOURS: Monday–Friday 9:00–5:30; Saturday 9:00–2:00; November 29th to December 23rd 9:00–6:00

CREDIT CARDS: American Express, Barclaycard, MasterCard, Diners Club

PRODUCTS: The General Trading Company was founded in 1920 by the Part family. This department store has merchandise arranged attractively in various specialty areas. On the first floor is an antique department filled with eighteenth- and nineteenth-century English furniture as well as a selection of high-quality reproduction furniture. Also on the first floor, the modern living area sells contemporary furniture and offers a range of upholstered pieces with co-ordinating accessories. On the ground floor are four separate gift departments. The china and glass department has top quality English and European manufacturers. The linen and cutlery departments offer both traditional and modern cutlery and linen from France and Ireland. They carry elegant antique lace tablecloths. The garden department sells garden furniture, plants, and gardening aids. The stationery department offers a wide range of paper, pens, and books. On the lower ground floor the kitchen department sells cooking utensils, cookbooks, herbs, sweets and preserves, toiletries, and potpourri.

Prices vary from the inexpensive to the expensive—in general the merchandise is in a middle range that most of us can afford. It is a pleasure to shop here. A charming cafe was added in 1978, and in the summer months it extends into the garden.

MAIL ORDER: The General Trading Company does have a lovely catalog that is mailed to its customers twice a year.

LOCATION: Sloane Square is in the southwest part of downtown, at the south end of Sloane Street. The Sloane Square underground station is here.

LONDON   *Glass*

The Glasshouse (craft centre)
65 Long Acre
London WC2, England
Tel. 01-836-9785

HOURS: Monday–Friday 10:00–5:30; Saturday 11:00–4:00
CREDIT CARDS: Access, Visa

PRODUCTS: The Glasshouse is a gallery where seven members hand-blow glass and sell their products. The "hot glass" workshop provides the public with the chance to watch the glassblowers. Prices ranged from £11 for a paperweight to £500 for pieces of glass that are works of art. An oval bowl by Annette Meech was priced at £230. Steven Newell was selling a flat jug for £45. An unusual scent bottle by Catherine Hough was being sold for £70. A glass plate by Fleur Tookey was listed at £130. A sale is held in January. The Glasshouse will ship items.

LOCATION: From the Covent Garden underground station, walk east about a block down Long Acre Street. The shop is on the right.

LONDON   *Diamonds*

The London Diamond Centre (factory outlet)
10 Hanover Street
London W1R 9HF, England
Tel.01-629-5511

HOURS: Sales Showroom: Monday–Friday 9:30–5:30; Saturday
       9:30–1:30
       Exhibition: Monday–Friday 9:30–5:30
CREDIT CARDS: All major credit cards

PRODUCTS: The London Diamond Centre calls itself the largest retail diamond outlet in Great Britain. Besides diamonds, they sell other precious and semi-precious stones at factory prices. A large selection of jewelry is also available. If you would like to create your own piece of jewelry, you may select a stone and a mounting, consult with the designer, and have a unique piece created. Often, when a diamond is purchased, a special design can be created for you within 48 hours.

An inventory is available for any budget. The least expensive diamond pendant is $60, while the biggest selection is between $300 and $5,000 (they welcome American dollars).

All items from the London Diamond Centre come accompanied with a diamond guarantee certificate. At the customer's request (you) can receive an insurance valuation certificate, which is recognized in America, as our company is a member of the American Appraiser Association. We also operate a limited credit scheme. We have a trade-in policy, in which clients can trade in any item purchased from us at its original retail price or at the-then prevailing sales price if it is higher.

For all visitors the purchases are tax free. The London Diamond Centre will be happy to mail your purchases home fully insured.

TOURS: The visitor is guided by a resident expert through an exhibition where the story of a diamond from the mine to the finished jewel unfolds. By experiencing the atmosphere of a diamond mine in life-size construction, watching diamonds being mined in a film, and watching the diamond progress through cutting, shaping, and faceting—as it is demonstrated by skilled craftsmen—a unique insight is given into the secrets of the world's most coveted gem-stone. After the tour, you will be led into the exclusive salesroom.

LOCATION: Hanover Street is two blocks south of Oxford Circus, running west from Regent Street.

LONDON   *Linens*

The Monogrammed Linen Shop
168 Walton Street
London SW3 2JL, England
Tel. 01-589-4033

HOURS: Monday–Friday 10:00–6:00; Saturday 10:00–5:00
CREDIT CARDS: Access, American Express, Barclaycard, Diners Club

PRODUCTS: This charming store carries household linens for bedrooms, bathrooms, and dining rooms. Many accessories, such as shoebags, toiletry bags, gifts, and children's items, are also sold. The best part of shopping here is that everything can be monogrammed, with 20 different kinds of lettering and over 100 colors. Special orders will also be taken.

This is a new shop; it opened in October 1983, and they plan to expand their range of goods. Everything is top quality, and the store carries a number of exclusive items. Sales are held in January and July. The VAT will be refunded to Americans, and the store will ship goods home.

MAIL ORDER: A catalog is available, and mail orders will be accepted.

LOCATION: Walton Street is between Brompton Road and Sloane Street, just behind Harrods.

LONDON   *Men's Clothing*

Tommy Nutter (retail store)
18/19 Savile Row
London W1X 2EB, England
Tel. 01-734-0831

HOURS: Monday–Saturday 9:00–6:00
CREDIT CARDS: Access, American Express, Barclaycard, Carte Blanche, Diners Club

PRODUCTS: Tommy Nutter was trained as a designer at G. Ward & Company in London's Savile Row. For those unfamiliar with Savile Row, the tailoring in this area is known as the best in the world. For over 100 years men have traveled to London from all over the world to have their suits custommade. The tailors receive excellent training, pay attention to details often ignored by competitors, and have a selection of some of the best worsted wool fabrics in the world.

Tommy Nutter has years of experience and training behind him. In 1982 he opened his own stylish store where he has assembled a team of the finest craftsmen and women. They have been trained to use only the best cloth and to fit the customer to perfection.

He has a collection of his own ready-to-wear clothing, which includes suits from £250, jackets from £160, trousers from £40, designer jeans from £29.50, shirts from £45, and knitwear from £50.

For those on an unlimited budget, he offers a custommade suit, shirt, and shoe service. (All of the prices quoted below do include the VAT.) Two-piece suits are £650, three-piece suits are £475; trousers are £195 and waistcoats are £130. Elegant dinner suits are £840. Shirts start at £60, and custommade shoes begin at £250.

If you become addicted to custommade clothing, you'll be glad to know that Tommy Nutter sends his tailors to the States each spring and autumn to visit his American clients.

Sales are held in January and July of each year.

The VAT refund scheme is offered to visitors from the States.

Tommy Nutter will be happy to mail your purchases home, although the customer will be required to pay for this service.

In this age of plastic, computers, and mass production, it is nice to know that people still take the time to create products of outstanding quality.

LOCATION: Savile Row is one block west of Regent Street, and one block north of Piccadilly (halfway between Regent Street and Old Bond Street).

LOW BENTHAM
Pottery

Bentham Pottery (craft workshop)
Oysterber Farm
Low Bentham, Lancaster LA2 7ET, England
Tel. (0468) 61567

HOURS: Monday–Friday 8:30–4:00; shop open longer in summer
CREDIT CARDS: None

PRODUCTS: Bentham Pottery sells unique individually made pottery.

The pottery is thrown in the studio and is available in a variety of colors and textures. Prices were very reasonable, from £1.20 for a cup to £23.30 for an entire coffee set. They have a good variety of well-made items: teapots, jugs, bowls, small animals, casseroles, plates, etc. They do offer seconds at their studio. Their workshop can hold up to 30 people. Arrangements can be made to mail your purchases home for you.

LOCATION: Low Bentham is in the northwest of England, about 12 miles northeast of Lancaster. From Lancaster take the A683 east toward Hornby. Just before reaching Hornby, turn onto the B6480. See the map below.

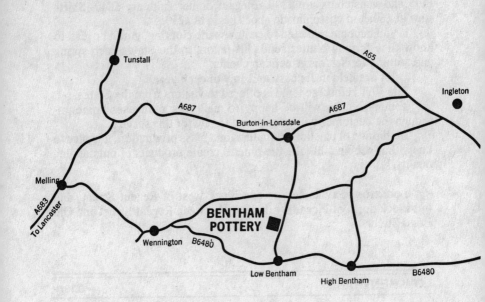

MALVERN   *Porcelain*

Boehm of Malvern England Ltd. (retail store)
Tanhouse Lane
Malvern, Worcestershire WR14 1LG, England
Tel. (0886) 32111

HOURS: Monday–Friday 9:00–4:30
CREDIT CARDS: Access, American Express, Barclaycard

PRODUCTS: Boehm Porcelain is among the most elegant in the world. In 1950 Edward Boehm began sculpting woodland and farm animals from the New Jersey countryside. The Boehm pieces soon gained world-wide recognition for their excellent quality and were sought after by art connoisseurs. Boehm received commissions from

Presidents Eisenhower and Nixon, and his works have been given as gifts by heads of state. Since the death of Edward Boehm in 1969, his wife, Helen, has carried on the tradition of quality for which the firm is famous.

The Boehm products include realistic sculptures of birds, flowers, wildlife, and figurines, dinnerware, and a special group of porcelain and bronze flowers and animals. There are over 150 objects that represent years of creative expression.

The Dove of Peace, produced in 1983 as a special edition, is £425. A Screech Owl is £75. A Gardenia with Violets produced in 1983 is £220. La Pietà Madonna, first produced in 1952, is an exceptional piece listed at £140.

LOCATION: Malvern is in western England, about 10 miles southwest of Worcester on the A449 road. However, the better approach to the Boehm shop is on the A4103. See the map below.

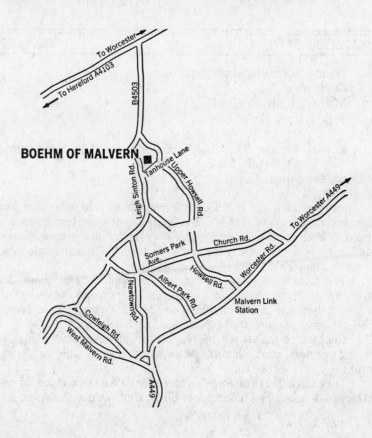

MARLOW   *Kitchen Shop*

Scoops (retail store)
4 West Street
Marlow, Buckinghamshire SL7 3HH, England
Tel. (06284) 75161

HOURS: Monday–Saturday 9:30–6:00; summer (June–July): Sunday 12:00–6:00

See the listing under STRATFORD-UPON-AVON.

LOCATION: Marlow is due west of London about 15 miles. It is between High Wycombe and Maidenhead on the A404 road.

MATLOCK BATH   *Stoneware*

Denby Seconds Shop (retail shop)
44 North Parade
Matlock Bath, England
Tel. Matlock Bath 56408

HOURS: Monday–Thursday 10:00–5:00; closed Friday; Saturday 10:00–5:00; Sunday 1:00–6:00
CREDIT CARDS: None

PRODUCTS: Since 1809 Denby Pottery has made stoneware from an exceptionally pure clay, which is fired at a very high temperature, to make it both attractive and durable—it is oven, microwave, freezer, and dishwasher safe. Giftware items are available in addition to tableware products.

The stoneware place settings are in beiges, grays, blues, and whites with decorative designs of flowers, leaves, and lines. Each set of tableware has a full matching set of cookware (e.g., casserole dishes), meat platters, fruit bowls, and flan dishes.

Denby also makes a large variety of gift merchandise such as vases, planters, candle lamps, ashtrays, nut dishes, table lamps, and mugs.

They sell a line of children's stonewear called Once Upon a Time, which is decorated with designs of birds, fruit, wild animals, the four seasons, or London scenes. The sets in this line include a plate, a bowl, and a mug, and cost £11.45. Pieces were sold separately for £3.35 to £4.25 each.

Greystone, a simple tableware pattern in beiges and browns, would fit into any decor. A teacup was £2.99, a tea saucer £2.05, a dinner plate £4.70, a cereal bowl £3.50, and an oval platter £13.85.

Planters in the Daybreak pattern ranged from £8.35 to £10.80. Lamp bases ranged in price from £31.20 to £41.45.

All the above prices are for first-quality merchandise and include the 15% VAT. The Denby Seconds Shop sells only seconds. The savings are substantial but due to a request from the factory, I am unable to release seconds prices.

LOCATION: Matlock Bath is located in central England, approximately 16 miles north of Derby, and 1½ miles south of Matlock on the A6. See the map below. The shop is on the main street through town.

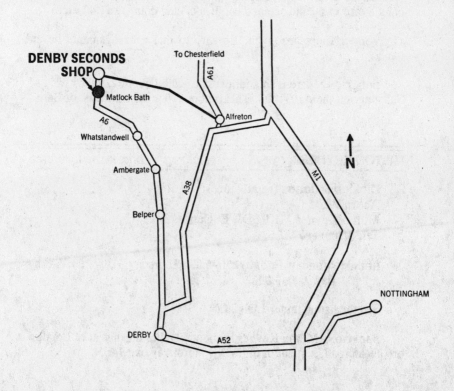

MERE   *Candles*

Ethos Candles Limited (factory outlet)
Quarry Fields
Mere, Wiltshire, England
Tel. (0747) 860960

HOURS: Monday–Friday 9:00–5:00
CREDIT CARDS: Access, Barclaycard, Visa

PRODUCTS: Candles, candles and more candles! Visitors will find garden, dining, hand-dipped taper, classical, ornamental, scented, floating, and Christmas candles. The candle colors are red, yellow, orange, dark and light blue, green, honey, cream, brown, white, pink, maroon, turquoise, and purple. Second-quality candles are also carried. Candleholders are also sold at this factory. Large garden flare candles are £1.25 each. Mini nightjar candles are £1.25 each. Teardrop candles are £1.80 and scented candles in clay pots are £1.40 each.

TOURS: Tours are given. Be sure to make arrangements in advance.

LOCATION: Mere is in southwest England about 22 miles west of Salisbury on the A303 road. This is about 20 miles southeast of Bath.

MILTON KEYNES   *Clothing, Fabric, Items for Home*

Dickins & Jones (retail store)
Acorn Walk
Milton Keynes MK9 3DJ, England
Tel. (0908) 662727

HOURS: Monday–Friday 9:30–6:00; Thursday 9:30–8:00; Saturday 9:00–6:00

See the listing under LONDON.

LOCATION: Milton Keynes is about 40 miles northwest of London on the A5 road, just south of the M1 motorway exit 14.

MILTON KEYNES   *Kitchen Shop*

Scoops (retail store)
85 Silbury Arcade
Milton Keynes, Buckinghamshire MK9 3AG, England
Tel. (0908) 606677

HOURS: Monday–Saturday 9:30–6:00; summer (June–July): 12:00–6:00

See the listing under STRATFORD-UPON-AVON.

LOCATION: Milton Keynes is about 40 miles northwest of London on the A5 road, just south of the M1 motorway exit 14.

MINEHEAD   *Clothing, Welsh Crafts*

Celtic Crafts Ltd. (retail shop)
57, The Avenue
Minehead, Somerset, England
Tel. Minehead 3853

HOURS: Monday–Saturday 9:00–5:30
CREDIT CARDS: Access, American Express, Visa

PRODUCTS: Reasonably priced woolen clothing is the specialty at this shop. A good selection of sweaters, kilts, capes, jackets, hats, and ties is nicely displayed. There is also a selection of Welsh craft items.
Sweaters and vests started at £8. Wool kilts were priced from £16.99 and wool hats from £9.99. Much of the wool carried at this shop is from Moffatt Weavers.

LOCATION: Minehead is in southwest England, on the Bristol Channel, about 25 miles northwest of Taunton on the A358 and the A39 roads. The shop is on the left of the main road as you go through the center of town toward the beach.

MORCOMBELAKE, NEAR BRIDPORT — *Biscuits, Shortbread*

S. Moores, Dorset Biscuits
Morcombelake, Near Bridport
Dorset DT6 6ES, England
Tel. (029-789) 253

HOURS: Monday–Friday 9:00–5:00
CREDIT CARDS: None

PRODUCTS: Moores Dorset Biscuits began in 1850 on a farm where local farmers gathered for tea and lunch. Today sweet biscuits are made, each individually molded by hand with three separate baking techniques that take four hours. Up to 60,000 biscuits a day are produced. Dorset Shortbread, Butter Biscuits, Dorset Gingers, Walnut Crunch, Chocolate Chip, and Golden Cap Biscuits, priced from 38p, are sold at the biscuit bakery.

TOURS: Tours, given during the hours the factory is open, last about 10 minutes; maximum group size is 20 people.

LOCATION: Morcombelake is in the southwest, four miles west of Bridport on the A35 road. Bridport is on the south coast of England about 15 miles west of Dorchester. The bakery is on the south side of the A35.

NEWCASTLE-UNDER-LYME — *Pottery*

Portmeirion Potteries Ltd.
25 George Street
Newcastle-under-Lyme, Staffordshire, England
Tel. 615192

HOURS: Monday–Friday 9:30–5:00 (Wednesday only until noon);
    Saturday 9:30–4:00

See the listing under STOKE-ON-TRENT.

LOCATION: Newcastle is in west central England, just to the west of Stoke-on-Trent. This is just off the M6 at exit 15. From the M6, exit going east onto the A500. Go east one mile. At the roundabout, take the first left onto the A34 (Stone Road) toward Newcastle. Go north about two miles. At the roundabout, go almost all the way around and exit onto Barracks Road. At the next roundabout take the fifth exit onto Brunswick. This will be the A52 toward Stoke-on-Trent. This road becomes George Street in about one-quarter mile.

NEWCASTLE-UNDER-LYME — *China, Porcelain, Earthenware*

The Potteries Centre at Keele (factory outlet)
M6 Motorway Services Area
Keele, Newcastle-under-Lyme, Staffordshire, England
Tel. (0782) 638783

HOURS: Monday–Sunday 9:00–9:00 (closes earlier in winter)
CREDIT CARDS: American Express, Diners Club, MasterCard, Visa

PRODUCTS: The Potteries Centre represents ten pottery and china manufacturers from Stoke-on-Trent, all under one roof. They carry first- and second-quality tableware and giftware in china, porcelain, and earthenware.

LOCATION: This shop is in the Keele Service Area on the M6 Motorway, between junctions 15 and 16 near Newcastle-Under-Lyme. This is in west central England just to the west of Stoke-on-Trent.

NEWENT — *Glasses, Vases, Paperweights*

Cowdy Glass Workshop (factory/showroom)
Culver Street, Newent
Gloucestershire GL18 1DB, England
Tel. (0531) 821173

HOURS: Glassblowing and Shop: Monday–Friday 10:00–12:30, 1:30–5:00. Shop only: Saturday 10:00–12:30
CREDIT CARDS: Access

PRODUCTS: This glassblowing workshop produces handmade colored glassware. Visitors are welcome to watch glass blowing in progress. The same types of tools have been used for centuries. Color is introduced in various ways with powdered glass or fine strands of colored glass known as Canes. Cowdy is known for its contemporary designs.

At the outlet shop, both first- and second-quality items are sold. Seasonal sales are held at Easter, July/August, and December. A selection of glass items sold at the shop includes glasses, decanters, candlesticks, perfume bottles, mini-vases, paperweights, and bowls. Second-quality items offer a substantial savings. A first-quality polychrome scent bottle was £34.60, while a second was £22.85. A first-quality terrazzo paperweight was £6.70, with a second costing £4.45. A first-quality cane paperweight was £15.40; second quality was £10.15. A plain goblet was £17.20 for a first and £11.35 for a second, while a matching decanter of first quality was £52.40 and of second quality £34.60.

TOURS: Group tours are welcome if arrangements are made in advance with the factory. The tours take approximately one hour.

LOCATION: Newent is in the southwest, about eight miles northwest of Gloucester on the B4215 road. From the B4215, turn toward the town center. In Newent, turn right off the main street by the Barclays Bank. The factory is 150 yards down on the right.

NORTH WOOTTON, NEAR SHEPTON MALLET *Wine and Cider*

Wootton Vineyard
North Wootton, Shepton Mallet
Somerset BA4 4AG, England
Tel. (074989) 359

HOURS: Monday–Saturday 10:00–1:00 and 2:00–500
CREDIT CARDS: None

PRODUCTS: Wine and cider are sold at this vineyard, which encompasses six acres. The three varieties of grapes grown here—Muller Thurgau, Seyval, and Schonburger—produce a dry crisp wine and a sweeter wine. Wine may be purchased by the bottle or by the case. Visitors are welcome to walk through the vineyard.

Wine was approximately £3.95 per bottle, Somerset punch £3.50 per bottle, and cider (alcoholic) about £1.75 for a half-gallon jug. A case of wine, which holds 12 bottles, was about £41.

TOURS: From June to September, a wine-tasting evening can be arranged for groups of 25 to 40 persons. Reservations need to be made in advance. The evening includes a visit to the vineyard, the winery, and samples of wine plus dinner. A 1½-hour tour of the vineyard and winery can also be booked for groups of 20 to 50.

LOCATION: Shepton Mallet is in the southwest, about 17 miles south of Bath on the A37 road. The winery is between Shepton Mallet and Wells. See the map below.

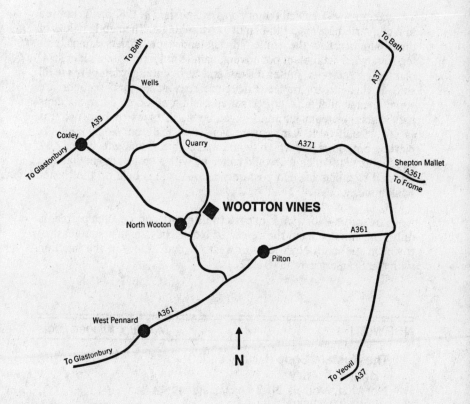

NORWICH   *Pottery*

Le Dieu Pottery (factory outlet)
Trowse
Norwich, Norfolk, NR14 8SR England
Tel. (0603) 24067

HOURS: Tuesday–Saturday 9:30–5:00
CREDIT CARDS: None

PRODUCTS: Le Dieu Pottery was established in 1967 and is housed in a converted seventeenth-century coach house. The subtle colors of the products reflect the gentle Norfolk landscape. Dishes, lamps, coffee sets, wine sets, plant pot covers, candle holders, vases, cider sets, planters, weed pots, butter dishes, and terra cotta garden pots are all sold at this factory outlet. Prices are reasonable, and seconds are sometimes available. A coffee set consisting of a coffee jug, six cups and saucers, cream jug, and sugar bowl, in blues or browns, was £15.60. Small table lamps were very reasonable at £6.20 each. A pierced potpourri jar, which would make an unusual gift, cost £2. A large cider set (which we would call a jug with a spigot) might make an unusual wedding gift and cost only £30. A sale is held on the Easter bank holiday.

LOCATION: Norwich is in eastern England, and Le Dieu pottery is only five minutes from the center of Norwich. It is just southeast of town on the main Norwich—Lowestoft road (A146) at the junction with the Bramerton road (B1332).

NORWICH   *Mustard, Kitchen Items*

The Mustard Shop (factory outlet)
3 Bridewell Alley
Norwich, Norfolk NR2 1AQ, England
Tel. (0603) 27889

HOURS: Monday, Wednesday, Friday, Saturday 9:00–5:30; Tuesday 9:30–5:30. Closed all day Thursday.
CREDIT CARDS: None

PRODUCTS: On February 15, 1823, Jeremiah Colman took his nephew James into partnership and created the famous firm of J & J Colman. To mark the 150th anniversary of this event, Colman's opened a mustard shop in 1973. It is the only one of its kind in Britain. (This company is the same one that owns R.T. French in the States.)

The premises have been restored and decorated in late nineteenth-century style. Many of the articles offered for sale are based on old designs taken from Colman's archives and are unique to this shop.

They sell 18 different varieties of mustard, plus many commemorative kitchen accessories often featuring the Colman name and design. Some of these items include: mustard pots, wooden spoons, cruet sets, spoon rests, hot pad holders, cookbooks, tea towels, aprons, posters, and mugs. Mustard is priced from approximately £1.05 to £2.10, mustard pots range from £3.10 to £13, a Colman's mustard thimble is £3.85, and a mustard label apron sells for £2.80.

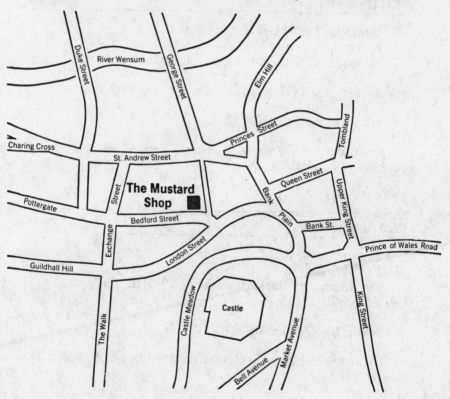

TOURS: The Mustard Museum, located at the rear of the Mustard Shop, is free and open to all visitors during business hours. With prior advance notice (a phone call is all that is necessary), the manager and staff would be happy to show small parties around the museum.

MAIL ORDER: They will mail orders all over the world. They have a United Kingdom mail order catalog, and will provide prices for overseas shipment when customers indicate which items they wish to purchase.

LOCATION: Norwich is in the eastern part of England. The Mustard Shop is in the center of town near the castle. See the map below.

NOTTINGHAM   *Crystal*

Cumbria Crystal Ltd. (factory outlet)
Broadmarsh Centre
Nottingham, Nottinghamshire, England

HOURS: Monday–Friday 9:00–5:00; Saturday 9:00–4:00

See the listing under ULVERSTON.

LOCATION: Nottingham is in central England about 50 miles northeast of Birmingham.

OLD AMERSHAM   *Kitchen Shop*

Scoops (retail store)
29 The Broadway
Old Amersham, Buckinghamshire HP7 OHL, England
Tel. (02403) 21733

See the listing under ABINGDON.

LOCATION: Old Amersham is ten miles northwest of London on the A413 road.

OLD CLEEVE   *Sheepskin Products*

John Wood & Son Ltd. (factory/showroom)
Linton, Old Cleeve, Minehead
Somerset TA24 6HT, England
Tel. (0984) 40291

HOURS: Monday–Friday 9:00–4:30; Saturdays and public holidays 10:00–4:00 (March–December only)
CREDIT CARDS: Access, Visa

PRODUCTS: In the quiet countryside of Somerset, the firm of John Wood & Son Ltd. has been processing hides and skins for over 100 years. This factory makes sheepskin coats, moccasins, booties, hats, toys, rugs, gloves, mitts, and seat covers. Sample prices include: moccasins £3.45 to £15.95; footmuffs £11.65 to £33.65; rugs £7.95 to £20.50; hats £5.95 to £9.45; and gloves £7.95 to £13.95. Most items come in two grades, A or B quality. The B merchandise is lower priced. A variety of colors and shades is available, and some products can also be made to order.

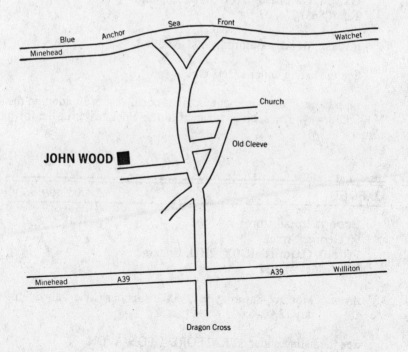

MAIL ORDERS: The company will mail orders anywhere.

TOURS: Visitors are welcome to tour the tannery and see sheepskins being processed. Factory tours are given Monday through Friday from April to October at no charge. The tours start at 10:45 and 11:30 a.m., and 2:15 and 3:00 p.m. Groups should make an advance appointment.

LOCATION: Old Cleeve is in the southwest of England, a few miles east of Minehead near the Bristol Channel. It is about one mile north of the A39 road, about three miles west of Williton. This is about 20 miles northwest of Taunton on the A358. The factory is in Linton, just to the west of Old Cleeve down a narrow country lane. See the map above.

OXFORD   *China, Crystal, Figurines*

Reject China Shop
54 Cornmarket Street
Oxford, Oxfordshire OX1 3HB, England
Tel. (0865) 724301

HOURS: Monday–Saturday 9:00–6:00

See the listing under LONDON.

LOCATION: Oxford is about 55 miles northwest of London on the M40 motorway. The shop is adjacent to the clock tower in the town center.

OXFORD   *Kitchen Shop*

Scoops (retail store)
50 George Street
Oxford, Oxfordshire OX1 2BU, England
Tel. (0865) 242837

HOURS: Monday–Saturday 9:30–6:00; summer (June–July): Sunday 12:00–6:00

See the listing under STRATFORD-UPON-AVON.

LOCATION: Oxford is about 55 miles northwest of London on the M40 motorway.

PENRITH
Woolen Products

The Sheepskin Warehouse Shop
15 Devonshire Street
Penrith, Cumbria A11 7SR, England
Tel. (0768) 66066

HOURS: Monday–Saturday 9:00–5:30

See the listing under KIRBY LONSDALE.

LOCATION: Penrith is in northwest England, just off the M6 motorway at exit 40 (about 15 miles south of Carlisle). The shop is in the center of town. See the map below.

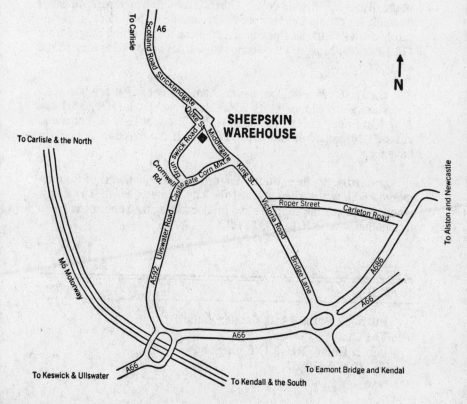

POOLE   *Pottery, Ceramics*

Poole Pottery Ltd. (factory/showroom)
The Quay
Poole, Dorset BH15 1RF, England
Tel. (0202) 672866

HOURS: Monday–Saturday 9:00–5:00; open later in summer and Sundays in August. Closed some Bank Holidays and Christmas.

CREDIT CARDS: None

PRODUCTS: Poole Pottery sells pottery from their factory plus souvenir items. In their seconds shop, one of the largest in the United Kingdom, prices are a real savings, usually 45% to 50% off the retail list prices; some firsts are sold also. Their main sale is held in January.

Various ceramic products, oven-to-tableware, bone china decorative items, and a variety of functional pieces are manufactured. Some of the dishes are in solid colors, others have a flowered pattern. Mugs were £2.75, candle lamps were £6.20, souffle dishes £5.45, and casserole dishes £9.05. The price for a 20-piece place setting ranged from £14.40 to £40. Most of the seconds were a 45% to 50% savings off the list price.

TOURS: Over a million visitors came to Poole Pottery last year. Tours are given Monday through Friday from 10:00–11:30 and 1:15–3:30. (On Friday the last tour is at 11:30.) The tour lasts 1¼ hours and costs £1.30 per adult and 65p per child. It is advisable to book in advance.

LOCATION: Poole is on the English Channel just west of Bournemouth. Follow the signs toward the city center then to The Quay, where you'll see the shop in a red brick building with enormous green letters that say "POOLE POTTERY."

POOLE   *Pottery*

Purbeck Pottery Ltd. (factory outlet)
The Quay
Poole, Dorset BH15 1RF, England
Tel. (0202) 670867

HOURS: January–April: Monday–Sunday 9:00–5:30; summer; 9:00–10:00
CREDIT CARDS: Access, Visa

PRODUCTS: This shop sells first- and second-quality pottery made from clays mined in the Purbeck Hills. Visitors will find a good selection of teapots, bowls, plates, vases, lamp bases, and animal figurines at up to a 50% discount on normal prices. Pottery colors are grays, browns, blues, greens, and beiges. The pottery is oven and dishwasher proof. A special bargain table offers even greater savings.

A 50-piece matched dinner service was £66—quite a bargain for this century. A 12-inch hand-painted fruit dish was £12, while a candleholder on a stand was £2.60. A ten-inch lamp base, slip decorated, was £16.50, while a six-inch wall plaque with a four seasons design was only £2.50. For those of you on a tight budget, there were a number of appealing decorative items for under £2.

LOCATIONS: Poole is on the English Channel just west of Bournemouth. Follow the signs toward the city center, then to The Quay. Purbeck Pottery is on The Quay facing the water.

RAVENSHEAD   *Craft Items*

Longdale Rural Craft Centre
Longdale Lane
Ravenshead, Nottinghamshire, England
Tel. Mansfield 794858

HOURS: Open daily throughout the year 9:30–6:00. Closed Mondays. Open Bank Holidays.
CREDIT CARDS: None

PRODUCTS: Longdale Rural Craft Centre has handcrafted gift items: wood carvings, wood and metal sculpture, furniture, copper, silver, leather, drawings, paintings, models, pottery, toys, pressed flowers, basket work, upholstery, wrought iron work, apple sculpture, graphics, embroidery, weaving, glass, corn dollies, printing, and herb and metal sculptures. A pottery coffee service was priced at £26.50. A hand-turned wooden bowl was £9.50, and a blown glass bird on a tree branch was £6.60. Oil paintings began at about £100. Pottery seconds are sold at the craft centre.

The museum workshop is an absolute must to visit. Authentic

doors, windows, and bricks have been used to re-create an ancient village. For a small charge craftsmen in each workshop may be observed at work—it is well worth the price. The most unusual of all the craft centers we visited!

Also on the premises is a licensed Coffee Lounge/Restaurant that is very good and reasonably priced. (Egon Ronay recommended.) In 1983 the Craft Centre was awarded a Certificate of Merit in the "Come to Britain" Trophy run by the English Tourist Board for outstanding tourist attractions.

Disabled visitors are welcome—the centre is on one level. They will ship purchases home.

LOCATION: Ravenshead is in central England, about ten miles north of Nottingham on the A60 road. See the map below.

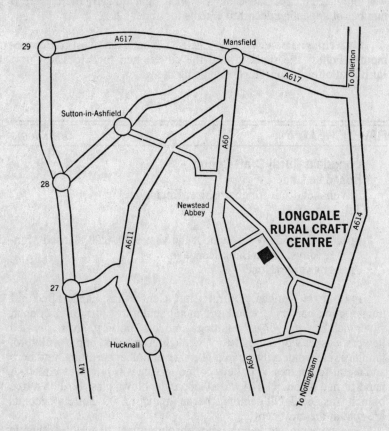

RICHMOND   *Clothing, Fabric, Items for Home*

Dickins & Jones (retail store)
George Street
Richmond, Surrey TW9 1HA, England
Tel. 01-940-7761

HOURS: Monday–Thursday 9:00–5:30; Friday 9:30–5:30; Saturday
9:00–5:30

See the listing under LONDON.

LOCATION: Richmond is in north central England about ten miles
southwest of Darlington.

RYE   *Pottery*

Rye Pottery (factory outlet)
Ferry Road
Rye, East Sussex TN31 7DJ, England
Tel. 0797-22-3363

HOURS: Monday–Friday 9:00–12:30 and 2:00–5:00; Saturday
9:30–12:30 and 2:30–5:00
CREDIT CARDS: None

PRODUCTS: Potters have worked in this area since the middle
ages. Rye Pottery was an offshoot of an eighteenth-century brick-
works and pottery at Cadborough Farm. The Mitchell family managed
both and remained the chief potters for over 100 years.
  This pottery was reopened after World War II by John and Walter
Cole. The style of decoration totally changed but many of the traditional shapes were retained. The decoration technique adopted was
known as "delft," "majolica," or "faience" and was in the same tradition as the seventeenth-century English Delftware potters of Lambeth,
Liverpool, and Bristol. Brush decoration is applied on the surface of
the glaze when it is fired, giving it a soft color.
  Each piece of pottery is hand produced, which makes each piece
unique. The Royal Family still purchases Rye Pottery, which has won
many awards over the years for its charm and design.

My favorite designs were the Chaucerian figures from *The Canterbury Tales*. Visitors will also find tea sets, coffee sets, bowls, cups and saucers, mugs, fruit bowls, vases, bathroom accessories, lamp bases, plates, banks, wedding plates, house plaques, and loving cups.

A ten-inch wedding plate was £27.50. A nine-inch house plaque was £28. A rimmed ten-inch fruit bowl was £17. The Chaucer figurines were well priced at £20.90 each. There are nine figures in this grouping.

LOCATION: Rye is near the southeast coast, about 11 miles north of Hastings on the A259 road.

RYE   *Ceramic Tiles*

Rye Tiles Ceramic Consultants Ltd. (factory outlet)
The Old Brewery
Wishward
Rye, Sussex TN31 7DH, England
Tel. 0797-223038

HOURS: Monday–Friday 9:00–12:30 and 2:00–5:00; Saturday 9:30–12:30 and 2:30–5:00
CREDIT CARDS: None

PRODUCTS: Rye Tiles is a company catering to the individual who wants quality tile with an emphasis on color and fine design. Tiles are made for walls, floors, and fireplaces.

The hand-painted Bodiam tiles are plain or have birds and flowers. They are shaded in subtle colors and the designs are exquisite. A series of eighteenth-century designs with flowers, birds, and boats are rendered in subtle colors on either Rye or Bristol white glazed tiles. Over 90 border tiles are available in a wide range of colors and designs. Tailored plaids, conservative stripes, bold art deco, and geometric patterns are also sold in all colors and variations.

The quality and detail of their workmanship is excellent! However, due to the handmade nature of the product, variations in shades do occur. Therefore when purchasing tiles, make sure to order enough to cover a complete area as a color variation may occur in the next batch ordered.

For prices please refer to LONDON Rye Tiles Ceramic Consultants Ltd.

LOCATION: Rye is near the southeast coast, about 11 miles north of Hastings on the A259 road.

SCARBOROUGH   *Wool Clothing, Scottish Crafts*

Clan Royal (retail store)
20 Westborough
Scarborough, North Yorkshire, England
Tel. 0723-71400

HOURS: Monday–Saturday 9:00–5:30

See the write-up under EDINBURGH, Scotland.

LOCATION: Scarborough is on the northeast coast of England about 40 miles northeast of York on the A64.

SHEFFIELD   *Pewter*

I. Gibson & Son Ltd. (factory outlet)
63, St. Mary's Road
Sheffield, S2 4AN, England
Tel. 79264

HOURS: Monday–Friday 10:00–4:30
CREDIT CARDS: American Express

PRODUCTS: This company makes an extensive range of pewter mugs, goblets, and flasks. They also sell pewter figures, candlesticks, bowls, cups, and other items. Many items are etched and/or engraved to the customer's specification. Both a shiny and satin finish are available.

Modern pewter is an alloy of at least 90% tin combined with copper and antimony. There is no lead content in modern pewter. The finish will resist tarnishing and can be maintained with warm water and a mild detergent.

Many of their products are truly unique, with graceful handles, and unusual curves and lines. For those of you who collect pewter, I. Gibson & Sons Ltd. could prove to be a great stop.

For that special college student, buy a Georgian lidded tankard for £17.78. A six-ounce plain flask was an excellent buy at £9.98. A pewter goblet was £7.98. For £68 the elegant three-piece coffee set was definitely my favorite.

LOCATION: Sheffield is in north central England just west of the M1 motorway. St. Mary's road is a main east–west road on the south side of the central city area.

SHEFFIELD   *Cutlery, Silverplate*

Schofields of Sheffield Ltd. (retail store)
50 Howard Street
Sheffield S1 2LX, England
Tel. 0742-21568

HOURS: Monday, Tuesday, Wednesday, and Friday 8:00–5:00; Thursday and Saturday 8:00–4:00
CREDIT CARDS: Access, Visa

PRODUCTS: This small shop specializes in Sheffield-made products such as cutlery, knives, silverplate, tea sets, and tankards. The shop specializes in special orders such as handmade staghorn knives or sterling silver sugar spoons. They also have a small selection of antique silver items.

Most of the kitchen knives were priced well under £20. We bought three knives, which we mailed home, and found them to be of exceptional quality. Tankards in all sizes and styles were £14 to £16. An antique meat carving set with detailed engravings in silverplate was a work of art and well priced at £110. Trays started at £28, and a half dozen table spoons ranged from £24 to £26.

LOCATION: Sheffield is in north central England just west of the M1 motorway. This store is within 200 yards of the main bus and railway stations in Sheffield. See the map.

SHEFFIELD   *Cutlery, Pewter*

Sheffield Scene (retail shop)
49 Surrey Street
Sheffield S1 2LG, England
Tel. 0742-731723

HOURS: Monday–Saturday 9:15–5:15
CREDIT CARDS: Access

PRODUCTS: The Sheffield Scene is a small shop which carries stag, stainless steel, rosewood, silver plate, and white-grained handled cutlery, scissors, thimbles, mugs, knives, goblets, and pewter pieces. All items are very reasonably priced. Knives are a specialty in Sheffield, and prices for good cutlery are far below those in the States. This shop specializes in selling pen knives handmade by the "little mesters," who are a group of senior craftsmen. Even though this shop is small, they have a good selection of products with a wide range of prices.

LOCATION: Sheffield is in north central England just west of the M1 motorway. The store is near the town centre. See the map.

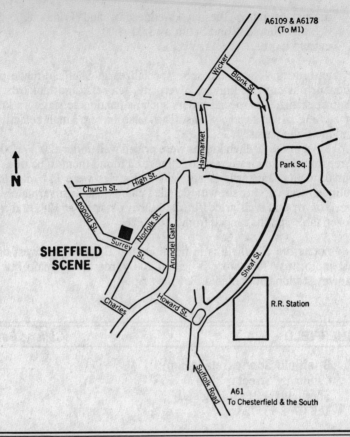

SHIPLEY *Clothing, Fabrics*

The Llama Shop (mill/showroom)
Salts of Saltaire
Victoria Road, Saltaire
Shipley, West Yorkshire BD18 3LB, England
Tel. 0274-582222

HOURS: Monday 2:00–5:30; Tuesday 9:30–5:30; Wednesday closed; Thursday 9:30–5:30; Friday and Saturday 9:30–12:30 and 1:30–5:00; Sunday closed.
CREDIT CARDS: None

PRODUCTS: Men's and ladies' outerwear including suits, jackets, coats, skirts, and knitwear are featured. Also fabrics for making suits and ladies' clothing. Sample prices: men's 3½-yard suit-length fabric £15; ladies' pure wool 2-piece suit £27.50; lambswool sweaters £8.95; ladies' skirt lengths from £4.

TOURS: Tours of the mill and museum, with refreshments, can be arranged in advance. Minimum group size is 15 people. The tour takes about one hour.

LOCATION: Shipley is about four miles north of Bradford in central England. This is just west of Leeds. Saltaire is a small resort on the north side of Shipley near the junction of the A657 and A6038 roads (just east of the A650). Drive across the north part of Shipley on the A657 road. You will see a small sign pointing north to Saltaire Village. The shop is down this street (Victoria Road) almost at the end of the street on the right.

SILVERDALE   *Pottery, Paintings, Wood, Weaving, Crafts*

Wolf House Gallery (craft workshop)
Near Jenny Browns Point, Gibraltar
Silverdale, Camforth, Lancashire LA5 0TX, England
Tel. 0524-701405

HOURS: Summer: Daily except Monday 10:30–1:00 and 2:00–5:30
Autumn: Tuesday–Friday 2:00–5:30; Saturdays and Sundays 10:30–5:30; closed Mondays.
Winter: Saturdays and Sundays only 10:30–5:30; closed Christmas week; open New Year's Eve and New Year's Day.
CREDIT CARDS: Access, American Express, Barclaycard

PRODUCTS: The Gallery is in an old barn where the original beams remain and the stalls provide natural dividers for displays. This gallery has been selected by the Crafts Advisory Council for its quality and regional significance. A variety of craft items are available.

Frank Irving, the resident potter, can usually be found in his workshop. His designs often feature details of blackberries and apples on creamware pots. Most of the pottery goods sold in the shop are "one-ofs" made in small professional workshops.

Wooden rocking horses come in three sizes with real manes and tails. Saddles and tack are made from leather hide by craftspeople/saddlers.

The Gallery also specializes in original paintings, which are framed in the workshop. Pictures range from £35 to £400. Sculpture sells for £30 to £500. Mugs start at £1. A few seconds are available, and occasionally merchandise is sold at reduced prices. It is possible to have items shipped abroad.

Summer courses available at the studio include painting, pottery, batik, stained glass, Ruskin lace, embroidery, crochet, spinning, weaving, and calligraphy.

The Gallery has a tea shop with its own blend of filtered ground coffee, fresh double cream, homemade biscuits and scones.

TOURS: Groups should give prior notification for tours which last from ½ to 2 hours, depending on the visitor's interest.

LOCATION: Silverdale is located on the northwest coast of England, halfway between Kendal on the north, and Lancaster on the south. Silverdale is just about ten minutes west from exit 35 of the M6 motorway. The Gallery is just south of town. Watch for the signs.

SOUTH MOLTON   *Honey, Beeswax Products*

Quince Honey Farm
North Road, South Molton
North Devon Ex 36 3AZ, England
Tel. 076 95-2401

HOURS: "Open all day, every day." Easter to October 8:00–6:00; November to Easter 9:00–5:00
CREDIT CARDS: None

PRODUCTS: Quince Honey Farm is the largest honey farm in Britain, and also the single largest producer of finest pure beeswax. In a 25,000 square foot warehouse, visitors in a glass booth can view an indoor apiary where bees buzz about making honey. Very interesting! At Quince Honey Farm a visitor can buy honey, beeswax candles, and creams. Honey is £1.15 per pound.

TOURS: Visitors may take a self-guided tour of the honey-making process areas, which takes about 1½ hours. Adults are charged £1 and accompanied children are free. Group rates are available for 20 or more.

LOCATION: South Molton is in the far southwest of England, about 38 miles west of Taunton on the A361 road. See the map below.

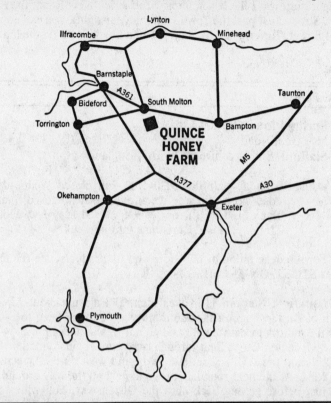

SOUTHPORT   *Clothing*

Lakeland Sheepskin Centre (retail store)
355/357 Lord Street
Southport, Lancashire PR8 1NH, England
Tel. 0704-32030

HOURS: Monday–Saturday 9:00–5:30

See the write-up under ALTRINCHAM.

LOCATION: Southport is on the northwest coast just north of Liverpool on the A565. The shop is situated halfway down Lord

Street, which is the main shopping street in Southport, and which is also the A565. If entering town from the east on the A570, continue straight on toward the beach along Scarisbrick New Road, then East Bank Street. Just past the Town Hall (on your right), you will come to Lord Street. Turn right. The shop is half a block down on the left.

STAFFORD   *Pottery*

Portmeirion Potteries Ltd.
56A Goal Road
Stafford, Staffordshire ST16 3AJ, England

HOURS: Monday–Saturday 9:30–5:00 (but closed Wednesdays). Also closed for one week over Easter; closed Summer Bank Holiday for one week; closed May Day Holiday Monday; closed Christmas for one week.

For the description of this store and its products, see the listing under STOKE-ON-TRENT.

LOCATION: Stafford is in west central England about 25 miles north of Birmingham on the M6 motorway. Coming from the south, take the motorway exit No. 13 and go north two miles on the A449 to the town center. Go straight through two roundabouts (junctions with the A34 and the A518). Continue north and west on the Queensway ring road. At the next roundabout, go almost all the way around, but exit just before getting back onto the Queensway. You will see the Portmeirion shop and car park on the left.

ST. JOHNS, ISLE OF MAN   *Crystal*

St. Johns Crystal Ltd. (craft workshop)
Tynwald Mills
St. Johns, Isle of Man, England
Tel. 0624-71-256

HOURS: Open seven days a week during summer season between 10:00 and 5:00.
CREDIT CARDS: None

PRODUCTS: Decorative and functional crystal glassware. Visitors are welcome to watch the creation of these hand-blown crystal items. Unique decorative crystal animals are available for collectors. Paperweights and unusual crystal fruit are also sold. Bathroom sets, lounge sets, and elegant perfume sets make fun and unusual gifts for that special person at home. Prices range from £2.50 for a small vase to £7.25 for a crystal pear.

LOCATION: The Isle of Man is off the northwest coast of England. St. Johns is in the west-central part of the Isle of Man about seven miles west of Douglas on the A1.

ST. JOHNS, ISLE OF MAN   *Wool Items, Craft Items*

Tynwald Woollen Mills (I.O.M.) Ltd. and Craft Centre
St. Johns, Isle of Man, England
Tel. 0624-71213

HOURS: Monday–Saturday 9:00–5:30; handspinning demonstrations on Tuesday and Thursday; pottery and pyrography demonstrations given daily.
CREDIT CARDS: MasterCard

PRODUCTS: The Tynwald Woollen Mills have woven Manx tweeds for 150 years. The subtle colors and texture of the cloth have made the fabric famous throughout the world. At the factory visitors are able to see the full range of woolen products, and they may purchase the fabric by the yard.

Visitors will find elegant fabric, rugs, kilts, jackets, sheepskin, coats, and sweaters of all colors for men and women in cashmere and Shetland wool.

Cashmere overcoats for men or for women were £152. A handwoven Manx tweed sports coat was a good buy at £52. Pringle lambswool sweaters are priced from £15 to £30. Pure wool kilts in Manx tweeds start at £14.50.

Second-quality woolen items are available all year long. An annual sale is held for four weeks in January and February.

In the craft center you'll find hand-blown glass products, pottery, herbal creams and perfumes, costumed dolls, soft toys, a silversmith, paperweights, screen-printed textiles, and books on weaving and spinning.

They will ship your purchases. On purchases over £40, they will arrange for the 15% VAT to be refunded to you.

LOCATION: The Isle of Man is off the northwest coast of England. St. Johns is in the west central part of the Isle of Man about seven miles west of Douglas on the A1. The mill is on the north side of the A1 road next to a church. The craft centre is just to the north of the mill.

STOKE-ON-TRENT

Stoke-on-Trent is the center of the pottery and porcelain industry in England. The town has several suburbs, which we have grouped together for ease of shopping. The suburbs are Barlaston, Burslem, Fenton, Hanley, Longton, and Meir Park. The shopping is great, but these industrial towns are not glamorous.

Following is a general map of the Stoke-on-Trent area, showing the locations of all the outlets. A description of each outlet, with specific directions, is then given.

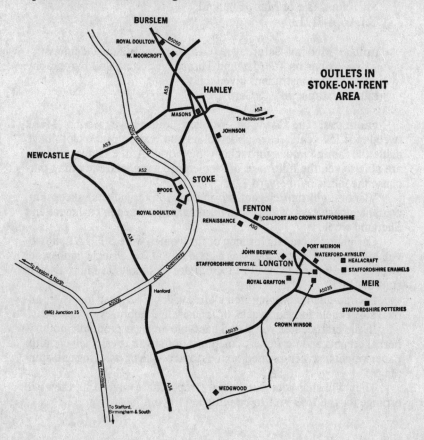

STOKE-ON-TRENT   *China, Crystal, Giftware*

Royal Doulton
Minton, London Road
Stoke-on-Trent, Staffordshire ST4 7QD, England
Tel. 0782-47771

HOURS: Monday–Friday 9:00–12:15, 1:30–3:30
CREDIT CARDS: Access, American Express, Diners Club, Visa

PRODUCTS: Minton was founded in 1793. Minton is one of five Royal Doulton factories where a large variety of china, crystal, and giftware is manufactured. Seconds are sold at the factory showroom. Some mugs, figures, children's dishes, and serving pieces were also being sold. Visitors can also order first-quality items for shipment home.

Royal Doulton first-quality bone china figures include Balloon Girl at £73, the Lobster Man £82.50, Santa Claus £121, and the Jester £102. The cost for shipment to the States for one or two figures is an additional £15. The duty on the Royal Doulton figures is £3.10 on every £100 spent.

Minton's Grasmere and Standwood five-piece bone china place settings are £64.50.

Royal Doulton bone china is truly elegant, but visitors can expect to pay extra for this. Prices are far below those in the States but still somewhat steep for a number of us. A five-piece Clarendon place setting was £55 while the sophisticated gold-trimmed Belmont pattern was £92.

All prices quoted do not include the 15% VAT.

TOURS: Tours of the Minton factory are conducted at 10:30 and 2:00 weekdays. The maximum number for tour parties is 20 for the morning tour and 40 for the afternoon tour. The cost is £1 per person. In two hours it is possible to tour the tableware factory, visit the museum with exhibits dating back to the 1790s, and visit the factory shop. Catering facilities are available.

LOCATION: Stoke-on-Trent is in west central England about half-way between Manchester on the north and Birmingham on the south, just east of the M6 motorway exit 15. The factory is in the center of Stoke-on-Trent. See the map next page.

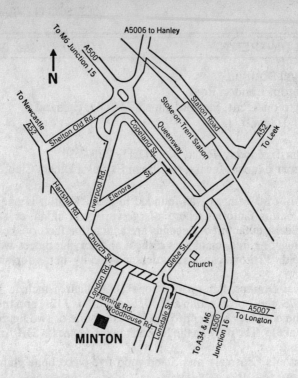

MINTON

STOKE-ON-TRENT   *Bone China*

Spode Limited (factory/showroom)
Spode Seconds Shop, Church Street
Stoke-on-Trent, Staffordshire ST4 1BX, England
Tel. 0782-46011

HOURS: Monday–Thursday 8:30–5:00; Friday 8:30–4:00; Saturday 9:00–1:00
CREDIT CARDS: Access, Visa

PRODUCTS: Spode Limited is a world-renowned china company founded in 1770. Josiah Spode perfected the process of blue underglaze printing, which was a major technical, artistic, and commercial success. He created the first bone china, which (through the addition of bone ash) was stronger, whiter, and more translucent than any other china previously produced. In 1813 he introduced a fine stone china which was an opaque, hard ceramic. Today over 200 years later, fine bone china, stone china, and imperial earthenware still form the basis for the Spode tableware, cookware, and giftware.

Spode creates tableware in fine bone china with all of the matching serving pieces. They also sell stone china Imperial cookware in 10 patterns. The dishes are safe for the oven, freezer, microwave, and dishwasher. Not only do they have tableware but they have functional and beautiful serving pieces. Cooking would become a real pleasure!

Spode is also the creator of the famous Christmas Tree pattern with a wide range of cutlery, cookware, and tableware to match. (Savings on purchasing seconds were fantastic! The factory asked that I not publicize the prices. We shipped home eight boxes of dishes if that gives you an indication of prices.)

Spode's boxed giftware is available in all styles, sizes, shapes, and prices. Presentation plates, coffee cups, Christmas miniatures, and bridge sets are just a few of the many items available. You cannot leave England without a visit to this famous factory.

If you want to do serious buying at the seconds shop, get there first thing before the tours arrive as they will, in this small shop, create chaos. It is better if you can shop off season when the tourists are still at home. The selection will be much larger.

They will ship all but the largest items and will deduct the VAT from items shipped. If you take more than £50 worth of items with you, they will give you the form to obtain a VAT refund on your return home. The women who work there are extremely helpful, courteous and patient. If you purchase quantities, plan on spending an hour due to the pricing system.

TOURS: A factory tour lasts about 1½ hours. Children under 12 are not allowed. There are two tours a day, Monday through Friday at 10:00 and 2:00. The tour costs 75 pence per person, which is refundable at the seconds shop on purchases over £3. Please remember that all bookings must be made in advance by writing to Spode Limited, Church Street, Stoke-on-Trent ST4 1BX England.

A museum which displays Spode factory wares is on the premises. Visits are made by appointment only although all factory tours begin at the museum.

LOCATION: Stoke-on-Trent is in west central England about halfway between Manchester on the north and Birmingham on the south, just east of the M6 motorway exit 15. Drive to the center of town. Then see the map below.

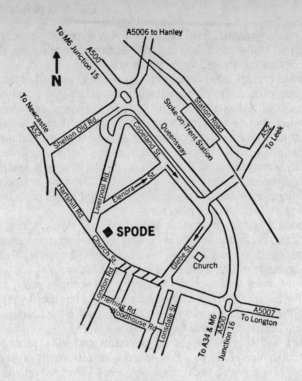

STOKE-ON-TRENT (BARLASTON)   *Fine Bone China, Oven-to-Tableware, Stoneware*

Josiah Wedgwood and Sons, Ltd.
Wedgwood Visitor Centre (factory/shop)
Barlaston, Stoke-On-Trent ST12 9ES, England
Tel. 078-139-3218 or 4141

HOURS: Monday through Friday 9:00–5:00 (last complete tour at 3:15) and open most bank holidays (except Christmas week and New Year's Day)

CREDIT CARDS: Access, American Express, Diners Club, Visa

PRODUCTS: Josiah Wedgwood and Sons Ltd. was founded in 1759. Today Wedgwood and its group of companies employ 10,000 people in 20 factories. It accounts for about 20% of the British ceramic tableware industry's output, and for about 25% of its exports. There is a huge selection of designs and patterns of plates, cups, bowls, saucers, and other tableware with matching serving pieces. Also available is an extensive collection of oven-to-table ware in every size, shape, color, and dimension. They also carry Mason's ironstone, Wedgwood crystal, Coalport figurines, Crown Staffordshire china and other products. There is also a limited selection of slightly imperfect items.

Peter Rabbit Nurseryware in Wedgwood Queen's ware has both words and pictures to be enjoyed by children and adults. A four-piece boxed set with a seven-inch plate, mug, porringer, and eggcup is £14.72. Wedgwood miniatures in white-on-blue jasper are perfect for that special doll house. A teacup and saucer are £13.80, a tiny heart box is £9.50, and a miniature teapost is £15.50.

Wedgwood bone china in the Medici pattern was £40 for a five-piece place setting. The Bianca pattern was £62, the Candlelight pattern was £20 and the Mirabelle pattern was £40, all of which are prices for a five-piece place setting.

If you are planning on shopping at this outlet, plan on a minimum of an hour due to the large selection. It is difficult to make a decision with so much lovely merchandise staring at you.

The VAT will be refunded on purchases over £50, or automatically deducted on items shipped directly home. Highly recommended!

The jasper and black basalt stoneware is made into busts, figures, and other ornamental items as well as functional pieces. It is beautifully detailed.

The Visitor Centre at Wedgwood has been designed for visitors to see the craftspeople at work. An 18-minute color film explains the creation of this famous pottery. Visitors may also watch the process of making Wedgwood at the demonstration hall, which includes throwing on the potter's wheel, turning, figure making, and ornamenting. The casting of busts, figures, and ornamental items is also shown. The decoration of fine bone china is also demonstrated, including hand lining, raised enameling, and multicolor transfer application.

In 1975 a museum was opened which occupies nearly 3500 square feet. It has been acknowledged as the most comprehensive collection of early and modern Wedgwood. The exhibits illustrate the founding and development of the company.

TOURS: Groups of 12 or more are advised to book in advance with the tours supervisor. Be sure to give three alternate dates when making bookings. Every care is taken that your reservation will be kept. However, Wedgwood reserves the right to vary or cancel without notice your reservation. Children under five are not admitted, and children between five and fifteen must be accompanied by an adult. There is a minimal charge of 50 pence for adults and 25 pence for children.

It is suggested that you time your arrival to coincide with the showing of the film, which is at 9:55, 10:30, 11:15, 11:50 a.m., and 1:15, 2:00, 2:45, and 3:30 p.m.

To avoid delays, tour organizers are asked to pay group charge at reception. Also, coaches should depart no later than 4:45 to avoid traffic congestion with the factory personnel who leave at 5:00.

Light refreshments are available in the refreshment lounge but again for groups, please make reservations.

LOCATION: Stoke-on-Trent is in west central England about halfway between Manchester to the north and Birmingham to the south, just east of the M6 motorway exit 15. Barlaston is a town five miles south of Stoke-on-Trent. The best route from London is to take the Finchley Road, turn left at Brent Cross intersection onto North Circular, Westbound. Keep to the inside lane. Follow the signs through the

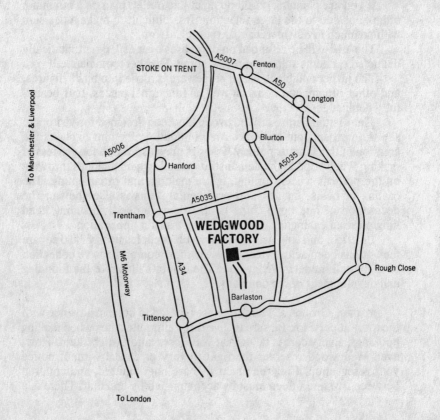

roundabout to M1 (signs "The North"). Continue on the M1 to the junction with the M6, and leave at Exit 14, following signs "Stone A34." Proceed for eight miles along the A34, bypassing Stone, and look for a right turn with the sign "Wedgwood and Barlaston."

Visitors traveling from the north should leave the M6 at Exit 15, then turn onto the A34 Southbound. Go through Trentham, and at Tittensor turn left at the signs to Barlaston and Wedgwood. See the map above.

STOKE-ON-TRENT (BURSLEM)   *China*

Royal Doulton (factory outlet)
Nile Street, Burslem
Stoke-on-Trent, Staffordshire ST6 2AJ, England
Tel. 0782-84271

HOURS: Monday–Friday 9:00–4:30
CREDIT CARDS: Access, American Express, Visa

PRODUCTS: Royal Doulton has for 150 years maintained an outstanding reputation for sculptural ceramic works of art. Since the Great Exhibition of 1871, special groups of collectors have been interested in acquiring jugs, plates, and various items from the Royal Doulton line. An International Collectors' Club arranges exhibitions for collectors each year.

Early examples of Royal Doulton are found in museums and private collections. Many of the auction houses specialize in antique Royal Doulton figures. Many rare pieces have become extremely valuable.

C. J. Noke, the Royal Doulton Art Director, has revived figure modeling and painting. He rediscovered the oriental flambé glazing technique, trained a group of artists, and developed a group of figures and jugs which were totally handmade by one individual. There are many series of figures including Fair Ladies and Children, Vanity Fair, Childhood Days, Tolkien Figures, Dickens Figures, Character Studies, Prestige Figures, etc.

An Anne Boleyn character jug in the large size is £24. Amy from the Kate Greenaway Collection is £39. The Judge from the Character Studies series is £69. Gandalf the Wizard from the Tolkien group is £23.

If you are interested in joining the Collector's Club, be sure to ask for details while you are here.

For further information, please also see Stoke-on-Trent, Royal Doulton on London Road.

Visitors will find fine tableware as well. Items available vary daily. Royal Doulton remains a company known for quality, detail, and design.

TOURS: Two-hour tours are given Monday through Friday at 10:15 and 2:00. Advance bookings must be made for all tours. The cost is £1 per person, but reduced rates can be obtained for parties of students and retired persons. No one under 14 may be allowed due to government safety regulations. Several stairways must be negotiated.

LOCATION: Stoke-on-Trent is in west central England about halfway between Manchester on the north and Birmingham on the south, just east of the M6 motorway exit 15. Burslem is to the north of Stoke-on-Trent. See the map below.

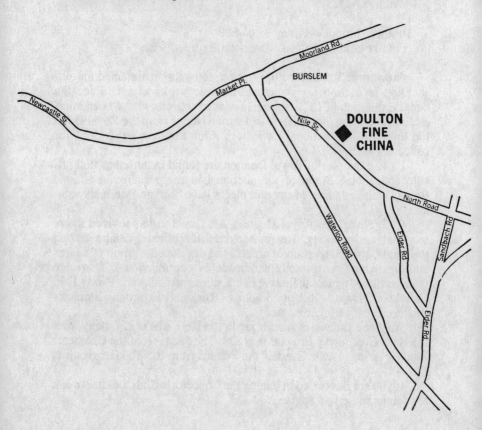

STOKE-ON-TRENT (BURSLEM) *Pottery*

W. Moorcroft Limited Potters (factory outlet store)
Bottle Oven and Seconds Shop
Sandbach Road, Cobridge
Burslem, Stoke-on-Trent ST6 2DQ, England
Tel. 0782-24323

HOURS: Monday–Friday 10:00–4:00; Saturday 9:30–12:30; closed
      on holidays.
CREDIT CARDS: None

PRODUCTS: Moorcroft Pottery is a form of ceramic art with a
special glaze as the finishing touch. Each piece is handpainted and put
through a kiln several times until the piece emerges looking like
translucent glass. The seconds shop carries the full range of Moorcroft

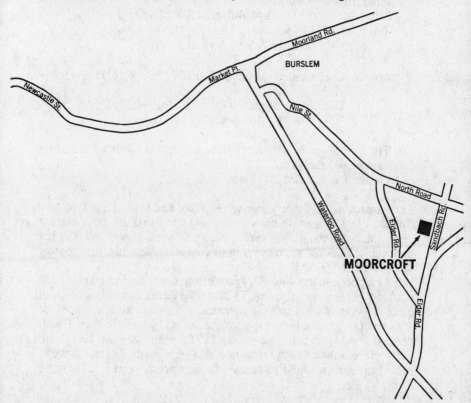

products, including lamps, bowls, plates, platters, ginger jars, and mini boxes. A small magnolia vase is £3.20, a small plate is £7.50, a ginger jar with a hibiscus motif is £13.80, a large bowl is £37.40, and a small bowl is £5.45. The entire process of making the pottery is explained with enlarged pictures. The pottery is unique, brightly colored, and unusual. Very exceptional!

LOCATION: Stoke-on-Trent is in west central England about halfway between Manchester to the north and Birmingham to the south, just east of the M6 motorway exit 15. This shop is in the town of Burslem in the northeast part of Stoke-on-Trent. See the map above.

STOKE-ON-TRENT (FENTON) — *Bone China*

Coalport and Crown Staffordshire (factory/showroom)
King Street, Fenton,
Stoke-on-Trent, Staffordshire ST4 3JB, England
Tel. 0782-45274 Tours
     0782-49174 Gift Shop

HOURS: Craft Center: Monday–Thursday 9:30–4:30, Friday 9:30–12:30
Gift Shop: Monday–Thursday 9:30–4:30, Friday 9:30–3:30, Saturday 10:00–5:00

The Gift Shop is open every weekday except Christmas, Boxing Day, and New Year's Day.
CREDIT CARDS: Access, Visa

PRODUCTS: Coalport (founded in 1750) and Crown Staffordshire (founded in 1801) are famous throughout the world for their elegant bone china tableware, giftware, delicate flowers, birds, and detailed handpainted collectors' pieces. Both companies are now divisions of the Wedgwood Group.

Coalport exports 46% of its production overseas and employs 550 craftspeople in three factories. Their unique pieces include small handpainted bone china Coalport cottages, which are reproductions of 19th-century pastille burners, once used to rid homes of odors. Handpainted floral studies have been created for more than 200 years with each piece meticulously designed and rendered. Vases, flowers, brooches, earrings, and place card holders are sold with these same floral designs. They also feature an extensive variety of figurines for collectors.

Crown Staffordshire sells tableware, ginger jars, planters, bowls, vases, bells, coasters, tiny boxes, cups and saucers, thimbles,plaques, christening sets, anniversary and wedding sets, motto boxes, mini floral clusters for each month of the year, floral arrangements, floral jewelry, napkin rings, and knife rests. Many of these items are small and easy to pack and perfect for a special gift.

The craft centre was established to help visitors see the manufacturing process. The company would like to emphasize that no appointment is necessary, and children are welcome.

The gift shop has a selection of slightly imperfect giftware (including Wedgwood Crystal) and tableware at reduced prices. Seasonal sales normally take place two weeks after Christmas, and the last two weeks in July.

FACTORY TOURS: Parties from 10 to 50 in number may take a full factory tour. Parties of less than 10 may be included on a tour if prior arrangements are made with the factory. Tours take about 1½ hours. Tours commence at 10:30 and 1:45 Monday through Thursday, and at 10:30 on Friday. Admission is 35 pence per person, and children must be over 14 years of age to be included on a tour. The factory tour is not suitable for the handicapped since there are many stairs. It is advisable to book your tour several months in advance, giving a choice of a second date. No date can be confirmed until the factory has received your written request.

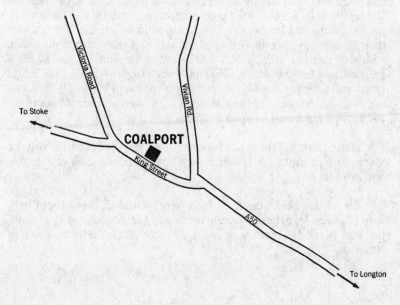

LOCATION: Stoke-on-Trent is in west central England about half-way between Manchester to the north and Birmingham to the south, just east of the M6 motorway exit 15. Fenton is a town to the south of Stoke-on-Trent. The factory is on the A50 road. From the south, leave the M6 motorway at Junction 15. From the north use Junction 16. Follow the A500 to the junction with the A50 (City Road). Turn onto the A50 toward Fenton. See the map above.

STOKE-ON-TRENT (FENTON) *China Figurines, Giftware*

Renaissance International Limited (factory outlet)
Dewsbury Road, Fenton Industrial Estate
Stoke-on-Trent, Staffordshire ST4 2TB, England
Tel. 0782-413518

HOURS: Monday–Friday 9:00–5:00
CREDIT CARDS: Access, MasterCard

PRODUCTS: This small company manufactures a variety of hand-painted figurines, including women in authentic period costumes, wildlife, and thimbles featuring portraits of famous composers. They also sell figurines personalized to order. On their Bride and Bridesmaid set, a first name and wedding date can be handpainted and fired into the base. On their Childsplay series, which is on a larger scale than the Bride, the child's hair and eye coloring can be specified in addition to the first name and birthday, which are fired into the base. The Edwardian Costume Series figurines sell for £60.50 if painted in colors, and £56.40 if painted black and white. Composer thimbles are £7.90 if painted, and £3.50 if white. Childsplay sculptures with the child's first name and birthday are £49. A round bud vase sells for £4.80. Seconds are available occasionally at reduced prices. Renaissance products are packed, insured, and shipped to all parts of the world.

MAIL ORDER: They accept mail orders. Mail orders will be shipped on receipt of payment, which should include cost of shipping and insurance.

LOCATION: Stoke-on-Trent is in west central England about half-way between Manchester on the north and Birmingham on the south, just east of the M6 motorway exit 15. Fenton is a town to the south of Stoke-on-Trent.

STOKE-ON-TRENT (HANLEY)   *Stoneware, Earthenware*

Johnson Brothers Works Shop (factory outlet)
Lichfield Street, Hanley
Stoke-on-Trent ST1 3LN, England
Tel. 0782-263934

HOURS: Monday–Saturday 10:00–5:15
CREDIT CARDS: Access, Visa

PRODUCTS: Five top china manufacturers sell their tableware seconds for as little as half price at this outlet. The tableware is from Johnson Brothers, J. & G. Meakin, Midwinter, William Adams, and Crown Staffordshire. The tableware is high quality. The designs are outstanding! For example, they carry the famous Willow pattern, Laura Ashley, Jessie Tait, and Mary Quant designs. Wedgwood Crystal, as well as some gift linens and trays, are sold. Highly recommended as an exceptional place for shopping! Prices are on typed lists which are well displayed. The staff will be happy to pack your pur-

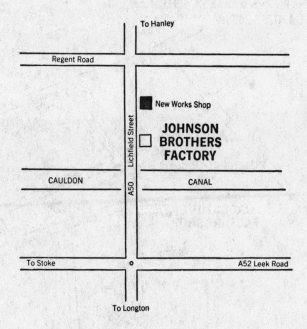

chases for shipping, but ask that you take your own items to a professional shipper.

At this outlet, visitors choose design of the dishes they like. The patterns are then classified by the shape. For example, the Willow pattern is in the Liberty Shape. A dinner set with 25 pieces is £68. Berries and Bonjour patterns, designed by Jessie Tait, belong to the Heirloom series. A 25-piece dinner set is £70.35. Some of my favorite patterns were sold at this well organized outlet.

LOCATION: Stoke-on-Trent is in west central England about halfway between Manchester to the north and Birmingham to the south, just east of the M6 motorway exit 15. This outlet is in the town of Hanley, which is just north of the center of Stoke-on-Trent. See the map above.

STOKE-ON-TRENT (HANLEY)   *Ironstone*

Mason's Ironstone Factory Shop
Broad Street, Hanley
Stoke-on-Trent ST1 4HH, England
Tel. 0782-264354

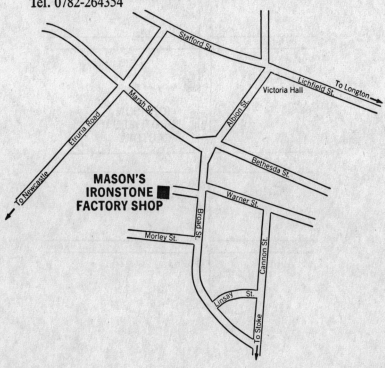

HOURS: Monday–Saturday 10:00–4:00
CREDIT CARDS: None

PRODUCTS: Ironstone tableware and giftware are sold at this small factory outlet store, which is a division of Josiah Wedgwood & Sons Ltd. The items are all second quality. Prices cannot be quoted. Bowls, plates, cups, serving dishes, and small decorative accessories are sold.

LOCATION: Stoke-on-Trent is in west central England about halfway between Manchester to the north and Birmingham to the south, just east of the M6 motorway exit 15. This shop is in the town of Hanley to the northeast of Stoke-on-Trent. See the map above. Note that there is no parking outside the shop. The nearest parking is at the Unity House and Broad Street car parks.

STOKE-ON-TRENT (LONGTON) *Ceramics*

Crown Winsor Sylvac Ceramics (factory outlet)
Sylvan Works
Normacot Road
Longton, Stoke-on-Trent, Staffordshire ST3 1PW, England
Tel. 0782-313037

HOURS: Monday–Saturday 10:00–4:00
CREDIT CARDS: Visa

PRODUCTS: This company is a manufacturer of earthenware, giftware, and bone china. Adjoining the factory is a retail outlet which sells first- and second-quality items. Hand-decorated character mugs, Tudor-style tableware, Zooline nursery ware, and Supreme Dogs are a few of the items.

Many of the items sold are carried in souvenir shops throughout England. The shop carries mostly second-quality goods and they are offered to the visitor at 50% off the normal retail selling price. The Staffordshire character jugs are £4.25 for Henry VIII, £4.55 for a Grenadier Guardsman, and £4.05 for a Churchill jug. Tudor cottage ware, which consists of seven pieces in the shape of thatched roof cottages, is priced at £3.05 for the salt and pepper set, £3.50 for a honey jar, £5.55 for a butter dish, and £7.50 for a matching teapot.

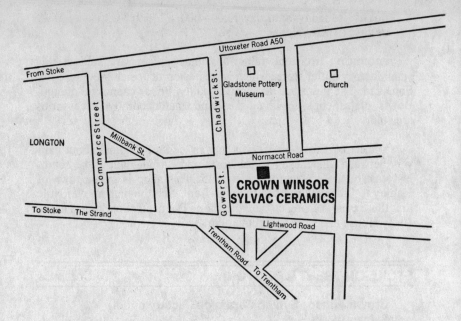

TOURS: Tours of the factory are given to groups of 12 three times a day at 10:30, 1:30, and 3:00. The tours take 20 to 30 minutes. There is a slight charge. A booking form is available from the factory.

LOCATION: Stoke-on-Trent is in west central England, about half-way between Manchester to the north and Birmingham to the south, just east of the M6 motorway exit 15. Longton is a town just to the south of Stoke-on-Trent on the A50 road. See the map above.

STOKE-ON-TRENT (LONGTON)   *Bone China*

Healacraft China Ltd. (factory)
New Park Works, Weston Coyney Road
Longton, Stoke-on-Trent
Staffordshire ST3 5EX England
Tel. 0782-332621/2

HOURS: Factory: Monday–Friday 8:30–4:00. Factory Tours: Tuesday, Wednesday, Thursday at 2:00. For tour groups only by prior arrangement.
CREDIT CARDS: Access, Visa

PRODUCTS: This company produces fine bone china flowers and various small gift items. One section of the company specializes in traditional free-hand painting. They produce containers filled with bone china flowers, which have the look of spring in blues, yellows, and pinks, or an autumnal look in yellows, golds, and browns. Tiny bouquets of white, yellow, pink, or red roses in tiny vases would make darling gifts. Birthday Blooms and Brooches are flowers designed for each month of the year. Handmade fine bone china flowers are made into pendants, earrings, and brooches. Prices for those products seemed very reasonable with most items priced under £7.50. (This factory also has a permanent factory shop at the Potteries Centre, located at the Keele Service Station on the M6 motorway, north of Junction 15.)

TOURS: Factory tours for groups of 30 to 50 people are given at 2:00 on Tuesday, Wednesday, and Thursday. Tours must be arranged in advance. After the tour, refreshments are available with tea. During the tour the company's products are offered for sale at factory prices, together with any seconds which may be available.

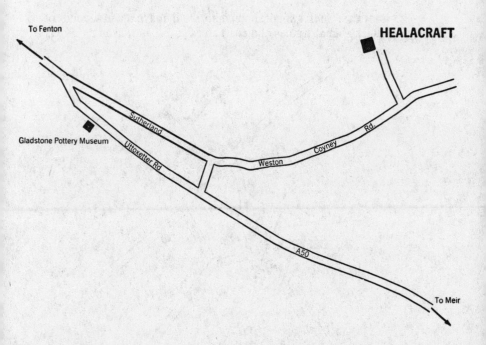

LOCATION: Stoke-on-Trent is in west central England about half-way between Manchester to the north and Birmingham to the south, just east of the M6 motorway exit 15. This factory is in the town of Longton, in the southwest part of Stoke-on-Trent. See the map above. When you enter the Cinderhill Industrial Estate, drive to the end of the road, then turn right and go all the way around the building. Healacraft is at the far end at the rear of the building.

STOKE-ON-TRENT (LONGTON)   *China, Porcelain*

John Beswick Ltd. (factory outlet)
Barford Street, Longton
Stoke-on-Trent, Staffordshire ST3 2JP, England
Tel. 0782-33041

HOURS: Monday–Friday 9:00–4:30
CREDIT CARDS: Visa

PRODUCTS: In this small shop visitors will find first and seconds of the Beswick animal studies and character figures, as well as the Royal

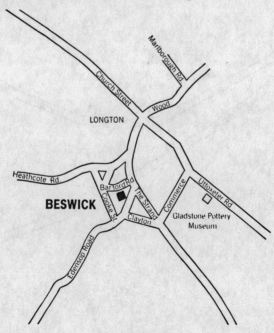

Doulton character jug collection. Also available are a wide range of various inexpensive souvenir gift items.

For further information, see the write-up under STOKE-ON-TRENT (Burslem) on Nile Street. Prices and details are the same.

TOURS: Tours must be booked in advance. The cost is £1 per person, and special reduced rates are given to groups. Tours begin at 2:00 p.m. and last about two hours. Tour groups are limited to 30.

LOCATION: Stoke-on-Trent is in west central England about half-way between Manchester on the north and Birmingham on the south, just east of the M6 motorway exit 15. Longton is to the south of Stoke-on-Trent. See the map above.

STOKE-ON-TRENT (LONGTON)   *Pottery*

Portmeirion Potteries Ltd. (factory outlet)
523 King Street, Longton
Stoke-on-Trent, Staffordshire, England
Also at: 167 London Road
              Stoke-on-Trent, Staffordshire, England

HOURS: Monday–Wednesday and Friday 8:30–4:00; Thursday
                  8:30–3:00; Saturday 9:30–1:00
CREDIT CARDS: Access, Visa

PRODUCTS: This shop sells seconds from the Portmeirion Potteries, which employs over 200 people. They have a wide range of bowls, vases, plates, casseroles, planters, and serving dishes. Their designs are boldly rendered plants, flowers, birds, and fruit. The prices are very low and many of the pieces quite large. All of the pottery is dishwater, microwave, and freezer safe.

Summer Strawberries, a design created by Angharad Menna in 1980, offers the freshness of summer mornings in your kitchen all year long. A large serving bowl was £10.75, a planter sold for £6.25, and a quiche dish was priced at £6.55. Susan William-Ellis designed Botanic Gardens in 1972, which is a design consisting of 34 different plants and butterflies, taken from nineteenth-century natural history books. A dinner plate was priced at £2.35, a teapot at £8.95, and a large vase at £7.15. Cookware, influenced by French functional cooking pieces, is available with all of the Portmeirion patterns—Botanic Gardens, Birds of Britain, Summer Strawberries, and Pomona.

A rectangular dish was £7.35, a cake plate server was £9.90, and a large serving plate a reasonable £5.95. Pomona, introduced in 1982 and designed by Susan William-Ellis, is a fruit motif derived from English gardens in the days of George IV. A full collection of tableware, kitchenware, and matching cookware is available in this pattern, which happens to be one of my favorites. A rolling pin in porcelain was £5.55, a planter £6, a rectangular dish was £5.10, an oval serving tray was £5.10, plates started at £1.65, and a quiche dish was £6.55. The items available for sale vary weekly.

Visitors will find themselves wondering how they can sell their products for such low prices and manage to stay in business. An exceptional value for your money!

LOCATION: Stoke-on-Trent is in west central England about halfway between Manchester on the north and Birmingham on the south, just east of the M6 motorway exit 15. Longton is to the south of Stoke-on-Trent.

STOKE-ON-TRENT (LONGTON)   *China*

Royal Grafton (factory/showroom)
Marlborough Road, Longton
Stoke-on-Trent, Staffordshire ST3 1ED, England
Tel. 0782-315667

Also: 33 Uttoxeter Road
          Longton, Stoke-on-Trent

HOURS: Monday–Friday 9:00–5:00; Saturday 10:00–4:30
CREDIT CARDS: Access, Barclaycard, Visa

PRODUCTS: Royal Grafton produces inexpensive bone china, tableware, and serving pieces. They make dozens of accessory pieces such as bells, vases, candlesticks, eggcups, napkin rings, and bowls. Both first- and second-quality items may be purchased. There are also periodic special sales. Most items are priced under £10.

TOURS: Factory tours are available by appointment only. Contact Mrs. Machin at 0782-315667 Monday through Friday. Tours last approximately one hour. There is an admission charge of 50 to 70 pence, which is redeemable against goods purchased at the factory shop. Salad lunches can be arranged for visitors upon prior notice.

LOCATION: Stoke-on-Trent is in west central England about half-way between Manchester on the north and Birmingham on the south, just east of the M6 motorway exit 15. The factory and shops are in the town of Longton, which is in the southern part of Stoke-on-Trent. See the map below.

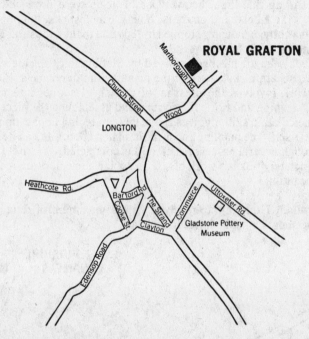

STOKE-ON-TRENT (LONGTON)   *Copper Enamel Boxes*

Staffordshire Enamels Ltd.
Cinderhill Industrial Estate
Weston Coyney Road
Longton, Stoke-on-Trent, Staffordshire ST3 5JT, England
Tel. 0782-322948

HOURS: Monday–Friday 9:00–4:00
CREDIT CARDS: None

PRODUCTS: At Staffordshire Enamels visitors will find beautiful copper enamel boxes for £12 to £50. The price depends on the complexity of the design. Perhaps of all the British products, these beautifully painted and designed boxes are my favorite.

The process for making handpainted enamel boxes was developed in Staffordshire during the eighteenth century, with a combination of metalworking and ceramic skills. The boxes were originally intended as a substitute for the elaborate gold enamels created on the Continent. During this time, many types of items were produced—snuff boxes, wine labels, and coasters, bowls, candlesticks, bonbonnieres; etc. This cottage industry stopped in 1804 due to the Industrial Revolution and the Napoleonic Wars.

Today the art has been revived by Staffordshire Enamels. There are two separate skills used in the manufacture of enamels: First, the metalwork involves the pressing of thin sheet copper into lids and bases, cleaning and firing the copper, and assembling the pieces. Second the ceramic skill involves the manufacture and application of the enamel itself. The painting and firing is all hand done, and an item must go through several processes before it is completed.

Each tiny box is a work of art. The detail and colors are indescribably beautiful.

TOURS: Hour tours are given with a maximum of four people. Arrangements must be made in advance.

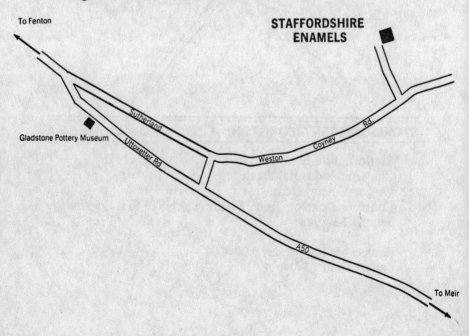

LOCATION: Stoke-on-Trent is in west central England about halfway between Manchester to the north and Birmingham to the south, just east of the M6 motorway exit 15. Longton is to the south of Stoke-on-Trent.

STOKE-ON-TRENT (LONGTON)   *Crystal*

Staffordshire Crystal Ltd. (factory shop)
Gladstone Museum Centre
Uttoxeter Road, Longton
Stoke-on-Trent, Staffordshire ST3 1PQ, England
Tel. 0782-334194

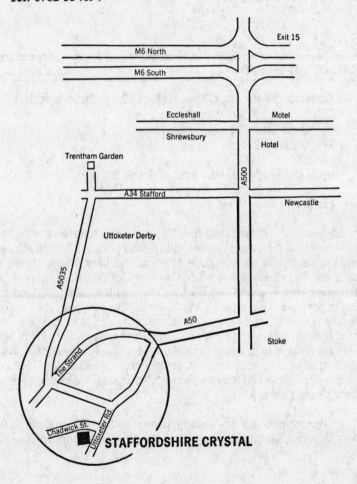

HOURS: Monday–Saturday 9:00–5:00
CREDIT CARDS: Access, American Express, Visa

PRODUCTS: At this small shop crystal is handcut or sandblasted with more detailed cutwork than most of the mass-produced crystal. Bowls, vases, glasses, and decanters were for sale. A beautifully detailed, intricately cut large bowl was £125. Shipping can only be done for purchases over £250.

LOCATION: Stoke-on-Trent is in west central England about halfway between Manchester on the north and Birmingham on the south, just east of the M6 motorway exit 15. Longton is to the south of Stoke-on-Trent. This shop is next to the entrance to the Gladstone Pottery Museum. See the map above.

STOKE-ON-TRENT   *Bone China*

Waterford-Aynsley China Reject Shop (factory outlet)
25 Uttoxeter Road, Longton
Stoke-on-Trent ST3 1HS, England
Tel. 0782-319216

HOURS: Monday–Friday 9:00–1:30 and 2:00–5:30; Saturday 9:00–
         1:30 and 2:30–5:00; closed on Thursdays.
CREDIT CARDS: None

PRODUCTS: Established in 1775, Aynsley produces a wide range of bone china tableware, serving pieces and giftware. This small outlet sells seconds and discontinued items at excellent prices. (More seconds are in the back if you ask.) It is one of my favorite outlets as I feel the prices are some of the lowest. They will not ship but will wrap items for you. (Waterford Crystal owns this company but unfortunately you will find no crystal at this shop.)
A small tray was £6.50, and a tiny bud vase was £4.75. A lovely serving bowl, which later became my Christmas present, was £16.80. Almost all of the pieces in the store were priced well under £15. Just be sure to leave some of the merchandise at the outlet so I can shop next time I'm in England.

LOCATION: Stoke-on-Trent is in west central England about halfway between Manchester on the north and Birmingham on the south, just east of the M6 motorway exit 15. The shop is directly across the street from the Gladstone Pottery Museum in Longton to the south of Stoke-on-Trent. See the map below.

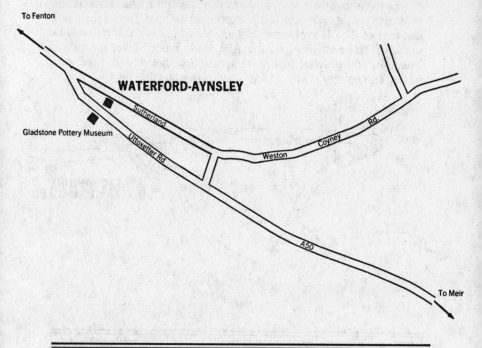

STOKE-ON-TRENT (MEIR PARK)   *Pottery*

Staffordshire Potteries Limited (factory outlet)
Meir Park, Stoke-on-Trent
Staffordshire ST3 7AA, England
Tel. 0782-315251

HOURS: Monday–Saturday 9:30–5:30
CREDIT CARDS: Access, American Express, Diners Club, Visa

PRODUCTS: This is an outlet for Staffordshire Potteries Limited. It is stocked with a selection of Kilncraft tableware and stoneware produced at the factory. The dinnerware designs have been created to appeal to all age and income groups. Tea and coffee sets and a huge variety of coffee mugs are available. Kilncraft is available in both firsts and seconds, at a substantial savings. Most dinner plates were £1 and a 30-piece dinnerware set was £16. Also in stock you will find a selection of Royal Winton planters, vases, and glassware, all at reasonable prices.

LOCATION: Stoke-on-Trent is in west central England about half-way between Manchester to the north and Birmingham to the south, just east of the M6 motorway exit 15. Meir Park is a few miles to the south of Stoke-on-Trent on the A50 road. From Stoke, go through Longton, and proceed to the intersection of the A50 and the A520 roads. The pottery is just a short way further, on the right.

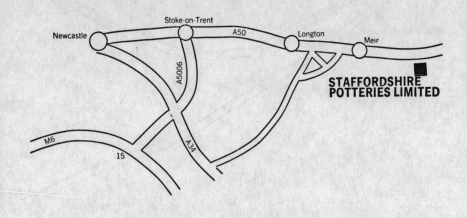

STOKE ST. GREGORY, TAUNTON

Willow Baskets, Artist's Charcoal

P. H. Coate & Son (workshop/showroom)
Meare Green Court
Stoke St. Gregory, Taunton, Somerset TA3 6HY, England
Tel. 0823-490249

HOURS: Monday–Friday 10:00–1:00 and 2:00–4:00
CREDIT CARDS: None

PRODUCTS: The Coate family has been growing willow for baskets for 150 years. Willow growing and basket making are among the oldest industries in Somerset. At the P. H. Coate & Son workshop, you can tour the facility and see baskets being made. The company has an excellent brochure which explains the entire process. In addition, you can see the preparation and burning of willow charcoal which is used by artists. Willow baskets, which are all handmade and of an excellent quality, are for sale. They also have some furniture pieces. A wicker basket with a handle is £10, a round bread tray is £4.35, a child's chair is £14.35, a two-person picnic basket is £14.13, and an 18-inch animal carrier is £15.95. You will absolutely love the workmanship of their products. A most enjoyable place to visit!

LOCATION: Stoke St. Gregory is in southwest England, a few miles due east of Taunton, and 1.5 miles north of the village of North Curry. Watch for the sign "Willow Craft Industry" on the left. See the map below.

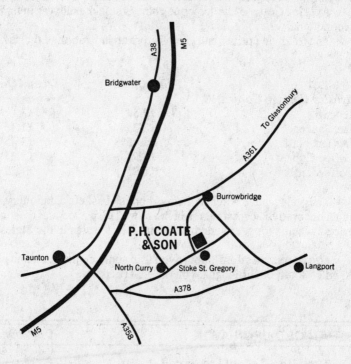

STRATFORD-UPON-AVON *Kitchen Shop*

Scoops (retail store)
26 Henley Street
Stratford-upon-Avon, Warwickshire CV37 6QW, England
Tel. 0789-68758

HOURS: Monday–Saturday 9:30–6:00; June–July, Sunday 12:00–6:00

CREDIT CARDS: MasterCard, Visa

PRODUCTS: Scoops sells first- and second-quality glassware, crystal, and china. They carry the same brand names all year long. A partial list of their suppliers includes Edinburgh Crystal, Dartington Glass, Aynsley, Duchess Bone China, Denmark Furnivals Ltd., and Colclough Bone China.

Scoops can save you 10% to 30% off the retail price on seconds. They often carry groups of discontinued items at a substantial savings.

Aynsley Cottage Garden bone china is stocked all year in first and second quality.

The following prices can give visitors an indication of the savings:

Aynsley Cottage Garden	First Quality	Second Quality
Teacup	£4.50	£3
Tea Saucer	£2.25	£1.40
Dessert Plate	£5.15	£3.45
Coffee Cup	£3.90	£2.35
Coffee Saucer	£1.95	£1.20

They also have kitchen items, books, baskets, stationery, and small decorative accessories, which are well displayed and reasonably priced. Their shops reminded me of the Pier 1 stores in the States.

LOCATION: Stratford-upon-Avon is in south central England about 20 miles south of Birmingham on the A34 road.

STRATFORD-UPON-AVON   *Gift Items*

The Little Gallery Ltd. (retail shop)
37 Henley Street
Stratford-upon-Avon, Warwickshire CV37 6PT, England
Tel. 0789-293742

HOURS: Monday–Sunday 9:30–6:00
CREDIT CARDS: Access, American Express, Eurocard, Visa

PRODUCTS: In this small shop visitors will find a good cross section of better quality British gift products—Tudor houses, Victorian dolls, Caithness glass, crystal, pewter, tin soldiers, and enameled coins. They will ship for you and the goods are received in about four weeks when shipping to the States.

Hand-enameled British coin pendants, which are an exclusive at this shop, start at £32.95. Handmade musical thatched-roof cottages by Pauline Ralph are £21.95 to £26.95. Bossons character heads, which many people collect, are £5.95 to £19.95. Porcelain dolls handmade by Catriona Beerli range between £59.95 and £99.95. The dolls are dressed and designed after pieces from the Edwardian and Victorian eras. For those of you who collect dolls, these are of exceptional quality and detail and found only at this shop. The walls and shelves are packed in this shop, and plan on spending at least 20 minutes looking for all of the special items found here.

LOCATION: Stratford-upon-Avon is in south central England about 24 miles south of Birmingham on the A34 road. The shop is across the street from Shakespeare's birthplace. See the map below.

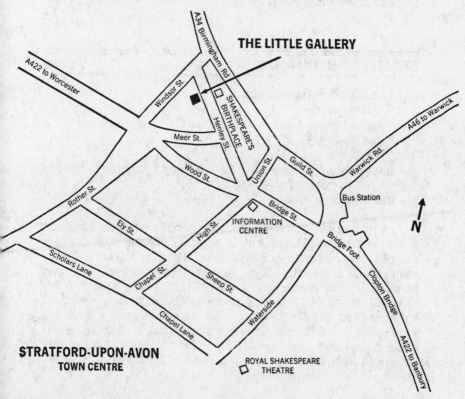

THE LITTLE GALLERY

STRATFORD-UPON-AVON
TOWN CENTRE

STRATFORD-UPON-AVON   *Woolen Items*

The Mulberry Tree Craftware
34 Bridge Street
Stratford-upon-Avon, Warwickshire CV37 6AD, England

HOURS: Monday–Saturday 8:30–5:30; Monday–Sunday (Easter until October) 8:30–5:30

See the write-up for Moffat Woollens Limited in the town of MOFFAT, SCOTLAND.

LOCATION: Stratford-upon-Avon is in south central England about 20 miles south of Birmingham on the A34 road. From Shakespeare's birthplace, walk down Henley Street to the center of town. Go straight on down Bridge Street and you will find this shop on the left at the bottom of the street. If coming into town from Oxford and the south on the A34, after you cross the bridge into town continue straight on and you will be on Bridge Street.

STRATFORD-UPON-AVON   *Pewter*

The Tappit Hen (retail shop)
57 Henley Street,
Stratford-upon-Avon, Warwickshire CV37 6PT, England
Tel. 0789-69933

HOURS: Monday–Saturday 9:00–5:30; Sundays: June 15 through October 12:00–5:30
CREDIT CARDS: None

PRODUCTS: At this shop, modern and reproduction hand-cast pewter pieces are sold. Some of the original gunmetal molds in which this pewter is cast are now 200 years old. Products include tankards, candlesticks, chess sets, plates, christening mugs, trays, vases, and pendants. Pewter napkin rings are £2.95 each, pewter jewelry is between £2.95 and £4.95, handpainted Victorian miniatures are priced between £4.55 and £16.95 while a reproduction hand-cast James II candlestick is £29.75. A three-ounce pewter flask is £9.25 and a six-ounce pewter flask is around £11.25. Pewter tea sets and coffee sets are priced from £65.25. Pewter was made in Britain as early as the

Roman conquest from tin mined in Cornwall. Pewter has always remained in style and today is lead free and safe to use for eating and drinking. You will enjoy visiting this shop if you enjoy pewter.

MAIL ORDER: Mail order is available. Brochure of products available.

LOCATION: Stratford-upon-Avon is in south central England about 20 miles south of Birmingham on the A34 road. Henley Street is the street on which Shakespeare's birthplace is located.

STRATFORD-UPON-AVON   *Artwork, Crafts*

Peter Dingley Gallery (retail shop)
8 Chapel Street,
Stratford-upon-Avon CV37 3EP, England
Tel. 0789-205001

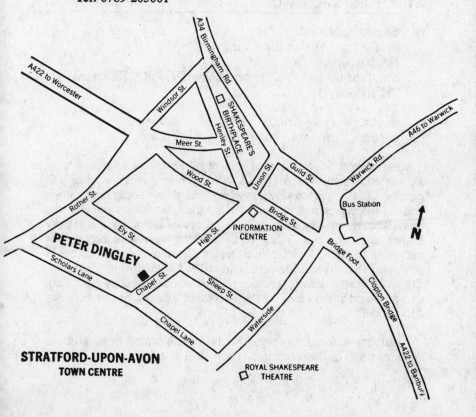

HOURS: Daily 9:30–1:30 and 2:30–5:30; closed Sundays and Thursday afternoons
CREDIT CARDS: None

PRODUCTS: All goods are handmade in England by artists and craftspeople. The items are of the best workmanship and well displayed. Prices range from £5 for a small pottery vase to £1000 for a collector's piece of pottery created by a leading artist. No two pieces in his shop are ever alike. He claims his turnover to be so rapid that it would be useless to quote specific prices. Many of his items are more for the serious buyer than the casual shopper. Shipping available.

LOCATION: Stratford-upon-Avon is in south central England about 20 miles south of Birmingham on the A34 road. The shop is opposite the Shakespeare Hotel on Chapel Streeet. See the map above.

STRATFORD-UPON-AVON   *Handcrafted Items*

Sentre Arts (craft centre)
Studio One, Centre Craft Yard
Henley Street
Stratford-upon-Avon, Warwickshire CV37 6QW, England
Tel. 0789-68731

HOURS: Weekdays 10:00–5:30; Sunday 10:30–5:00
CREDIT CARDS: American Express, MasterCard, Visa

PRODUCTS: Sentre Arts has a small gallery of items handmade by British craftsmen. Products sold include: blown glass, stained and painted glass, wood carvings, pewter jewelry, toys, puzzles, greeting cards, lithographs, and etchings. In Sentre Arts visitors will find peg dolls, sachets or tiny animals, created out of fabric by a company known as Mole End. Prices for these small decorative accessories vary from £1.50 to £5. Colin Reid creates a hand-blown perfume bottle in various shapes and iridescent lustres. The bottles are approximately £12 each. Just Balancing creates colored wooden puzzles intricately designed and intertwined in the shapes of animals priced between £2.75 and £7.

LOCATION: Stratford-upon-Avon is in south central England about 24 miles south of Birmingham on the A34. See the map.

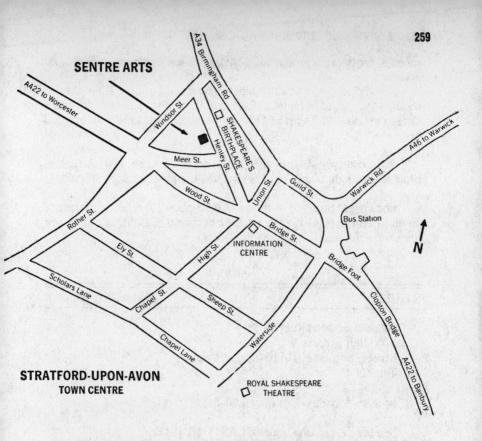

SENTRE ARTS

A422 to Worcester

A34 Birmingham Rd.

Windsor St.

SHAKESPEARE'S BIRTHPLACE

Henley St.

Meer St.

Union St.

Guild St.

A46 to Warwick

Warwick Rd.

Wood St.

Rother St.

Bus Station

Bridge St.

Ely St.

High St.

INFORMATION CENTRE

N

Scholars Lane

Chapel St.

Sheep St.

Bridge Foot

Chapel Lane

Waterside

Clopton Bridge

STRATFORD-UPON-AVON
TOWN CENTRE

ROYAL SHAKESPEARE THEATRE

A422 to Banbury

STREET *Handmade Footwear*

Adams and Jones (craft workshop)
Crispin Hall, High Street
Street, Somerset BA16 0EZ, England
Tel. 0458-45441

HOURS: Monday–Saturday 9:30–5:30
CREDIT CARDS: Access, American Express, Diners Club, Visa

PRODUCTS: This small, unique company has been making made-to-measure footwear since 1975. They make shoes and boots not only for problem feet, but also for individuals who are seeking something different in color and style. They also make children's shoes. The customer provides measurements to the shop, and the shoes are mailed back within about three weeks. Natural material is used. A full range of footwear is produced, including shoes, boots, moccasins, and sandals.

Adult sizes 3 to 14 can be made. The ankle boot is £33.99, the "s" sandal £29.99, the hill boot £38.99, and the oxford £39.50. Children's shoes in sizes 4 to 7 start at £15.50 for a moccasin, to £25.50 for a full boot.

MAIL ORDER: Most of their business is done by mail. A helpful brochure with detailed sketches explains the procedure for shipping.

LOCATION: Street is in the southwest about 20 miles northeast of Taunton on the A361 road. The A361 becomes High Street, on which the shop is located.

STREET   *Sheepskin Products*

Avalon Sheepskin Shop
124 High Street
Street, Somerset BA16 0EX, England
Tel. 42045

HOURS: Monday–Saturday 9:00–5:30

See the description under GLASTONBURY.

LOCATION: Street is in the southwest of England about 20 miles northeast of Taunton on the A361 road. The A361 becomes High Street, on which the shop is located.

STREET   *Sheepskin Products*

D.T. Bayliss & Son (factory outlet)
147 High Street
Street, Somerset BA16 0EX, England
Tel. 0458-42164

HOURS: Monday–Saturday 9:00–5:30
CREDIT CARDS: Access, Visa

PRODUCTS: Men's and women's sheepskin coats and jackets are made at this factory. They have racks of coats starting at £110. Leather coats and jackets are also carried. Excellent selection and top quality! Mittens, hats, gloves, and rugs are also sold. Ladies three-quarter-length sheepskin coat prices range from £115 to £125. Ladies full-length coats are from £145 to £249. Men's three-quarter-length coats are £135 to £150; and full-length coats start at £249. There is a very good variety of styles and colors, with matching pile collars.

LOCATION: Street is in the southwest, about 20 miles northeast of Taunton on the A361 road. The A361 (A39) becomes High Street, and the shop is on the east side of this street.

STREET   *Shoes*

Fine Shoes (factory outlet)
111/113 High Street
Street, Somerset BA16 0EY, England
Tel. 0458-43603

Also at:
  Durstons Clark Centre
  92 High Street
  Street, Somerset BA16 0EN
and
  Mr. D's
  119 High Street
  Street, Somerset BA16 0EY

Also:
  Jobbers
  136 High Street
  Street, Somerset
BA16 0ER
and
  Fine Shoes
  30–34 High Street
  Street, Somerset
BA5 2SG

HOURS: Monday–Saturday 9:00–5:30
       British Bank Holidays 10:00–5:00
       Some Sundays 10:00–5:00
CREDIT CARDS: Access, Diners Club

PRODUCTS: Fine Shoes is a factory outlet shoe shop selling name brand shoes at discount rates, with savings of between 10% and 50% off the normal price for discontinued, clearance, sample line, and sub-standard shoes. Further 10% discounts are given six times a year. Write the store for the exact dates.

A leather open-toed sandal with a small heel was £29.99. A casual leather tie shoe was also £29.99. A very fashionable two-tone gray and beige pump was £31.99.

The following shoe lines are carried at their store. Brief descriptions with the possible savings on each brand are listed below.

Bally: Ladies fashion boots, shoes, sandals, with savings from £5 to £35.
Barkers: Traditional men's and ladies' walkers with savings of £5 to £35.
Clarks: Men's, women's, and children's seasonal shoes with savings of £5 to £25.
Grenson: Supremely styled men's shoes, made in England with savings of £5 to £30.
Morlands: Renowned for men's and women's sheepskin boots and slippers with savings of £3 to £30.
Wallabees: Casual shoes and moccasins with savings of £5 to £10.

The store is extremely busy and almost everyone seems to leave with a pair of shoes. The shoes are displayed so you can try them on without waiting for a clerk.

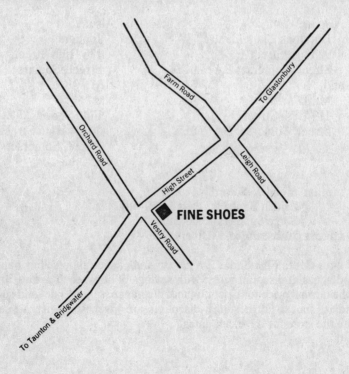

LOCATION: Street is in the southwest about 20 miles northeast of Taunton on the A361 road. The A361 becomes High Street, on which the shop is located.

STREET   *Sheepskin Products*

STOP—Sheepskin Discount Centre (factory outlet)
146 High Street
Street, Somerset BA 160EX, England
Tel. 42858

HOURS: Monday–Saturday 9:00–5:00
CREDIT CARDS: Barclaycard, Visa

PRODUCTS: This shop is the factory outlet of O.H.C. Barry & Co. Ltd. They specialize in making men's and women's coats and jackets in sheepskin and curly lamb. They have a special sale rack on seconds and discontinued coats. Also available: sheepskin hats, berets, gloves, mittens, moccasins, rugs, men's and women's leather coats. Sweaters and kilts are also sold at very reasonable prices.

LOCATION: Street is in the southwest, about 20 miles northeast of Taunton on the A36 road. The A361 becomes High Street, on which the shop is located.

STROUD   *Pottery*

Inderwood Pottery (craft workshop)
Michael and Barbara Hawkins
Stroud, Gloucestershire GL5 5ND, England

HOURS: Monday–Friday 9:00–5:00
CREDIT CARDS: None

PRODUCTS: Inderwood Pottery specializes in large plant pots priced from £3 to £10. There are also glazed pottery vases, plant stands, and teapots. Prices on all of the items were very reasonable. Many of the pots would be great for outdoor plants or trees.

LOCATION: Stroud is in the southwest about 10 miles south of Gloucester on the A4173. Inderwood Pottery is just behind the Rooksmoor Mills furniture outlet on the A46 to the south of Stroud. See the map below.

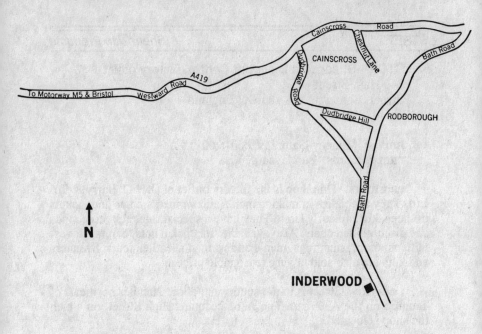

STROUD   *Wine*

Raffles Wine Co. (Wholesale Wine Warehouse)
Rooksmoor Mills
Bath Road, Woodchester
Stroud, Gloucestershire GL5 5ND, England
Tel. 045 387-2717

HOURS: Monday–Friday 9:30–1:00 and 2:00–5:00; Saturday 10:00–1:00 and 2:00–4:00; closed Sundays and Bank Holidays.
CREDIT CARDS: None

PRODUCTS: Wine and champagne may be purchased from the Raffles Wine Co. at wholesale prices if you purchase a case which is 12 bottles. The company specializes in French wines from two companies: Dulong Frères in Bordeaux and Marcilly in Beaune. They specialize in wines which cost between £2 and £4.50. You will also find a small selection of Italian, Spanish, and German wines.

Bin ends and fine and rare wines, which change weekly, are also sold. These wines are often not a full case and can be purchased by the bottle.

For special parties and weddings wines purchased here could be a real savings!

LOCATION: Stroud is in the southwest, about 10 miles south of Gloucester. Raffles Wine Co. is on the south side of town, on the A46 just behind the Rooksmoor Mills furniture outlet. See the map below.

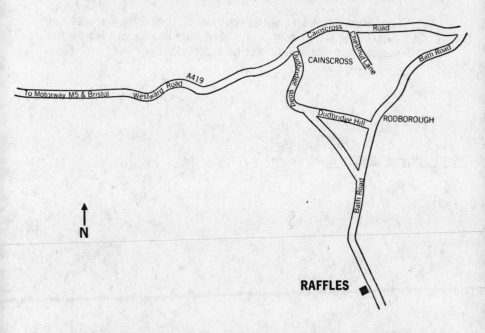

STROUD   *Furniture, Kitchen Gift Items*

Rooksmoor Mills (factory showroom)
Bath Road, Stroud
Gloucestershire GL5 5ND, England
Tel. 045387-2577

HOURS: Monday–Saturday 9:00–4:30; Sunday 10:00–4:30
CREDIT CARDS: Access, Visa

PRODUCTS: At this huge showroom visitors will find couches, chairs, dining room sets, end tables, and china cabinets. Pine and wicker furniture is sold in all price ranges. Carpeting, kitchens, mattresses, and accent rugs are abundant. There is a nice selection of unusual pottery pieces at good prices. Various accent and accessory items are also sold.

All prices include the VAT. A stained pine blanket chest was £104.95. A ladies wardrobe in natural pine was £285. A Welsh country-style pine dresser with a two-drawer dresser with an open shelf unit measuring 72″ × 37″ × 20″ was £199.95. They have an excellent color catalog but they cannot fill international mail orders.

LOCATION: Stroud is in the southwest about 10 miles south of Gloucester. The Rooksmoor Mill is on the south edge of town on the A46 road toward Nailsworth. See the map below.

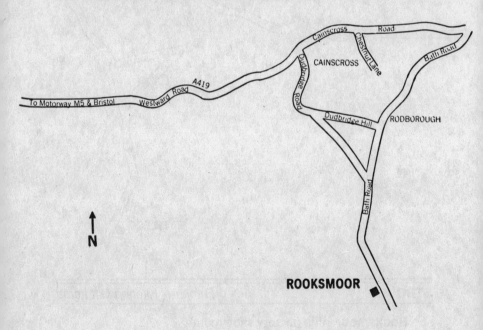

STROUD   *Clothing, Fabrics*

West of England Woollen Mills
Frome Hall, Chestnut Lane
Stroud, Gloucestershire, England
Tel. 04536-77301

HOURS: Monday–Saturday 9:00–4:30

CREDIT CARDS: Access, Eurocard, MasterCard, Visa

PRODUCTS: A wide range of suitings and fabrics in pure wool, wool mixtures, cotton, and synthetics. Also ladies' readymade outerwear, and knitwear for men and ladies. Woolen accessories and scarves, gloves, car rugs, and more. Sample prices: men's 3½-yard suit length £25; ladies' pure wool two-piece suit £27.50; lambswool sweaters £8.95; ladies' skirts from £4. They have a good selection of high quality items. Wool blankets are £6.95 and are made from woolen yarns at the factory. A super buy and excellent quality.

LOCATION: Stroud is in the southwest of England about 10 miles south of Gloucester on the A46 road. The woollen mill is near the center of town. See the map below.

TAUNTON	*Sheepskin Products*

Tanns of Taunton Factory Shop
Tancred Street
Taunton, Somerset TA1 1SP, England
Tel. 0823-51752

HOURS: Monday–Friday 8:00–5:00; Saturday 9:30–5:00
CREDIT CARDS: Access, Barclaycard, MasterCard

PRODUCTS: Tanns sells high-quality fashionable sheepskin coats at factory prices. They also sell sheepskin rugs, mittens, hats, toys, moccasins, umbrellas, handbags, leather goods, and other natural products. The factory is right behind the store, so you can watch them work.

Women's and men's sheepskin coats range in price from £99 to £149. Seconds and discontinued sheepskin coats are £75 each. Sheepskin rugs are £13.75, ski hats are £7.95, steering wheel covers are £1.99, and lambskin toys are £5.99.

LOCATION: Taunton is in the southwest of England, just off the M5 motorway. Leave the motorway at Exit 25, and drive toward the center of town on the A358. You will be on East Reach, and the factory shop will be on your right down a side street. See the map below.

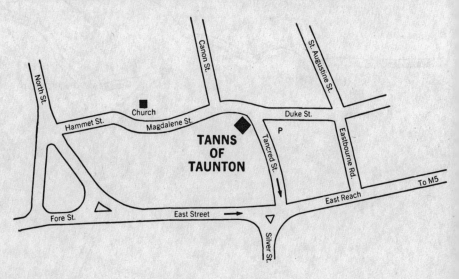

THORNHAM MAGNA, NEAR EYE   *Herb Teas, Herbs*

The Suffolk Spice and Herb Company (factory outlet)
Thornham Herb Garden
The Walled Garden
Thornham Magna, Near Eye, Suffolk IP23 SHA, England
Tel. Mellis 510

HOURS: Tuesday–Friday 10:00–4:00
CREDIT CARDS: Visa

PRODUCTS: The eighteenth-century walled herb garden devoted to the medicinal use of plants was founded by Jill Davies, a herbologist, in 1978. It now houses a growing number of plants and trees and serves as a sanctuary for a number of endangered herb species. The garden includes a wild garden for bees, butterflies, and insects, an astrological herb garden, a Wildflower Garden and the largest Knot Garden built in recent times.

This company sells a variety of herb teas blended in flavors such as lemon leaf, Jamaican spice, peppermint, and rose hip; also a variety of cooking mixes for vegetables and meats made from herbs. They also sell herbs, herb seeds, and spices, and a line of herbal skin and hair care products such as astringents, oils, shampoos, and hair coloring products. A four-ounce package of blended tea is £1.28, herb roots are priced at approximately 25 to 40 pence per ounce, and a bottle of chamomile shampoo is £2.07.

MAIL ORDER: They operate a worldwide mail service and can provide a brochure for this purpose. Their mail order address is Suffolk Spice & Herb Company, c/o Fir Tree Cottage, Dennington, Suffolk 1P13 8JF, England

TOURS: The 2½-acre garden is open without charge to the public during the day. A conducted tour around the garden is provided on request, and there is a small charge. Coaches must book in advance. All disabled groups are welcome.

LOCATION: Thornham Magna is in the east of England. From Bury St. Edmunds, take the E143 northeast to Diss. Continue on the A143 for one mile east, and then take the A140 south for about five miles. Thornham Magna will be on a side road going west.

TORQUAY   *Ceramics*

Philip Laureston Designs (factory shop)
Torquay Pottery and Craft Centre
16/17 Braddons Hill Road West
Torquay, Devon TQ1 1BG, England
Tel. 0803-211629

HOURS: Monday–Friday 9:30–1:00 and 2:00–5:00
CREDIT CARDS: None

PRODUCTS: This company makes hand-painted miniature pottery
animals and houses, ceramic greeting cards, local hand-thrown pottery
mugs, cups, vases, and blown glassware. Animals are priced from 35
pence to 95 pence, houses from 75 pence to £1.85, and ceramic greeting cards range from 85 pence to £1.85. They will ship items.

MAIL ORDER: They will accept mail orders. Details are available
upon request.

TOURS: Forty-five minute tours are available for groups of up to
50. Arrangements must be made in advance.

LOCATION: Torquay is in the far southwest of England on the
English Channel about 20 miles east of Plymouth. It is easier to approach Torquay from the north (from Exeter and Newton Abbot) on
the 380. Go toward the harbor on Newton Road, then Union Street (a
one-way shopping street) until the Post Office roundabout is reached.
Twenty yards further toward the harbor, there is a side road bearing off
to the left of Fleet Street. One hundred yards up this road, visitors will
see the pottery with its large parking lot. In general Torquay Pottery is
300 yards from the harbor, 120 yards from the post office, and opposite
Dingles Department Store.

TROWBRIDGE   *Clothing, Fabrics*

West of England Woollen Mills (factory outlet)
Stone Mills, Court Street
Trowbridge, Wiltshire, England
Tel. Trowbridge 3765

HOURS: Monday–Friday 9:30–1:00 and 2:15–5:00; Saturday 9:30–12:30
CREDIT CARDS: Access, Eurocard, MasterCard, Visa

PRODUCTS: You'll find a wide range of suitings and fabric in pure wool, wool blends, cotton, and synthetics, as well as ladies ready-made outerwear, and knitwear for men and ladies, plus scarves, gloves, and car rugs. Sample prices: men's 3½-yard suit length £25; ladies' pure wool two-piece suit £27.50; lambswool sweaters £8.95; ladies' skirts from £4.

LOCATION: Trowbridge is in the southwest of England on the A361, about 10 miles southeast of Bath.

TUTBURY, NEAR BURTON-ON-TRENT   *Crystal*

Georgian Crystal (Tutbury) Ltd. (factory outlet)
Silk Mill Lane
Tutbury, Near Burton-on-Trent, Staffordshire, England
Tel. 0283-814534

HOURS: Monday–Saturday 9:00–5:00;
                closed for lunch 12:00–1:00
CREDIT CARDS: Diners Club, Visa

PRODUCTS: Georgian Crystal manufactures lead crystal glasses, decanters, bowls, vases, honey jars, ring holders, baskets, and ring stands. Sales are held in February and July of each year. They will ship purchases home for you.
   The Elvaston crystal pieces were £2.53 for the liqueur glass, £3.37 for the nine-ounce rummer, £4.60 for the goblet and £30 for the wine decanter. The Fancies crystal pattern has 36 functional pieces. A small rose bowl was £8.40, a candlestick £5, a honey pot £5.85, and a large basket £30.

TOURS: Tours are given to groups of up to 40. Arrangements must be made in advance.

LOCATION: Burton-on-Trent is in central England about 25 miles northeast of Birmingham on the A38 road. Tutbury is a few miles north of Burton-on-Trent on the A50 road. See the map below.

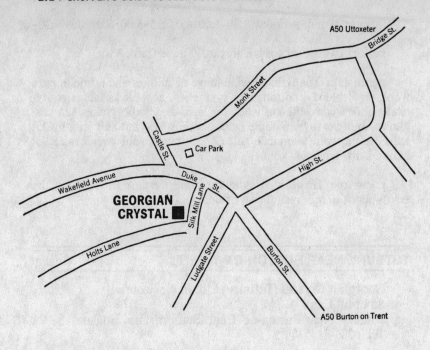

ULVERSTON   *Crystal*

Cumbria Crystal Limited (factory/outlet)
Lightburn Road
Ulverston, Cumbria LA12 ODA, England
Tel. 0229-54400

HOURS: Factory: Monday–Friday 8:00–4:00
Shop: Monday–Friday 9:00–5:00; Saturday 10:00–4:00;
May to September open Sunday 10:00–1:00.
CREDIT CARDS: Access, American Express, Visa

PRODUCTS: In 1975 Cumbria Crystal Ltd. was established by five friends who were concerned about the modernization of crystal making techniques. All of their items are based on authentic seventeenth- and eighteenth-century patterns. Their detail and quality is absolutely magnificent! Cumbria Crystal is purportedly the only crystal company in Great Britain which sells full lead crystal in a clear, uncut form. Cumbria Crystal has won international fame for its designs and quality. Each piece is skillfully hand engraved using diamond points and carborundum wheels. Each piece is a work of art. There are over 54 different processes which must be completed before a crystal piece is ready.

Vases, decanters, bowls, candlesticks, glasses, jugs, and tumblers, are just a few of the pieces they manufacture. A few samples of the savings:

ITEM	CRYSTAL STYLE	FIRST QUALITY	FACTORY PRICE
Whisky Tumbler	Lakeland Cut	£ 8.50	£ 4.50
Brandy Glass	Clear	£15.05	£ 8.70
Large Violet Vase	Keswick Cut	£17.10	£ 9.65
Trifle Dish	Hawkshead Cut	£46.25	£27.75
Rose Bowl	Hawkshead Cut	£51.50	£28.15

In their two retail shops and factory, crystal with slight imperfections is available at substantial discounts from normal retail prices. They also offer a VAT refund. They will be happy to mail your purchases. Highly recommended!

TOURS: There are no guided tours offered, but an information pamphlet is given to each person. The pamphlet is extremely descriptive and explains the history of glass as well as the entire process of making crystal. There is no restriction on party size.

LOCATION: Ulverston is in the northwest of England eight miles north of Barrow-in-Furness on the A590. This is northwest of Lancaster across Morecambe Bay.

Approaching Ulverston from the east, enter town on the A590, go straight across a roundabout, and then turn left at the first set of traffic lights. Take the next left and you will be in front of the factory. See the map below.

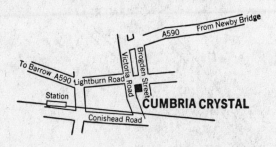

UPPERMILL NR. SADDLEWORTH   *Craft Items*

J. Bradbury & Co. (Saddleworth) Ltd.
The Alexandra Craft Centre
Dam Head
Uppermill, Oldham OL3 6LB, England
Tel. 04577-5984

HOURS: Wednesday–Sunday 11:00–4:30
CREDIT CARDS: None

PRODUCTS: Visitors will find a craft center filled with 30 independent tenants. A sampling of products available: wooden items, soft
toys, pottery, china, kilts, butterflies, paintings, stationery, perfumes,
flowers, jewelry, books, decorative glass, frames, and wood-turned
products. Prices vary greatly. Two tearooms help to create a warm and
relaxing atmosphere in this former woolen mill.

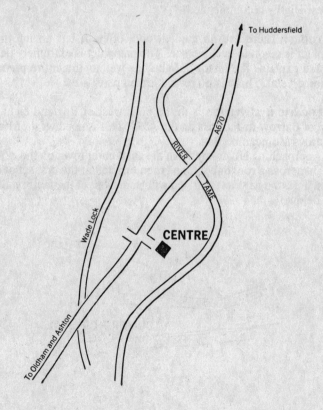

LOCATION: Uppermill near Saddleworth is in west central England about 10 miles northeast of Manchester on the A670. This is five miles due east of Oldham. See the map.

VENTNOR, ISLE OF WIGHT *Hand-blown Decorative Glassware*

Isle of Wight Glass
Old Park, St. Lawrence
Ventnor, Isle of Wight, England
Tel. 0983-853-526

HOURS: Glassworks: Monday–Friday 9:00–4:00, year 'round.
Showroom: Monday–Friday 9:00–5:00; 10:00–5:00 Saturday and Sunday in summer.
CREDIT CARDS: Access, Barclaycard, Visa

PRODUCTS: Isle of Wight Glass produces some of the most exquisite hand-blown vases, goblets, bottles, and figurines seen anywhere. These artfully hand-blown pieces are available in quite a range of sizes and finishes, from iridescent blues shot through with streaks of gold to marbelized and crackled surfaces. Their Minimal and Maximal glass creatures look as if they've just crept out of the forest; the Golden Peacock and Kyoto collections have the opulence yet restrained beauty and simplicity of form of the finest Oriental pottery; the Meadow Garden, Seascape, and Landscape series draw their influence from the mossy greens, blues, and slate grays of the local fields, forests, and coastline. Prices quoted at the showroom are all wholesale, which means you'll pay the same prices as a dealer. You'll pay as much as £60 for a 35 cm-tall Seascape vase to £6.50 for a small Golden Peacock bowl, or £4.20 for a glass mushroom. There are some lovely Golden Rain and Firecracker perfume vials for about £15.

LOCATION: The Isle of Wight is off the southern coast of England, near Southhampton. Take the car or passenger ferry into Ryde, on the northern side of the Isle, then drive south to Ventor (about 40 minutes). Isle of Wight Glass is on route A3055 in Ventnor.

WATTISFIELD   *Pottery*

Henry Watson's Potteries Limited (factory/outlet)
Wattisfield, Suffolk IP22 1NH, England
Tel. 0359-51239

HOURS: Monday–Saturday 9:30–5:00
CREDIT CARDS: Access

PRODUCTS: Henry Watson's Potteries Limited is a 180-year-old
company which sells a wide variety of domestic terra-cotta pottery
items such as vases, planters, candelabras, clocks, and condiment
sets. They also manufacture Suffolk Kitchen oven-to-table ware along
with a wide range of pottery gift items such as wine coolers, spice
bottles, clocks. Their terra-cotta kitchen items are simple and elegant—very country in feeling. A retail shop at the factory sells only
factory seconds. Highly recommended!
  The following prices are all second prices. The most expensive
item I could find was the bread crock for £13.74. Over 80% of the items
were priced below £7.50.
  A small tea jar was £3.08, a flan dish was £3.92, a candle lamp was
£3.94, and a wine cooler was £2.06.

TOURS: Tours are available by prior appointment at 11:00, 2:00,
and 3:15. A tour and visit to the seconds shop takes about 1¼ hours.

LOCATION: Wattisfield is in eastern England about halfway between Bury St. Edmunds and Diss on the A143 road. (It is slightly
closer to Diss.) Bury St. Edmunds is about 28 miles east of Cambridge
on the A45. From Cambridge go east on the A45 to Bury St. Edmunds.
Then go northeast on the A143 about 12 miles.

WELLS   *Shoes*

Fine Shoes
30–34 High Street
Wells, Somerset BA5 2SG, England

HOURS: Monday–Saturday 9:00–5:30

Please see the description of this store under STREET.

LOCATION: Wells is in the southwest of England, about 22 miles south of Bath on the A39 road. See the map below.

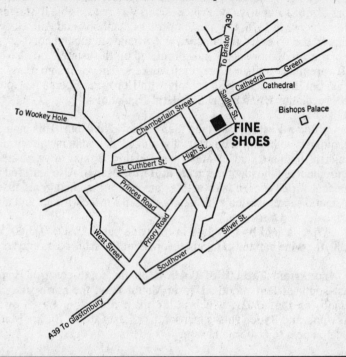

WHIPPINGHAM, ISLE OF WIGHT   *Wines, Giftware*

Barton Manor Vineyard and Gardens
Whippingham, East Cowes
Isle of Wight PO32 6LB, England
Tel. 0983 292835

HOURS: May 1st to September 30th: Monday–Saturday 11:30–
        5:30. Open Sundays in April, and open Easter Monday
CREDIT CARDS: None

PRODUCTS: The history of Barton Manor is almost as long as that of England, beginning with its first mention in the Doomsday Book of

1086. In 1275, an Augustinian Oratory was founded here, portions of which are still in existence. Many years later, the lands were annexed by Winchester College and rented out as an agricultural estate. In 1845, Queen Victoria purchased the property, using it to house members of European royalty. Prince Albert was responsible for laying out the gardens. In 1976, the present owners, Anthony and Alix Goodard, planted the vineyard and opened the grounds to the public.

Barton Manor sells wines produced on the estate, and also some giftware made by Isle Island craftworkers. They will ship items overseas, but their wine labels comply with European Economic Community regulations, and not U.S. federal regulations.

TOURS: Visitors may take their own walking tour. This includes a woodland walk with a quarter of a million daffodils in the spring, an English vineyard and estate winery with a display of wine-making equipment and a videotape made at Barton Manor. Also featured are a magical water garden lake with swans and a thatched boathouse, an aromatic secret garden with plants chosen for their scent, and a wine bar, cafe, and gift shop.

Wine is sold by the glass in the wine bar from 12:00–3:00. After 3:00, the wine bar and cafe remain open for the sale of teas and snacks.

LOCATION: The Isle of Wight is off the south coast of England, just south of Portsmouth. Barton Manor is on the north side of the island, on the A3021, which is the main road from East Cowes to Newport and Ryde. This is just south of East Cowes. Barton Manor is located next to Osborne House.

WILLITON   *Thimbles, Spoons, Miniatures*

The Paddingham Collection (factory showroom)
Station Road, Industrial Estate
Williton, Somerset TA4 4RF, England
Tel. 0984-32072

HOURS: Monday–Friday 9:00–5:00
CREDIT CARDS: MasterCard, Visa

PRODUCTS: Visitors will find bone china thimbles, silver-plated teaspoons, collector spoons, pewter thimbles, and display cabinets for all of the above. Factory seconds are also sold.

All prices include the VAT, postage, and packing charges. Henry VIII thimbles are £5.90 each. Animal thimbles are £2.50 each. The Royal Family thimbles are £2.10 each. A spoon rack for 18 is £12.90 and a thimble rack for 12 is £4.90.

MAIL ORDERS: Goods are sent to all parts of the world.

LOCATION: Williton is in southwest England near the Bristol channel, about 16 miles northwest of Taunton on the A358 road. See the map below.

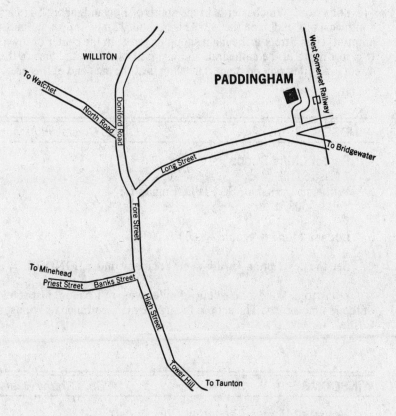

WINCHESTER   *Clothing*

Lakeland Sheepskin Centre (retail store)
25 High Street
Winchester, Hampshire SO23 9BL, England
Tel. 0962-60743

HOURS: Monday–Saturday 9:00–5:30

See the write-up under ALTRINCHAM.

LOCATION: Winchester is in the south of England, about 50 miles southwest of London on the M3. This is about 12 miles north of Southampton. High Street is the main shopping street in the center of town. It is just north of the cathedral, and just east of the castle. Part of the street is a pedestrian precinct. The shop is at the east end of this area.

WINDSOR   *China, Crystal, Figurines*

Reject China Shops
1 Castle Hill
Windsor, Berkshire SL4 1PD, England
Tel. 95-50870

HOURS: Monday–Saturday 9:00–6:00

See the description for this same company under LONDON.

LOCATION: Windsor is about 15 miles west of London, just south of the M4 motorway. The shop is facing the main entrance to Windsor Castle.

WINSCOMBE   *Dolls, Teddy Bears*

House of Nisbet, Limited (factory outlet)
Dunster Park
Winscombe, Avon BS25 1AG, England
Tel. 0934-84-2905

HOURS: Monday–Thursday 8:30–5:00; Friday 8:30–2:00
CREDIT CARDS: American Express, Diners Club, MasterCard, Visa

PRODUCTS: The first Nisbet doll was made in 1953, at the time of the coronation of Her Majesty, Queen Elizabeth II. Mrs. Peggy Nisbet made a dressed figurine of the Queen in coronation robes as her first portrait doll. Since 1953, there have been hundreds of different dolls and soft toys made in the Nisbet workrooms.

Today the Nisbet collection also features many eight-inch Portrait and Costume Dolls such as Princess Diana, Prince William, the Reagans, Charlie Chaplin, Sitting Bull, Abraham Lincoln, other British royalty, and Bozo the Clown. Others include a series of wax dolls reviving an old doll-making technique, the Alison Nisbet vinyl fashion dolls, the My Little Girl series of vinyl dolls, and others.

The Nisbet bears are a collection of stuffed and costumed teddy bears inspired by *The Teddy Bear Book* by Peter Bull. There is also a series of Zodiac Bears costumed according to the personality traits of the different signs of the zodiac.

Doll prices range from $24.95 to $275. Bears are priced from $32.95 to $89.95. They will ship items to the States, and the above prices include shipping costs and duty.

TOURS: Tours are available by appointment. They request advance notice of one day. Maximum tour group size is 10.

LOCATION: Winscombe is in the southwestern corner of England. The town is southwest of Bristol on the A38 about 13 miles.

WINTON   *Pottery*

Langrigg Pottery (craft workshop)
Winton, Kirkby Stephen
Cumbria CA17 4HL, England
Tel. 0930-71542

HOURS: Easter to mid-October: every day 9:00–5:00; winter: Tuesday–Saturday 9:00–5:00.
CREDIT CARDS: None

PRODUCTS: Langrigg Pottery is a small one-room studio/

showroom where stoneware and earthenware are sold. You will find tableware, cooking pots, lamp bases, plant pots, vases, and plates glazed in subdued greens, browns, and whites decorated with brush strokes. Mugs begin at £1.80, coffee sets at £31, and vases from £1.75.

For a week at Easter, seconds are sold as well as miscellaneous items, and there is a 10% reduction on normal stock.

TOURS: Demonstrations for 15 to 20 people can be booked in advance.

LOCATION: Winton is in north central England just south of Brough. Brough is about 21 miles southeast of Penrith on the A66 road. See the map below. The studio is on the upper floor of an old hay barn.

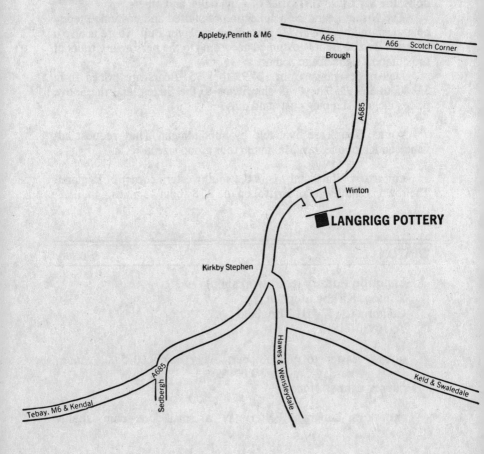

WOODSTOCK   *Kitchen Shop*

Scoops (retail store)
58 Oxford Street
Woodstock, Oxfordshire OX7 1TT, England
Tel. 0993-812128

HOURS: Monday–Saturday 9:30–6:00; June–July: Sunday 12:00–
6:00

See the write-up under STRATFORD-UPON-AVON.

LOCATION: Woodstock is in south central England eight miles
northwest of Oxford on the A34. Oxford is 55 miles northwest of
London on the M40.

WORDSLEY, NEAR STOURBRIDGE   *Crystal*

Stuart Crystal (factory outlet)
Redhouse Glassworks
Wordsley, Stourbridge, West Midlands DY8 4AA, England
Tel. 0384-71161

HOURS: Monday–Saturday 9:00–5:00
CREDIT CARDS: American Express, Visa

PRODUCTS: A room full of crystal seconds at greatly reduced
prices—a must for every visitor. Decanters, bowls, honey pots, vases,
glasses, and pitchers were lining the shelves. Decanters started at £22
and honey pots at £5. They will ship and insure your purchases and
deduct the VAT. This outlet is a popular one so try to be there before
the bus tours arrive. The selection is better and you do not have to
wait to pay. Highly recommended!

TOURS: Tours are Monday through Friday at 10:00, 11:15, 2:00,
and 3:15. Children under 14 must be with an adult. Parties of more
than six must book in advance.

LOCATION: Wordsley is in west central England just to the north
of Stourbridge on the A491 road. Stourbridge is about five miles west
of Birmingham. See the map below.

WORDSLEY, NEAR STOURBRIDGE   *Crystal*

Tudor Crystal Factory Shop
Junction Road, Wordsley
Stourbridge, West Midlands DY8 4YG, England
Tel. 038-43-4805

HOURS: Monday–Friday 9:15–5:00; Saturday 10:00–5:00. Also on
Sunday from the third Sunday in May for 18 consecutive
Sundays from 10:00–5:00.
CREDIT CARDS: All major credit cards.

PRODUCTS: Tudor Crystal is a manufacturer of full lead crystal
tableware and accessory pieces with simple designs. Each piece is
handled by a minimum of 20 people. The small factory shop sells

seconds as well as first-quality items at factory prices. Decanters, stemware, bowls, pitchers, vases, paperweights, birds, and bells were only a few of the items. Paperweights in eight animal shapes were £15 each. A honey jar was £22. A medium rose bowl was £22.50. The day we visited, their selection was rather small.

TOURS: Tours of the factory are available by prior appointment.

LOCATION: Wordsley is in west central England two miles north of Stourbridge on the A491 road. Stourbridge is about five miles directly west of Birmingham. See the map below.

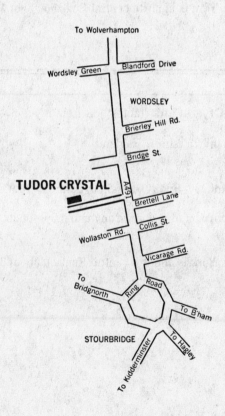

YORK   *Wool Clothing, Scottish Crafts*

Clan Royal (retail store)
38 Stonegate
York, England
Tel. 0904-22165

HOURS: Monday–Saturday 9:00–5:30

See the write-up under EDINBURGH, Scotland.

LOCATION: York is in north central England about 20 miles northeast of Leeds.

YORK   *Crystal*

Cumbria Crystal Ltd. (factory outlet)
8 Stonegate
York, North Yorkshire, England
Tel. 32382

HOURS: Monday–Friday 9:00–5:00; Saturday 10:00–4:00

For a description of this company and its products, see ULVERSTON.

LOCATION: York is in north central England about 20 miles northeast of Leeds.

SCOTLAND

WELCOME TO SCOTLAND

Scotland is a country filled with heather, manicured gardens, the sound of bagpipes, rugged mountains, deep valleys, swift moving rivers, calm blue lakes, and centuries of rich history. Scotland is divided into three regions: the Northern Highlands, the Central Lowlands, and the Southern Uplands. Scotland has over 800 islands off her broken 2300-mile coastline. The country's total length is 274 miles, and at the widest point it's 154 miles. The Scots, Picts, Britons, and Angles have intermarried to create the Scotland of today.

The two major cities of Scotland are Edinburgh and Glasgow. Edinburgh, a city famous for its tartan-clad bagpipers and the Edinburgh Castle which overlooks the city, is only 375 miles north of London. Edinburgh has a romantic air about it which makes you wish you could stay forever. Glasgow is the manufacturing and population center of Scotland. It is a city of contrasts—rich in history yet modern and hardworking.

Scotland has a hearty cuisine with many excellent specialties including: cock-a-leekie soup (chicken and leek), kippers, trout, neeps (turnips), poacher's soup, Aberdeen Angus filet steak, scones, and shortbread. In restaurants you'll find the food served in generous portions. The meat, as well as the vegetables, are often fresh and carefully seasoned.

Scotland offers visitors a vast range of activities: salmon fishing, curling, pony trekking, rock climbing, grouse shooting, golfing, visits to woolen mills, museums, castles, and much more.

SHOPPING IN SCOTLAND

Scotland offers the visitor some very special buys on her world-renowned products.

Craft centres and shops, where you will find unique and one-of-a-kind items, are abundant throughout Scotland. Many smaller businesses create quality products which are displayed only in these shops. Mass production is not their goal! Instead they prefer to emphasize creativity and individual expression. You will find pottery, leather,

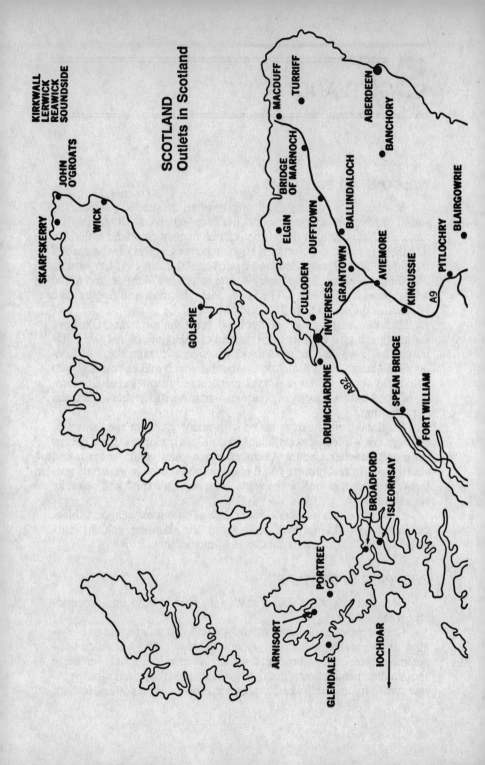

SCOTLAND
Outlets in Scotland

KIRKWALL
LERWICK
REAWICK
SOUNDSIDE

JOHN O'GROATS
SKARFSKERRY
WICK
GOLSPIE

MACDUFF
TURRIFF
ABERDEEN
BANCHORY
BRIDGE OF MARNOCH
ELGIN
DUFFTOWN
BALLINDALOCH
CULLODEN
GRANTOWN
AVIEMORE
BLAIRGOWRIE
PITLOCHRY
INVERNESS
KINGUSSIE
A9

DRUMCHARDINE
A82
SPEAN BRIDGE
FORT WILLIAM

BROADFORD
ISLEORNSAY
PORTREE

ARNISORT
GLENDALE
IOCHDAR

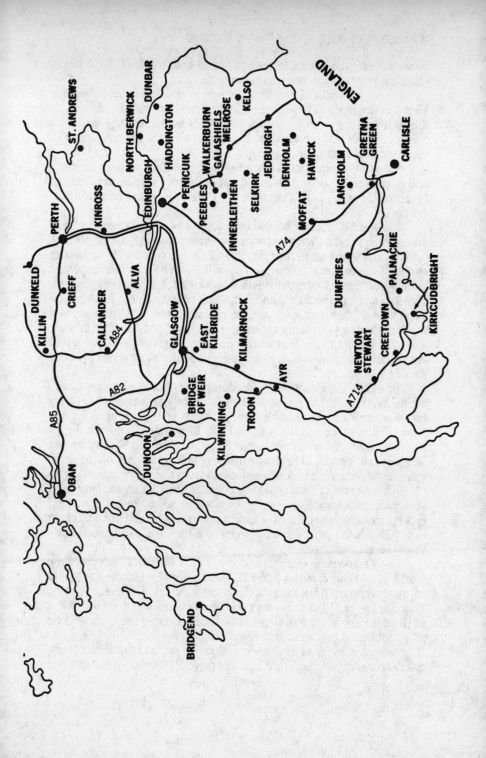

bone, silver, wood, pebble jewelry, hand-knit woolens, food items, glass, and more displayed from floor to ceiling.

Of course, Scotland always brings to mind the rich, haunting sound of bagpipes. These ancient instruments are also handmade. In the 19th century a strong revival in folk music helped bagpipe music attain international recognition. Be sure to visit the manufacturers of these unusual instruments.

Scotland has famous factories which manufacture crystal, glass, and paperweights of superb quality and unusual shapes and designs. Much of the work is still completed by hand, as it has been for centuries.

Perhaps Scotland is best known for the beautiful woolen tartans and tweeds woven at the factory mills throughout the country, which visitors are welcome to tour. You will find as many as 750 tartans to choose from at some factories. You will also find cashmere, mohair, lambswool, Harris tweeds, Shetland and Fair Isle woolens, angora, cheviot, and merino wool, and Aran knitwear available in sweaters, kilts, skirts, blazers, coats, jackets, trousers, ties, and knitwear, and for the seamstress a seemingly endless choice of 100% woolen fabrics. The mill shops' prices are reasonable and the choices for the most part are superb! Shop selectively and take home the best, which will last for years to come.

To weave all of that wool, Scotland needs flocks of sheep. Sheep are all over the barren plains of Scotland in breeds which are not very common in other parts of the world. Keep your eyes open for the North County Cheviot, the Shetland, the Border Leicester, the Rough Fell, the Suffolks and Lonks, the Herwick, and the Teeswater and Wensleydale breeds. There are many others, but most of the wool spun for woven cloth or knitwear comes from the above breeds.

Where there are sheep, you also find available an abundance of sheepskin products. Factories process sheepskins into quality coats, jackets, rugs, mittens, boots, slippers, gloves, hats, and purses. There is a wide choice of colors and styles available for purchase directly from the manufacturers.

One of Scotland's largest exports is malt whisky. (The rest of the world knows this drink as Scotch). It is created by blending a variety of malt whiskies from many different distilleries with grain whisky. There are over 110 of these malt whisky distilleries in Scotland. Most of them do not allow tours. We have listed some of the ones who do allow tours and of course give samples.

Antiques are easily found in Scotland. You can hunt for cherry, oak, and mahogany furniture in cities or small towns. Whimsical and decorative accent pieces, books, and jewelry are found in markets, shops, and stalls all over the Scottish countryside.

Enjoy shopping for Scotland's quality products at affordable prices as well as the warmth of the Scottish people plus the beauty of the rolling green plains and heather-covered moors.

Best Buys in Scotland

ABERDEEN   *Wool Clothing, Scottish Crafts*

Clan Royal (retail store)
35–41 Bridge Street
Aberdeen, Grampian, Scotland
Tel. 0224-51883

HOURS: Monday–Saturday 9:00–5:30

See the write-up under EDINBURGH.

LOCATION: Aberdeen is a large city on the northeast coast of Scotland.

ALVA   *Wool Sweaters*

Raymond Hodgson & Co. Ltd. (factory outlet)
Ochilvale Mills, Alva,
Clackmannanshire FK12 5HW, Scotland
Tel. 0259-61600

HOURS: Monday–Friday 10:00–4:30; Saturday 9:30–5:00; Sunday
10:30–5:00
CREDIT CARDS: MasterCard, Visa

PRODUCTS: This company sells vests and sweaters for men and
women that are made from merino wool or two-ply lambswool. Seconds are available from £5.95 to £7.45 for women's clothing, and from
£9.45 for men's. Prices for first-quality women's sweaters start at
£9.95. The quality, prices, and selection are excellent. Highly recommended.

LOCATION: Alva is in central Scotland about six miles east of Stirling on the A91 road. The mill shop is on the right at the far (east) end of town.

ARNISORT, ISLE OF SKYE   *Candles*

Skye-Lytes Candlemaker (craft workshop)
"Three Rowans"
Kildonan, Arnisort
Isle of Skye IV51 9PU, Scotland
Tel. 047082-286

HOURS: Monday–Saturday 10:00–5:30; Sunday 12:00–5:30; evenings by appointment only.
CREDIT CARDS: None

PRODUCTS: Skye-Lyte Candles are handmade in this factory high above the sea. They make a variety of candles: carved designs which are cut freehand; ceilioh lanterns, which are carved shells of wax in which a small 12-hour candle burns; Skye flower candles, which are surrounded with sand sealed on them; sand candles encased in sand and stone; chunky candles which are hand carved; cuillin candles colored with the gentle hues of the mountains; and lichen candles containing tiny chips of wax to give an impression of the island mosses and lichens. Prices of the candles range from £2.60 to £15 for the 240-hour burning candle—which is enormous. Seconds are available occasionally. All orders over £100 receive a 20% discount. Sky-Lytes Candlemakers will mail your candles abroad for you.

TOURS: Visitors are free to watch the candles being created. About 15 people may watch in one room.

LOCATION: The Isle of Skye is off the northwest coast of Scotland. The town of Arnisort is about halfway between Portree and Dunvegan on the A850 road. From the ferry, take the A863 to Broadford and then Portree. From Portree take the A850 to Broadford toward Dunvegan, past Skeabost and Bernisdale and onto a new stretch of road. At the end of the new road (where the single track begins again) is a right-hand turn to Fanks. Take this turn and it will lead to Three Rowans restaurant and Skye-Lytes Candles.

AVIEMORE *Whisky, Gifts*

Cairngorm Whisky Centre
Inverdruie, Aviemore
Inverness Shire PH22 1QU, Scotland
Tel. 0479-810574

HOURS: Monday–Saturday 10:00–6:00 (later in summer season);
       Sunday 12:30–2:00
CREDIT CARDS: Access, Visa

PRODUCTS: This firm sells a large selection of malt Scotch whiskies. Their shop also sells gifts and whisky-related products as well as over 300 different Scotch whisky miniatures. Their brochure states that prices are kept as low as possible. (They are unable to quote prices.)

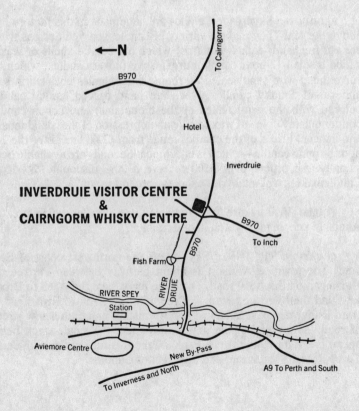

TOURS: Their museum and audiovisual presentation are open during regular hours, with an admission price of 50 pence per person. Their tasting room features over 75 different malt whiskies. Charge for the tasting room is £1.25 per person.

LOCATION: Aviemore is in north central Scotland, about 25 miles southeast of Inverness on the A9 road. See the map below.

AYR   *Sweaters*

Aran International Knitwear (factory outlet)
Unit 22, Ayr Harbour Industrial Estate
Ayr KA7 4LN, Scotland
Tel. 284245

HOURS: Monday–Friday 8:30–5:00
CREDIT CARDS: Access, Barclaycard, MasterCard, Visa

PRODUCTS: As far back as the ninth century Aran sweaters were worn only by the people and fishermen of the Aran Islands off the coast of Connemara, Ireland. Each family designed its own pattern of stitches which became its own trademark. Soon families were remembered simply by the pattern. The cable stitch stood for the fisherman's rope (it's also supposed to bring good luck), and the trellis stitch represented the familiar stone walls. Using unique combinations of these intricate stitches, fishing villages created designs that made it possible for the body of a drowned fisherman to be identified and returned to his hometown for burial. Originally, the sweaters were knit by men, women being relegated to the task of spinning the wool. The authentic Aran sweaters are handknit in a dense, water resistant, off-white wool. There are many adaptations today, in colors, lighter-weight wools, and in less expensive versions they have machine-finished details. The weight, texture, and label (it should always read handknit, *not* handloomed or machine knit) should tip you off as to whether or not it's the authentic item.

Aran knitwear is 100% pure new wool which is made into cardigan and pullover sweaters for men, women, and children. Aran International also makes Icelandic handknit sweaters from wool which is lightweight yet extremely warm. Handloomed sweaters are also available in Shetland wool.

Prices for children's sweaters range from £15.80 to £17.25, women's from £26.70 to £27.30, and men's from £26 to £28.

Visitors can special order colors. Quality merchandise at low prices.

MAIL ORDER: Aran International will take mail orders. They have a full color brochure with a price list.

LOCATION: Ayr is on the west coast of Scotland about 30 miles southwest of Glasgow on the A77. See the map below.

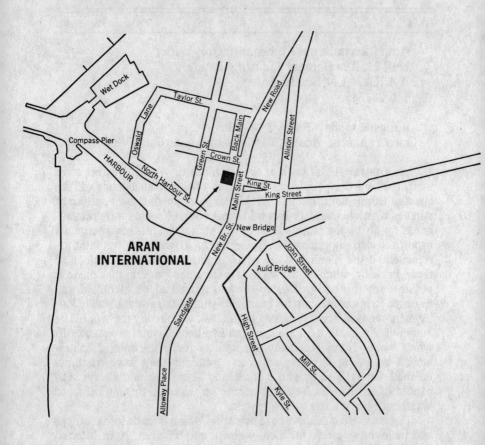

BALLINDALLOCH   *Whisky*

J. & G. Grant (factory/showroom)
Glenfarclas Distillery
Ballindalloch, Banffshire AB3 9BD, Scotland
Tel. 080-72-209

HOURS: Monday–Friday 9:00–5:00; July–September: Saturday
     9:00–5:00
CREDIT CARDS: None

PRODUCTS: In 1836, a tenant farmer decided to build a small still
on the land he rented for his herd of cattle. John Grant bought the
tenancy in 1865, and with it, the distillery. In 1870, the Grants began
distilling, and the business is still owned by their family. The distillery
was completely rebuilt by 1897, yet the Glenfarclas stills, replaced

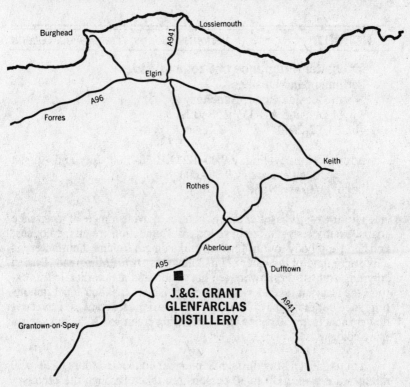

every 20 years or so, are exactly the same shape and size as when originally introduced.

This distillery sells Glenfarclas single malt whisky, at various ages from 8 to 25 years old. A bottle of 8-year-old whisky costs from £11 to £25, while a bottle aged 21 years is priced from £16 to £50. The distillery has a visitor's centre, an exhibition museum, and craft shop.

TOURS: Tours of the distillery take place Monday–Friday from 9:00–5:00 and also on Saturdays from July to September. The average length of a tour is 45 minutes. For groups of more than 20, advance notice would be appreciated.

LOCATION: The Glenfarclas Distillery is in the north of Scotland near the town of Marypark. This is about halfway between Grantown-on-Spey and Rothes on the A95 road. See the map above.

BANCHORY   *Perfumed Soaps, Aftershaves, Lotions*

Ingasetter (Fragrance of Scotland) Ltd.
Perfumers and Distillers
North Deeside Road, Banchory
Royal Deeside AB 33YR, Scotland
Tel. 03302-2600

HOURS: Monday–Friday 9:00–12:30, 1:30–5:00; July and August
        open every day 9:00–5:00
CREDIT CARDS: None

PRODUCTS: Ingasetter manufactures a wide range of fragrance soaps, beauty soaps, aftershave lotions, foundation creams, colognes, and hand and body lotions for men and women. Behind their factory is a five-acre field of lavender plants known as Dwarf Munstead. During July and August the flowers are harvested and steam-distilled to extract the fragrant lavender oil. Lavender is perhaps their most famous fragrance but they also create Islay and Catriona fragrances. Lavender flower sachets are 50 pence each, cleansing cream is £1.25, and a mini-Islay cologne is £1.

TOURS: From May through September conducted tours of 20 to 30 minutes are given. Up to 50 persons are taken through the premises and shown a film on the production operations. Groups must make advance reservations.

LOCATION: Banchory is in the northeast part of Scotland about 16 miles west of Aberdeen on the A93. See the map below.

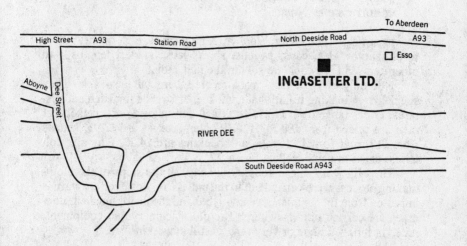

BANCHORY

High Street   A93   Station Road   North Deeside Road   A93

To Aberdeen

Aboyne   Dee Street

☐ Esso

INGASETTER LTD.

RIVER DEE

South Deeside Road A943

BLAIRGOWRIE   *Woolen Products*

Moffat Weavers
20 Wellmeadow
Blairgowrie, Perthshire PH10 6AS, Scotland
Tel. 382-3463

HOURS: Monday–Saturday 9:00–5:30; Monday–Sunday (Easter until October) 8:00–5:30

See the write-up for Moffat Woollens Limited in the town of MOFFAT.

LOCATION: Blairgowrie is in central Scotland 16 miles north of Perth on the A93.

BRIDGEND, ISLE OF ISLAY   *Woolen Items*

The Islay Woollen Mill Co. Ltd.
Bridgend, Isle of Islay
Argyll PA44 7PJ, Scotland
Tel. 049681-563

HOURS: Monday–Saturday 10:00–6:00
CREDIT CARDS: None

PRODUCTS: The Islay Woollen Mill weaves high-quality 100% wool scarves, ties, caps, tweeds, sports jackets, skirt lengths, and other items, all of which are sold in the mill shop.

Not only is pure new wool created here but also silk. They specialize in making traditional gamekeeper tweeds for Highland Estates. Prices range from £13.75 to £19.50 per meter. Sports jackets for men are priced from £80 to £120. Woolen scarves are £3.95, shawls from £17, rugs for £16 to £25, and neckties are £4.20. Pure silk collarless shirts are an excellent buy at £35.

The Mill was built in 1883. Originally, all the steps of the cloth-making process were carried out in the mill. Now, however, the yarn is imported from the mainland, ready-dyed, and the major finished processes are carried out elsewhere. The old machinery and equipment, much of it now unique or very rare, is still in working order.

TOURS: Visitors are welcome to look around the premises.

LOCATION: The Isle of Islay is about 60 miles due west of Glasgow. Bridgend is in the central part of the island. The Woollen Mill is about 1½ miles north of Bridgend on the A846. Watch for a sign directing you to turn east. Follow the lane about 200 yards.

BRIDGE OF MARNOCH, NEAR HUNTLY   *Wool Products*

Coleman-Chambers Weavers (craft workshop)
Hazelbrae House
Bridge of Marnoch, Aberdeenshire AB5 5RL, Scotland
Tel. 046 683-252

HOURS: Monday–Saturday 9:30–6:00; other times open by appointment

CREDIT CARDS: None

PRODUCTS: You will find handwoven tweeds created out of pure Scottish wool for sale at this country workshop. The tweeds are sold in skirt lengths, or made into hats, caps, scarves, rugs, and ties. Skirt lengths are from £10, hats and caps from £15, scarves from £3, and ties from £3.50. Demonstrations of handweaving are given every Monday through Friday at 10:30. There is a slight charge for large group demonstrations, which should be arranged in advance. They will ship your items for you if you wish. A residential weaving course very popular with Americans is taught. The £25 per day includes tuition, accommodation, and full board. Definitely a bargain for anyone interested in learning the art of weaving! Also available are watercolors by J. Michael Chambers.

LOCATION: From Aberdeen in the northeast of Scotland, take the A96 road northwest to Huntly (about 38 miles). Then go north on the A97 10 miles. The Coleman-Chambers Weavers is on the right just after you cross the River Deveron. See the map below.

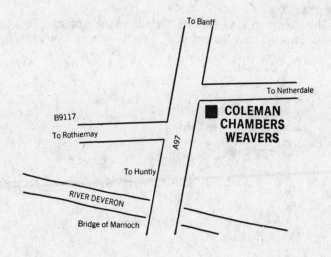

BRIDGE OF WEIR   *Soft Toys*

Dormouse Designs
Toy Design Workshop "The Store"
Quarriers Village, By Bridge of Weir
Renfrewshire PA11 2SX, Scotland
Tel. 0505-690435

HOURS: Monday–Friday 10:00–4:00
CREDIT CARDS: None

PRODUCTS: Sue Quinn has a small workshop where she makes small detailed soft animals, many with darling clothing. Her bunnies with tiny carrots are delightful. In 1984 she was awarded the Toymaker of the Year award by the British Toymakers Guild.

Biddy and Bud are tiny jointed squirrels made in woven fur fabric. Each is fully clothed and holding a tiny leather bag. They sell for £20 each. Teddy bear is very traditional and jointed and sells for £20. Jointed hare is in complete school uniform and sells for £48. Hand puppets (dog, rabbit, and hedgehog), all with distinct personalities, are £6.90 each. Habbie Hedgehog is holding a sack of leaves and is cute as a bug at £5.40.

The store is in the Quarriers Village, which is an excellent collection of Victorian architecture in a beautiful setting. Founded by Wil-

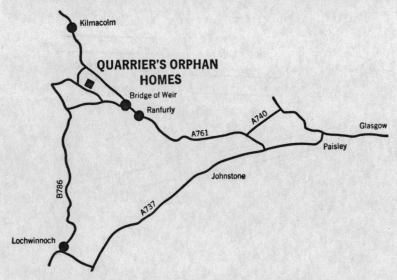

liam Quarrier, it was originally a home for orphans. Now several small businesses have workshops in the buildings.

LOCATION: Bridge of Weir is in central Scotland toward the western coast, about 10 miles west of Glasgow on the A761. Quarrier's Village is about 1½ miles further west. On your map it may be labeled Quarrier's Orphan Homes. Dormouse Designs occupies the old Drapery, above the village shop, which is the third building on the right through the main gate of the village.

BROADFORD, ISLE OF SKYE   *Knitwear*

Skye Crotal Knitwear Mill Shop (factory outlet)
Broadford, Isle of Skye IV43 8QR, Scotland
Tel. 04712-529

HOURS: April–October: Monday–Friday 9:00–5:00; Saturday 9:30–4:00
CREDIT CARDS: Access, MasterCard, Visa

PRODUCTS: This shop sells 100% pure wool knitwear manufactured by their knitters. Their specialty is sweaters ranging from traditional oiled fishermen's sweaters in Harris wool to modern picture jacquard knits. Hats, scarves, and tweed skirt lengths are also sold. Retail prices vary from £18 to £40 per sweater. Seconds are often available for £10. There is usually a sale during the month of October.

Three types of wool are used at the mill: Shetland, Harris, and Gotland. Shetland wool is universally known. Harris is rough but very warm and hard-wearing; ideal for outdoor use. Gotland wool is a soft, silky wool from Swedish sheep now being reared in Skye.

All of the sweaters may also be made from lambswool by special request.

There is a wide color range on the sweaters—naturals, blues, greens, berrys, whites, grays, and browns. They will ship sweaters anywhere in the world, or make any sweater to order for mailing later at very little extra cost.

MAIL ORDER: Visitors may leave their names and addresses to receive their informative winter mail-order brochure each year by which you may order the color and the style of sweater you wish. All orders do take from four to ten weeks. The company's mail order address is: Skye Crotal Knitwear, Camus Chros, Isle of Skye IV43 8QR, Scotland.

TOURS: Visitors may tour the factory and see the sweaters being knitted. There is an adjoining coffee room featuring home baked goods.

LOCATION: The Isle of Skye is off the northwest coast of Scotland. Broadford is in the southern part of the island about eight miles west of Kyle of Lochalsh on the A850 road. The mill shop is in the middle of town on the left as you go north by the river.

CALLANDER *Woolen Items*

Kilmahog Woollen Mill
Callander, Perthshire FK17 8HB, Scotland
Tel. 0877-30268

HOURS: Monday–Saturday 9:00–5:30; Monday–Sunday (Easter until October) 9:00–5:30

Also: Moffat Weavers
38 Main Street
Calander, Perthshire, Scotland
Tel. 0877-30921

See the write-up for Moffat Woollens Limited in the town of MOFFAT.

LOCATION: Callander is in central Scotland 15 miles northwest of Stirling on the A84 road.

CREETOWN *Jewelry, Silverware*

Creetown Gold and Silversmith Workshops (craft workshop)
93 St. John's Street

Creetown via Newton Stewart, Wigtownshire DG8 7JE,
  Scotland
Tel. 067-182-396

HOURS: Monday–Saturday 9:00–5:00
CREDIT CARDS: None

PRODUCTS: John Prince studied silversmithing at Manchester
College of Art and has received numerous awards for his work. Gold
and silver jewelry and silverware are made on the premises at
Creetown Gold and Silversmithing Workshops. Jewelry made by various Scottish craftspeople is also sold. Silver charms sell from £3, and
gold and larger silver items are in the £100 price range. He will mail
purchases for visitors.

TOURS: Any time by appointment. Explanatory talk about materials, machinery, and procedures in the workshop lasts about an hour.
Maximum group size is 12 persons with a 50 pence charge per person.

LOCATION: Creetown is on the southwestern coast of Scotland
eight miles southeast of Newton Stewart on the A75. See the map
below.

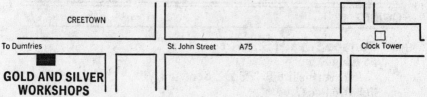

CRIEFF   *Hand-Painted Pottery*

A. W. Buchan and Co. Ltd. (factory/showroom)
Thistle Potteries
Muthill Road
Crieff, Perthshire PH7 4AZ, Scotland
Tel. 0764-3515

HOURS: April to December: Monday–Friday 9:30–5:00; Saturday
     10:00–5:00; Sunday 10:00–5:00. Closed Christmas Eve
     until January 1.
CREDIT CARDS: Access, Visa

PRODUCTS: Thistle Potteries is a company which still uses hand painting on all of its products. The pieces are all decorated with thistle, heather, or bluebell Scottish flowers. Each piece is initialed by the artist, and subtle color variations are achieved through a difference in reaction of the paint during firing. Thistle Pottery is chip resistant and dishwasher safe. They have a very complete line of place settings, coffee and tea sets, unusual serving pieces with elegant shapes, accessories and pitchers. The factory only sells second-quality items at very low prices from £1.50 for tiny vases, up to £25 for large bowls. They have a yearly seasonal sale around Christmas. Highly recommended.

TOURS: Factory tours are given Monday to Thursday from 10:15–11:30 and 1:30–4:00, and on Friday mornings only from 10:15–11:30. Tours last about 15 minutes. Coach tours are welcome if prior notice is given.

LOCATION: Crieff is northwest of Edinburgh, about 15 miles west of Perth on the A85 road. The factory is just south of town on the west side of the A822 road toward Muthill.

CRIEFF   *Sweaters*

Dorraga Sweater Shop (retail shop)
55 King Street
Crieff, Perthshire PH7 3AX, Scotland
Tel. 0764-4647

HOURS: Monday–Tuesday 9:30–5:00; Thursday–Sunday 9:30–5:00. Winter: closed on Sundays.
CREDIT CARDS: American Express, Visa

PRODUCTS: Dorothy Smith designs sweaters which she sells at her shop. She creates hand-knit and hand-loomed sweaters made from 100% wool, mohair, Shetland, lambswool, or cashmere. The sweaters range in price from £20 to £100 depending on the design, complexity, and the type of wool used. Seconds are carried. Special orders can be taken for those who would like special colors or styles. Garments will be shipped home for customers. Visitors will also find other designer sweaters—Bill Baber, Margaret Hund, Sally's Woollies, Ganzies, David Scott Designs, and Ardfern Knitwear.

LOCATION: Crieff is northwest of Edinburgh, about 15 miles west of Perth on the A85 road. Coming from Perth, turn left onto King Street at James Square (a parking area). This is just before the Tourist Information Office. The shop is on the right, at the corner of King Street and Commissioner Street.

CRIEFF   *Distillery*

Glenturret Distillery
Crieff, Perthshire PH7 4HA, Scotland
Tel. 0764-2424

HOURS: March–October: Monday–Friday 10:00–12:30 and 1:30–4:00; July–August: Monday–Saturday 9:45–4:30; November–February: Monday–Saturday 2:00–4:00
CREDIT CARDS: None

PRODUCTS: Glenturret makes an excellent malt Scotch whisky, which is world renowned. They are Scotland's oldest working distillery, established in 1775. At the retail shop you may purchase the malt whisky as well as decanters, glasses, flasks, and various souvenir items. The Glenturret Pure Single Highland Malt Scotch Whisky is 86° proof. An eight-year-old bottle is £11.99, a twelve-year-old bottle £13.99, and a fifteen-year-old bottle is £16.49. Miniature bottles of Scotch are sold for between £1.15 and £1.75 each.

TOURS: A 15-minute movie is presented which gives the history of whisky and the Glenturret Distillery. A free guided tour is given. A free tasting dram of the Glenturret eight-year-old-Scotch whisky is given to each visitor taking a tour. An exhibition museum is attached to the building. The last tour is 30 minutes before closing.

LOCATION: Crieff is northwest of Edinburgh, about 15 miles west of Perth on the A85 road. From Crieff take the A85 toward Comrie/Lochearnhead for ¾ mile. Turn right at the crossroads (where you will see a Glenturret Distillery sign) toward Monzie and Loch Turret. The distillery is ¼ mile down the road.

CRIEFF	Glass, Paperweights

Perthshire Paperweights Ltd. (factory/showroom)
Muthill Road
Crieff, Perthshire PH7 4AZ, Scotland
Tel. 0764-2409

HOURS: Monday–Friday 9:00–12:30 and 1:00–4:00
CREDIT CARDS: Access, MasterCard, Visa

PRODUCTS: Glass paperweights have their origin in the mid-nineteenth century where the most famous were created in the three French factories of Baccarat, Clichy, and Saint Louis. Today, Perthshire Paperweights has recreated this art form in limited editions. They are elegant collectors' items with unique and fascinating designs which can only be seen to be appreciated. A few inkwells and perfume bottles have also been designed by their talented staff. The items are priced between £7.50 and £200, and no seconds are available. They do not want prices on specific items listed.

TOURS: Tours are not practical except for small groups by prior appointment.

LOCATION: Crieff is northwest of Edinburgh, about 15 miles west of Perth on the A85 road. The factory is just south of town on the A822 road toward Muthill.

CRIEFF	Crystal

Stuart Strathearn Limited (factory/showroom)
Muthill Road
Crieff, Perthshire PH7 4HQ, Scotland
Tel. 0764-2942

HOURS: Seconds Shop: Monday–Saturday 9:00–5:00; Sunday 12:00–5:00 (June to September till 5:30)
Factory: Monday–Friday 8:00–12:00 and 12:45–4:30
CREDIT CARDS: Access, American Express, Diners Club, MasterCard, Visa

PRODUCTS: Stuart Strathearn produces an extensive selection of crystal giftware, including vases, decanters, beer mugs, and whisky tumblers. The etched crystal is beautiful. The quality and design of their items are exceptional. Second-quality items are available at their shop. Small five-inch vases start at £7.95, medium oval vases are £12.50, and large oval vases start at £37.50. A whisky decanter is £34.95 and many have matching glasses. Rum glasses start at £6.95 each. Highly recommended!

There is a picnic area and a children's playground in front of the factory.

TOURS: A video is available for visitors to see how handmade crystal is produced. You can also walk through the factory, which has signs explaining the process. A demonstration is usually given by a craftsworker.

LOCATION: Crieff is about 15 miles west of Perth on the A85 road. Upon entering Crieff, turn south on the A822 road toward Muthill. Stuart Strathearn is just south of Crieff.

CULLODEN   *Wool Clothing, Scottish Crafts*

Clan Royal (retail store)
Battlefield Site, Keppoch Inn
Culloden, Inverness, Scotland
Tel. 0463-792615

HOURS: Monday–Saturday 9:00–5:30

See the write-up under EDINBURGH.

LOCATION: From Inverness in northern Scotland, take an unnumbered road east across the A9 about four miles to the Culloden National Trust Battlefield.

DENHOLM   *Sweaters*

The Mill Shop
Main Street
Denholm, Borders, Scotland
Tel. 0450-87-531

HOURS: Monday–Saturday 9:00–4:30
CREDIT CARDS: None

PRODUCTS: Cashmere, lambswool, and Shetland wool sweaters
for men, women, and children are sold at this tiny shop. Allegedly, all
of the products are made in their own factory and therefore their prices
are lower. Lambswool sweaters started at £16.99 and Shetland sweaters at £15.99.

LOCATION: Denholm is in southern Scotland, five miles north of
Hawick on the A698.

DRUMCHARDINE   *Toiletries*

Highland Aromatics, Ltd. (factory outlet)
Drumchardine, Kirkhill, Inverness Shire IV5 7PX, Scotland
Tel. 0463-83-625

HOURS: Monday–Friday 10:00–4:00
CREDIT CARDS: None

PRODUCTS: Highland Aromatics originated after Nan McDougall
studied plants and perfumes and blended a variety of wildflowers and
plants growing naturally in the Highlands of Scotland into soaps. A
local village church that seemed ideal for her work was offered for
sale. During the summer of 1975, while the church was refurbished, all
the ingredients she proposed to use were tested by experts in the field
of perfumery and skin care. That autumn, production of small batches
of hand-finished soaps had begun.
Highland Aromatics is still located in the former church in Drumchardine. Today they manufacture soaps, herb pillows, talcum pow-
ders and perfumes, and have a retail outlet located on the factory

premises. They also sell Cairngorm Perfume, and a range of decorated porcelain soap pots.

The soaps sell for £1.30. Prices are slightly higher for soaps in cotton or satin bags. Herb pillows are £1.20, and perfume sachets are £1.

TOURS: Visitors may watch soaps being made during regular hours. Maximum group size is 50. Please make arrangements in advance for groups over 10.

LOCATION: Drumchardine is in northern Scotland on the A9 road seven miles west of Inverness.

DUFFTOWN   *Distillery*

The Glenfiddich Distillery
Dufftown, Scotland
Tel. 0340-20375

HOURS: Monday–Friday 9:30–4:30 all year
Saturday 9:30–4:30; Sunday 12:00–4:30 May 26 to September 30; closed from December 24 to January 6.
CREDIT CARDS: None

PRODUCTS: The Glenfiddich Distillery was founded in 1887 and makes wonderful Scotch. It is the only distillery where malt whisky is bottled. They did not wish to advertise their Scotch prices.

TOUR: Visitors can view the entire process of brewing from the barley to the bottle. Each visitor is given a dram to taste. In the theater (in six different languages) the history of Scotland and whisky and its heritage is traced. Large groups must make arrangements in advance.

LOCATION: Dufftown is in northern Scotland. It is about 17 miles southeast of the town of Elgin on the A941. The distillery is on the north side of Balvenie castle on the northern outskirts of Dufftown.

DUNBAR   *Wool Clothing, Scottish Crafts*

Clan Royal (retail store)
53 High Street
Dunbar, East Lothian, Scotland
Tel. 0368-63734

HOURS: Monday–Saturday 9:00–5:30

See the write-up under EDINBURGH.

LOCATION: Dunbar is 28 miles east of Edinburgh on the A1 road.

DUMFRIES   *Sweaters*

Drumohr Knitwear Millshop
Robertsons of Dumfries
Balmoral Road
Dumfries, Scotland
Tel. 55413

HOURS: Monday–Saturday 10:00–4:00
CREDIT CARDS: Access, American Express, Diners Club, Visa

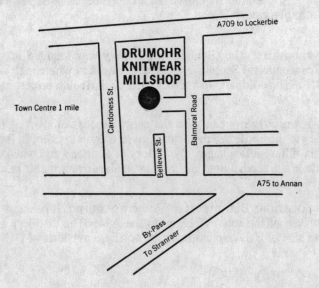

PRODUCTS: Drumohr Knitwear makes a wide variety of men's and women's sweaters. The sweaters are of first and second quality with a large percentage being Shetland wool, cashmere, camel hair, or lambswool. A cashmere sweater as a second was selling for £17.50. They have a good selection of quality sweaters.

LOCATION: Dumfries is in the south of Scotland just across the border. As you enter town from the south on the A75 road, go through the first roundabout, then take the first right turn onto Balmoral Road. The mill shop is halfway down the block on the left. See the map.

DUNKELD   *Deerskin Products*

Jeremy Law (Scotland) Ltd. (workshop/showroom)
City Hall, Atholl Street
Dunkeld, Perthshire PH8 OAR, Scotland
Tel. 03502-569

HOURS: April to October: Monday–Sunday 8:00–5:00; November to March: Monday–Friday 8:00–5:00.
CREDIT CARDS: None

PRODUCTS: Jeremy Law is a deerskin leather workshop with handcrafted leathergoods. Most of the items are designed and made in the Highlands. All of the deerskin handbags, wallets, and purses have clasps and fastenings fashioned from hand-polished staghorn. Also available are deerskin belts, mittens, slippers, gloves, sheepskin coats, horn-trimmed walking sticks, cutlery, and tableware. Jewelry pouches, key cases, tobacco pouches, eyeglass cases, pencil holders, and passport cases are created out of elegant deerskin. The quality found at this family-owned business is superb!

Prices cover a wide range. A fully lined shoulder handbag with two smaller compartments is £35.50. A fully-lined classic handbag with two small handles and four smaller compartments is £43. A passport case with an outer pocket for airline tickets is £8. A ladies wallet purse fully leather lined and with three compartments is £10.50. Deerskin gloves, tanned and finished to perfection, were £19.50 per pair. A carving set in stainless steel with staghorn handles included a carver, fork (with guard) plus sharpening steel packed in a velvet- and silk-lined box for £33. An exceptional buy! This shop will complete the paperwork necessary for a VAT refund. Seconds and rejects are always available at a real savings.

MAIL ORDER: Jeremy Law will mail order their products. They have an excellent, well-organized brochure. An explanation for sizing gloves is included. Please remember to order very early for Christmas, as each item is handcrafted, and this is a small family business.

TOURS: All visitors are welcome to watch the manufacturing process from the showroom. Fifteen-minute guided tours are available if arrangements are made in advance.

LOCATION: Dunkeld is in central Scotland about 14 miles north of Perth on the A9 road. See the map below.

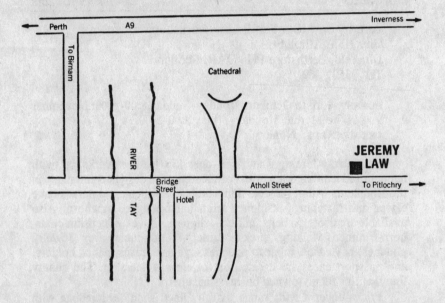

DUNOON   *White Heather, Plants, Gifts*

The Scottish White Heather Farm (factory outlet)
Toward, Dunoon, Argyllshire PA23 7UA, Scotland
Tel. 036-987-237

HOURS: Monday–Friday 9:00–5:00. Visitors coming from a distance are advised to phone beforehand.

CREDIT CARDS: None

PRODUCTS: The Scottish White Heather Farm offers visitors an old Celtic tale: "The story of the white heather is an old, old tale and a sad one. The Celtic Bard Ossian had a daughter, Malvina, who was as fair as the dawn and gentle as the dew. She was betrothed to Oscar, a warrior as gallant as he was handsome. Though he had wandered far in search of fame and beauty, no one held chief place in his heart save Malvina the fair.

"Once in the glory of autumn, Malvina and her father were sitting on the moor's edge talking of Oscar's return from some warlike expedition. Over the heather came limping to them a ragged messenger. Wounded and weary he knelt before them. Holding out a spray of purple heather to Malvina, he told her that it came from Oscar as a last token of his love for he was slain in battle and his henchmen had barely escaped to bring the news.

"As Malvina listened, her tears fell on the purple heather which immediately became white.

"Ossian made mournful music for his daughter's dead lover and, as they wandered over the moors, her tears often fell upon the clumps of purple heather which immediately turned white. Then, even in the bitterness of her own sorrow, wishing that others may be happier than she, Malvina said, 'Although it is the symbol of my sorrow, may the white heather bring good fortune to all who find it.'"

The Scottish White Heather Farm wants you to have good fortune and sells white heather horseshoes and sprays, white heather plants, colored heathers and conifers. They also sell paperweights and key rings made with white heather preserved in resin that are decorated with various tartan designs. White heather buttonhole sprigs sell six for £4.50, paperweights are £4, and key rings cost £1.

TOURS: Visitors are welcome to enjoy the extensive gardens.

LOCATION: Dunoon is in western Scotland across the Firth of Clyde from Greenock. From Dunoon take the A815 south about five miles just past the town of Innellan. Watch for the sign and the car park at the side of the road.

EAST KILBRIDE   *Bagpipes and Accessories*

Grainger and Campbell Ltd. (factory outlet)
42 Westgarth Place
College Milton North, East Kilbride
Glasgow G74 5NT, Scotland
Tel. East Kilbride 46516

HOURS: Monday–Friday 9:00–5:00
CREDIT CARDS: Barclaycard, Visa

PRODUCTS: This company manufactures and sells Highland bagpipes, Scottish small bagpipes, chanters, reeds, pipe bags, bag covers,
ribbons, seasoning, and pipe cases. They sell a Bagpipe Tutor Kit,
which consists of a practice chanter made from African Blackwood,
and a reed, a tape, and a tutor book. Bagpipes are priced from £345 to
£360, practice chanters range from £27.50 to £44.95, practice chanter
tutor kits from £39.95, pipe gabs from £30, and pipe chanter reeds run
£1.95. They will ship goods to the U.S. and Canada.

LOCATION: East Kilbride is about five miles southeast of Glasgow
on the A749 road. To reach the shop, head out from Glasgow to Clark-
ston, then pass through Busby which takes you on to the dual carriageway to East Kilbride. You will pass the Philipshill Hospital on the right
side. Keep on the left side of the carriageway and you will approach a
sign marked "College Milton." Turn left onto Glenburn Road. Turn at
the second left marked "Westgarth Place." Keep going right around
Westgarth Place until you come to a cul de sac. Grainger and Campbell's premises are at the end of the cul de sac.

EDINBURGH   *Sweaters*

Canongate Jerseys (factory outlet-retail shop)
166 Canongate
Edinburgh EH1 1SR, Scotland
Tel. 557-2967

HOURS: Monday–Saturday 10:00–5:30; open Sunday during Edin-
        burgh Festival
CREDIT CARDS: American Express, Visa

BEST BUYS IN SCOTLAND / 317

PRODUCTS: At this small shop three people sell sweaters mainly made of Shetland wool. They make the sweaters and mark them up slightly over wholesale. Seconds are carried occasionally. Prices range from £10 to £50. Fair Isle crew neck sweaters are priced from £33 while vests are priced from £27. Hats, scarves, and leg warmers are priced between £6 and £15. Some children's wear is carried. Both traditional and current sweater styles are sold.

LOCATION: From the castle, go east down High Street toward Holyrood Palace. High Street becomes Canongate. The shop is on the south side of the street across from the Old Toll Booth.

EDINBURGH   *Woolen Items*

Clan Royal (retail store)
449 Lawnmarket
Edinburgh, Lothian, Scotland
Tel. 031-2265366

Also at:
134C Princess Street
Edinburgh, Lothian, Scotland
Tel. 031-225-2319

HOURS: Monday–Saturday 9:00–5:30; Sunday (this store only) 11:30–4:00
CREDIT CARDS: Access, American Express, Diners Club, Visa

PRODUCTS: In this well organized shop, visitors will find all types of woolen items at reasonable prices: sweaters, blankets, kilts, and blazers. The prices are much lower than in similar stores. Please note that this is one of a chain of stores. A complete list of the stores can be found under CHAIN STORES in the front of this book.

LOCATION: The shop is just east of the entrance to Edinburgh Castle. Lawnmarket Street leads directly to the Castle.

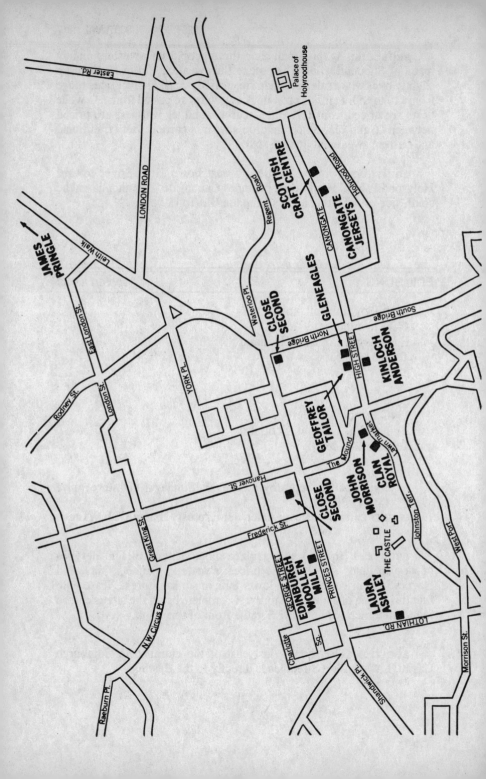

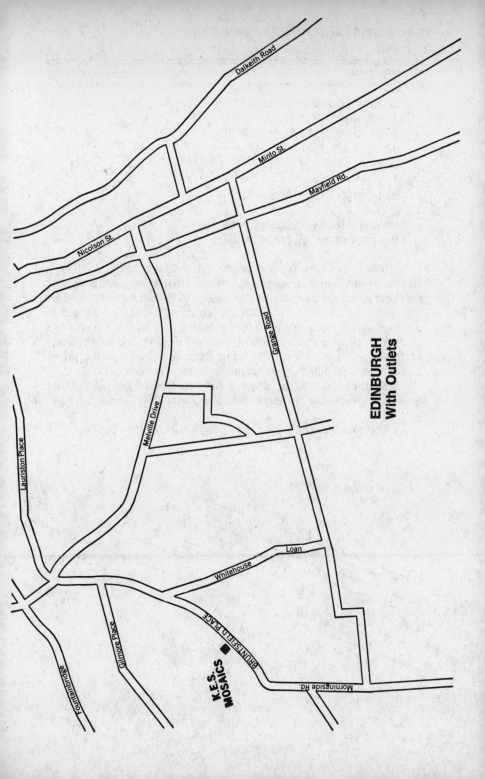

EDINBURGH
With Outlets

Dalkeith Road

Minto St.

Mayfield Rd.

Nicolson St.

Grange Road

Melville Drive

Lauriston Place

Loan

Whitehouse

Fountainbridge

Gilmore Place

BRUNSFIELD PLACE

K.E.S.
MOSAICS

Morningside Rd.

EDINBURGH
Knitwear, Crystal

Close Second (retail shop)
108 A Rose Street
Edinburgh EH2 3JF, Scotland
Tel. 031-225-5551
Also at:
10 North Bridge
Edinburgh EH2 3JF, Scotland

HOURS: Monday–Saturday 9:00–5:00
CREDIT CARDS: All credit cards

PRODUCTS: Close Second, which is a small shop, sells Edinburgh Crystal seconds at a great savings. They also sell slightly imperfect knitwear garments at a substantial savings. The majority of the items are half price or less. All of the merchandise for sale is knitted in Scotland by world-famous producers (a few Fair Isle and Irish knits also). You will also find available discontinued colors and styles. Some perfect stock is also sold. The shop will not release specific prices since the merchandise varies according to what is available.

All purchases will be shipped for you free of the VAT. Close Second is a subsidiary of the well-known Tartan Gift Shops.

LOCATION: For the locations in Edinburgh, see the map below.

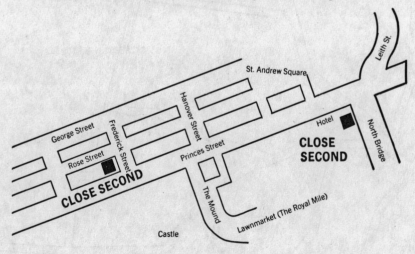

EDINBURGH   *Highland Press*

Geoffrey (Tailor) Highland Crafts Ltd.
(retail shop/manufacturer)
57–59 High Street
The Royal Mile
Edinburgh EH1 1SR, Scotland
Tel. 031-557-0256

HOURS: Monday–Saturday 9:00–5:30; Sunday 10:00–5:00
CREDIT CARDS: Access, American Express, Barclaycard, Diners
Club

PRODUCTS: Geoffrey (Tailor) Highland Crafts Ltd. is a retail shop
that manufactures many of their own Highland dress products. They
sell clothing for men, women, and children. They specialize in selling
Highland dress for bands. The 15% VAT is deducted from all sales
over £20. All materials used in kiltmaking are 100% pure wool. All
tartans are not available in all qualities of wool. If you do not know the
name of the tartan you want, please request the color combinations.
There are literally hundreds of different tartans available. If groups
order kilts or any other items, quantity discounts are available. A good
selection of woolen sweaters and rugs are also sold as well as souvenir
gift items.

All prices quoted include the 15% VAT. Postage, packing, and
insurance are of course extra. Dress kilts for men made from seven
yards of fabric range from £87.95 to £153.95. Kilt jackets run from
£85.95 to £102.95. Tartan sports jackets are priced from £123.95 to
£141.95. Tartan slacks, which are great for golfing, are priced between
£51.95 and £62.96. Kilted skirts for women with three yards of fabric
are priced from £38.95 to £69.95. A velvet kilt jacket runs £102.95. An
A-line woman's evening skirt starts at £51.95. A child's kilt with four
yards of fabric will cost about £47.80.

MAIL ORDERS: This company specializes in mail orders. They
have a very complete booklet with mail ordering information, measuring instructions, and payment requirements. Overseas customers are
not charged the 15% VAT. You will find budget and executive Highland
Dress. Extra large sizes can be made for men and women with a slight
increase in cost. A fun way to shop for authentic Scottish dress from
the comfort of your own home.

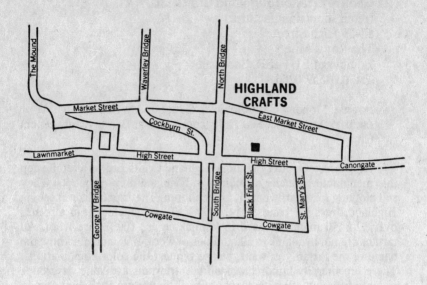

EDINBURGH

Woolen Items

Gleneagles of Scotland
371 High Street
Edinburgh EH1 1PW, Scotland
Tel. 031-557-1777

HOURS: Monday–Saturday 9:00–5:30; Monday–Sunday (Easter
until October) 9:00–5:30

See the write-up for Moffat Woollens Limited in the town of
MOFFAT.

LOCATION: From the castle, go east down Lawnmarket, which
becomes High Street.

EDINBURGH *Woolen Products*

James Pringle Woollen Mill and Clan Tartan Centre
70-74 Bangor Road
Leith, Edinburgh EH6 5JV, Scotland
Tel. 031-553-5100

HOURS: January–May: Monday–Saturday 9:00–5:30; November–
December: Sunday 10:00–5:30; June–October: Monday–
Saturday 9:00–6:00, Sunday 10:00–6:00
CREDIT CARDS: Access, American Express, Visa

PRODUCT: The *Clan Tartan Centre* was created in response to the
worldwide interest of people of Scottish descent in tracing their ances-
try. Today an archive computer is presented with your surname. It
takes seconds to search five million units of information before it
prints out your official certificate detailing any clan connection, with
its chief, origins, heraldic crest, plant badge, warcry, tartan, and other
historic information. You will also be able to see a free audiovisual
presentation which shows the history and the development of the tartan. A fun place to visit before you buy your tartans!

The *Woollen Mill* produces a large variety of top-quality woolen
items. In the mill shop there is a comprehensive range of Scottish
knitwear including cashmere, lambswool, and Shetland. Ladies' coats
and skirts, gentlemen's sports jackets and trousers, and an endless
range of travel rugs, knee rugs, shawls, socks, tartan and tweed ties,
tartan and tweed scarves, wooly mufflers, tweed hats, tam o'shanters,
Fair Isle caps and mitts, wool gloves, sheepskin rugs, knitting wool,
and wool packs are all found at mill prices. Highly recommended! It is
the largest outlet with the largest selection of any we visited.

Cashmere sweaters are found for men and women in every color
of the rainbow with prices starting at £50. There was a huge selection
of Shetland sweaters with both crew and V-necks starting at £9.95.
Soft lambswool sweaters in muted or traditional colors started at
£15.75. Mohair knitwear started at £25 and lovely Aran sweaters were
priced from £27.50. Men's sports coats started at £52.95, and tartan
slacks at £59.95. Tartan travel rugs were abundant and priced from
£8.95. Thick and luxurious sheepskin rugs started at £25.

If you only want to make one stop for woolen products in Scotland, this one outlet may be your best bet.

LOCATION: Northeast part of Edinburgh. See the map below.

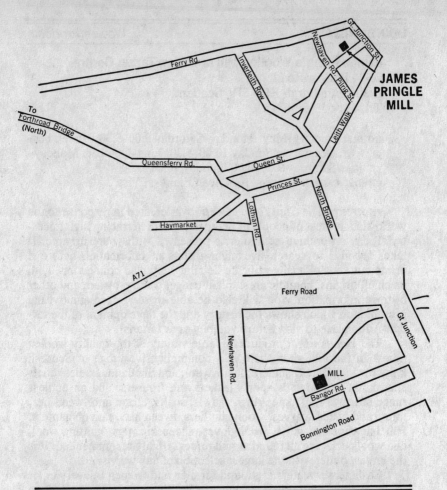

EDINBURGH   *Woolen Items*

John Morrison (Highland Outfitters) Ltd. (retail shop)
461 Lawnmarket
Edinburgh EH1 2NT, Scotland
Tel. 031-225-8149

HOURS: Monday–Saturday 9:00–5:00; April to September, Sundays 11:00–5:00.
CREDIT CARDS: Access, American Express, Barclaycard, Diners Club, Visa

PRODUCTS: John Morrison Ltd. is a retail shop which specializes in high-quality woolen items. Full Highland dress for ladies and gentlemen in all styles and colors of tartans are sold. Ladies' kilted skirts with all of the matching accessories—cardigans and pullovers in cashmere, lambswool, and pure virgin wool, and tartan material, Saxony and worsted wool, line the walls waiting to be taken home. Tartan rugs, scarves, and stoles are available in plaids, cashmeres, lambswool, and pure new wool. Miscellaneous souvenir items are also available. Men's regulation hand-tailored kilts range in price from £85 to £185. Women's kilted skirts are available in a wide range of tartans, tweeds, and cashmeres from £28. Ladies' kilts in all types of wool plaids start at £60. Men's and women's wool sweaters begin at £21. Silver kilt pins are priced from £17.50 while skean dhus (stocking daggers) start at £20. An enjoyable place to be outfitted from head to toe in the traditional Scottish dress.

MAIL ORDERS: They have a mail order service available which ships all over the world.

LOCATION: Lawnmarket is part of the Royal Mile which stretches from Edinburgh Castle to Holyrood Palace. The shop is on the left descending from the castle to the palace.

EDINBURGH   *Art, Craftwork*

K.E.S. Mosaics Studio Gallery (craft centre)
43 Bruntsfield Place
Edinburgh EH10 4HJ, Scotland
Tel. 031-229-6464

HOURS: Monday–Friday 9:30–5:30
CREDIT CARDS: Access, American Express, Diners Club, Visa

PRODUCTS: This craft centre features permanent and special exhibitions of fine art and artist's craftwork. They sell crystal ornaments and jewelry, paintings, sculpture, tapestry, pottery, glass, and mosaics made by Scottish craftsmen.

A unique type of mosaic by Katherine Steele is made from old wooden type blocks which are transformed into mosaic tables, lamps, ornamental boxes, and wall panels. Wall hanging blocks are priced from £21. Boxes range from £80 to £125. Lamps range from £39 to £89. Tables are priced from £300. Crystal jewelry starts at £3.

They hold seasonal sales periodically and are willing to ship goods overseas.

LOCATION: Southwest of the Edinburgh city center. See the map below.

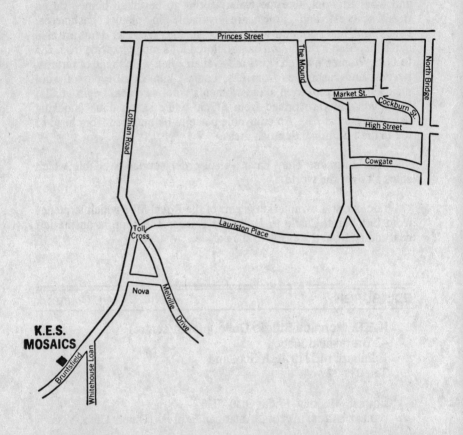

EDINBURGH   *Kiltwear*

Kinloch Anderson Ltd. (retail store)
John Knox House
45 High Street
Edinburgh EH1 1SR, Scotland
Tel. 031-556-6961

HOURS: Monday–Saturday 9:00–5:30
CREDIT CARDS: Access, American Express, Barclaycard, Diners Club, Eurocard, MasterCard, Visa

PRODUCTS: Kinloch Anderson is synonymous with the best in Highland dress. It is a firm of Scottish tailors and outfitters who have built up a reputation of supreme craftsmanship in the making of kilts, coats, and accessories for over 100 years. Their modern workshops are in Edinburgh.

Kinloch Anderson will coordinate your entire Scottish outfit with expertise. They'll advise you about which tartans are to be worn in the evening, the correct sash, the jacket, the pin, etc. They dress His Royal Highness the Duke of Edinburgh and His Royal Highness the Prince of Wales, so you know you are in the best of hands.

The kilt is the focal point of the outfit. Worsted tartans make the finest kilts for men, as the material takes and holds pleats better. Each kilt takes seven to eight yards of fabric. All of the kilts come with a traditional blanket kilt pin. (For people on a lower budget, the Lochan kilt has been designed to give the appearance of a full kilt, but less yardage is used.)

For day wear, a complete outfit consists of the kilt, tweed jacket or sweater, leather sporran and strap, hose, and tweed tie to blend with the jacket, garters and flashes and Brogue shoes. For evening wear, the kilt should be made from material in a lighter texture.

Kinloch Anderson sells the coat and vest, the Argyll jacket, kilt stockings, shoes, garters, traditional bonnets (the Balmoral and the Glengarry), the Sporran, and the Skean Dhu (Black Knife). Sash brooches are available with citrine, smoky topaz, amethyst or agate stones. Kilt pins are offered in sterling silver with citrine, smoky topaz, or amethyst stones.

Skirts, sweaters, blazers, hats, and scarves are sold in women's wear.

Ladies' kilted skirts range from £53 to £77. A kilted skirt in a maxi-length will cost about £98 in a worsted wool. Sweaters in lambswool and Shetland wool ranged from £25 to £30. A plain jacket in dark gray with a waistcoat was £147. Kilts for boys in a fine Saxony tartan begin at £57. Kilt pins range from £5.75 for a pewter pin to £49.50 for a Celtic pin with a large stone. Skean dhus are priced from £20 for one which has a carved handle with a brass mount to £183 for an engraved silver one. Kilts for men range from £100 for a standard kilt in Saxony cloth to £195 for a custommade kilt in worsted cloth. Fine Saxony wool in over 360 tartans sells for £15 per meter. Medium worsted wool sells for £18.50 per meter.

Highland dress for men, women, teenagers, and children is sold all year long. An excellent selection and superb quality!

MAIL ORDER: Kinloch Anderson has a mail order division. Exact instructions are included on measuring for your kilts, jackets, or skirts. The brochure *Tartans and Highland Dress* is excellent for those people unsure of what items to purchase.

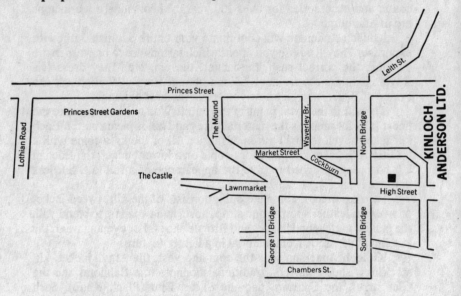

EDINBURGH   *Women's and Children's Clothing*

Laura Ashley Bargain Shop
43/45 Lothian Road
Edinburgh, Lothian, Scotland
Tel. 031-229-5135

HOURS: Monday–Friday 9:30–5:30; Saturday 9:00–5:00
CREDIT CARDS: Access, Visa

PRODUCTS: Laura Ashley's clothing has a feminine, nostalgic look with full skirts, smocks, and dresses in tiny floral prints and lace.

At this shop visitors will find discontinued and seconds in clothing items for women and children at a real savings. Blouses, skirts, dresses, blazers, jackets, and nightgowns were available in cotton, velvet, or corduroy. Blouses started at £10 and skirts about £20. A *real* savings! Be sure to check your merchandise carefully as some flaws were very noticeable—dye mistakes, torn waists, or crooked pockets.

If you would like a unique, country-fresh look that will win you compliments, try wearing a Laura Ashley. Her clothing seems to stay in style, which is wonderful on your pocketbook. Many of the colors she uses are very memorable . . . rich teal and cornflower blues, poppy reds, or soft roses, etc.

Highly recommended if you like the Laura Ashley look! One of my favorite shopping days was spent here. I took two full hours trying everything on I thought I liked even a little. I came home with sacks of outfits that I could mix and match. Be careful about taking a friend who is the same size. Both of you end up wanting the same ensemble. Have a wonderful time!

Laura Ashley has a chain of stores, though this is the only one in which seconds are sold. For a list of the others, see "Chain Stores" in the front of the book.

LOCATION: Just west of, and at the bottom of, the hill from the castle, on the east side of Lothian Road.

EDINBURGH   *Craft Items*

Scottish Craft Centre
140 Canongate
Edinburgh EH8 8DD, Scotland
Tel. 031-556-8136/7370

HOURS: Monday–Saturday 10:00–5:30
CREDIT CARDS: Access, American Express, Visa

PRODUCTS: The Scottish Craft Centre offers top-quality work in every area of crafts. A committee reviews the items, and only products which meet the highest standards of workmanship and design are accepted. Visitors will find a gallery filled with jewelry, batiks, glassware, rugs, crystal, pottery, textiles, wood, weaving, ceramics, leather goods, needlepoint, etc. Very well done and pleasant surroundings!

Sterling silver rings begin at £2. Rugs in all combinations of wool blends start at £65. Smaller pottery pieces start at £4 while many expensive pieces are also available for the serious collector. Handknit sweaters in exquisite textures begin at £65. One could easily label these "designer sweaters" as the chance of seeing another one like it is very remote.

The Scottish Craft Centre gives the visitor in a hurry an overview of the many Scottish products which are produced throughout the country.

LOCATION: On the Royal Mile near Holyrood Palace. See the map below.

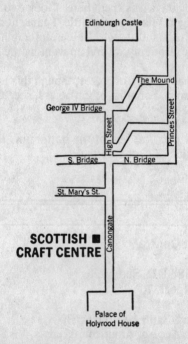

EDINBURGH *Woolen Clothing*

The Edinburgh Woollen Mill (retail shop)
139 Princes Street
Edinburgh, Scotland
Tel. 031-226-3840

Also: Romanes & Paterson
      62 Princes Street
      Edinburgh, Scotland
      Tel. 031-225-4966

      51 Hi Street
      Edinburgh, Scotland
      Tel. 031-556-9786

      453/455 Lawnmarket
      Edinburgh, Scotland
      Tel. 031-225-1525

HOURS: The Princes Street branches are open: Monday–Saturday 9:00–5:30; Sunday 1:00–5:00.
The Royal Mile and Lawnmarket branches are open: Monday–Saturday 9:00–5:30.

CREDIT CARDS: Access, Visa

PRODUCTS: The Edinburgh Woollen Mill carries a large variety of woolen products at excellent prices. Visitors will find sweaters, vests, kilts, blazers, scarves, coats, socks, and numerous other woolen items. The stores are easy to shop. The quality, detail, and workmanship of their items will always be dependable and consistent. Prices at the end of the season fall drastically. Clothing is available for men, women, and children.

All wool tartan kilts beautifully made start at £19.99. They usually have many styles from which to choose. Lambswool sweaters begin at £11.99. Sweaters can be found with collars, crew and V-necks, in any number of wonderful colors. Cashmere sweaters, as soft as silk, start at £45. As you may know, cashmere sweaters in the States only *start* at £100. All wool tartan travel rugs begin at £12.99. Due to the high volume of this chain of stores, they are able to offer exceptional savings on much of their merchandise.

This is one of a chain of stores. For other locations see CHAIN STORES in the front of the book.

LOCATIONS: The shop on 139 Princes Street is located at the west end of Princes Street opposite the Caledonian Hotel.

The shop at 51 High Street is located below John Knox's home, which was built in the fifteenth century, one of the oldest of its type in Edinburgh.

The Lawnmarket Shop is located on Castle Hill 200 yards from the famous Edinburgh Castle.

The shop at 62 Princes Street is part of the original Edinburgh Woollen Mill group first established in 1808. This store is located opposite the Scott Monument in the center of Princes Street.

ELGIN   *Wool Clothing, Scottish Crafts*

Clan Royal (retail store)
25 Batchen Street
Elgin, Scotland
Tel. 0343-3381

See the write-up under EDINBURGH.

LOCATION: Elgin is in the north of Scotland about 37 miles northeast of Inverness on the A96 road.

ELGIN   *Scotch Whisky*

Gordon and MacPhail (whisky distributor)
58–60, South Street
Elgin, Morayshire IV30 1JY, Scotland
Tel. 0343-45111 (seven lines)

HOURS: Mondays and Tuesdays 9:00–5:15; Wednesday 9:00–1:00; open all day 9:00–5:15 in summer months; Thursday and Friday 8:30–5:15; Saturday 9:00–5:00
CREDIT CARDS: Access, MasterCard

PRODUCTS: Gordon and MacPhail established themselves at their present location in 1895. They are a wine, spirit, and grocery shop which specializes in Scotch malt whiskies and miniature bottles of whisky and other drinks. Stocked in the shop are 353 different bottles of whiskies, and 545 different miniatures.

A bottle of MacPhail's single malt Scotch whisky distilled in 1964 is £14.85. A bottle of Glen Calder blended Scotch whisky is £8.85. Dunkeld Atholl Brose, a Scotch liqueur, is about £9.90 per bottle. A miniature bottle of 1938 MacPhail's single malt Scotch whisky is £2.50. A full range of wines, spirits, groceries, Scottish shortbread, oatcakes, cheeses, and honey are also stocked. Many of the whiskies for sale have been matured, blended, and bottled by Gordon and MacPhail. Never again will you see such a selection of alcoholic beverages. Have yourself a picnic in the quaint countryside with "wine, cheese, and thee." Goods can be shipped subject to the local regulations. A price list is available for the asking.

LOCATION: Elgin is near the north coast about 37 miles northeast of Inverness on the A96 road. See the map below.

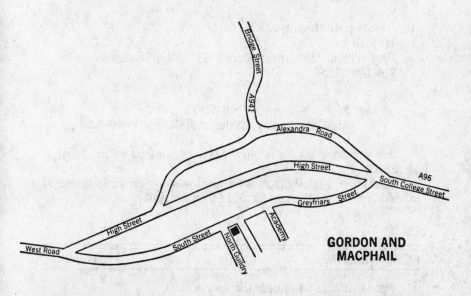

FORT WILLIAM · *Wool Clothing, Scottish Crafts*

Clan Royal (retail store)
Unit 1 Playhouse, High Street
Fort William, Inverness Shire, Scotland
Tel. 0397-3325

HOURS: Monday–Saturday 9:00–5:30

See the write-up under EDINBURGH.

LOCATION: Fort William is in northwestern Scotland, about 32 miles due north of Oban on the A828 then the A82.

FORT WILLIAM   *Woolen Items*

Moffat Weavers
35 High Street
Fort William, Inverness Shire PH33 6DH, Scotland
Tel. 0397-2991

Also: Mairi Macintyre Ltd.
High Street
Fort William, Inverness Shire PH33 6DH, Scotland
Tel. 0397-2058

HOURS: Monday–Saturday 9:00–5:30
        Monday–Sunday (Easter until October) 9:00–5:30

See the write-up for Moffat Woollens Limited in the town of MOFFAT.

LOCATION: Fort William is in northwestern Scotland about 32 miles due north of Oban on the A828 then the A82.

FORT WILLIAM   *Woolen Items*

Nevis Bridge Clanwear (factory outlet)
Belford Road
Fort William, Inverness Shire PH33 6B2, Scotland
Tel. 0397-4244

HOURS: Monday–Saturday 9:00–5:30; Monday–Sunday (Easter until October) 9:00–5:30

PRODUCTS: For the full description of items carried at this factory, please see the write-up for Moffat Woollens Limited in the town of MOFFAT, Scotland. They have a vast selection of ladies' kilted skirts in all of the tartans since they manufacture the skirts at this outlet. Visitors can watch the manufacturing of kilts Monday to Friday between 9:00 and 5:00. This will definitely make one appreciate the meticulous workmanship involved.

LOCATION: Fort William is in northwestern Scotland, about 32 miles due north of Oban on the A828 then the A82.

GALASHIELS   *Woolen Items*

Andrew Stewart Woollens and Crafts Shop (mill shop)
The Pirns, King Street
Galashiels, Selkirkshire TD1 1QH, Scotland
Tel. 0896-2226 and 2227

HOURS: Monday–Friday 9:00–1:00 and 2:00–5:00; Saturday 9:30–
1:00 and 2:00–4:00
CREDIT CARDS: Access, Visa

PRODUCTS: At this neatly organized mill shop visitors will find shelves of colorful woolen sweaters, mohair capes and jackets, and woolen women's suits. Andrew Stewart was founded in 1905 and has maintained its quality and detail since that time.

Cardigan and pullover sweaters begin at £29. They carry a large selection of sweater styles with unique details such as tie necks, round necks with pleats, scalloped collars, turtlenecks, and shawl collars. The color ranges are excellent and range from birsay blue to briar rose. Fully lined wool skirts in quality wool tweed fabric begin at £31. Most of the skirts are fully lined and beautifully made. A stylish detailed two-piece Aran suit totally lined and made of a wool loop tweed fabric was £114. This suit was truly an exceptional value. The same suit in the United States would cost $300.

In 1933, Andrew Stewart began to produce mohair due to a worldwide demand. The AF13 mohair fabric is still produced today and only top quality mohair is used. They have become experts at creating the fabric and the rich colors. The Andrew Stewart Mohair collection not only coordinates with the Pirnspun tweed garments but also with the entire collection of their lambswool knitwear. This allows the customer a great deal of versatility when color coordinating a new wardrobe.

Mohair capes begin at £43. Mohair coats begin at £108. Fully lined mohair coats start at £126. The coats are very chic and many have top stitching detail with belted waists.

Fully lined wool slacks are also sold which match the soft lambswool sweaters.

At this outlet there is a comprehensive selection of top-quality woolen products available for the well-dressed woman of today.

LOCATION: Galashiels is 32 miles south of Edinburgh on the A7 road. See the map below.

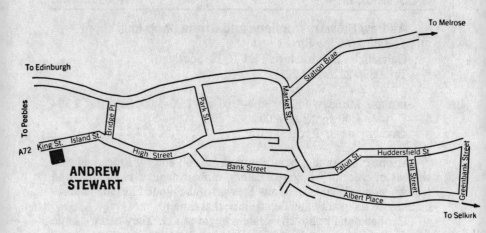

GALASHIELS   *Wool Clothing, Scottish Crafts*

Clan Royal (retail store)
Channel Street
Galashiels, Borders, Scotland
Tel. 0896-2253

HOURS: Monday–Saturday 9:00–5:30

See the write-up under EDINBURGH.

LOCATION: Galashiels is about 32 miles south of Edinburgh on the A7 road.

GALASHIELS   *Woolen Items*

Peter Anderson Ltd. (factory/shop)
Nether Mill
Huddersfield Street
Galashiels TD1 3BA, Scotland
Tel. 0896-2091

HOURS: Museum: April–October: Monday–Saturday 9:00–5:00;
June–September: Sunday also 12:00–5:00.
Mill Shop: Monday–Saturday 9:00–5:00; Sunday 12:00–
5:00 from June to September.
CREDIT CARDS: Access, American Express, Diners Club, Visa

PRODUCTS: Peter Anderson Ltd. produces high-quality natural
fiber cloth and knitwear, such as cashmere, mohair, and wool. They
allegedly produce the world's largest selection of pure wool worsted
tartans in over 670 designs. They specialize in making fabric into
ladies' wear and gents' highland dress. Products include vests, skirts,
sweaters, hats, coats, ties, capes, scarves, jackets, blazers, women's
suits, kilts, etc. Their quality is known throughout the world.
They offer excellent prices at their mill shop. Their annual mill
sale starts the last week in November and lasts 14 days. A wool kilted
skirt in the Blue Glen Stewart plaid was listed at £56.24. The classic V-
neck Shetland sweater in soft jade was £10.98. The Shetland Fair Isle
sweater with a decorative yoke was attractively priced at £21.90. A
mock turtleneck sweater in scarlet made of a washable super merino
was a good buy at £15.98. A three-piece lambswool ensemble in sap-
phire sold for £72.90. A skirt, sweater, and cardigan was included for
the one price. Definitely a good buy if you were to comparison shop in
the States. They will ship all of your purchases home for you.

TOURS: From April to October there are two mill tours Monday
through Friday at 10:30 and at 2:00. The free tour lasts 40 minutes.
Individuals as well as bus parties should make advance reservations.

MAIL ORDERS: Peter Anderson Ltd. has a complete mail order
business. Write and ask for the mail order brochure which has complete instructions. There is a size conversion chart.

LOCATION: Galashiels is 32 miles south of Edinburgh on the A7
road. See the map below.

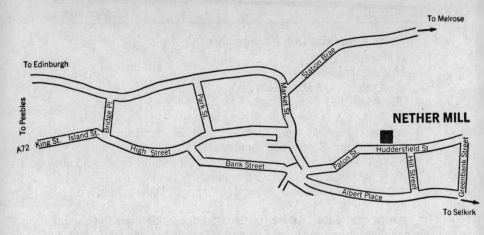

GLASGOW   *Knitwear*

M & B Anson, Ltd. (retail shop)
1145 Cathcart Road
Glasgow G42 9HD, Scotland
Tel. 041-632-5950 and 041-632-4818

HOURS: Monday–Friday 9:30–5:00
CREDIT CARDS: None

PRODUCTS: This company sells an extensive variety of men's, women's, and children's knitwear. The company normally distributes these goods to retail stores throughout Scotland with the "Maban" and "Top Kids" labels. They also sell directly to the public at this outlet. Products include mohair jackets, waistcoats, capes and carcoats, lambswool cardigans, Botany wool sweaters, Shetland and Fair Isle sweaters, and numerous jumpers, pullovers, and other knitwear. They also sell accessories such as gloves, hats, and scarves. Prices range from £6 to £40. Since this outlet sells to other retail outlets, we can only give a range of prices. Special prices are available on various styles which have been discontinued. They will ship goods worldwide.

LOCATION: From the center of Glasgow, take the A726 (Cathcart Road) south to Hampden Park. See the map.

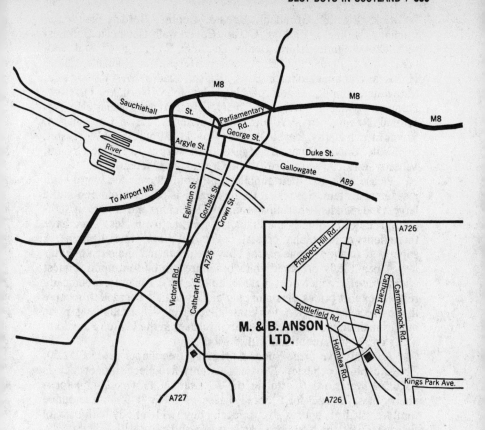

GLASGOW   *China, Crystal*

Stockwell China Bazaar (retail store, mail order)
67-77 Glassford Street
Glasgow G1 1UB, Scotland
Tel. 041-552-5781

HOURS: Monday–Saturday 9:30–5:30
CREDIT CARDS: All major credit cards

PRODUCTS: Stockwell China Bazaar is a retail store which sup-
plies customers with a choice of the world's most famous fine bone
china and crystal. They stock: Albany, Aynsley, Baccarat, Beleek,

Beswick, Bing & Grondahl, Bochm, Booths, Border Fine Arts, Buchan, Caithness, Carlton, Cavan, Caverswall, Coalport, Connoisseur, Crown Staffordshire, Denby, Duchess, Edinburgh Crystal, Galvani, Galway, Guzzinni, Hammersley, Heredities, Highland China, Hornsea, Hummel, Johnson Bros., Kaiser, Lladro, Masons, Meakin, Midwinter, Minton, Moorcroft, Nicholas John, Noritake, Orrefors, Paragon, Pendelfin, Perthshire Paperweights, Poole, Renaissance, Rosenthal, Rosina, Royal Albert, Royal Brierley, Royal Copenhagen, Royal Crown Derby, Royal Doulton, Royal Grafton, Royal Worcester, St. Louis, Spode, Stuart Crystal, Sutty, Swarovski, Tyrone Crystal, Villeroy & Boch, Waterford, Webb Crystal, and Wedgwood.

Please note that their suppliers are from all over the world—not just Great Britain. Stockwell China Bazaar is 60 years old and is the largest independent specialist retailer of fine china and crystal in Scotland. They offer quality merchandise at attractive prices. They have three floors of fine china, crystal, collectors' pieces, and gift items. A super way to shop at one place! They are organized and most helpful.

A beautifully prepared color brochure can be sent upon request with a price list which does include the 15% VAT. You must specifically request export prices plus shipping and insurance charges to receive the correct information for Stateside prices. The following price quotes include the VAT and are for purchases in the United Kingdom. The savings are exceptional either way!

A twenty-five-piece Spode Christmas Tree dinner set is £252.50. The Royal Worchester Evesham twenty-five-piece dinner set is £178.50. Waterford Crystal in the Lismore pattern is £14.50 for a sherry glass, £23.95 for a brandy glass, and £13.95 for a five-ounce tumbler. Lladro's figures are wonderful buys with a Lady with Parasol figurine at £99, the Newborn Lamb at £47, and a Girl with Lilies at £49. Spode's Blue Italian was very reasonable. An eight-inch plate sold for £3.45, a six-inch plate was £2.90, a nine-inch flan dish was £8.95, and a four-pint casserole was £21.50.

MAIL ORDERS: Stockwell China Bazaar ships all over the world and provides free breakage insurance to all overseas destinations. Simply write to them and include a list of the products which you wish to purchase and they will send a price quote to you. For customers from the U.S. there is an office available for all questions: United States Customer Service Office, 9335 El Cajon Blvd., La Mesa, California 82041; telephone 714/698-6981.

Only first-quality items are carried. Shipping time varies from eight to ten weeks after the order is received. A catalog of all products is not available, but catalogs can be sent on specific items and products.

LOCATION: In the southern part of Glasgow. See the map below.

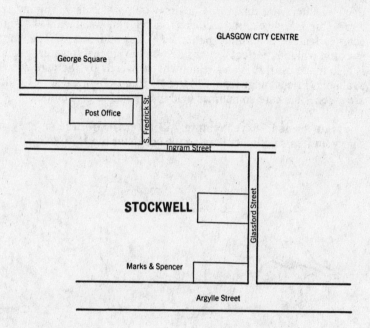

GLENDALE BY DUNVEGAN, ISLE OF SKYE   *Sweaters*

Skye Venture Cottage Industry
W. MacKenzie
18, Holmisdal, Glendale By Dunvegan
Isle of Skye, Scotland
Tel. 047-081-316

HOURS: Monday–Saturday 10:00–6:00
CREDIT CARDS: MasterCard, Visa

PRODUCTS: Handknit sweaters in undyed natural colors are the specialty at Skye Venture. The garments are hand finished—necks are sewn down by hand, and the edges of all raglan sleeves, cuffs, and hats are individually hand-crochet finished. The high-quality wools used are worsted spun for the longest possible retention of natural oils. The dyed sweaters are made of Cheviot wool, which is warm and soft. Aran Fair Isle sweaters, cardigans, slipovers, waistcoats, hats, and scarves feature beautifully patterned yokes and details. The Vargan sweater, which is perfect for outside weather since it is water resistant, is also made on this island. Handwoven tweeds by the yard are also available. Prices range from £18 to £45. Handweaving demonstrations are given. Sales are sometimes held in September or October.

MAIL ORDER: Skye Venture will accept mail orders. They will ship your items without charging the customer the 15% VAT.

LOCATION: The Isle of Skye is off the west coast of Scotland. Glendale is on the far northwest end of the Isle of Skye near the town of Dunvegan. From Dunvegan take the B884 road west about six miles. After coming down the *brae* into Glendale, cross the River Hamara and turn left when you reach the post office. The road has a sign to Holmisdal. The shop is at the end of the road in an old black house. See the map.

GOLSPIE   *Stone Gift Items*

Orcadian Stone Company Limited (craft workshop)
Main Street, Golspie
Sutherland KW10 6RH, Scotland
(also at the Highland Craft Centre, Aviemore)
Tel. 040-83-3483

HOURS: Monday–Saturday 9:30–5:30
CREDIT CARDS: None

PRODUCTS: The Orcadian Stone Company is a family business founded in 1970 by Anne and Don Shelley, with a workshop and showroom at Golspie, and a retail outlet at the Highland Craft Centre in Aviemore. The workshop at Golspie is open to the public, and visitors may watch stonecutting and polishing. There is also a collection of mineral specimens, with particular emphasis on British and local rocks, minerals, and fossils.

Products include stone giftware such as clocks, barometers, lamps, bookends, penholders, thermometers, vases, planters, and sundials in Scottish highland and imported stones. There are also tables and tabletops, semiprecious stone jewelry, mineral specimens, geological specimen cards (local), books, and maps.

Stone lamp bases are priced from £7.50, stone planters from £2.50, and stone clocks average £25. They are willing to post and ship goods abroad.

TOURS: Twenty-minute tours of the workshop at Golspie are available during working hours. Large parties are divided into groups of 10 and advance arrangements must be made.

LOCATION: Golspie is in the far north of Scotland on the east coast about five miles south of Brora on the A9. See the map below.

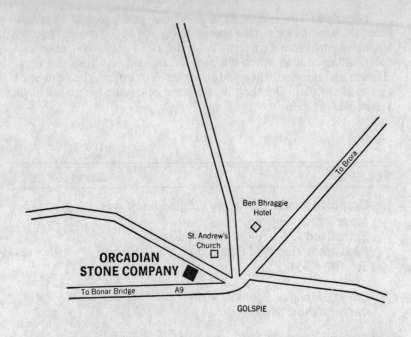

GRANTOWN-ON-SPEY   *Furniture*

Robadina Woodworking
Craigbegg Smithy Cottage
Grantown-on-Spey, Morayshire, Scotland
Tel. 0479-3106

HOURS: Monday–Friday 9:00–5:00
CREDIT CARDS: None

PRODUCTS: Furniture is the specialty at Robadina Woodworking—especially poster beds which begin at £350. Dressers, garden furniture, and custommade furniture are also manufactured. Dressers begin at £130. Visitors are welcome to watch production.

LOCATION: Grantown-on-Spey is in north central Scotland on the A95 road. It is about 25 miles southeast of Inverness. From Grantown, take the A939 road north toward Nairn and Forres about one and a half miles. Turn right at the telephone box, and go down to the bottom of the hill. The Craigbegg Smithy Cottage is on the righthand side.

GRETNA GREEN   *Woolen Items*

Gretna Green Woolen Mill
Gretna Green, Dumfriesshire, Scotland
Tel. 0461-38297

HOURS: Monday–Saturday 9:00–5:30; Monday–Sunday (Easter
until October) 9:00–5:30.

See the write-up for Moffat Woolens Limited in the town of MOF-
FAT.

LOCATION: Gretna Green is in the far southwest on the Scottish
border just north of Carlisle, England, on the A74.

HADDINGTON   *Sweaters*

Ewe Nique Knitwear (factory shop)
Primrose Gallery
3, Lodge Street, Haddington,
East Lothian EH41 3DX, Scotland
Tel. 062 082-2199/4398

HOURS: Tuesday–Saturday 10:00–1:00 and 2:30–5:00
CREDIT CARDS: None

PRODUCTS: At Ewe Nique Knitwear visitors will find sweaters
and vests knitted in 100% Shetland wool featuring multicolored jacquard designs, some of which depict animals such as sheep, dogs, and
camels. Prices for adult sweaters range from £24 to £44. Children's
sweaters are priced from £10 to £20. Also sold are mohair handknit
sweaters. The designs are excellent as is the craftsmanship. If you
would like a truly unusual sweater with wonderful colors and fascinating designs, I would definitely recommend a stop at this shop. She has
a limited production which assures the visitor that the same sweater
will not be everywhere. (She wholesales many of her sweaters to
famous department stores in the United Kingdom and in the States.)

MAIL ORDER: Mail order is available.

LOCATION: The market town of Haddington is located 17 miles east of Edinburgh on the A1. See the map below.

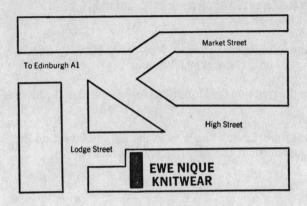

HADDINGTON   *Pottery, Ceramics*

Margery Clinton Ceramics
The Pottery, Newton Port
Haddington, East Lothian EH41 3DX, Scotland
Tel. 062-082-3584

HOURS: Gallery: Tuesday–Saturday 10:00–1:00 and 2:30–5:30; workshop: Saturday mornings or by appointment.
CREDIT CARDS: None

PRODUCTS: In 1978 Margery Clinton Ceramics was started in restored seventeenth-century cottages. Today she has four parttime assistants. She specializes in the creation of iridescent luster pottery and tiles, an art which was all but forgotten until recently. Her work has been influenced by the art nouveau glasswork of Louis Comfort Tiffany. She sells bowls, lamps, and designer pieces. A large vase with a black matt glaze and an iridescent silver luster finish is £19.40. A 27-inch slimline lamp with a shade in a green silver luster glaze is £73.50. Her work is very unusual and I have never seen anything like her fascinating work in all of our travels. Her pieces border on the contemporary.

LOCATION: Haddington is about 17 miles east of Edinburgh on the A1. See the map below.

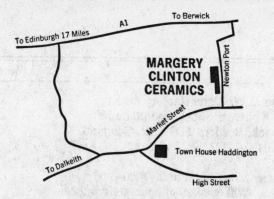

HAWICK *Animal Figurines*

Arista Designs Limited (factory outlet)
Unit 2, Eastfield Mills, Mansfield Gardens
Hawick, Roxburghshire TD9 8AN, Scotland
Tel. 0450-75272

HOURS: Monday–Friday 9:00–12:00 and 1:30–5:00
CREDIT CARDS: None

PRODUCTS: Arista Designs Limited manufactures realistic animal and wildlife figurines. The dogs are especially well done and all are hand painted by Scottish artists. Miniature dogs are £1.50, rabbit figurines are £17, gold figurines are £125 and a Scottish terrier figurine was £41.

TOUR: Tours can be given if arrangements are made in advance. Groups of up to 30 can be handled with ease.

LOCATION: Hawick is in the south of Scotland on the A7 about 20 miles north of the English border. When approaching Hawick from the north, take the A7 from Edinburgh. Upon entering town, turn right at the traffic lights. Go along the river's edge and turn right again at the garage. Then turn left at the Presto Supermarket. The shop is 100 yards further on the right.

Approaching from the south on the A7, turn left at the traffic lights and cross the river. You will be on Albert Road. Take the first left at the Presto Supermarket onto Victoria Road. The shop is 100 yards down on the right.

HAWICK   *Woolen Items*

Chas N. Whillans (factory outlet)
The Knitwear Shop, Teviotdale Mills
Hawick, Borders TD9 7BR, Scotland
Tel. 0450-73128

HOURS: Monday–Saturday 9:00–5:00
            Will open other hours for coaches
CREDIT CARDS: Access, American Express, Visa

PRODUCTS: This family-owned business carries their own brand of sweaters as well as those of Pringle, Lyle and Scott, and others. There are baskets of sweaters which are seconds or discontinued styles sold at a large discount. They also sell first-quality sweaters in Shetland wool, cashmere, and lambswool.

Men's or women's V-neck pullover sweaters in two-ply cashmere are sold for £39.95. (I have seen a similar sweater on sale in a depart-

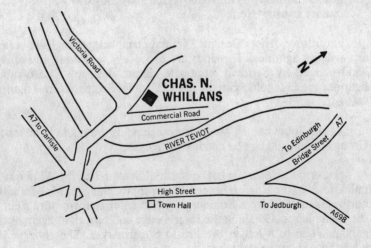

ment store in the States for $110.) A woman's pullover turtleneck lambswool sweater was £16.95. A men's round neck lambswool pullover sweater was £23. Children's new wool V-neck pullover sweaters are priced between £11.95 and £12.50.

The quality and color choices of sweaters are outstanding. Definitely a must to visit if you are in the market to increase your sweater wardrobe.

MAIL ORDERS: This company has a mail order catalog in color and they welcome inquiries.

LOCATION: Hawick is in the south of Scotland on the A7 about 20 miles north of the English border. The store is opposite the Tourist Office and a large car park. See the map.

HAWICK   *Sweaters*

White of Hawick (retail store)
Victoria Road
Hawick, Roxburghshire TD9 7AH, Scotland
Tel. 0450-73206

HOURS: Monday–Saturday 9:00–5:15
CREDIT CARDS: Access, American Express, Visa

PRODUCTS: Shelves and shelves of woolen sweaters in lovely colors and textures are sold. Boxes of sweaters which are seconds, and end-of-the-lines for men and women are under all of the tables. Most of them are priced under £10—an exceptional buy!

This shop specializes in cashmere sweaters which start at £27.95. A 100% pure cashmere sweater with a round neck for £37.95 was an outstanding buy for any woman.

A lambswool turtleneck sweater was priced at £16.95. A mohair jacket was £37.95. A men's double lambswool machine washable V-neck sweater was £16.95. A men's double cashmere V-neck pullover sweater with turn-back cuffs was £45.95. (Men's sizes range from 38″ to 46.″) A men's two-ply Botany wool long-sleeved pullover with suede trim was only £22.95.

For all purchases over £40 by overseas customers, the 15% VAT amount is deducted. For postage, packing, and insurance add £1.80 per sweater.

MAIL ORDERS: White of Hawick has a mail order division and will send brochures upon request.

LOCATION: Hawick is in the south of Scotland on the A7 about 20 miles north of the English border. See the map below.

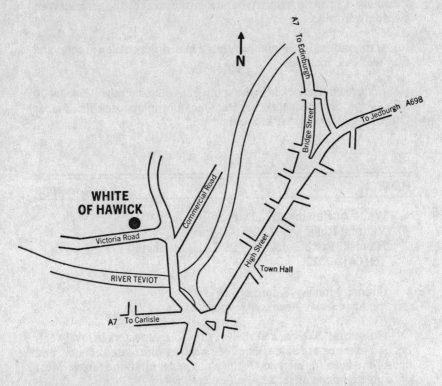

HAWICK *Woolen Items*

Wrights of Trowmill Ltd. (woolen mill)
Hawick, Roxburghshire TD9 8SU, Scotland
Tel. 0450-728145

HOURS: Monday–Friday 9:00–5:00; Saturday–Sunday 10:00–5:00.
CREDIT CARDS: Access, Visa

PRODUCTS: At this woolen mill, visitors will find exceptional buys on full-length wool coats for £57, women's suits, skirts, wool rugs, sweaters, some fabric, and men's sport coats at £40. Tartan wool 60″ wide was £6.95 per yard, Shetland wool 60″ wide was £7.95 per yard and lambswool 60″ wide was £7.95 per yard and lambswool 60″ wide was £8.95 per yard. Scarves went from £3 to £3.50 and men's ties averaged £2.75. Shetland cardigan sweaters for women started at £13.95. A men's Norwegian crew neck sweater was £19.95. Men's and women's lambswool sweaters were priced between £11.95 and £18.95. Fully lined wool skirts ranged from £11.95 to £17.95. Kilted skirts started at £18.95. Not a large selection but definitely good prices.

TOURS: Visitors are allowed to walk through the mill at their leisure. An informative brochure explains each step in the weaving process.

LOCATION: Hawick is in southern Scotland about 50 miles south of Edinburgh on the A7 road. The Trow Mill is just north of town on the A698 toward Denholm, on the west side of the road. Coming from Hawick, you must make a hairpin turn to the left.

INNERLEITHEN   *Woolen Items*

Neidpath Knitwear Ltd. (mill shop)
Peebles Road
Innerleithen, Peeblesshire, Scotland
Tel. 0896-830446

HOURS: Monday–Friday 9:00–5:00
CREDIT CARDS: Access, Visa

PRODUCTS: In a quaint old church visitors will find a nice selection of sweaters, blankets, ties, scarves, purses, and gifts. Sweaters start at £14.99, blankets at £10.99 and ties at £4.99.

LOCATION: From Edinburgh take the A703 south about 22 miles to Peebles. Then take the A72 road about six miles east to Innerleithen. The shop is on the left as you enter town.

INVERNESS   *Wool Clothing, Scottish Crafts*

Clan Royal (retail store)
23 High Street
Inverness, Inverness Shire, Scotland
Tel. 0463-220653

HOURS: Monday–Saturday 9:00–5:30

See the write-up under EDINBURGH.

LOCATION: Inverness is in north central Scotland at the north end of Loch Ness, at the junction of the A9, A82, and A96 roads.

INVERNESS   *Scottish Highland Clothing*

Duncan Chisholm & Sons, Limited (factory outlet)
47–51 Castle Street
Inverness, Inverness Shire IV2 3DU, Scotland
Tel. 0463-234599

HOURS: Monday–Saturday 9:00–9:00; off season: Monday–
     Saturday 9:00–5:30
CREDIT CARDS: Access, American Express, Diners Club, Visa

PRODUCTS: Scotland is one of the few countries in Europe where men wear national dress as part of their everyday lives. In the year 1822 King George IV visited Edinburgh attired in full highland dress, and almost overnight the wearing of tartans became popular. It is from this time that so many clan and family tartans date. Most clans have several different designs and hues of tartan plaids, and there are nearly 700 authentically named tartans in existence.

For everyday wear, highland dress consists of a kilt, jacket, or jacket and vest, brogue shoes, knitted hose and garters, a sporran, a plain tweed tie, and a leather waist belt with a brass buckle. A silver kilt pin completes the outfit.

Duncan Chisholm sells the above-mentioned items, plus tartan fabric, scarves, sashes, ties, travel rugs, Scottish wall plaques, bagpipes, swords, and Scottish books.

Men's kilts range from £155–£215, women's kilts from £137–£190, kilt hose range from £5.50–£26.50, dancing pumps for adults sell for £15.25, and ties range from £4.25–£4.95.

MAIL ORDER: They have a mail order service. A brochure and order form are available. They are able to supply individuals with a tartan pattern of the clan with which they are associated if their family either has a clan or is a sect of a particular clan.

TOURS: Tours of the working area are available by prior arrangement.

LOCATION: Inverness is in north central Scotland at the north end of Loch Ness. See the map below.

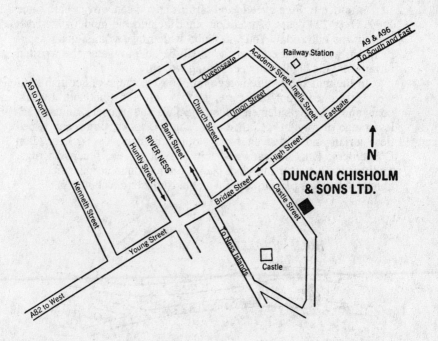

INVERNESS *Woolen Products*

James Pringle Ltd., Holm Woollen Mills
Dores Road
Inverness, Inverness Shire 1V2 4RB, Scotland
Tel. 0463-223311

HOURS: June–September: Monday–Friday 8:30–6:00; Saturday 9:00–5:00; Sunday 10:00–5:00.
October–November: Monday–Friday 9:00–5:30.
December–March: Monday–Friday 9:00–5:00; Saturday 10:00–12:30.
April–May: Saturday 9:00–5:00.

CREDIT CARDS: All types of payment are accepted.

PRODUCTS: Fine tweeds and tartans have been woven here since 1780. Over 200 years of tradition stand behind the modern methods used in the mill today. You will find a wide range of high-quality garments in wool. At the factory you will be able to watch the worsted tartans and the highland tweeds being woven.

In the mill shop there is a comprehensive range of Scottish knitwear fashioned from cashmere, lambswool, and Shetland. Ladies' coats and skirts, gentlemen's sports jackets and trousers, and an endless range of travel rugs, knee rugs, shawls, socks, tartan and tweed ties, tartan and tweed scarves, woolly mufflers, tweed hats, Tam O'Shanters, Fair Isle caps and mitts, wool gloves, sheepskin rugs, knitting wool, tweed and wool packs, are all found at mill prices. An annual sale takes place from November to the end of January.

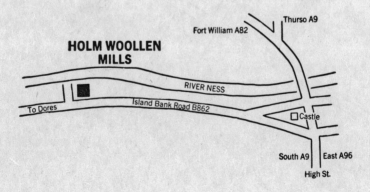

Women's single-ply cashmere sweaters start at £50. Tartan kilts begin at £26.95. Ladies wool coats and jackets start at £65. Men's two-ply cashmere sweaters begin at £65. Sports jackets are an especially good buy at £54.95. Men's slacks begin at £18.95. For that price, you could buy a pair in every color. A wonderful shopping experience for everyone!

TOURS: The factory tours at Inverness are fascinating. There is no limit on the group size.

LOCATION: Inverness is in the north of Scotland at the north end of Loch Ness. Follow the sign posts marked Dores A862. The mill is approximately 1½ miles from the town center. See the map below.

IOCHDAR, SOUTH UIST ISLAND   *Jewelry*

Hebridean Jewellery (retail shop)
Garrieganichy, Iochdar, South Uist PA81 5OX, Scotland
Tel. 08704 288

HOURS: Monday–Saturday 9:00–5:00
CREDIT CARDS: Access, Barclaycard, Visa

PRODUCTS: Hebridean Jewellery manufactures mainly silver and some nine-carat gold jewelry. The shop specializes in Scottish and Celtic designs. They feature new versions of the heart-shaped lucken-booth brooch which became popular in Scotland in the early eighteenth century. They also sell brooches, kilt pins, crosses, charms, tie tacks, cufflinks, chains, bracelets, and pendants with earrings resembling other ancient Celtic styles, often with interlocking designs and borders. The designs are very unique and the workmanship is excellent. Silver charms, which can also be used as pendants, range in price from £3.60 to £5.60. Silver earrings for pierced ears or with screw fittings were £7.60 to £10.40. Rings were an outstanding buy at £5.75 with the most expensive one only £13. Silver crosses, many of which feature the symbolic Celtic tree of life, are priced from £5.60 to £28.40. Brooches and kilt pins vary between £11.60 and £30.40.

MAIL ORDER: A catalogue plus mail order service to all parts of the world are available. Postage and packing £1 per order. Wholesale and retail export.

TOURS: Small groups can be shown around almost any time. Advance notice is required for larger groups.

LOCATION: This workshop is on the northern tip of South Uist Island in the Outer Hebrides. (This is a group of islands off the northwest coast of Scotland.) On the A865 road, turn west just before crossing over to Benbucia Island—the shop is about one mile away.

ISLE OF SKYE

See ARNISORT
BROADFORD
GLENDALE BY DUNVEGAN
ISLEORNSAY
PORTREE

ISLE OF ISLAY

See BRIDGEND

ISLEORNSAY, ISLE OF SKYE   *Sweaters*

Skye Crotal Knitwear Mill Shop
Isleornsay, Isle of Skye IV43 8QR, Scotland
Tel. 04713-271

HOURS: Monday–Friday 8:30–5:30; Saturday (April–October) 9:30–4:00; Sunday (April–October) by request—knock at adjoining house
CREDIT CARDS: Access, MasterCard, Visa

PRODUCTS: Pure wool knitwear is made in this shop. Knitwear consists mainly of sweaters ranging from traditional oiled fishermen's sweaters in Harris wool to modern "picture knits." Visitors will also find hats and scarves plus a small selection of other local craft goods. Tweed lengths for making skirts are also available. Prices vary from £18 to £40 per sweater. Seconds are often available from £10. They will mail sweaters anywhere, or make sweaters to order for later mailing.

Visitors can stand behind a glass door and see the sweaters being knitted.

LOCATION: The Isle of Skye is off the northwest coast of Scotland. Isleornsay is in the southernmost parish of the island about seven miles south of Broadford on the A851 road. The mill shop is in the old school house on the hill overlooking Isleornsay Bay.

JEDBURGH   *Woolen Items*

Jedburgh Kiltmakers (factory outlet)
Bankend North
Jedburgh, Roxburghshire TD8 6EB, Scotland
Tel. 0835-63585

HOURS: Monday–Saturday 9:00–5:30; Monday–Sunday (Easter until October) 9:00–5:30

See the write-up for Moffat Woollens Limited in the town of MOFFAT.

LOCATION: Jedburgh is 50 miles south of Edinburgh on the A68.

JOHN O'GROATS   *Candles*

Caithness Candles
John O'Groats
Wick, Caithness KW1 4YS, Scotland
Tel. 095-581-238

HOURS: Monday–Sunday 1:00–6:00; June to September evenings until 9:00.
CREDIT CARDS: Visa

PRODUCTS: Perfumed and decorative candles are all handmade at Caithness Candles. You will find candles fused, marbled, layered, multicolored, streaked, and flowered. The candles are molded into squares, cones, cratered, cylindrical, rounded, and spherical forms. Prices range from £1.50 to £15. Seconds in candles are sold at a large savings. Each candle is hand dipped and made with the finest waxes. They will ship orders for you.

MAIL ORDERS: They have a mail order business and a small catalog.

LOCATION: John O'Groats is at the north tip of Scotland, about 17 miles north of Wick on the A9 road. At the crossroads with the A836 (by the post office) turn right toward Duncansby Head, then take the next right. Caithness Candles is down this street on the right.

KELSO   *Jewelry*

Norman Cherry (craft shop)
36-38 Woodmarket
Kelso, Roxburghshire TD5 7AX, Scotland
Tel. 0573-240032

HOURS: Monday–Tuesday 10:30–12:30 and 1:30–5:00; Thursday–Saturday 10:30–12:30 and 1:30–5:00; Wednesday 10:00–12:30
CREDIT CARDS: None

PRODUCTS: Visitors will find quality in hand-designed jewelry made by Norman Cherry. The jewelry is in silver, gold, and titanium. In 1984 this jeweler received the award given by the Society of North American Goldsmiths' Platinum Design Competition. Sample prices: silver pendants from £21; silver rings from £17; and a gold ring set with an amethyst at £70.
Items created by other local craftsmen such as paintings and ceramics are also displayed.

LOCATION: Kelso is about 44 miles southeast of Edinburgh on the A68, then the A697, then the A6089 roads. The shop is on Woodmarket Street just behind the Town Hall.

KELSO   *Pottery*

The Kelso Pottery (craft workshop)
The Knowes, Kelso
Roxburghshire TD5 7BH, Scotland
Tel. Kelso 24027

HOURS: Monday–Friday 10:00–1:00 and 2:00–5:00
CREDIT CARDS: None

PRODUCTS: Ian and Elizabeth Hird established the Kelso Pottery in 1970 and have developed a simple range of domestic stoneware pottery including mugs, jugs, plates, and whisky tots. The pots are hand thrown, decorated with colored clay mixed to a creamy consistency, and fired to 960° centigrade. They are then glazed and sometimes decorated further before being fired to 130°. The kiln is starved of oxygen during certain stages of the firing. This pulls the many colors through the glaze and develops the speckle characteristic of reduced stoneware. Kelso pottery designs are based on the border country landscape: a snowstorm or rainshower sweeping across the Scottish hills is often combined with a solitary pine tree or branch. Mugs are £2.50, and bowls range from £3.50 to £6. Seconds are available. They are unable to ship, but they will supply you with names of shippers and packers.

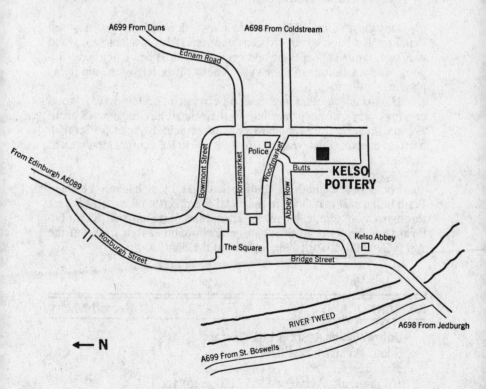

TOURS: Groups of up to 12 may visit and a tour will last 10–15 minutes.

LOCATION: Kelso is about 44 miles southeast of Edinburgh on the A68, then the A697, then the A6089 roads. See the map above.

KILLIN   *Handcrafted Scottish Goods*

Ben Ghlas Workshops (craft workshop)
Tomocrocher
Killin, Perthshire FK21 8TX, Scotland
Tel. 05672-527

HOURS: April–November 10:00–6:00
CREDIT CARDS: Diners Club

PRODUCTS: Ben Ghlas has their own flock of sheep. They sell handknit and handwoven woolens and rugs. Also available are wood carvings, tanned sheepskins and original watercolors. They have on-going demonstrations of canework. They will be happy to ship items abroad.

Handspun woolens are priced between £12.50 and £65. Wood carvings vary in price according to their detail but begin at £8 each. Pressed flower pictures and pewter picture frames begin at £4. Scottish heritage chests, which vary in size from 400 to 800 centimeters, start at £285.

LOCATION: Killin is in central Scotland about halfway between Perth in the east and Oban in the west. From Perth, take the A85 west through Crieff about 40 miles. Then turn north on the A827. Go through Killin (two miles), then go north another four miles on the A827. Ben Ghlas Workshops will be on the right.

KILMARNOCK   *Scotch Whisky*

John Walker & Sons Ltd. (factory)
Scotch Whisky Distillers
Hill Street
Kilmarnock, Ayrshire KA3 1HD, Scotland
Tel. 0563-23401

HOURS: Tours are given Monday through Friday at 10:15 and 2:00; closed first two weeks in July and other statutory holidays.
CREDIT CARDS: None

PRODUCTS: John Walker and Sons Ltd. makes some of the best Scotch whisky in the world. Unfortunately it is not sold at the factory. They do allow visitors to tour the factory and a tasting is given after the tour. The tours take about 2½ hours. Visitors can watch the whisky blending and bottling processes. No children under 14 may be admitted. Visitors must book tours in advance. Groups of 40 or under are preferred, but adjustments can be made for different group sizes. A small gift shop sells various souvenir items.

LOCATION: From Glasgow, take the A77 road toward Ayr. The junction for Kilmarnock is about 20 miles from Glasgow and 15 miles before reaching Ayr. Head for the town center, and look for the Kilmarnock railway station. The factory is across the railroad tracks from the station.

KILWINNING · *Knitting Wool, Knitting Yarn, Sweaters*

Mill Shop,
Busby Spinning Co. Ltd.
Bridgend Mills
Kilwinning, Ayrshire KA13 7JD, Scotland
Tel. 0294-57743 and 0294-52132

HOURS: Monday–Saturday 10:00–1:00 and 2:00–5:00; Sunday 12:00–4:00.
CREDIT CARDS: None

PRODUCTS: The Busby Spinning Mill Shop is located on the grounds of the Busby Woollen Spinning Mills. They claim to have the best Aran handknitting wool at low prices since they spin it themselves. They have a variety of machine-knitting yarns as well. Quantity discounts are available. I would recommend this shop only to the knitter. The shop also carries some sweaters. Skirts, skirt lengths, sheepskin rugs, horncraft, jewelry, and pottery are also sold.

The 100% wool Aran handknitting wool is available on 1000 gr. cones which are priced at £10.40 each. Fully-lined wool kilts and skirts begin at £12.95 while Andrew Stewart wool sweaters begin at £14.35. Celtic jewelry, which makes a thoughtful gift for that person at home, ranges from £2.25 to £10.

LOCATION: Kilwinning is about 30 miles southwest of Glasgow, just north of Irvine. See the map below.

KINGUSSIE *China, Earthenware*

Highland China Limited (factory/showroom)
Kingussie, Inverness Shire PH21 1PH, Scotland
Tel. 05402-576

HOURS: Factory: Monday–Friday 9:00–5:00.
       Shop: Monday–Friday 9:00–5:00; Saturday 10:00–4:00;
       evenings July and August until 9:00.
CREDIT CARDS: Access, Visa

PRODUCTS: This firm sells Highland China, a line of fine bone china which has been developed over the last few years. These light, delicate pieces are available in a variety of patterns and colors. They also carry a line of their own earthenware, Aviemore Pottery, with hand-painted decorations reflecting the colors of the Highland scenery. In addition to the variety of dishes, thimbles, letter openers, and miniatures, other pieces are available. Prices start at £1 and they sell both first-quality and seconds in this shop. They will ship first-quality goods.

The Cairngorm Animals, which are designed by Tom Mackie, are hand-modeled miniatures in protective boxes that would be perfect for packing in suitcase corners. Included in the collection are 14 animals which range in price from £3.45 for an Old English Sheepdog to £4.95 for a highland bull. The bone china West Highland pattern has 33 separate pieces ranging in price from £1.50 for a thimble to £5.20 for a sugar and cream set. You would have to really look to find any item over £10.

MAIL ORDER: They will accept mail orders.
TOURS: Tours of the factory are available by appointment.

LOCATION: Kingussie is in north-central Scotland about 70 miles northeast of Perth on the A9 road. It is also about 46 miles south of Inverness. See the map below.

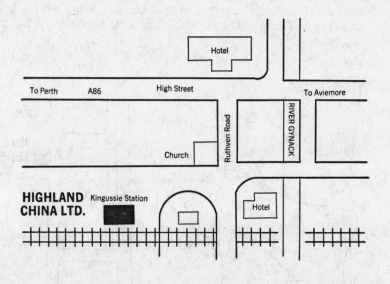

KINROSS *Cashmere Garments, Tweed Skirts, Jewelry, Handbags*

Lochleven Mill Shop
Lochleven Mills
Kinross, Tayside KY13 7DH, Scotland
Tel. 0577-63521

HOURS: Summer daily 9:00–5:00; winter Monday–Saturday 9:00–5:00 (closed on Thursday afternoon).

CREDIT CARDS: American Express, Diners Club, Eurocard, MasterCard, Visa

PRODUCTS: Lochleven Mill Shop offers a wide selection of quality products. Superb cashmere and lambswool sweaters and other garments are sold, as well as tweed skirts, jewelry, handbags, and other Scottish souvenirs. This outlet is not for those on a limited budget! The prices are somewhat steep but the quality is exceptional. Lochleven Mill Shop specializes in sweaters and cardigans in cashmere and lambswool. Lambswool garments begin at £22.50 and cashmere garments at £65.

LOCATION: Kinross is about 25 miles north of Edinburgh on the M90 motorway. At the No. 6 junction, take the exit to the east onto the A922 road. Go to the center of town. Then turn right onto the B996 road. The mill shop will be on your left near the edge of town. See the map below.

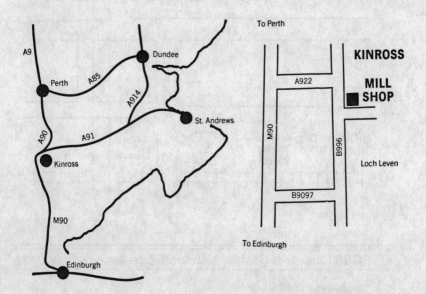

KIRKCUDBRIGHT   *Engraved Glass*

David Gulland Engraved Glass (craft workshop)
Skairkilndale
6, Barrhill Road
Kirkcudbright, Galloway DG6 4BG, Scotland
Tel. 0557-31072

HOURS: Monday–Friday 2:30–5:30 or by appointment
CREDIT CARDS: None

PRODUCTS: David Gulland started his studio in 1979. He uses the copper wheel to engrave crystal so that it reflects light to create the impression of sculptured images. He also uses sandblasting to decorate windows, mirrors, and glass.

Visitors are welcome to view the work, to purchase, or to order. Designs may be chosen from simple lettering and heraldry to wildlife, botanical subjects, or more elaborate figurative and architectural themes. He has a wide range of crystal pieces, paperweights, and

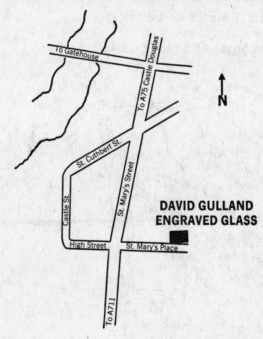

sculptured blocks which he can individually decorate. He will ship items for you.

Each piece he creates is a work of art. His crystal is well-priced for the work but the larger pieces are not inexpensive. The most detailed elegant workmanship we have ever seen anywhere in the world is to be found here. A small engraved posy bowl is £5.50, a set of six whisky glasses is £30, an engraved decanter is £120, vases from £30 and elaborately detailed crystal bowls £250. He will do special commissioned works, which may range in price from £50 to £500. The cost of the piece depends on the crystal piece chosen as well as the detail of the scene. If you would like something truly exceptional and one-of-a-kind, be sure to visit here.

LOCATION: Kirkcudbright is on the southwest coast of Scotland about 30 miles southwest of Dumfries on the A711. See the map below.

KIRKCUDBRIGHT   *Jewelry*

Michael Gill (craft workshop)
80 High Street
Kirkcudbright, Galloway DG6 4BG, Scotland

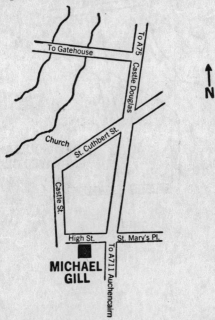

HOURS: Monday–Saturday 9:00–5:00; closed Thursday at 12:00; closed two days a week in winter; days vary.
CREDIT CARDS: None

PRODUCTS: Handcrafted jewelry is made at this tiny workshop. Most items are in sterling silver and they are priced under $20. Rings, pendants, charms, necklaces, pins, and earrings are attractively displayed in cases.

LOCATION: Kirkcudbright is on the southwest coast of Scotland about 30 miles southwest of Dumfries on the A711. Coming into town from the north on the A711 road, go through the center of town and turn right on High Street.

KIRKWALL, ORKNEY ISLANDS   *Jewelry*

Ortak Jewellery (factory/showroom)
Hatston Industrial Estate
Kirkwall, Orkney Islands KW15 1RH, Scotland
Tel. 0856-2224

HOURS: Monday–Friday 9:00–1:00 and 2:00–5:00; closed from Christmas to New Year's Day.
CREDIT CARDS: Access, American Express, Visa

PRODUCTS: Ortak Jewellery is a manufacturer of sterling silver and nine-carat gold jewelry. Their jewelry is made with precious and semiprecious stones, agates, and cultured pearls. Their variety of styles is enormous—from Celtic to traditional—and their quality exceptional.

Kilt pins, brooches, charms, pendants, cuff links, earrings, and necklaces are all available in sterling silver and in gold. Many of the pieces are set with large bold pieces of agate. The price range on their jewelry is from £5 to £500. The company will not list specific prices due to a large volume wholesale business. If they do have a sale, it is usually held during the month of January.

TOURS: Tours can be taken at 11:00 and 4:00. The tours last from 30 minutes to 1 hour. Parties of up to 20 can be taken on the tour, and two parties can usually be handled per tour.

LOCATION: The Orkney Islands are off the northern coast of Scotland. Kirkwall is the main city on Mainland Island. From the ferry terminal turn right (west) down Harbour Street. Continue west down Ayre Road, past the Peerie Sea (a lake) which will be on your left. Just past the Ayre Mills, and just before the Esso station, which will both be on your left, turn right onto Sparrowhawk Road. Ortak Jewellery will be a short way down on the left.

There is also a retail store just a block from the ferry terminal. From the ferry, go straight down Bridge Street to Albert Street. The store will be on the other side of the intersection, a short distance to the right.

KIRKWALL, ORKNEY ISLANDS   *Orkney Chairs*

Robert H. Towers (craft workshop)
"Rosegarth" St. Ola
Kirkwall, Orkney Islands KW15 1SE, Scotland
Tel. 0856-3521

HOURS: Monday–Friday 9:00–5:00
CREDIT CARDS: None

PRODUCTS: Robert H. Towers makes handmade Orkney chairs in pine or in walnut. The chairs can be made with or without hoods and with or without drawers. Each chair is fitted with sea grass seats. Shipping time varies depending on the time of the year. The pine chairs are priced from £265 to £364. The walnut chairs, which are of a harder wood, start at £299 and go up to £439.50. A child's chair, which is almost certain to become an heirloom, is available at £212.

MAIL ORDER: Mail orders are welcome. A black-and-white brochure with dimensions and the terms of business is sent with a price list and delivery instructions. All chairs are delivered free (and insured in transit) to the United Kingdom mainland only. Overseas orders will be delivered to any United Kingdom port. Customers must make their own overseas shipment arrangements.

TOURS: A maximum of five people may visit the shop by appointment. The tour is 15 to 20 minutes.

LOCATION: The Orkney Islands are just to the north of the Scottish mainland. Kirkwall is the main city on Mainland Island. From the center of town, with the St. Magnus Cathedral on your left, go straight along Broad Street, into Victoria Street, and into Main Street. At the junction, go straight up Wellington Street and High Street. When the road forks at the top of High Street take the left fork and go about one and a quarter miles along the A964. The shop is in the center of an S-bend, next to the entrance of the Scapa Distillery.

KIRKWALL, ORKNEY ISLANDS   *Jewelry*

The Longship (retail outlet for manufacturer)
7–9 Broad Street
Kirkwall, Orkney Islands KW15 1RH, Scotland
Tel. 0856-3251

HOURS: Monday–Saturday 9:00–5:00 (except Wednesday 9:00–1:00).
CREDIT CARDS: Access, Barclaycard, Visa

PRODUCTS: The Longship is the retail outlet for Orkney Jewellery. They have been making jewelry for 20 years and have a reputation for quality work and for attractive designs. Many of the designs are based on stone carvings which have been found in Scotland. They also have jewelry designs based on wildlife and modern lines. Their products are very well done. For specific prices and products, see the write-up: KIRKWALL, ORKNEY ISLANDS—Robert H. Towers.

MAIL ORDER: The Longship offers to ship your purchases for you. They have a mail order division.

TOURS: A viewing area in the workshop is accessible to visitors, where one can see work in progress along with photographs and explanations of the processes involved. Groups of up to 12 can be taken on a tour but larger groups must make advance appointments.

LOCATION: The Orkney Islands are just north of the northern tip of Scotland. Kirkwall is the main city on Mainland Island. See the map below. From the pier take Bridge Street into town, and bear right onto Albert Street, which becomes Broad Street. The shop is on the right, across from the Tourist Information Centre and the twelfth-century St. Magnus Cathedral.

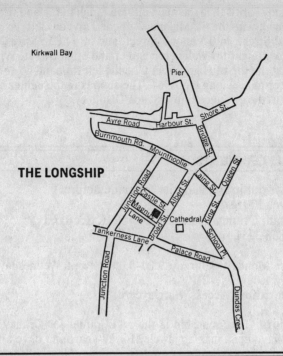

LANGHOLM   *Figurines*

Border Fine Arts Company Limited
Langholm, Dumfriesshire DG13 0ET, Scotland
Tel. 0541-80524

HOURS: Monday–Friday 9:00–5:00; Saturday and Sunday 10:00–
12:00
CREDIT CARDS: MasterCard, Visa

PRODUCTS: Border Fine Arts figurines are acclaimed as some of
the most authentic animal and bird sculptures ever produced. Some of
the animals depicted include dogs, cats, ducks, horses, mice, rabbits,
ducks, butterflies, and birds. Some pieces have limited editions and
they will be replaced with new designs.

Because each figurine is handpainted with as many as twelve
applications of translucent enamel, no two figurines are alike. Each
piece is signed, and a Certificate of Authenticity is issued with limited
edition sculpture. This company will undertake special commissions,
and will be pleased to sculpt a customer's dog, horse, or farm animal

from suitable photographs. There is an extra charge for this service.

There is a very small outlet store at the factory, with a limited amount of merchandise which varies depending on what is available. Figurine prices range from £13.50 for a 1½″ sculpture of a cat to £245 for a limited-edition sculpture of several ospreys. Discontinued lines are available at reduced prices.

All figurines are also available in cold cast bronze, foundry bronze, and precious metal.

MAIL ORDER: They have a mail brochure available.

LOCATION: Langholm is in the southwest of Scotland, just a few miles north of the English border—about 20 miles north of Carlisle on the A7 road. See the map below.

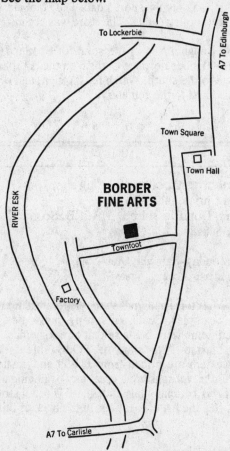

LANGHOLM   *Woolen Items*

Eskvalley Knitwear Co. Ltd. (retail store)
Skipper's Mill
Langholm, Dumfriesshire DG13 0LH, Scotland
Tel. 0541-80309

HOURS: Monday–Friday 9:00–5:00; Saturday 10:00–4:00; Sunday
    1:30–4:00
CREDIT CARDS: Access, Visa

PRODUCTS: Visitors will find a *large* selection of woolen garments
and accessories such as lambswool kilts starting at £14.99, women's
two-piece suits £35, men's sport coats £30, mohair rugs £16, and
shelves of all styles of sweaters. The store was organized and roomy.

LOCATION: Langholm is in the south of Scotland very near the
English border, 20 miles north of Carlisle on the A7 road. The store is
just out of town to the south. Watch for the sign, and drive up a steep
hill to the store, next to the cemetery.

LANGHOLM   *Woolen Items*

The Edinburgh Woollen Mill (mill shop)
64/66 Old Christchurch Road
Langholm, Dumfriesshire DG13 0EB, Scotland
Tel. 0541-80812

HOURS: Monday–Saturday 9:00–5:00
CREDIT CARDS: Access, Visa

PRODUCTS: At this small mill shop, visitors will find some seconds
and salesmen's samples. Coats, kilts, caps, socks, ties, sweaters, and
various woolen items were being sold at a real savings.
    All wool tartan kilts start at £19.99. Men's and women's
lambswool sweaters are priced from £11.99 and cashmere sweaters
from £45. Tartan travel rugs are a great buy beginning at £12.99.
    Note that this company has a chain of 77 retail stores in England
and Scotland. See the list of locations in the back of this book.

LOCATION: Langholm is in the far south of Scotland just a few miles inside the border on the A7 road.

LERWICK, SHETLAND ISLANDS *Woolen Items*

Anderson & Co.
The Shetland Warehouse
60 Commercial Street
Lerwick, Shetland Islands ZE1 0BD, Scotland
Tel. 0595-3714

HOURS: Monday–Tuesday 9:00–1:00 and 2:00–5:00; Thursday–Saturday 9:00–1:00 and 2:00–5:00
CREDIT CARDS: Access, Eurocard, MasterCard, Visa

PRODUCTS: At this factory Shetland knitting yarn which is 100% pure wool is sold by the ounce or the pound. Color swatch cards are available. Men's, women's and children's jackets, cardigans, pullovers, hats, scarves, gloves, and vests, mostly handknit by people in their homes, are also sold by Anderson & Company. Sheepskin rugs and various knitting accessories are also available. Two-ply natural jumper yarns cost approximately £8.10 for a cone weighing one pound, while colors will cost about £8.40 per cone. Two-ply lace yarn is £2.88 for four ounces in the naturals and £3.04 for the colors. Shetland shawls were between £12.90 and £16.25, travel rugs £16.95 and £21.95, men's gloves £4.20, and hats from £4.95 to £5.35. They had some quality children's sweaters starting at £6.45 up to £29.50 for Fair Isle sweaters. Children's hats were £3.10 for a darling Fair Isle beret. Fair Isle slipover sweaters were £26.35 to £32.45 while a Fair Isle sweater with a yoke made by knitting machine was £16.35.

MAIL ORDER: Mail orders are welcomed, and a color brochure plus a price list is available. The company does have a money-back guarantee on all purchases.

LOCATION: The Shetland Islands are off the coast of northern Scotland. Lerwick is the main city on the mainland of the Shetland Islands. Anderson & Company is near the small boat harbor on Commercial Street, directly across from the Tourist Information Centre.

MACDUFF   *Sweaters*

Jennie Ross Classic Knitwear
Macduff Industrial Estate
Macduff, Banffshire AB4 1QD, Scotland
Tel. 0261-33035

HOURS: Monday–Saturday 9:00–5:00
CREDIT CARDS: American Express

PRODUCTS: Jennie Ross creates pullover and cardigan sweaters
for women. Prices start at £21. Many of the sweaters have intricate
designs woven into them. A limited number of seconds are available.
Visitors may walk through the factory area.

LOCATION: Macduff is on the north coast of Scotland just east of
Banff on the A98. From the town center, go east on the A98 about one
mile. Turn right directly across from the Tarlair Golf Club. Follow the
road as it curves to the right, then turn right into the Macduff Industrial Estate. Go left at the roundabout, and to the end of the street. The
shop will be on your left.

MELROSE   *Woolen Items*

The Abbey Mill
Annay Road
Melrose, Roxburghshire, Scotland
Tel. 089-682-2138

HOURS: February 4 to March 3: 10:00–4:00; March 11 to Decem-
      ber 23: 9:00–5:30

See the write-up for Moffat Woollens Limited in the town of
MOFFAT.
    Visitors will find a restaurant on the premises serving soups,
salads, hot dishes, desserts, local cream pastries, and delicious
homemade scones. Relax and enjoy a cup of hot tea and a scone while
shopping. Car and coach parking is available. The Abbey Mill will be
happy to send your purchases home.

LOCATION: Melrose is just east of Galashiels, which is 30 miles south of Edinburgh on the A7. The mill is 150 yards from the main Abbey gates on the Melrose–Newstead road. See the map.

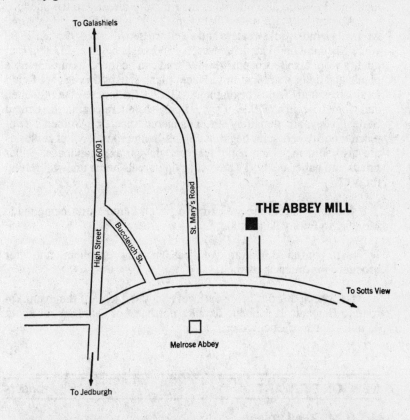

MOFFAT   *Woolen Items*

Moffat Woollens Limited (factory outlet)
Ladyknowe
Moffat, Dumfriesshire DG10 9EP, Scotland
Tel. 0683-20134

HOURS: Monday–Friday 9:00–5:00
CREDIT CARDS: Access, American Express, Carte Blanche, Diners Club, Visa

PRODUCTS: Moffat Woollens manufactures and sells top-quality sweaters, vests, skirts, kilts, suits, coats, and blouses for the well-dressed woman. Men's vests, sweaters, sheepskin coats, kilts, and full highland dress are also offered at their factory directly to the public.

Woolen kilts are priced between £12.99 and £29.99. Men's and women's lambswool sweaters and vests are between £10.99 and £25.99 while Shetland and Fair Isle sweaters and vests begin at £13.99. Top-quality wool blankets begin at £10.99 and can be found in innumerable plaids and color combinations. Thick, plush sheepskin rugs are found in all sizes and shapes beginning at £19.99. Cashmere coats for men and women begin at £79.99. (Try to find a cashmere coat in the United States! They are definitely an endangered species.) Women's two-piece wool tweed suits begin at £31.99. Numerous wool accessories are also sold including hats, scarves, gloves, and handbags. Super prices and super quality! They will ship parcels home and will refund the VAT.

TOURS: Visitors are welcome to watch kilted skirts being made Monday to Friday 9:00–5:00.

MAIL ORDERS: Moffat Woollens has an excellent full-color brochure for ordering by mail.

LOCATION: Moffat is in southwest Scotland just off the main A74 road to England. It is about 20 miles northeast of Dumfries, or about 15 miles north of Lockerbie.

NEWTON STEWART   *Mohair Products*

Glen Cree Limited
Weaving Mill and Mill Shop
King Street
Newton Stewart, Wigtownshire DG8 6DH, Scotland
Tel. 0671-2990

HOURS: Easter to end of October: Monday–Saturday 9:00–5:00;
            November to Easter: Monday to Friday only.
CREDIT CARDS: None

PRODUCTS: Glen Cree Ltd. sells mohair products such as scarves, stoles, knee rugs, travel rugs, blankets, capes, and a large selection of plaid and solid woolen fabrics. Sample prices include: a travel rug at a regular price of £50, a discontinued style for £25 and a second at £15. A good selection of sweaters is also sold. Children's sweaters and kilts are available in a variety of colors and styles. Most items are sold at slightly below normal retail. Some seconds are sold when available. Slow moving items are continuously reduced. An annual sale is held in November. The company will mail your purchases home.

TOURS: Continuous tours are held Monday through Friday in the summer. Tours in the winter are only available upon request. The tour is 20 minutes and the maximum group size is 15.

LOCATION: Newton Stewart is in the southwest of Scotland in the center of the beautiful Galloway district. The mill is on the riverbank just off the A714 road. See the map below.

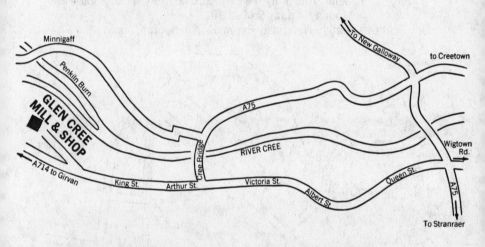

NORTH BERWICK   *Wool Clothing, Scottish Crafts*

Clan Royal (retail store)
Fishermen's Hall, The Harbour
North Berwick, Lothian, Scotland
Tel. 0620-3030

HOURS: Monday–Saturday 9:00–5:30

See the write-up under EDINBURGH.

LOCATION: North Berwick is east of Edinburgh along the coast about 20 miles on the A198 road.

OBAN   *Glass Items, Paperweights*

Caithness Glass P.L.C. (factory/shop)
Oban Glassworks
Lochavullin Estate
Oban, Argyll, Scotland
Tel. 0631-63386

HOURS: Shop: Monday–Friday 9:00–5:00 (Also Saturday 9:00–12:00 from May 1st to September 30th); Glassblowing: Monday–Friday 9:00–4:30
CREDIT CARDS: American Express, Diners Club, Visa

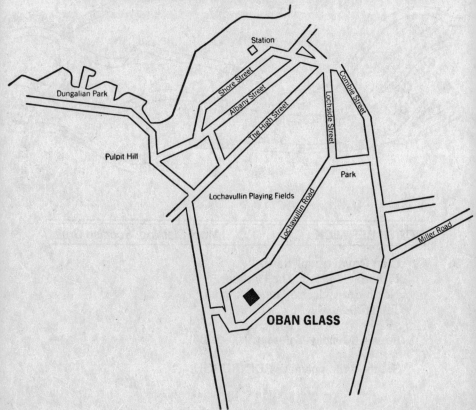

PRODUCTS: Caithness Glass was founded in Wick, Scotland in 1960. They make a large variety of glass vases, bowls, goblets, perfume bottles, paperweights, and other items. The company began by producing hand-blown glassware only, but in 1968 expanded to include engraving. They now allegedly employ the largest group of engravers in Britain. In 1969 the company began making glass paperweights, specializing in abstract designs rather than the more traditional designs. However, they do make traditional styles and have also developed a range of jewelry using intricate "canes" of multicolored molded glass. Many of the other products are made of colored glass. The factory shop sells mostly second-quality items.

The Oban factory specializes in paperweight production, and is the *only* Caithness Glass factory at which visitors can watch this fascinating process, and will find a large selection of unique paperweights. The limited-edition designs of no more than 750 have prices that vary between £37.95 and £65. The mass-produced versions range in price from £17.95 to £131.

LOCATION: Oban is in the west of Scotland on the coast. It is due west of Perth on the A85. See the map.

OBAN   *Woolen Items*

MacDonald's Tweeds Ltd.
Soroba Road
Oban, Argyll PA34 4YY, Scotland
Tel. 0631-63081

HOURS: Monday–Saturday 9:00–5:30
Monday–Sunday (Easter until October) 9:00–5:30

See the write-up for Moffat Woollens Limited in the town of MOFFAT.

LOCATION: Oban is in the west of Scotland on the coast, due west of Perth on the A85.

ORKNEY ISLANDS

See KIRKWALL

PALNACKIE   *Glassware*

North Glen Gallery (craft workshop)
Castle-Douglas
Palnackie, Kirkcudbrightshire DG7 1PN, Scotland
Tel. 05560-200

HOURS: Most days 10:00–6:00, especially summer.
CREDIT CARDS: None

PRODUCTS: At this craft workshop visitors will find decorative glassware handblown by Ed Iglehart, an American living in Scotland. The form and color of the pieces are influenced by early Mediterranean and art nouveau glass as well as Japanese decorative arts and ceramics. Influence is also drawn from Scottish wildlife. Mushrooms are a recurring theme. Vases, goblets, wind chimes, and glass mushrooms are available. Mushrooms range in price from £3.50 to £17.50.

MAIL ORDER: He will mail order. Any item may be returned for credit or refund at any time for any reason.

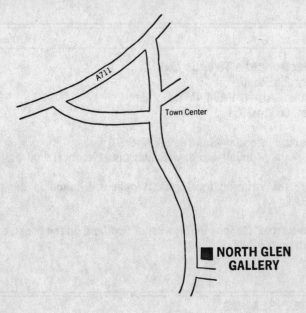

TOURS: Groups of up to 40 may take a tour, which lasts approximately 45 minutes. Advance notice is recommended. Admission is 40 pence for adults, and 10 pence for children. Admission charge is refunded upon purchase.

LOCATION: Palnackie is in the southwest of Scotland, about 16 miles southwest of Dumfries on the A711 road. See the map below.

PEEBLES   *Wool Clothing*

Clan Royal (retail store)
14 High Street
Peebles, Peeblesshire, Scotland
Tel. 0721-21461

HOURS: Monday–Saturday 9:00–5:30

See the write-up under EDINBURGH.

LOCATION: Peebles is 23 miles south of Edinburgh on the A703 road.

PEEBLES   *Woolen, Worsted, and Cashmere Fabric*

Robert Noble (factory/showroom)
March Street Mills
Peebles EH 45 8ER, Scotland
Tel. 0231-20146

HOURS: April to September Monday–Friday 10:00–4:00; September to March hours as above but only on request from factory reception office
CREDIT CARDS: None

PRODUCTS: The Robert Noble Company has been weaving wool and cashmere fabrics since 1666. Their products are sold worldwide. They sell woolen, worsted, and cashmere woven fabrics by the yard for men's and women's outerwear. They have very discounted prices such as skirtings £2 per meter to cashmeres at £12 per meter. Also sold at this factory outlet are woolen and cashmere scarves, and woolen travel picnic rugs.

LOCATION: Peebles is 23 miles south of Edinburgh on the A703 road. See the map below.

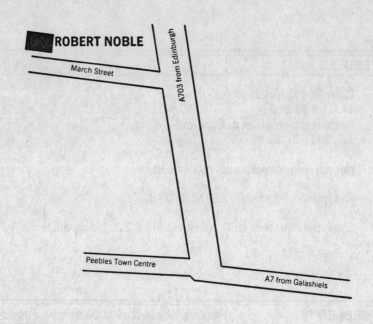

PENICUIK   *Crystal*

Edinburgh Crystal (factory/showroom)
Eastfield, Penicuik
Midlothian EH26 8HB, Scotland
Tel. 0968-75128

HOURS: Gift Shop: Monday–Saturday 9:00–5:00; factory tours available from 9:15–11:00 and 1:15–3:00 Monday–Friday
CREDIT CARDS: None

PRODUCTS: Edinburgh Crystal is entirely handmade crystal glassware. The shop provides a chance for a visitor to purchase items slightly below the normal Edinburgh Crystal quality. A great deal of their crystal is elegantly etched. Edinburgh Crystal offers a variety of stemware, vases, bowls, bells, miniatures, salt and pepper sets, decanters, pitchers, and more. Their pieces are elegant and bold. A certain amount of their crystal glassware—particularly specially commissioned commemorative pieces or unique limited editions—is engraved. These pieces have become collector's items. The company does not want their seconds prices disclosed due to their large wholesale business. The company cafeteria offers a variety of food from 9:00 to 5:00.

TOURS: Visitors are welcome to tour the factory without advance notice. Groups of 12 or more must book in advance. Children under 10 years of age cannot be admitted to the factory. There is a small charge except for disabled persons. For safety reasons, photography is not permitted in the factory. Edinburgh Crystal reserves the right to refuse admission, vary prices, or cancel any visit without notice even if such visits have been confirmed in advance.

LOCATION: Penicuik is about 10 miles south of Edinburgh just off the A701 to Peebles. See the map below.

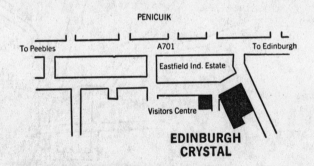

PERTH   *Glass Items, Paperweights*

Caithness Glass, P.L.C. (factory/shop)
Inveralmond Industrial Estate
Inveralmond, Perth, Perthshire PH1 3EE, Scotland
Tel. 0738-37373

HOURS: Shop and Cafe: Monday–Saturday 9:00–5:00; Sunday 1:00–5:00.

Glassblowing: Monday–Friday 9:00–4:30.

CREDIT CARDS: Access, American Express, Diners Club, Master-Card, Visa

PRODUCTS: Caithness Glass was founded in Wick, Scotland in 1960. They make a large variety of glass vases, bowls, goblets, per-fume bottles, paperweights, thimbles, stemware, bells, mugs, and other items. The company began by producing hand-blown glassware only, but in 1968 expanded to include engraving. They now allegedly employ the largest group of engravers in Britain. In 1969 the company

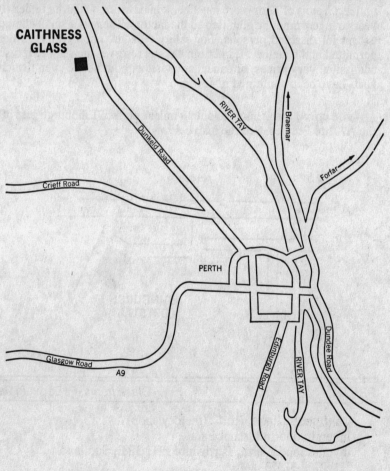

began making glass paperweights, specializing in abstract rather than the more traditional designs. However, they do make traditional styles, and have also developed a range of jewelry working with intricate canes of multicolored molded glass. Many of the other products are also made of colored glass. The factory shop sells mostly second-quality items. The items are well displayed and there is an excellent selection in all price ranges. A paperweight entitled Whispers comes in a limited edition of 500 at £52.50. A paperweight labeled Fireball in an unlimited edition is £18.95. Perfume bottles are £15.95 while perfume atomizers are £25. Delicate jewelry varies from a lapel pin for £3.50 to a pendant which is £7.95. A posy vase is £6.95, a rose bowl is £12.95, and a very elegant fruit bowl is £22.50. Highly recommended!

The Perth factory was opened in July 1979. The factory has a shop, viewing gallery, and visitors' cafe.

LOCATION: Perth is about 42 miles north of Edinburgh on the M90 motorway. The factory is just north of town on the A9 road. See the map.

PERTH   *Woolen Items*

Gleneagles of Scotland
45 High Street
Perth, Perthshire PH1 5TT, Scotland
Tel. 0738-31572

HOURS: Monday–Saturday 9:00–5:30; Monday–Sunday (Easter to October) 9:00–5:30

See the write-up for Moffat Woollens Limited in the town of MOFFAT.

LOCATION: Perth is about 42 miles north of Edinburgh on the M90 Motorway.

PERTH   *Whisky, Gifts*

John Dewar & Sons, Ltd. (retail shop)
Inveralmond, Perth, Perthshire PH1 3EG, Scotland
Tel. 0738-21231

HOURS: Monday–Friday 9:00–5:00, except Bank Holidays
CREDIT CARDS: None

PRODUCTS: This company sells the famous Dewar's whiskies, and also many gift items which carry the Dewar name. Some sample products and prices include: water jugs £2.20, ashtrays £1.60, and glasses £2.30. They also sell many smaller items, some priced under £1. They did not release their Scotch whisky prices.

TOURS: There are two tours each day at 10:15 and 2:15. The tour includes views of blending of the whisky, the repair of casks, plus the bottling and dispatch operations. Tours last 1½ hours. The maximum tour group size is 40, and children are not allowed. As much prior notice as possible is requested for groups.

LOCATION: Perth is about 42 miles north of Edinburgh on the M90 motorway. The John Dewar factory is just north of town on the A9 road.

PERTH   *Handmade Craft Items*

Perth Craft Centre (workshops and showroom)
38 South Street
Perth, Perthshire PH 28PG, Scotland
Tel. 0738-38232

HOURS: Monday–Saturday 10:00–5:30
CREDIT CARDS: None

PRODUCTS: The Perth Craft Centre sells a wide range of handmade Scottish goods. Products available: leaded glass mirrors, cushions, jewelry, shortbread, leather belts, pottery, wooden boxes, prints, honey, purses, jams, paperweights, knitwear, sculpture, and other items. Model boats are £1.05, sterling silver jewelry from £2.50, honey and jams from £1.15, paperweights from £3.95 and 100% wool sweaters from £18. There are six separate craft businesses under one roof. Visitors can often see the craftspeople at work. Items will be shipped overseas.

LOCATION: Perth is about 42 miles north of Edinburgh on the M90 motorway. The Craft Centre is in the center of town. See the map below.

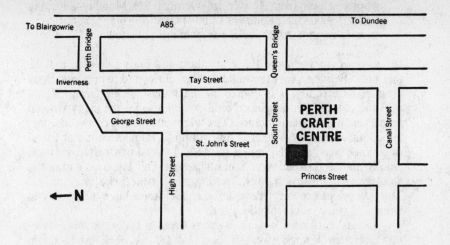

PITLOCHRY   *Woolen Items*

Atholl Woollens
45 Atholl Road
Pitlochry, Perthshire, Scotland
Tel. 0796-2801

HOURS: Monday–Saturday 9:00–5:30; Monday–Sunday (Easter until October) 9:00–5:30

See the write-up for Moffat Woollens Limited in the town of MOFFAT.

LOCATION: Pitlochry is in central Scotland 26 miles north of Perth on the A9 road.

PORTREE, ISLE OF SKYE   *Woolen Items*

Skye Woollen Mill Ltd.
Dunvegan Road
Portree, Inverness Shire IV51 9HG, Isle of Skye, Scotland
Tel. 0478-2889

HOURS: Open from Easter till October 31: Monday–Saturday 9:00–5:00; Sundays 12:00–4:00 during high season.

CREDIT CARDS: All types of payment are accepted

PRODUCTS: For over 100 years there has been a woolen mill on this site. Over the years the mill has been converted to create various products. Currently, it is owned by the James Pringle Group which uses the old mill buildings as a retail warehouse for the many woolen items which they manufacture. The warehouse is full of tweeds, tartans, knitwear, and garments. You will find a large selection of travel rugs, knee rugs, shawls, socks, tartan and tweed ties, tartan scarves, woolly mufflers, tweed hats, tam o'shanters, Fair Isle caps and mitts, wool gloves, sheepskin rugs, knitting wool, tweed and wool packs. The mill prices are very reasonable, and all items have the quality in wool that you expect from Scotland.

Ladies' cashmere V-neck sweaters begin at £60 while men's two-ply cashmere V-neck sweaters begin at £85. A Shetland Fair Isle sweater is £14.50 and a men's fisherman's knit sweater is £17.25. Ladies' kilts in various tweeds and tartans range in price from £26.95 to £60. Men's tweed sport coats in numerous qualties and tweeds vary between £46.95 and £115. Wool travel rugs, which come in very handy during the windy and rainy seasons, are £17.50. Skye Wool Mill Ltd. does offer a mailing service to all of its visitors.

LOCATION: The Isle of Skye is to the west of the mainland. From the town of Portree, take the Dunvegan road (A850). About 500 yards up the road, take the second left. This turn is opposite the West End Garage, just before the Struan road junction (B885). See the map below.

REAWICK, SHETLAND ISLANDS   *Sheepskin Goods*

Reawick (Shetland) Lamb Marketing Company Ltd.
Skeld, Reawick, Shetland ZE2 9NJ, Scotland
Tel. 059-586-261

HOURS: Monday–Friday 8:00–5:00; Saturdays on request with advance notice.
CREDIT CARDS: None

PRODUCTS: Visitors will find over 300,000 sheep on the Shetland Islands. They live mostly on open hills exposed to severe gales and winter blizzards. They eat grass and heather and in the winter months seaweed and salt-sprayed grasses. The meat of Shetland lambs is extremely flavorful and Reawick specializes in preparing and selling it to customers. They also sell sheepskin products: rugs, waistcoats, hats, muffs, slippers, cushions, etc. They sell second-quality rugs. The sheepskins are hand cured to a high quality by island craftsmen and are fully washable. Colors available: whites, gray, black and moorit (light brown). Ladies' jackets are priced from £24.50 to £28.50, ladies' hats from £8.60, and children's colored muffs are £3.50. Sheepskins are priced from £15.70 for first quality to £12.50 for second quality. Treble sheepskins are from £46 and quadruple sheepskins are from £71. (These prices do not include the 15% VAT.) The prices here are exceptionally low. They will ship to any part of the world.

LOCATION: The Shetland Islands are to the far north of Scotland. Reawick is on the west side of the island about 30 miles from the main town of Lerwick. Take the A970 then the A971 west to Effirth. Then go about two miles south of Effirth on the B9071 road.

SCARFSKERRY   *Pottery, Craft Items*

Scarfskerry Pottery
Princes Street
The Moorings, Scarfskerry
Thurso, Caithness KW14 8XN, Scotland
Tel. Barrock 324

HOURS: Monday–Saturday 10:00–4:30; closed on Thursdays.

CREDIT CARDS: None

PRODUCTS: A complete range of hand-thrown stoneware for the kitchen and table is sold at this outlet. There are five different finishes available in quite a variety of pieces: jars, coffee pots, sugar bowls, cups and saucers, jam sets, honey pots, casseroles, mixing bowls, wine sets, mugs, and dinnerware. Coffee sets start at £38.15, small vases at £3.50, and mugs at £4. They have annual sales in January and at the end of September. They will be happy to mail items overseas.

LOCATION: Scarfskerry is on the far north coast of Scotland, about halfway between John O'Groats and Thurso. It is about one mile north of the A836 road.

SELKIRK   *Fabrics, Textile Products*

Atelier Fabrics (factory outlet)
Forest Mill, Station Road
Selkirk TD7 5DJ, Scotland
Tel. 0750-21236

HOURS: Monday–Thursday 9:00–5:00; Friday 9:00–4:00; Saturday 9:00–1:00.
CREDIT CARDS: None

PRODUCTS: A variety of hand-printed cotton furnishing and dress fabrics are sold here, plus household textile products such as tea towels, aprons, pot holders, tea cosys, tablecloths, napkins, patchwork cushions, sachets, and herbal pillows. Seconds are always available. They also carry a selection of remnants and discontinued lines at bargain prices. This company was selected by the Design Centre of London. Tea towels are priced at £1.80, and aprons at £3.50. Tea towel seconds cost £1, and apron seconds are priced at £2.90.

LOCATION: Selkirk is about 40 miles south of Edinburgh on the A7 road. See the map.

SELKIRK   *Fabrics, Knitting Wool*

Gardiner of Selkirk Ltd. (factory outlet)
Walter Turnbull Mill Shop
Tweed Mills
Selkirk TD7 5DZ, Scotland
Tel. 0750-20735

HOURS: Monday–Saturday 9:00–5:00
CREDIT CARDS: Access, Visa

PRODUCTS: The majority of merchandise on sale is produced in the factory next to this outlet store. This shop sells men's and women's tweeds in a variety of weights and designs, tartans, and Shetland hand or machine-knitting wool in shades coordinated with fabrics. There is a large selection of high-quality and well-coordinated tweeds! Highly recommended if you are a seamstress! Seconds are available at greatly reduced prices. They will ship goods to any destination at cost.
Prices are competitive with other tweed fabrics but Gardiner of Selkirk did not want their prices released.

TOURS: Tours of the factory are available by advance arrangement for groups of 12 to 24 people. Tours last approximately one hour.

LOCATION: Selkirk is about 40 miles south of Edinburgh on the A7 road. The shop is located on the A707/A708 about ¼ mile southwest of its junction with the A7 at the northern end of Selkirk. See the map below.

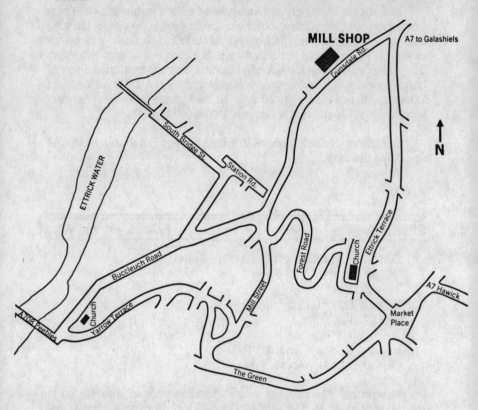

SHETLAND ISLANDS

See LERWICK
 REAWICK
 SOUTHSIDE

SOUNDSIDE, SHETLAND ISLANDS   *Jewelry*

Shetland Silvercraft
Soundside, Weisdale
Shetland, Scotland
Tel. 059572-275

HOURS: Monday–Friday 9:00–1:00 and 2:00–5:00
CREDIT CARDS: American Express, MasterCard, Visa

PRODUCTS: Shetland Silvercraft concentrates on producing silver and gold jewelry of the best quality and original design in their jewelry workshop. The jewelry is worked in unique motifs of Viking ships, cross and thistles, Shetland and birds, mythological characters, and Scandinavian designs. Visitors will find charms, pendants, earrings, cuff links, bracelets, tie tacks, etc. Sterling silver items are very reasonable. Brooches are priced between £5.47 and £19.25. Small pendants range from £3.40 to £6.25 while larger pendants begin at £5.97 and go up to £22.50. Stick pins are £3.75, charms £2.67, rings £7.75, and bracelets £22.50.

Nine-carat gold jewelry pieces are considerably more expensive. Brooches are between £30 and £160. Small pendants range from £5.75 to £16.75 while larger pendants are £6.75 to £46. Charms are £6.75 to £22.50, rings from £23.75 to £57.50, and bracelets from £47.50 to £215. They will be happy to ship any purchases abroad.

LOCATION: The Shetland Islands are to the far north of Scotland. (They're a 12-hour ferry ride from Aberdeen.) Weisdale is in the center of Mainland Island. From Lerwick take the A970 and then the A971 west about 11 miles. The shop is on the side of the road on the shore of Hellister Lock. These products are also sold in Lerwick at the shop of J.G. Rae Ltd. at 92 Commercial Street.

SPEAN BRIDGE   *Woolen Items*

Spean Bridge Woollen Mill (retail shop)
Spean Bridge, Inverness Shire PH34 4EP, Scotland
Tel. 039781-260

HOURS: Monday–Saturday 9:00–6:00, except during winter; winter: 10:00–5:00

CREDIT CARDS: Access, American Express, Diners Club, Visa

PRODUCTS: This shop belongs to the Pitlochry Knitwear Group, which has more than 40 shops throughout the United Kingdom. They sell women's sweaters, dresses, blouses, scarves, gloves, hats, leg warmers, tartans, and nightdresses in a variety of fabrics including Scottish wools and Shetland tweeds. They also sell children's sweaters and kilts, men's clothing, Scottish souvenirs, records and cassettes of Scottish music, and tartan rugs. Rugs range from £4.99 to £18.99, women's gloves are about £1.75, and women's sweaters are priced from £9.75. They usually hold a spring sale and sometimes a winter sale. If a garment is damaged in any way, it is sold at a reduced price. They ship items to other parts of the world. Prices are *very* reasonable.

For a list of other shops in the United Kingdom that sell these products, see CHAIN STORES at the front of this book.

MAIL ORDER: A catalog is available for ordering items from their mail order department, which is handled by their head office. The address is Pitlochry Knitwear Company Ltd., Scottish Woollens House, P. O. Box 8, East Kilbride, Glasgow G74 5QZ, Scotland.

LOCATION: Spean Bridge is in northwestern Scotland about 10 miles north of Fort William on the A82 road.

ST. ANDREWS   *Wool Clothing, Scottish Crafts*

Clan Royal (retail store)
113–115 Market Street
St. Andrews East Fifeshire, Scotland
Tel. 0334-76722

HOURS: Monday–Saturday 9:00–5:30

See the write-up under EDINBURGH.

LOCATION: St. Andrews is on the east coast about 12 miles south of Dundee.

TROON   *Wool Clothing, Scottish Crafts*

Clan Royal (retail store)
Ayr Street
Troon, West Ayrshire, Scotland
Tel. 0292-313515

HOURS: Monday–Saturday 9:00–5:30

See the write-up under EDINBURGH.

LOCATION: Troon is on the southwest coast about six miles north of Ayr on the A78.

TURRIFF   *Natural Fiber Clothing and Fabrics*

Russell Gurney Weavers (craft workshop)
Brae Croft, Muiresk
Turriff, Aberdeenshire AB5 7HE, Scotland
Tel. 0888-63544

HOURS: Monday–Saturday 9:30–5:30
CREDIT CARDS: None

PRODUCTS: Russell Gurney Weavers is a country workshop where visitors can see the processes of hand weaving and spinning demonstrated. Products include handwoven fabrics in natural fibers; wool, silk, plus wool and silk blends. Each fabric pattern designed is woven on a one off basis to maintain exclusiveness. Patterns are never repeated. Women's shawls and men's ties are produced in limited quantities. The fabric produced is about 28″ wide. Prices range from £5.64 to £6.72 per meter depending on the type of fabric. Goods shipped to other parts of the world by request.

TOURS: Maximum for tour groups is 16. Tours last 30 to 60 minutes. Prior arrangements must be made.

LOCATION: Turriff is in the north of Scotland, 36 miles northwest of Aberdeen on the A947 road. From Turriff, take the B9024 road west about 2½ miles.

WALKERBURN   *Wool Clothing and Knitwear*

Clan Royal of Scotland (factory outlet)
Tweedvale Mills
Walkerburn EH43 6AH, Scotland
Tel. 089-687-281/283

HOURS: Monday–Friday 9:00–5:30; Sunday (summer) Walkerburn 12:00–4:00, Edinburgh Lawnmarket 9:00–5:00
CREDIT CARDS: Access, American Express, Diners Club, Visa

PRODUCTS: Clan Royal is a new retail company that is part of a large textile group. They own 23 retail outlets throughout England and Scotland. At the headquarters in Walkerburn, there is a large mill shop and a Scottish Museum of Woolen Textiles which features a history of spinning and weaving. They sell knitwear and wool clothing including sweaters, skirts, kilts, tartans, and blouses. All clothing is made in Scotland. They also sell accessories such as gloves, slippers, and gifts. Fair Isle knitwear prices start at £13.99. Lambswool knitwear is priced from £11.99. Pure wool kilts are priced under £20. There are seasonal sales in July and January. Very stylish products of high quality.

TOURS: Tours are available by previous arrangement. The cost of a tour guide is £3. A tour of the spinning mill lasts 45 minutes.

LOCATION: Walkerburn is about 30 miles south of Edinburgh, halfway between Peebles and Galashiels on the A72 road.

WICK   *Glass Items, Paperweights*

Caithness Glass P.L.C. (factory/shop)
Harrowhill, Wick, Caithness, Scotland
Tel. 0955-2286

HOURS: Shop: mid-June to September 1 Monday–Friday 9:00–5:30; Saturday 9:00–4:30; rest of the year Monday–Friday 9:00–5:00, Saturday 9:00–12:00.
Glassmaking: Monday–Friday 9:00–4:30
CREDIT CARDS: American Express, Diners Club, Visa

PRODUCTS: Caithness Glass was founded in Wick, Scotland in 1960. They make a large variety of glass vases, bowls, goblets, perfume bottles, paperweights, and other items. The company began by producing hand-blown glassware only, but in 1968 expanded to include engraving. They now allegedly employ the largest group of engravers in Britain. In 1969 the company began making glass paperweights, specializing in abstract designs rather than the more traditional designs. However, they do make traditional styles and have also developed a range of jewelry using intricate canes of multicolored molded glass. Many other products are made of colored glass. The factory shop sells mostly second-quality items. A paperweight entitled Whispers with a limited edition of 500 is £52.50. A paperweight entitled Fireball in an unlimited edition is £18.95. Perfume bottles are £15.95 while perfume spray bottles are £25. Delicate jewelry varies from a lapel pin for £3.50 to a pendant which is £7.95. A posy vase is £6.95, a rose bowl is £12.95, and a very elegant fruit bowl is £22.50.

TOURS: Visitors are welcome to watch the glassmakers at work.

LOCATION: Wick is in the northernmost part of Scotland, on the northwest coast at the end of the A9. See the map below.

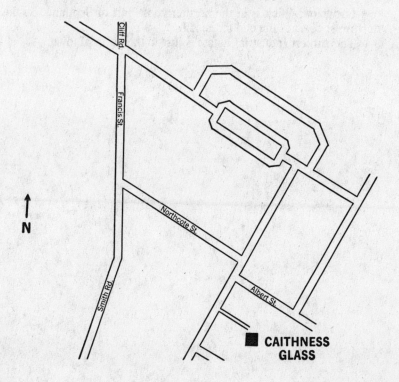

Caithness Leather Products (factory outlet)
Airport Industrial Estate
Wick, Caithness, Scotland
Tel. 0955-3169 and 4343

HOURS: Monday–Friday 9:00–4:30
CREDIT CARDS: None

PRODUCTS: At Caithness Leather Products visitors will find men's and women's wallets, checkbook holders, key cases, coin purses, credit card, and passport holders and other small leather goods. The products are made of either Montana calf, Arizona calf, pigskin or Finecell. A man's wallet is £10, a credit card wallet is £8, a woman's checkbook cover is £21 and a jewelry roll for traveling £15. These prices do not include the 15% VAT.

At the factory special discontinued items are always available at a special savings.

LOCATION: Wick is in the northernmost part of Scotland, on the northwest coast at the end of the A9.

The Airport Industrial Estate is just to the north of town.

Wales

WELCOME TO WALES

Wales is a small, scenic country only 150 miles long and 60 miles wide. The scenery varies from deep valleys to coastline resorts and green pastures to thickly wooded mountains. Much of the land is unspoiled by industrialization. The Welsh have their own Gaelic language as well as their own distinct culture, history, customs, and cuisine.

Wales has been called the land of the castles. The area has been a battleground for centuries, and castles had been erected at strategic points all over the country. The visitor will be delighted to find that over 100 castles can be toured.

Wales was once a rural, very isolated region supported mainly by small, family-run farms. Much of that flavor is still available to the visitor by staying on a working farm where bed and breakfast are offered, by sleeping in a quaint Tudor inn which is several centuries old, or by renting a horse-drawn caravan and touring the countryside at a leisurely pace.

The southeast of Wales is heavily industrialized due to the coal rush in the last century. Much of the population settled here to work the coal mines, steel making, and manufacturing. The Welsh slate quarries are largely in the north. However, both coal and slate mining have vastly declined during this century.

Every inch of Wales offers a new activity or attraction for the visitor. Visit the slate caverns, relax on one of the 100 golf courses, tour a woolen mill, visit a museum, dine at a castle, attend a sheepdog trial, shop at a craft workshop, ride on a narrow-gauge steam train, or just relax and enjoy the scenery.

Wales is quickly becoming a major tourist attraction. The people are warm, friendly, and helpful. Enjoy a visit into its colorful past where castles were once a reality of life.

SHOPPING IN WALES

Wales's wool is perhaps one of its most famous products. For centuries the woolen mills were run by water power, so that you will find many of the mills by streams. The colors and textures of the wool products are distinctively Welsh, each mill often developing their own style. At the mills visitors will find an immense range of woolen products from clothing to blankets to cloth.

Pottery in every form is abundant in Wales. The larger companies will be found near those sections of Wales where clay is abundant, as well as coal, which is used to stoke their kilns. In the country you will find many family-run potteries on farms and in smaller craft shops.

Woodworking has existed in Wales in one form or another for centuries. Today many antique buffs are looking for that special accent piece created years ago by skilled craftsmen. You will find that many of the woodworkers will create pieces of furniture to your specifications. The creation of cane furniture is a dying art but a few craftsmen still work in this area. Wooden bowl-turning, as well as the creation of many practical household items, will still be found in many shops.

My favorite Welsh wooden item is the lovespoon. Lovespoons were once upon a time created as a way to pass the time on bitter cold winter evenings. The spoons were elaborately carved and decorated by a man and then given as a token of affection to his sweetheart. The more intricate the design of the lovespoon, the more in love the man was supposed to be. Of course today, visitors will find lovespoons for sale all over Wales.

Slate products are found in a wide range of items from clocks to bowls. Slate was once used throughout Europe for roofs.

In Wales you will find a very large selection of very unique and creative jewelry designs worked in all types of metals.

Every mineral, semi-precious, and precious gem has been available in Wales throughout her long history. The Welsh have become very talented craftsworkers aided by the extensive choice of stones and minerals.

Wrought iron and metalwork are also made by the craftsmen in Wales.

By no means is this a complete list of all of the Welsh products. You will find an abundance of craft shops and craftsworkers throughout Wales. The Wales Tourist Board has encouraged craftsworkers to help create a new industry in Wales and keep traditional techniques alive. As far as we are concerned, they have done a very good job.

Have fun shopping in Wales! You can discover all types of new and exciting products.

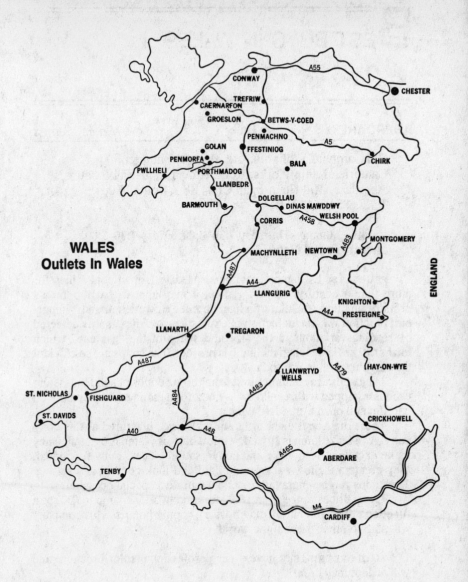

WALES
Outlets In Wales

CONWAY
TREFRIW
CAERNARFON
GROESLON
BETWS-Y-COED
PENMACHNO
GOLAN
FFESTINIOG
PENMORFA
PORTHMADOG
PWLLHELI
BALA
LLANBEDR
DOLGELLAU
BARMOUTH
DINAS MAWDDWY
CORRIS
WELSH POOL
MACHYNLLETH
NEWTOWN
MONTGOMERY
LLANGURIG
KNIGHTON
LLANARTH
PRESTEIGNE
TREGARON
HAY-ON-WYE
LLANWRTYD
WELLS
ST. NICHOLAS
FISHGUARD
CRICKHOWELL
ST. DAVIDS
ABERDARE
TENBY
CARDIFF
CHESTER
CHIRK
ENGLAND

A55
A5
A458
A483
A44
A487
A44
A487
A484
A483
A479
A40
A48
A465
M4

Best Buys in Wales

E. Thomas & Williams, Ltd. (factory showroom)
Cambrian Lamp Works, Robertstown Industrial Estate,
Aberdare, Mid Glamorgan CF44 8YY, South Wales
Tel. 0685-876107

HOURS: Monday–Thursday 7:30–4:00; Friday 7:30–3:00.
CREDIT CARDS: None

PRODUCTS: Oil lamps have been used in British coal mines for
more than a century. At first glance, it may appear that the lamp's
primary function was that of a light source. However, its most impor-
tant function was the detection of explosive gas. The gas was detected
by reading variations in the size and shape of the "gas cap" which
forms on the flame when methane is present. The lamps are so efficient
that they are still in use today.
The lamps are manufactured from three pounds of solid brass, and
each is equipped with a solid brass hook for handling. They operate on
paraffin and burn a standard wick.
There are about eight different styles manufactured at this company. A full-size lamp is 10″ tall, while a half-size lamp is 6½″ tall. They
make excellent decorative and conversation pieces. Fully functional,
they create a mellow background light and look good in any setting.
The lamps can be engraved to commemorate a special occasion.
Lamp prices range from £8.90 for a nonworking lamp to £30 for a
functional, paraffin burning lamp with a copper bonnet. This company
will ship to other parts of the world.

MAIL ORDER: They have a very professional color brochure and
will accept mail orders.

TOURS: Tours take place at 10:00–12:00 and 2:00–3:00 for groups
of six or less.

LOCATION: Aberdare is in south central Wales about 25 miles northwest of Cardiff on the A4059. It is about four miles west of Merthyr Tydfil, the legendary haunt of Merlin the magician.

BALA   *Welsh Crafts*

Craftcentre Cymru (retail store)
59 High Street
Bala, Gwynned LL23 7AF, Wales
Tel. 0678-520-510

HOURS: Monday–Saturday 9:00–5:30 (but closed on Wednesdays from November to March); in June, July, and August also open Sunday, Friday, and Saturday evenings.

See the write-up under PORTHMADOG.

LOCATION: Bala is in north central Wales about 18 miles northeast of Dolgellau on the A494 road. The shop is centrally located on High Street (Main Street) next to the White Lion Hotel.

BARMOUTH   *Welsh Crafts*

Craftcentre Cymru (retail store)
The Welsh Kitchen
High Street
Barmouth, Gwynedd LL42 1DS, Wales
Tel. 0341-280-245

HOURS: April through September: Monday–Saturday 9:00–5:30; closed during winter months.

See the write-up under PORTHMADOG.

LOCATION: Barmouth is on the northwest coast of Wales about 10 miles west of Dolgellau on the A496 road. The shop is situated halfway down the main street.

BETWS-Y-COED
Welsh Crafts

Craftcentre Cymru (retail store)
Talgarth House
Betws-y-coed, Gwynedd LL24 OAY, Wales
Te. 06902-284

HOURS: Spring and autumn: Monday–Saturday 9:00–8:00; July
and August: Monday–Saturday 9:00–9:30; winter: Monday–Saturday 9:00–5:30

See the write-up under PORTHMADOG.

LOCATION: Betws-y-Coed is in the northwest of Wales about 12
miles north of Blaenau Ffestinog on the A470. The store is east of the
Pont-y-Pair Bridge on the opposite side of the A5 road.

BLAENAU FFESTINIOG
Pottery

Ffestiniog Pottery (craft workshop)
Blaenau Ffestiniog
Gwynedd, LL41 3LZ, Wales
Tel. 0766-83061

HOURS: Monday–Sunday "until 10:00 p.m."
CREDIT CARDS: None

PRODUCTS: This small shop in the back of a home has country
earthenware products, including mugs, coffee pots, teapots, baking
sets, casseroles, bowls, plates, and a variety of other items. One pint
tankards were £3.40. A nest of three baking dishes were well priced at
£10. A three-pint casserole was £7.75. Many items were priced under
£10. They make a number of large pottery pieces, such as fruit bowls,
casseroles, vases, and storage pots. No VAT is charged. All items are
ovenproof and microwave safe. Visitors can watch traditional wood-
fired techniques used to make the pottery.

LOCATION: Blaenau Ffestiniog is in the northwest of Wales on the
A470. The pottery is just a few minutes walk from the town centre. See
the map below.

A470 Betws-y-Coed

"The Commercial"

Town Centre

Railway Station

FFESTINIOG
POTTERY

A496 To Porthmadog

To Ffestiniog A470

CAERNARFON   *Welsh Crafts*

Craftcentre Cymru (retail store)
7 Castle Ditch
Caernarfon, Gwynedd LL55 2AY, Wales
Tel. 0286-5939

HOURS: Monday–Saturday 9:00–5:30; also open Sunday from
Easter through October; in July and August open 9:00–
7:30; from November–March closed each Thursday.

See the write-up under PORTHMADOG.

LOCATION: Caernarfon is in the far northwest about eight miles
south of Bangor on the A487. The shop is situated immediately opposite the main entrance to Caernarfon Castle.

CHIRK   *Welsh Crafts*

Craftcentre Cymru (retail store)
2/3, Station Avenue
Chirk, Near Wrexham, Clwyd LL14 5LS, Wales
Tel. 0691-777-015

HOURS: Monday–Saturday 9:00–6:00; also open Sunday from
Easter to Christmas.

See the write-up under PORTHMADOG.

LOCATION: Chirk is on the northeast border of Wales about eight
miles south of Wrexham on the A483, then the A5 roads. The shop is
opposite the Hand Hotel and the War Memorial on the main A5 road.

CONWY   *Welsh Crafts*

Craftcentre Cymru (retail store)
Stanley Building
Castle Street
Conwy, Gwynedd LL32 8AY, Wales
Tel. 0492-63 3417

HOURS: Monday–Saturday 9:00–5:30; also open Sunday from
March to Christmas; evenings from July to September.
Closed Wednesday from January to March.

See the write-up under PORTHMADOG.

LOCATION: Conwy is on the north coast of Wales on the A55. The
shop is 100 yards from the Conwy Castle on Castle Street.

CORRIS   *Tweed, Rag Rugs*

Alison Morton (craft workshop)
1 Bron-y-Gan, Corris
Machynlleth, Powys SY20 9TN, Wales
Tel. 065473-629

HOURS: Monday–Friday 9:00–5:00
CREDIT CARDS: None

PRODUCTS: Alison Morton makes handwoven tweed cloth incorporating handspun wool with matching knitting wool. The tweed is woven with a commercial yarn for the warp (usually Jacobs yarn in natural colors) and the weft is handspun to give unique textural interest. The colors available are the five natural fleece tones—dark brown, moorit (brown), gray, cream, and mixed gray and white which gives the cloth random stripes.

The handspun knitting wool is a two-ply yarn. It is available in the same shades as the tweed.

The tweed woolen fabric and the knitting yarn are available in packs of two yards of tweed 36″ wide, and 12 ounces of matching yarn. Customers can order fabric and wool for their specific needs. Prices are from £10—£14 per yard.

Alison also makes rag rugs which begin at £40. The rugs have a strong linen warp with the weft of rag which is actually old clothing cut

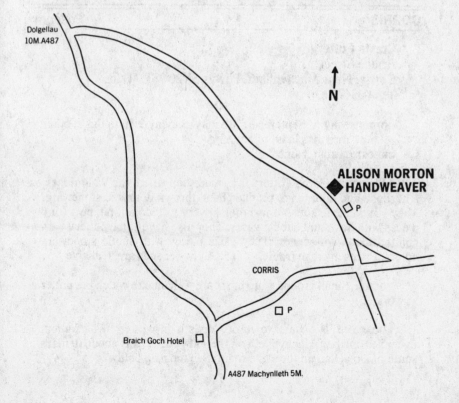

into one-inch strips and woven to form a brightly colored floor rug 36″ wide and between five and six feet long. A color scheme is chosen in advance for each rug. The color blends available are in shades of browns, greens, blues, or reds. The rugs are often used as wall hangings. Alison sometimes adds tufts across the width of the rug for added texture and interest.

The quality of the cloth and the color combinations are excellent. Her rag rugs are very country and I highly recommend them. Superb colors! Alison has an eye for detail! She will send you a brochure which will explain the colors of the products which she will make for mail orders.

LOCATION: Corris is in western Wales about five miles north of Machynlleth on the A487 road. (It is also about 10 miles south of Dolgellau on the same road.) See the map.

CORRIS   *Pottery*

Corris Pottery
Bridge Street
Corris, Near Machynlleth, Powys SY20 9SP, Wales
Tel. 065473-630

HOURS: May to September: Monday–Sunday 9:30 to dusk; other
months please phone.
CREDIT CARDS: None

PRODUCTS: Corris Pottery is a small shop where the Wallbridges, a husband and wife team, produce hand-thrown domestic stoneware. They specialize in sets of mushrooms (very well done), pin pots (tiny pieces with lids), and bubble vases. They also have some pottery with colored mountain scenes. They glaze pieces with subtle stoneware colors. Prices average from £1 to £5. A few seconds are available.

TOURS: Small groups of up to six are welcome to watch the potter at work.

LOCATION: The small town of Corris is in western Wales about five miles north of Machynlleth on the A487 road. (It is about 10 miles south of Dolgellau on the same road.) See the map below.

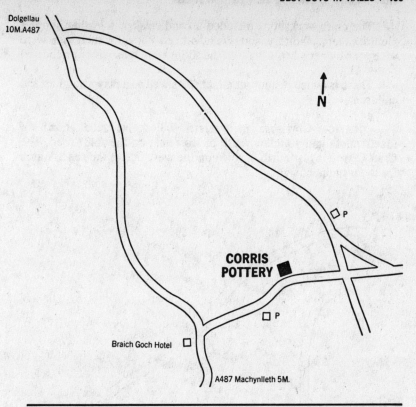

CORRIS *Craft Products*

Corris Craft Centre
Corris, Near Machynlleth, Powys, Wales
Tel. 065473-343

HOURS: April 1–May 31: Monday–Saturday 10:00–6:00; June 1–
September 15: Monday–Saturday 9:00–8:00; September
16–March 31: Monday–Sunday 10:00–4:00.
CREDIT CARDS: None

PRODUCTS: The Corris Craft Centre is an attractive new group of
buildings which house six separate craft workshops. It offers the
visitor a chance to see skilled craftsmen at work and to purchase their
products at the same time. The crafts vary according to the time of
year.

The craft workshops included a candlemaker, a leather shop, a picture gallery, a pottery, and several others. Prices for each shop were set by the owners. Most items in the shops were reasonably priced and below £15.

There is a nice restaurant attached as well as a playground for the children.

LOCATION: Corris is in western Wales five miles north of Machynlleth and 10 miles south of Dolgellau on the A487 road. The Craft Centre is just north of town on the west side of the road. Watch for the prominent sign.

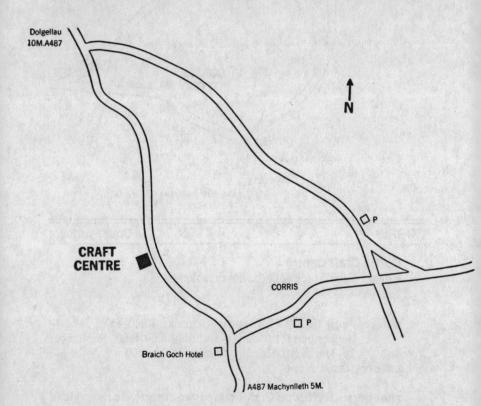

CORRIS *Ceramics*

Glandwyryd Stores Ceramics
Upper Corris, Near Machynlleth, Powys SY 20 9SP, Wales
Tel. 065473-297

HOURS: Open daily all year—but do not be surprised if they are
closed occasionally in the winter.
CREDIT CARDS: None

PRODUCTS: Don and Jacky Bennet have created stoneware
figures that are unique and extremely creative. They have tiny candle
snuffers as monks, lawyers, chefs, ballerinas, and over 45 other separate occupations. They make full nativity sets, equestrian candle snuffers, period nursery figurines, and large stoneware figures. Their designs, quality, and color selections are superb. Since they are selling
direct, their prices are at a substantial savings over the retail stores.

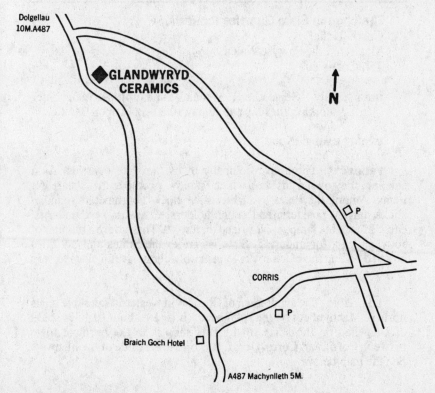

Their large pieces sold for approximately £80. Their candle snuffers were £3.50 each. I only bought six and wish I had purchased one of each.

Each item has its own personality and charm! A "highly recommended" is easily given for these two talented artists!

They also carry a pottery line from a talented friend. His items have tasteful colors, handsome design, and very reasonable prices.

LOCATION: Corris is in western Wales five miles north of Machynlleth and 10 miles south of Dolgellau on the A487 road. Upper Corris is a small group of buildings up the valley just north of the town of Corris. The shop is on the east side of the main road. Parking is across the street.

CORRIS UCHAF   *Slate Products*

Braichgoch Slate Quarries (craft shop)
Corris Uchaf
Machynlleth, Powys, Wales
Tel. Corris 602

HOURS: July 1–September 1: Monday–Sunday 10:00–5:00; winter
months: Tuesday and Friday 10:00–5:00; open Bank Holidays.
CREDIT CARDS: None

PRODUCTS: The above company owns the slate quarries. As a sideline, they own a gift shop which employs people to make slate gift items. Among the items available: slate clocks, barometers, candlesticks, lamps, coasters, and pencil holders. Coasters were under £2 each. Most slate lamps were priced under £40. There were a number of souvenir gifts for under £5. Slate is rare in the States and my boys enjoyed adding the black rocks to their collections. A fun place to stop if you enjoy slate.

LOCATION: The small town of Corris is in western Wales five miles north of Machynlleth on the A487 road. (It is also about 10 miles south of Dolgellau on the same road.) This shop is to the north of town between Corris and Corris Uchaf. It is on the east side of the highway. See the map below.

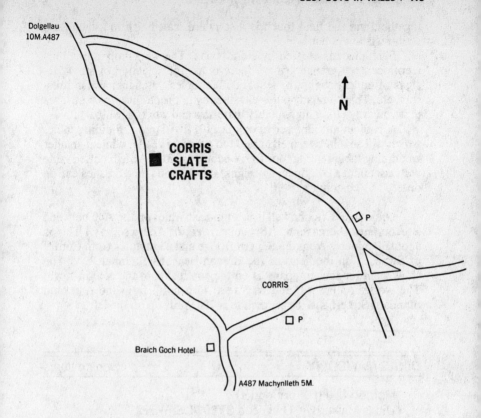

CRICKHOWELL   *Furniture*

Grahame Amey Ltd. Furniture Makers
   (workshop/showroom)
The Granary
Standard Street
Crickhowell, Breconshire NP8 1SY, Wales
Tel. 0873-810540

HOURS: Monday–Saturday 9:00–4:30
CREDIT CARDS: None

PRODUCTS: Grahame Amey Ltd. creates all handmade furniture
in solid hardwoods—mainly ash or oak. All of their items are screwed

414 / SHOPPER'S GUIDE TO BEST BUYS IN WALES

together, and the final touch is a standard matt finish in a heat- and stain-resistant polish which is handwaxed.

Each piece is created by a craftsman. The workshop is in a thirteenth-century granary where there is a large selection of stock designs of tables, chairs, benches, coffee tables, kitchens, Welsh dressers, etc. This company only sells directly to the public, which ensures that you are getting high-quality materials and workmanship.

A cabinet and dresser in oak is £1011. A large ash dining table, which will seat between eight and ten people, is £494, while a smaller oak dining table seating four to six people is £312. An ash coffee table will cost about £118. Special designs, stains, wood, and finishes can be ordered by customers.

LOCATION: Crickhowell is in southeast Wales on the A40 between Brecon and Abergavenny. (Six miles west of Aberqavenny.) This is about 30 minutes from the Severn Bridge and 45 minutes from Cardiff or Swansea, in the heart of the Brecon Beacons National Park. The showroom for this company is on the south side of the A40 in town. The workshop is on Standard Street: turn north from the A40 onto Standard Street, and the workshop is 100 yards up on the left.

DINAS MAWDDWY   *Woolen Items*

Meirion Mill (factory/outlet)
Dinas Mawddwy, Gwynedd SY20 9LS, Wales
Tel. 06504-311

HOURS: April to October: Monday–Saturday 10:00–5:00; Sunday 11:00–4:00; November to March: Monday–Saturday 10:00–4:00
CREDIT CARDS: American Express, Visa

PRODUCTS: Meirion Mill has a large shop which sells their merchandise at low mill prices. Much of the merchandise is unobtainable elsewhere. Meirion Mill makes beautiful bedcovers in pure virgin wool £40 to £56; travel rugs £16; lap rugs £8; capes £52 to £70; tunics from £33; skirts from £25; coats £59 to £70; place mats and tea cosys. A wide range of knitwear and other garments and gifts are also sold. About half of the goods sold at the Mill Shop are woven on the premises. There is a sale room where certain items are reduced all year long. A coffee shop, which is known for its freshly baked goods, is on the premises. The mill is in an old railway station and offers pleasant strolls for visitors and their pets, as well as a children's play area.

MAIL ORDERS: A mail order service is available for both domestic and foreign orders. Also, the Mill will mail items home for you which have been purchased at their shop.

TOURS: A self-guided tour of the factory is available for a nominal charge.

LOCATION: The Mill is in central western Wales about half a mile north of Mallwyd (about 10 miles east of Dolgellau) on the A470 road. See the map below.

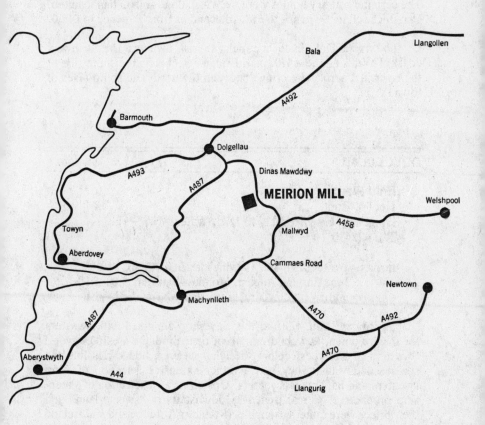

DOLGELLAU   *Welsh Crafts*

Bryn Melyn Studio (craft centre)
Bridge Street
Dolgellau, Gwynedd LL40 1AY, Wales
Tel. 034149-651

HOURS: April through October: Monday–Saturday 10:00–5:30
CREDIT CARDS: None

PRODUCTS: This small craft centre sells ceramics, candles, original paintings and other items, all produced locally. Work is done in the shop on all these products, and at least one craftsman is always there. The ceramic country homes were very well done and all handpainted. Ceramics sell for 90 pence to £18, and candles from 25 pence to £4.50.

LOCATION: Dolgellau is a popular tourist town near the northwest coast of Wales on the A470 road. Bridge Street is on the south side of the river just across the bridge between the north and south sides of town.

DOLGELLAU   *Sweaters*

Enid Pierce
Heol Y Bont
Dolgellau, Gwynedd LL40 1AU, Wales
Tel. 422430

HOURS: Winter 9:30–4:00 (Wednesday 9:30–12:30)
        June through August: Monday–Saturday 9:00–5:30
CREDIT CARDS: Barclaycard, Eurocard, MasterCard, Visa

PRODUCTS: You will find this tiny shop crammed with sweaters for men, women, and children. All of their products are 100% wool! Sweaters of all types, colors, designs, weaves, and styles line the shelves and walls. They had a rather extensive selection of Aran sweaters and handmade sweaters. Upstairs was a selection of sheepskin products. The real treat was downstairs in "sweaterland" and their prices were quite reasonable. (Sweaters from Iceland and Ireland were also sold.) Aran sweaters and natural wool sweaters are priced from £20. Lighter weight sweaters in Shetland wool begin at £9.99, and soft lambswool sweaters start at £12. Tweed hats are a store specialty from £3.95, and wool knee rugs from £3.99. Sheepskin slippers are from £6, gloves from £10.95, and sheepskin rugs from £14.

LOCATION: Dolgellau is in the northwest of Wales near the coast on the A470. This shop is on the south side of the river, on the left after you cross the bridge into town from the A470 road.

FISHGUARD   *Wool Goods, Clothing, Gifts, Pottery*

Tregwynt Textiles
6 High Street, Fishguard, Letterston
Haverfordwest SA 65 9AT, Wales
Tel. 872370

See the write-up under the town of ST. NICHOLAS.

LOCATION: Fishguard is in the far southwest of Wales on the north coast of the peninsula. It is about 19 miles southwest of Cardigan on the A487.

GOLAN   *Woolen Products*

Brynkir Woollen Mill Ltd. (factory/showroom)
Golan, Garndolbenmaen
Gwynedd LL51 9YU, Wales
Tel. 076-675-236

HOURS: Monday–Thursday 8:00–4:45; Friday 8:00–4:00; closed on public holidays, Saturdays, and Sundays.
CREDIT CARDS: American Express, Diners Club, MasterCard, Visa

PRODUCTS: Brynkir Woollen Mill Ltd. was originally in a corn mill which was converted into a woolen mill 150 years ago. A water wheel can still be seen turning, although its power is no longer utilized.
All of the items available from the gift shop have been spun from pure new wool which has been carded, spun, and woven on the prem-

ises. You will find a wide selection of woolen items. Tapestry bedspreads and blankets with traditional patterns are reversible and come in sizes up to 115 inches wide. Honeycomb bedspreads with hand-knotted fringes are available in a variety of colors. Blankets and traveling rugs are available in various sizes, weights, and patterns. Fabrics are sold by the yard—tweeds, Welsh flannels, and tapestry. Brynkir Tapestry is made into coats, capes, skirts, waistcoats, and hats. Knitting wools, socks, and numerous smaller items are also made from tapestry. Purses, place mats, and cushion covers are just a few of the small items available.

Bedspreads are found to be reasonably priced between £50 and £70. Warm wool blankets for the cold winter nights range between £20 and £40. Lap rugs, or travel rugs as they are sometimes known, are priced from £18 to £35. Wool fabric which is 56 inches wide is exceptionally well-priced between £10 and £15. For talented knitters, knitting wool is sold in 50 gram balls at £1 each.

Postal service is available to all parts of the world, as well as a VAT refund when applicable.

TOURS: Visitors are welcome to watch the process of making woolens on the complex machinery: tenterhook willey, carders, spinning mules, doubling and hanking machines, cheese and bobbin winder, warping mill and the looms. All children must be accompanied by adults. Coaches and organized parties must make prior arrangements with the factory.

LOCATION: Golan is in the northwest of Wales, just north of Porthmadog. From Porthmadog, take the A487 toward Caernarfon. Go through the villages of Tremadog and Penmorfa. You will then see a sign directing you to turn right toward Golan. The mill is a short way down this road on the right.

GROESLON   *Slate Items*

Inigo Jones & Co. Ltd. (factory outlet)
Tudor Slate Works
Groeslon, Caernarfon, Gwynedd LL54 7UE, Wales
Tel. 0286-830-242

HOURS: Monday 9:00–4:00; Saturday 9:00–12:00
CREDIT CARDS: Access, Barclaycard

PRODUCTS: Inigo Jones is a company of experienced craftsmen established since 1861. The slate they use is quarried from the hills of the Snowdonia Range and is about 500 million years old. They manufacture slate products such as clocks, dice, lamps, pen sets, chess sets, tabletops, fireplace hearths, floor tiles, and barometers. Of the many slate products in Wales, these are by far the nicest we saw. Prices range from £4 for a five-inch trophy to £32.25 for a hebog lamp. A mantel clock 5″ × 5″ × 3″ in natural black slate is £24.30. A slate solitaire board was £8. A calendar with a pen mount and a red silkscreened dragon was £7. They hold a seasonal sale at Christmas and are willing to ship items to other parts of the world.

MAIL ORDER: They have a mail order division.

LOCATION: Groeslon is in the northwest of Wales. It is on the A487 road between Caernarfon and Porthmadog, about five miles south of Caernarfon.

HAY-ON-WYE   *Books*

PRODUCTS: Hay-on-Wye is a small Welsh village known as the secondhand book capital of the world. Building after building is crammed with dusty old books, many of which have come from the States. Most of the stores are very basic and the town is not very pretty. We were somewhat disappointed, but the tourists throng to this city where used books cost from a few cents to thousands of dollars. The Guinness Book of World Records describes Richard Booth (Bookseller) Ltd. as the world's largest secondhand book dealer. His stores, which are all over Hay-on-Wye, have over 9.9 miles of shelving and between 900,000 to 1,100,000 volumes. In the summer season it is not uncommon to sell 5000 books a day to tourists. Parking lots are well marked. If you are a real book buff, plan on spending hours looking through the wealth of old books available here.

LOCATION: Hay-on-Wye is in the south, on the eastern border of Wales. It is about 21 miles west of Hereford (in England) on the A438 road. This is about 15 miles northeast of Brecon on the A470, then the A438. At the town of Clyro, turn east on the B4351, which will lead into town.

KNIGHTON   *Knitwear and Crafts*

Wendy Lawrence Ltd (retail store)
The Narrows Craft Shop
21 High Street
Knighton, Powys LD7 1AT, Wales
Tel. 0547-528018

HOURS: Monday, Tuesday, Thursday, Friday, Saturday 9:15–5:30;
        Wednesday, 9:15–1:00; closed Sunday.
CREDIT CARDS: Access, Barclaycard, Visa

PRODUCTS: The tiny shop where Wendy Lawrence knitwear is
designed, manufactured, and sold, was built in the early 1600's. In
addition to knitwear, other craft items such as Welsh love spoons,
pottery, patchwork, woodwork, and silver jewelry are sold. A long-

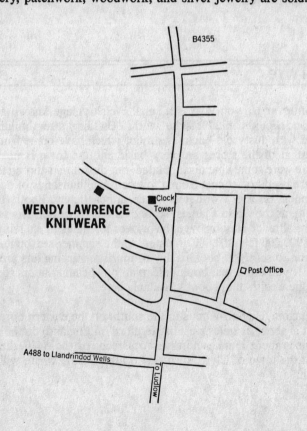

sleeved sweater retails for about £24.50, mug for £1.95, a patchwork cushion for £10, and seconds in sweaters for £10 to £15. Sales are held at the end of summer and after Christmas. Wendy Lawrence will ship to any part of the world.

LOCATION: Knighton is on the eastern border of Wales about 25 miles northwest of Hereford (in England) on the A488. It is about halfway between the towns of Knighton on the south and Bishop's Castle on the north. See the map.

LLANARTH   *Pottery*

Llanarth Pottery (John and Mary Lovett) (workshop)
Llanarth, Dyfed SA47 OPU, Wales
Tel. 0545-580584

HOURS: Monday-Sunday 9:00–7:00; closed at times in winter.
CREDIT CARDS: None

PRODUCTS: Handthrown stoneware and terracotta pots are the specialty of this pottery. Many items are priced under £1. There are pots, mugs, tea and coffee pots, casseroles, oven dishes, goblets, wine sets, bread crocks, butter and cheese dishes, salt pigs, jam pots, lamp bases, and a vast range of vases and flower pots. All items are oven, freezer, microwave, and dishwasher proof. A coffee set for six was £28, a cereal bowl £2, a dinner plate £4.40, a pie dish with handles £8, a posy pot £2, and a small lamp base £10.
All items come in four glazes—talc yellow, blue/gray, green, or speckled dolomite.
Children are welcome and visitors will find small bags of clay which they may purchase.

TOURS: Coach parties, mystery trips, and guided tours are welcome during the evening by appointment.

LOCATION: Llanarth is near the west coast of Wales about four miles south of Aberaeron (which is 16 miles south of Aberystwyth) on the A487. Watch for the sign to the pottery which is 100 yards from the main road.

LLANBEDR   *Wool Jackets*

Enoch Griffiths Ltd. (factory outlet)
Maes Artro Tourist Village
Llanbedr, Gwynedd LL45 2PZ, Wales
Tel. 034-123-447

HOURS: Monday–Friday 9:00–5:00
CREDIT CARDS: None

PRODUCTS: Visitors may watch the products being manufactured
in this tiny showroom-factory. Very nice woolen jackets for women
are made here. The wool is mostly beige, brown, and gray in a tailored
tweed which is very appealing to all ages. Prices vary from £20 to £40
on most jackets.

LOCATION: Llanbedr is on the A496 on the northwest coast of
Wales about halfway between Porthmadog on the north and Barmouth
on the south. Look for the Maes Artro Tourist Village sign on the west
side of the A496 road. There is an admission charge to enter the
Tourist Village, where several craft shops are located.

LLANGURIG   *Welsh Crafts*

Craftcentre Cymru (retail store)
Near Llanidloes
Llangurig, Powys SY18 6SG, Wales
Tel. 055-15-229

See the write-up under PORTHMADOG.

LOCATION: Llangurig is in central Wales 25 miles east of Aberystwyth on the A55 road. The shop is in the center of the village opposite
the Black Lion Hotel.

LLANWRTYD WELLS   *Welsh Tweeds*

The Cambrian Factory (factory/showroom)
Llanwrtyd Wells, Powys LD5 4SD, Wales
Tel. 05913-211

HOURS: Factory: Monday–Thursday 8:15–5:00; Friday 8:15–3:45.
Shop: Monday–Friday 8:15–5:30; Saturday 9:00–12:00
Saturday 9:00–4:30 May to September
CREDIT CARDS: Access, MasterCard, Visa

PRODUCTS: The Cambrian Factory Ltd. was established in 1918 to give employment to ex-servicemen and women disabled in World War I. Today the factory still employs ex-servicepeople and other disabled persons.

Visitors can see the entire Welsh Tweed manufacturing process of wool sorting, dying, carding, spinning, warping, winding, and weaving.

At the shop you may purchase woolen Welsh Tweeds or any number of completed woolen clothing items or accessories. A partial list of available items: ties, sport coats, men's trousers, sweaters, caps, socks, gloves, stockings, travel rugs, knee rugs, coats, women's slacks, handbags, etc. Travel rugs made from wool start at £25 while knee rugs (36″ × 54″) start at £13. They make special gifts and are easily put into a suitcase. Raglan herringbone tweed coats for women begin at £69. Lapland coats in natural undyed Welsh mountain wool are £36.30. Fully lined wool skirts are available in four color combinations at £24 each. Men's fisherman's knit pullover sweaters with suede elbow patches are £28. (I have seen these sweaters in exclusive department stores for well over $100.)

Tweed 100% Welsh wool fabric is sold to visitors. The fabric is 29 inches wide and approximate yardages needed for sewing will be found in the HELPFUL HINTS section. Wool for lightweight suits (Irfon) weighs about seven ounces per yard and is priced at £4.30 per yard. Wool for suits or skirts (Cledan) weighs about nine ounces per yard and is £5.60 per yard. Wool for coats (Cammarch) weighs eleven ounces and is £5.60 per yard. Dress-weight wool (Wye) is five ounces per yard and is £5.20 per yard. For those visitors who know how to sew, the savings on creating your own woolen garments can be substantial.

A designer collection of women's clothing fashioned by Eddie Newton has brought an elegant new look to traditional country tweeds. The outfits are flattering and stylish as well as comfortable. A classic blouson with leather inset trim and patch pockets is £47.95. A very well constructed button-down-the-front matching skirt, which has a gathered waist and suede trimmed side pockets, will run £32.40. For £80.35 a woman could have an ensemble which would be timeless and stunning.

MAIL ORDERS: A world mail order division is in operation. Their leaflets are easy to understand and most of their pictures are full color. If they are unable to deliver your order within 21 days, you will be notified.

TOURS: An eight-minute slide and sound introduction is given before the 30-minute tour begins. There is no group size limit.

LOCATION: Llanwrtyd Wells is in south central Wales on the A483 road about 40 miles north of Swansea (which is on the south coast). The factory is right beside the road, just north of town. See the map below.

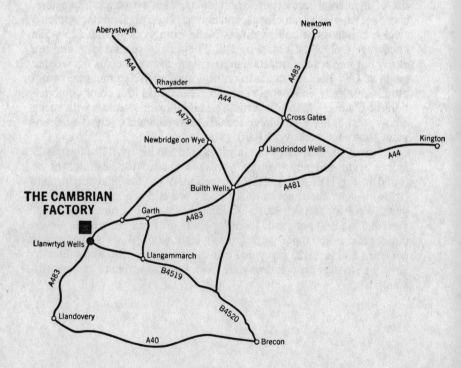

MACHYNLLETH   *Welsh Crafts*

Craftcentre Cymru (retail store)
Albert House
Penrallt Street
Machynlleth, Powys SY20 8AJ, Wales
Tel. 0654-2232

HOURS: Easter to Christmas: 9:00–5:30; open Bank Holidays.

See the write-up under PORTHMADOG.

LOCATION: Machynlleth is in west central Wales about 16 miles south of Dolgellau on the A487. The shop is only 50 yards from the clock tower.

MONTGOMERY   *Hand-Printed Textiles*

Plas Robin Products (factory/showroom)
The Chapel
Montgomery, Powys SY15 6QZ, Wales
Tel. 068681-459

HOURS: Monday–Friday 9:30–5:00; also May to September on Bank Holidays and Saturdays 10:00–4:00.

CREDIT CARDS: None

PRODUCTS: Plas Robin Products is a family-run business employing 15 people. There is a workshop, retail showroom, and coffee shop in a converted Welsh Chapel. Textile products are hand painted on the premises and made into gifts for the kitchen, bathroom, and other areas of the home. Pie covers, tea cosys, aprons, mitts, napkins, bed covers, and tablecloths are just a few of their many products. Hand-printed tea towels are £1.90, miniature teddy bears £2, sachets £1.25, towels £3.10, and a tea cosy £4.75. A seconds corner is always available where you can find extra savings. The showroom has a collection of mini-room settings which show you how to use the fabrics creatively in your home.

TOURS: Organized groups can be accommodated during the day or evening. A talk and demonstration of silk screening is given which lasts approximately 30 minutes. A delicious home-cooked meal follows. A menu can be requested from the factory. During November and December, a Christmas menu is offered. Please be sure to make advance arrangements for tours.

MAIL ORDERS: Products can be ordered by mail.

LOCATION: Montgomery is in east central Wales about six miles south of Welshpool. From Welshpool take the A490 south about 3½ miles, where you meet the B4388. Turn south onto the B4388 and go about three miles to Montgomery. You cannot miss this outlet as it is very well marked and on the main road going through town.

NEWTOWN   *Leather Clocks, Barometers*

Alaven Designs (factory/showroom)
Cymric Mill, Canal Road
Newtown, Powys SY16 2JH, Wales
Tel. 0686-26342

HOURS: Open all year Monday–Friday 9:00–5:00; open most
                Saturdays, but call first.
CREDIT CARDS: Access, Visa

PRODUCTS: Visitors are welcome to watch at the workshop as high-quality clocks and barometers encased in tooled, dyed, finely finished cowhide are created. Only the finest hides are selected. They are cut, tooled, dyed, and burnished. A large number of small leather goods are created from the off-cuts. You will also find craft items created by other companies. There is a bargain corner where discontinued leather items and seconds are sold at reduced prices.
    A round-cased clock with a battery quartz movement is £35. Limited-edition clocks are totally tooled by hand and fitted with solid brass numerals. Each clock is numbered and signed on the dial. The prices range from £65 for a 14″ clock with an edition of 1000 pieces to £195 for a large clock with a limited edition of 100. (Only one per month can be produced.) Barometers are priced from £28 to £31.

A leathercraft workbench is provided free of charge where you may make your own souvenirs. Kits are available for sale as well as leathercraft tools.

MAIL ORDER: Alaven Designs will ship orders. The address of their mail order division is: The Olive Branch, Freepost, Newton, Powys SY16 2JH, Wales.

TOURS: Group tours must be arranged in advance for parties of up to 40. The tour takes approximately 1½ hours.

LOCATION: Newtown is in central eastern Wales about 13 miles south of Welshpool on the A483 road. See the map below.

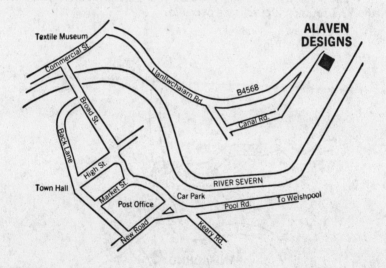

PENMACHNO, Near BETWS-Y-COED   *Woolen Products*

Penmachno Woollen Mill
Penmachno Nr. Betws-Y-Coed
Gwynedd LL24 OPP, Wales
Tel. 06902-545

HOURS: Easter to mid-November: Monday–Sunday 9:00–5:00
Weaving: Monday to Friday only.
Closed Sunday mornings in spring and autumn.
CREDIT CARDS: None

PRODUCTS: The mill stands beside the Machno River waterfall in beautiful Snowdonia. Visitors will find many types of wool tweeds which have been made into fashionable knitwear. Many of the products are exclusive only to this mill. Wool, tweed, and mohair are sold as well as hats, scarves, gloves, ties, rugs, skirts, jackets, and sweaters. Seconds and end-of-the-season products are usually available at a great savings. Sales are held in September and in October. A man's tweed hat will cost about £9.99, while a wool tweed sports coat is £44.99. A mohair wool jacket is a good buy at £49.99. Ladies' lambswool tweed skirts begin at £26.99.

The factory will be happy to mail your purchases home and offers the VAT refund on purchases over £25.

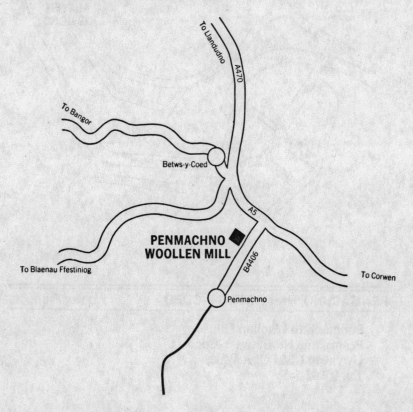

TOURS: Tours are offered to groups of 50 or less. The tour lasts about 15 minutes. Visitors are also welcome to watch the weavers.

LOCATION: Betws-y-Coed is in the northwest of Wales, about half-way between Conwy on the north and Ffestiniog on the south. From Betws-y-Coed follow the A5 road south toward Corwen for 1½ miles. Turn right at the Mill Cafe. The mill is ½ mile on the right. See the map.

PENMORFA NR. PORTHMADOG   *Pottery*

Tynllan Pottery & Farm Museum
Penmorfa
Porthmadog, Gwynedd LL49 9SG, Wales
Tel. 0766-2514

HOURS: Monday–Friday 9:30–6:00 from Easter through October; Saturday 9:30–5:00 from Easter through September. Open all Bank Holidays except Christmas and New Year.
CREDIT CARDS: Access, Barclaycard, MasterCard, Visa

PRODUCTS: At the end of a twisting, leafy lane nestled in a wooded hollow, visitors will find a group of old farm buildings which have been converted into a pottery, shop, and cafe. The pottery workshop is the oldest building, its roof being over 400 years old. Coffee sets, mugs, jars, and boxes are patterned with ancient Celtic designs: interwoven knots, mythical birds and figures. The designs have been taken from carved stone crosses found in Wales and from Celtic manuscripts. Coffee pots start at £9.50, milk jugs £2.80, coffee mugs £2.50, small trinket boxes £2, and sugar bowls £5. You'll also find other crafts in the barn. There is also a shelf full of second-quality items. The pottery pieces are glazed in beige, brown, and blue. On the wall are farm implements, all carefully labeled and arranged.

The owners will pack parcels for visitors so that they may mail them.

TOURS: Visitors are welcome to view the workshop all day.

LOCATION: Porthmadog is on the northwest coast of Wales. Penmorfa is about two miles northwest of Porthmadog on the A487. From Porthmadog, go north through Tremadog. Then watch for the sign directing you to turn left down a narrow road. See the map below.

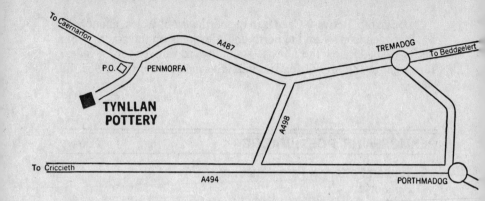

PORTHMADOG   *Welsh Crafts*

Craftcentre Cymru (retail shop)
Madog Harbour
High Street
Porthmadog, Gwynedd LL49 9LR, Wales
Tel. 0766-3834

HOURS: Monday–Saturday 9:00–5:30, open till 9:00 mid-May
through September; open Sunday from Easter through
October; open Bank Holidays.

CREDIT CARDS: Access, Barclaycard

PRODUCTS: In this neat and spacious shop visitors will find the
finest Welsh merchandise. Pottery, rugs, sweaters, woolen fabric,
woolen ties, capes, and food items are attractively displayed. Many of
the items are made just for this group of stores. The prices were very
good, the staff most helpful, and a VAT refund is offered to visitors. A
"highly recommended" if you do not want to visit each outlet or if you
want to get an excellent overview of Welsh products.

Small pottery candle snuffers were about £4.50 each. A ladies'
mohair wool cape in a wide range of colors was £49.99. Beautiful
lambswool tweed skirts were from £26.99. Very stylish men's tweed
hats were £9.99.

Do not drive through Wales without stopping at one of these
lovely shops. You will find it well worth your time!

LOCATION: Porthmadog is on the northwest coast of Wales on the A481. The shop is 50 yards from the Harbour Bridge on the south side of the main street next to the Tourist Information Centre.

PORTHMADOG   *Pottery*

Porthmadog Pottery
Snowdon Mill, Snowdon Street
Porthmadog, Gwynedd LL49 9DF, North Wales
Tel. 0766-2785

HOURS: April through October: Monday–Friday 9:00–5:30; June: Monday–Saturday; July to September: Monday–Sunday.
CREDIT CARDS: None

PRODUCTS: Porthmadog Pottery makes a large variety of decorative and functional pottery pieces with a distinctive blue and green glaze. They have a large craft and pottery seconds shop where the public may purchase items at a great savings. Each piece is hand painted and signed by the artist, making it unique. Most of the pottery pieces are designed for the tourist industry. They are smaller items and most are priced under £10.

You may throw a pot of your own on the potter's wheel and take it home with you.

TOURS: The factory offers 15-minute guided tours of the workshops. Coaches are welcome if advance reservations are made. Please call 0766-2785.

LOCATION: Porthmadog is on the northwest coast of Wales on the A481. Porthmadog Pottery is at the end of Snowdon Street opposite the post office or just outside the exit of the main car park.

PRESTEIGNE   *Welsh Crafts*

Presteigne Crafts (retail store)
3, Hereford Street
Presteigne, Powys LD8 2AW, Wales
Tel. 0544-267391

HOURS: Monday–Friday 10:00–1:00 and 2:00–5:00
CREDIT CARDS: None

PRODUCTS: Presteigne is a small country town with picturesque seventeenth-century half-timbered houses. Presteigne Crafts sells lithographs (many on Welsh slate plaques) and hand paintings on six- and nine-inch Welsh circular slate. The plaques have a leather hanging device on the back and are finished with a matt polyurethane varnish to protect the paint while leaving the natural quality of the slate. Prices including postage and packaging are £12 to £15.

Timber-framed doll houses built on a $\frac{1}{12}$th scale based on fifteenth-and sixteenth-century houses are also sold. The doll houses are works of art with solid oak beams, slate and oak floors, handcut roof tiles, oak staircases, etc. One medieval farmhouse was priced at £375. Other traditional Welsh craft items are sold. The shop is very small, although the items are well displayed.

LOCATION: Presteigne is just inside the Welsh border about half-way between Llandrindod Wells (in Wales) and Leominster (in England). Traveling from Leominster, take the A44 14 miles west to Kington. Turn north onto the B4355. Presteigne is seven miles north of Kington on the B4355 road.

PWLLHELI   *Welsh Crafts*

Craftcentre Cymru (retail store)
62, High Street
Pwllheli, Gwynedd LL53 5RR, Wales
Tel. 0758-612246

HOURS: Easter to Christmas: Monday–Saturday 9:00–5:30 and Bank Holidays.

See the write-up under PORTHMADOG.

LOCATION: Pwllheli is on the south coast of Lleyn Peninsula in the northwest of Wales. The town is on the south coast of the peninsula. The shop is in the center of the main shopping street 100 yards east of Woolworths and opposite the Tower Hotel.

ST. DAVIDS   *Wool Goods, Clothing, Gifts, Pottery*

Tregwynt Textiles
5 Nun Street
St. Davids, Dyffed SA62 6NS, Wales
Tel. 720386

HOURS: Monday–Friday 9:00–5:00.

See the write-up under ST. NICHOLAS.

LOCATION: St. Davids is on the A487 in the far southwest of
Wales, near the coast at the very western end of Dyffed.

ST. NICHOLAS, NEAR FISHGUARD   *Wool Goods Clothing*

Tregwynt Woollen Mill (factory outlet)
Near St. Nicholas, Letterston
Haverfordwest, Pembrokeshire SA62 5UX, Wales
Tel. 03485-225

HOURS: Mill: Monday–Friday 9:00–5:00
Mill Shop: Monday–Saturday 9:00–5:00
CREDIT CARDS: Access, American Express, Visa

PRODUCTS: The Mill is situated in a picturesque wooded valley
five miles from Fishguard and one mile from the Pembrokeshire coastline. The original buildings date from the eighteenth century and the
Mill has been owned by the same family since 1912.

The wool industry in Wales is over 2000 years old. In the four-
teenth-century Pembrokeshire was the main center of the woolen industry. The spinning wheel came into use and servants were hired to
work on the land and to spin and weave cloth.

With the invention of the loom, carding, spinning, and weaving
machinery, small factories began to appear in the 1800s. Woolen textiles became a large industry in Wales. In 1918, there were over 250
mills.

During the 1960s, tourism in Wales blossomed and many of the
old factories were reopened for tourists.

The Tregwynt Mill Shop sells fabric such as flannel, tweed, and tapestry weaves. Flannel fabric 56″ wide was £7.30 per yard, while tweed fabric 56″ wide was £7.80 per yard. Bedspreads, place mats, blankets, and rugs are sold. A fringed bedspread (120″ × 100″) was £55, while a smaller bedspread (72″ × 100″) was only £36.50. Place mats, to add a special touch to your table, were £1.30 each. A blanket (82″ × 96″) was £32, a traveling rug was £17, and a knee rug (48″ × 60″) was £12.

Visitors will also find car coats, skirts, tweed jackets, blouses, skirts, purses, stoles, and scarves.

TOURS: Tours may be arranged by appointment and last from 15–20 minutes.

LOCATION: St. Nicholas is in the far southwest of Wales, about five miles west of Fishguard. This is on the north side of the Dyffed peninsula. See the map below.

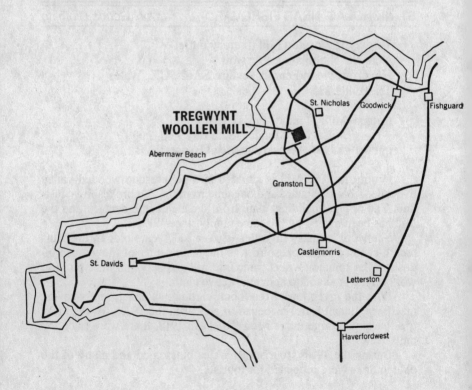

TENBY
Pottery

Tenby Pottery (workshop)
Upper Frog Street
Tenby, Pembrokeshire, Dyfed SA70 7JD, Wales
Tel. 0834-2890

HOURS: Monday–Saturday 10:15–12:00 and 2:15–5:30
CREDIT CARDS: None

PRODUCTS: This small workshop is owned by a husband and wife team. They make handthrown pottery which is individually glazed and decorated at their shop. Tiny miniature plates are 70 pence. Salad or fruit bowls are priced between £3 and £7.50. Plant pots with saucers range from £2.50 to £10. Small decorative vases are from 80 pence to £2 while larger vases are between £10 and £15. Ashtrays are from £1.95 to £2.95. Seconds are sometimes available on the day the kiln is unpacked.

LOCATION: Tenby is on the southwest coast of Wales on the A478. See the map below.

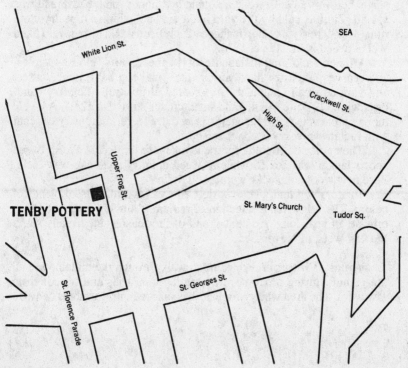

TREFRIW   *Woolen Goods*

Trefriw Woollen Mills Ltd.
Trefriw, Gwynedd LL27 0NQ, North Wales
Tel. Llanrwst 640462

HOURS: Mill: Monday–Friday 9:00–5:30 all year except Bank
Holidays and two weeks over Christmas. But please tele-
phone ahead and check hours off season.
Shop: Monday–Friday 9:00–5:30; Saturday 10:00–4:00;
Sunday in July and August 2:00–5:00.
CREDIT CARDS: Mastercard, Visa

PRODUCTS: Trefriw Woollen Mills is on the banks of the River
Crafnant. This site was chosen to use water from the river to drive the
water wheels and for washing wool and cloth. About 1900 the water
wheels were dismantled, and hydro-electric turbines were first installed. The turbines can be viewed through a window at the far end of
the shop.
Visitors will find tapestry-weave and honeycomb bedspreads,
blankets, knee rugs, and traveling rugs. A tapestry bedspread for a
single bed was £49.50, while a double bed honeycomb bedspread was
£51.50. Cloth is sold by the yard in 58″ and 60″ widths. Tapestry cloth
runs £14.95 per yard, herringbone (2 ply) runs £12.15 per yard, and
Welsh tweed is £12.15 per yard.
Women's clothing included coats, capes, skirts, blouses, stoles,
and scarves. Tapestry handbags, purses, makeup bags, pencil cases,
and various small containers are created at this mill. Tapestry handbags were £12.35 to £18.45, and small purses started at £2.95. A lovely
mohair stole was very reasonably priced at £11.70. A tapestry car coat
with raglan sleeves was about £66.50.
The choice of clothing for men was more limited. A Welsh tweed
sports jacket was £69.55 while a tweed country-style cap was £6.55.
Pure new wool golf socks were £4.30 per pair.
Visitors will find a large variety of weaves and unusual blends of
colors. There is often a selection of remnants and discontinued items
on sale all year long. An annual end-of-the-season sale usually starts
the first week in November.

TOURS: Visitors are welcome to walk through the mill and see all
the manufacturing processes for creating tapestries and tweeds from
raw wool. The area where wool cloth is tailored into garments can also

be seen. Other attractions during the season include a slide show explaining the processes, handspinning and handweaving demonstrations, a children's playground, and a cafeteria. Guided tours can be arranged in advance for parties over 25 people. The tour takes about 40 minutes.

LOCATION: Trefriw is in the northwest of Wales about 10 miles south of Conwy on the B5106. The mill is located in the center of Trefriw on the west side of the main street, which is the B5106 road between Conwy.

TREGARON   *Welsh Crafts*

Craft Design Centre of Wales
Tregaron, Dyfed SY25 6JL, Wales
Tel. 09744-415

HOURS: Monday–Saturday 9:30–5:30; open Sunday in the summer.
CREDIT CARDS: Access, Eurocard, MasterCard, Visa

PRODUCTS: This craft shop in Wales carries contemporary Celtic jewelry in gold and silver, traditional knit garments in natural color Welsh wool (mainly from pedigree Black Welsh Mountain sheep), authentic Welsh national costumes, and a full range of craft goods produced in Wales. These include leather goods, wood carvings, pottery, slate pictures, ceramics, and more. Traditional Welsh designs and more contemporary items are all available. Jewelry items run from £11, handknit sweaters £30 to £40, and cardigan sweaters from £40 to £50. Leather clocks are priced from £29. Lectures on Celtic design and Welsh crafts can be arranged for groups.

LOCATION: Tregaron is in the west of Wales, about 20 miles south of Aberystwyth (which is on the west coast) on the A485 road.

The Prentice Traders (retail shop)
10 High Street
Welshpool, Powys SD21 7TP, Wales
Tel. 0938-2055

HOURS: Monday–Saturday 9:00–5:30; June to September also open Sunday 10:00–7:00.

The Prentice Traders would be happy to open at different hours for coach parties if arrangements are made in advance.
CREDIT CARDS: MasterCard, Visa

PRODUCTS: The Prentice Traders is the local craft center, with mainly Welsh craft items for sale. Sheepskin rugs are priced from £12, sheepskin coats from £90, and Welsh tapestry bedspreads from £35.

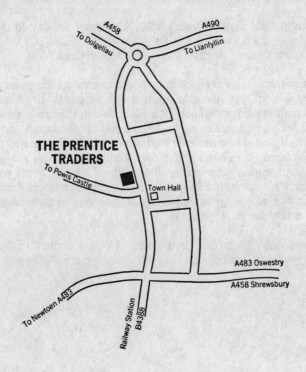

Various pottery items, slate coasters, love spoons, tapestry woolen purses, and tweed caps are just a few of the many items sold.

This is a small quaint shop with a good cross section of Welsh crafts. The shop has facilities for mailing and will arrange for VAT refunds.

LOCATION: Welshpool is on the east central border of Wales, about 20 miles west of Shrewsbury on the A458 road. See the map.

A SELECTION OF ESTABLISHMENTS FOR THOSE WITH LIMITED TIME

For those of you with limited time for shopping in Great Britain, the list below offers you a representative selection of the best buys in the establishments, shopping areas, and outlets recommended in this book.

Town Name	Company Name	Products
ENGLAND		
Bowness-on-Windermere	Lakeland Sheepskin Center	Leather, Clothing
Brierley Hill	Royal Brierley Crystal	Crystal
Glastonbury	Baily's of Glastonbury	Sheepskin items
Glastonbury	R. J. Draper & Co. Ltd.	Sheepskin items
Hornsea	Hornsea Pottery Co. Ltd.	Pottery
Lancaster	Hornsea Pottery Co. Ltd.	Pottery
London	Regent Street	Varied
London	Burlington Arcade	Varied
London	Brompton Road	Varied
London	Camden Passage	Antique Market
London	The London Silver Vaults	Silver, Antiques
London	Austin Reed	Clothing
London	Burberry's Ltd.	Clothing
London	Foyles	Books
London	Hamleys	Toys
London	Harrods	Everything
London	Henry Sotheran Ltd.	Maps, Rare Books, Engravings
London	Laura Ashley	Clothing, Fabric
London	Liberty & Co.	Dept. Store
London	Mothercare	Children's Everything
London	R. J. Draper & Co. Ltd.	Sheepskin Items
London	Lillywhites Ltd.	Sportswear
London	Reject China Shop	China, Crystal
Nottingham Ltd.	Cumbria Crystal	Crystal
Ravenshead	Longdale Rural Craft Centre	Craft Museums

Town Name	Company Name	Products
Stoke-on-Trent	Spode	Bone China
Stoke-on-Trent	Wedgwood	China, Stoneware
Stoke-on-Trent	Coalport and Crown Staffordshire	Bone China
Stoke-on-Trent	Portmeirion Potteries	Potteries
Stoke-on-Trent	Waterford-Aynsley China Reject Shop	Bone China
Ulverston	Cumbria Crystal	Crystal
Ventnor, Isle of Wight	Isle of Wight Glass	Handblown Glassware
Wordsley	Stuart Crystal	Crystal
York	Cumbria Crystal Ltd.	Crystal

SCOTLAND

Crieff	A. W. Buchan and Co.	Pottery
Crieff	Perthshire Paperweights	Paperweights
Crieff	Stuart Strathearn Ltd.	Crystal
Dunkeld	Jeremy Law	Purses, Deerskin Products
Edinburgh	Clan Royal	Woolen Items
Edinburgh	James Pringle Woollen Mill	Woolen Products
Edinburgh	Laura Ashley Bargain Shop	Clothing
Edinburgh	Scottish Craft Centre	Crafts
Galashiels	Peter Anderson Ltd.	Woolen Items
Hawick	White of Hawick	Sweaters
Inverness	James Pringle Ltd.	Woolen Items
Kirkcudbright	David Gulland	Engraved Glass
Penicuik	Edinburgh Crystal	Crystal
Perth	Caithness Glass	Glass, Paperweights

WALES

Bala	Craftcentre Cymru	Welsh Crafts, Clothing
Barmouth	Craftcentre Cymru	Welsh Crafts, Clothing
Betws-y-Coed	Craftcentre Cymru	Welsh Crafts, Clothing
Caernarfon	Craftcentre Cymru	Welsh Crafts, Clothing
Chirk	Craftcentre Cymru	Welsh Crafts, Clothing
Conwy	Craftcentre Cymru	Welsh Crafts, Clothing
Corris	Corris Craft Centre	Crafts
Corris	Glandwyrrd Stores Ceramics	Ceramics

Town Name	Company Name	Products
Dinas Mawddwy	Meirion Mill	Woolen Items
Dolgellau	Enid Pierce	Sweaters
Llangurig	Craftcentre Cymru	Welsh Crafts, Clothing
Machynlleth	Craftcentre Cymru	Welsh Crafts, Clothing
Porthmadog	Craftcentre Cymru	Welsh Crafts, Clothing
Pwllheli	Craftcentre Cymru	Welsh Crafts, Clothing

CHAIN STORES

The following companies own numerous stores throughout Great Britain. Rather than repeating the description for each store, we have listed all the locations below. These stores are all well worth visiting if you are in any of the cities listed.

AUSTIN-REED

Austin-Reed sells top-quality men's clothing, plus stylish women's clothing. See the write-up for this chain of stores under LONDON.

ENGLAND

BATH, 19 Milsom Street, Tel. (0225) 64340

BEVERLEY, Browns of Beverley, 58 Market Place, Tel. (0482) 881606

BIRMINGHAM, 3 North Court, Tel. (021) 643-0072/3 and 39 Auchinleck Square, Tel. (021) 6432621

BLACKPOOL, Abingdon Street, Tel. (0253) 28477/8

BOURNEMOUTH, Westover Corner, Tel. (0202) 20336

BRIGHTON, 1 Churchill Square, Tel. (0273) 25089

BRISTOL, Embassy House, Queen's Road, Tel. (0272) 20910

CAMBRIDGE, 16/17 Sidney Street, Tel. (0223) 356982

CANTERBURY, 2728 Burgate, Tel. (0227) 67146

CHELTENHAM, 62/64 The Promenade, Tel. (0242) 513090

CHESTER, 35 Bridge Street Row, Tel. (0244) 311068

COVENTRY, 12 Bull Yard, Tel. (0203) 23413

EXETER, 227 High Street, Tel. (0392) 70299

GUILDFORD, 218 High Street, Tel. (0483) 68510
HARROGATE, 15 James Street, Tel. (0423) 502753
IPSWICH, 25/29 Butter Market, Tel. (0473) 54425
LEEDS, 37/39 Bond Street, Tel. (0532) 430164
LEICESTER, 39 Belvoir Street, Tel. (0533) 551622
LIVERPOOL, 27/29 Bold Street, Tel. (051) 709 8123
LONDON
   103/113 Regent Street, Tel. (01) 734 6789
   163/169 Brompton Road, Tel. (01) 734 6789
   78 Cheapside, Tel. (01) 734 6789
   13/23 Fenchurch Street, Tel. (01) 734-6789
   The Brent Cross Shopping Centre, Tel. (01) 202 5677/8
MANCHESTER, 4 Exchange Street, St. Ann's Square, Tel. (061)
   834 1952
NEWCASTLE, 61/67 Grey Street, Tel. (0632) 321780
NORWICH, 38 London Street, Tel. (0603) 26141
NOTTINGHAM, 7 Angel Road, Tel. (0602) 417124
OXFORD, 38 Cornmarket Street, Tel. (0865) 244510
PLYMOUTH, 19 New George Street, Tel. (0752) 260404
SHEFFIELD, 10 Barkers Pool, Tel. (0742) 25949
SHREWSBURY, 25/26 The Square, Tel. (0473) 50477
SOLIHULL, 55 Mill Lane, Tel. (021) 705 2268
SOUTHAMPTON, 176/178 Above Bar, Tel. (0703) 23391
STRATFORD-UPON-AVON, 40 High Street, Tel. (0789) 68516
TUNBRIDGE WELLS, 35 High Street, Tel. (0892) 44009
WINDSOR, 137 Peascod Street, Tel. (95) 68788
WORCESTER, 14/14a Lychgate Centre, Tel. (0905) 26744
YORK, 8/9 Parliament Street, Tel. (0904) 22424

SCOTLAND

EDINBURGH, 124 Princes Street, Tel. (031) 225-6703
GLASGOW, 35 Gordon Street, Tel. (041) 248 3811/2
PERTH, 9/15 St. John Street, Tel. (0738) 28450

WALES

CARDIFF, 121/3 Queen Street, Tel. (0222) 28357

LAURA ASHLEY

Laura Ashley's women's and girls' clothing is feminine and fashionable. They also sell fabrics and decorative accessories. See write-up for this chain of stores under LONDON, ENGLAND and under EDINBURGH, SCOTLAND.

ENGLAND

AYLESBURY, 10 Hale Leys, Tel. (0296) 84574
BATH, Old Red House New Bond Street, Tel. (0225) 60341
BIRMINGHAM, 14/16 Priory Queensway, Tel. (021) 233-1499
BOURNEMOUTH, 80 Old Christchurch Road, Tel. (0202) 27572
BRIGHTON, 104/106 Queen's Road, Tel. (0273) 27431
BRISTOL, 62 Queen's Road, Clifton, Tel. (0272) 277468
CAMBRIDGE, 14 Trinity Street, Tel. (0223) 51378
CANTERBURY, 41/42 Burgate, Tel. (0227) 50961
CHELTENHAM, 1 Queen's Circus, Tel. (0242) 45500
CHICHESTER, 32 North Street, Tel. (0243) 775255
GUILDFORD, Old Cloth Hall North Street, Tel. (0483) 34152
IPSWICH, 17 Buttermarket, Tel. (0473) 216828
LONDON
   9 Harriet Street SW1, Tel. 01-235-9796
   35 Bow Street WC2, Tel. 01-240 1997
   157 Fulham Road SW3, Tel. 01-584-6939
   36 Hampstead High Street NW3, Tel. 01-431-3215
   75 Lower Sloane Street SW1, Tel. 02-730-5255
   183 Sloan Street SW1, Tel. 01-235-9728
MANCHESTER, 28 King Street, Tel. (061) 834-7335
NEWCASTLE-UPON-TYNE, 8 Nelson Street, Tel. (0632) 61595
NORWICH, 3/5 Dove Street, Tel. (0603) 26533
NOTTINGHAM, 58 Bridlesmith Gate, Tel. (0602) 5366
OXFORD, 26/27 Little Clarendon Street, Tel. (0865) 52477
SHREWSBURY, 65 Wyle Cop, Tel. (0743) 51467
TUNBRIDGE WELLS, 61 Calverly Road
WINCHESTER, 10 The Square, Tel. (0962) 55718
WINDSOR, 5 King Edward Court, Tel. (07535) 59560
WINDSOR, 17 King Edward Court, Tel. (07535) 65859
YORK, 7 Davygate, Tel. (0904) 27707

SCOTLAND

EDINBURGH
137 George Street, Tel. (031) 225 1121
43/45 Lothian Road, Tel. (031) 229 5135
GLASGOW, 215 Sauchiehall Street, Tel. (041) 333 0850

WALES

CARDIFF, 5 High Street, Tel. (0222) 40808
CHESTER, 17/19 Watergate Row, Tel. (0244) 316403
LLANIDLOES, 30 Great Oak Street, Tel. (05512) 2557

MOTHERCARE

The Mothercare stores have everything for mothers-to-be, mothers, and children. For a description of these stores, see LONDON.

ENGLAND

ALDERSHOT, Unit 11, The Wellington Centre, Victoria Road, Tel. 0252 315730
ALTRINCHAM, 58 George Street, Tel. 061-928 2928
ASHFORD, 32 Tufton Walk, The Tufton Centre, Tel. 0233 29424
ASHTON UNDER LYNE, 5–7 Staveleigh Way, Tel. 061-330 5910
AYLESBURY, 14 Hale Leys, Tel. 0296 83383
BARKING, 49 East Street, Tel. 01-594 3381
BARNET, 129 High Street, Tel. 01-449 0080
BARNSLEY, 8–12 The Arcade, Tel. 0226 81158
BASILDON, 21–22 East Gate, Tel. 0268 22473
BASINGSTOKE, 16–17 Paddington House, Hollins Walk, New Town Centre, Tel. 0256 26184
BATH, 44–48 Southgate, Tel. 0225 66245
BEDFORD, 16 Harpur Street, Tel. 0234 52874
BEXLEYHEATH, 42 The Mall, Broadway Shopping Centre, Tel. 01-303 7337
BIRKENHEAD, 19–21 Milton Pavement, Tel. 051-647 3676
BIRMINGHAM, 15–17 Central Square, High Street, Tel. 021-350 5937
BIRMINGHAM, 81 High Street, Tel. 021-643 8132

BISHOP AUCKLAND, 11 Newgate Street, Tel. 0388 604927
BLACKBURN, 36–38 King William Street, Tel. 0254 54980
BLACKPOOL, 32 Hounds Hill Centre, Victoria Street, Tel. 0253 26836
BOGNOR REGIS, 27 London Road, Tel. 0243 868135
BOLTON, 1 Market Street, Tel. 0204 24717
BOOTLE, 299–301 Stanley Road, Tel. 051 922 5464
BOURNEMOUTH, 35 Commercial Road, Tel. 0202 28351
BRACKNELL, 1 Charles Square, Tel. 0344-426323
BRADFORD, 41 Broadway, Tel. 0274 394112
BRENTWOOD, 3–4 Chapel High, Tel. 0277 233001
BRIGHTON, 59–60 Churchill Square, Tel. 0273 26826
BRISTOL, 23–25 Merchant Street, Tel. 0272 294035
BROMLEY, 90–92 High Street, Tel. 01-460 6730
BROMSGROVE, 138 High Street, Tel. 0527 76886
BURNLEY, 50 The Mall, Tel. 0282 25678
BURTON ON TRENT, 5 Underhill Walk, Tel. 0283 67472
BURY, 1A Union Street, Tel. 061 797 9404
BURY ST. EDMUNDS, 4 Brentgovel Street, Tel. 0284 701019
CAMBRIDGE, 12 Lion Yard, Tel. 0223 62001
CANTERBURY, 18 St. Georges Street, Tel. 0227 54382
CHATHAM, 159–163 High Street, Tel. 0634 45701
CHELMSFORD, 1A–2 High Chelmer, Tel. 0245 267480
CHELMSLEY WOOD, 14 Greenwood Way, Tel. 021-7706456
CHESTER, 29 Newgate Row, Tel. 0244-43485
CLACTON, 48 Pier Avenue, Tel. 0255 74243
COLCHESTER, 16 Culver Walk, Tel. 0206 573053
CORBY, 42 Queen's Square, Tel. 05366 3882
COVENTRY, 34–38 The Precinct, Tel. 0203 29713
CRAWLEY, 20 Haslett Avenue, Tel. 0293 544900
CREWE, 15 Victoria Centre, Tel. 0270 213227
CROYDON, 76 Whitgift Square, Tel. 01-686 2785
DARLINGTON, 66–68 Northgate, Tel. 0325 469743
DARTFORD, 36–38 North Mall, Amdale Centre, Tel. 0322 75813
DERBY, 10 Burrows Walk, Eagle Centre, Tel. 0332 44759
DEWSBURY, 34–36 Princess of Wales Precinct, Tel. 0924 455964
DONCASTER, 28–29 High Street, Tel. 0302 49388
DUDLEY, 195 High Street, Tel. 0384 211874
DURHAM, 3 Millburngate, Tel. 0385 62440
EASTBOURNE, 71 Eastbourne Arndale Centre, Tel. 0323 24880
ENFIELD, 4 Palace Gardens, Tel. 01-367 1188
EXETER, 12–13 High Street, Tel. 0392-59483

FAREHAM, 29 Westbury Mall, Fareham Shopping Centre, Tel. 0329 288945

GLOUCESTER, 9 Westgate Street, Tel. 0452 25713

GRAVESEND, 5 Kempthorne Street, St. Georges Centre, Tel. 0474 534885

GREAT YARMOUTH, 18 Market Gates, Tel. 0493 58850

GRIMSBY, 15 Friargate, Tel. 0472 52793

GUILDFORD, 23 The Friary, Tel. 0483 573953

HALIFAX, 14 Woolshops, Tel. 0422 44912

HANLEY, 13 East Precinct, Charles Street, Tel. 0782 262302

HARLOW, 17 Harvey Centre, Tel. 0279 24630

HARROGATE, 45–47 Station Parade, Tel. 0423 61265

HARROW, 336–338 Station Road, Tel. 01-427 7575

HARTLEPOOL, 87–88 The Shopping Centre, Middleton Grange, Tel. 0429 69131

HEMEL HEMPSTEAD, 164 Marlowes, Tel. 0442 52860

HEREFORD, 18 High Town, Tel. 0432 272665

HIGH WYCOMBE, 2 Paul's Row, Tel. 0494 35182

HORSHAM, 31–32 West Street, Tel. 0403 55360

HOUNSLOW, 133 High Street, Tel. 01-570 5996

HUDDERSFIELD, 36–38 Princess Alexandra Walk, Tel. 0484 26490

HULL, 57–60 Whitefriargate, Tel. 0482 223401

HUNTINGDON, St. Benedict's Court, Tel. 0480 57707

ILFORD, 114 High Road, Tel. 01-478 1953

IPSWICH, 21 Westgate Street, Tel. 0473 52049

KETTERING, 19 The Mall, Newborough Centre, Tel. 0536 513310

KIDDERMINSTER, 15 Vicar Street, Tel. 0562 751689

KINGS LYNN, 91–93 High Street, Tel. 0553 3327

KINGSTON, 107 Clarence Street, Tel. 01-546 4529

LANCASTER, 16–18 Cheapside, Tel. 0524 69163

LEAMINGTON SPA, 23–25 The Parade, Tel. 0926 312238

LEEDS, 1 Albion Arcade, Bond Street Centre, Tel. 0532 438927

LEICESTER, 1 Belgrave Gate, Tel. 0533 20768

LETCHWORTH, 13 Eastcheap, Tel. 04626 4067

LINCOLN, 6 Cornhill Pavement, Cornhill, Tel. 0522 21825

LIVERPOOL, 99–101 Lord Street, Tel. 236 1622/1856

LONDON, MARBLE ARCH, 461–465 Oxford Street, Tel. 01-629 6621

LONDON, OXFORD CIRCUS, 174–176 Oxford Street, Tel. 01-580 1688-9

LONDON, BRENT CROSS, Brent Cross Shopping Centre, Tel. 01-202 5377

LONDON, BRIXTON, 416 Brixton Road, Tel. 01-733 1494

LONDON, CLAPHAM, 71 St. John's Road, Tel. 01-228 0391

LONDON, EALING WEST, 64 The Broadway, Tel. 01-567 7067

LONDON, EAST HAM, 115 High Street North, Tel. 01-472 4948

LONDON, EDMONTON, 113 Fore Street, Tel. 01-803 9408

LONDON, HAMMERSMITH, 26 King's Mall, Tel. 01-741 0514

LONDON, HOLLOWAY, 448–450 Holloway Road, Tel. 01-607 0915

LONDON, KENSINGTON, 120 Kensington High Street, Tel. 01-937 9781

LONDON, KILBURN, 172 Kilburn High Road, Tel. 01-328 6466

LONDON, LEWISHAM, 41 Riverdale High Street, Tel. 01-852 2167

LONDON, PECKHAM, 203–205 Rye Lane, Tel. 01-639 0744

LONDON, STRATFORD EAST, 33–34 The Mall, The Stratford Centre, Tel. 01-534 5714

LONDON, TOOTING, 14 High Street, Tel. 01-672 3947

LONDON, WALTHAMSTOW, 253–255 High Street, Tel. 01-520 3573

LONDON, WANDSWORTH, 53 The Arndale Centre, Garrett Lane, Tel. 01-874 2699

LONDON, WOOD GREEN, 34 High Road, Tel. 01-888 6920

LONDON, WOOLWICH, 62 Powis Street, Tel. 01-854 3540

LUTON, 3133 Arndale Centre, Tel. 0582 28583

MACCLESFIELD, 30 Mill Street, Tel. 0625 611552

MAIDSTONE, 34 Week Street, Tel. 0622 54181

MANCHESTER, Store 6B, Arndale Centre, Tel. 061-832 2153

MANSFIELD, 22 Four Seasons Centre, Tel. 0623 25644

MARGATE, 79 High Street, Tel. 0843 25240

MIDDLESBROUGH, 6 Oberhausen Mall, Hill Street Shopping Centre, Tel. 0642 244201

MILTON KEYNES, 152 Midsummer Arcade, Secklow Gate East, Tel. 0908 607646

NEWCASTLE UPON TYNE, 2 Blacket Bridge, Eldon Square, Tel. 0632 612907

NORTHHAMPTON, 15 Abingdon Street, Tel. 0604 32428

NORWICH, 47–49 St. Stephen's Street, Tel. 0603 21075

NOTTINGHAM, 28 Maid Marian Way, Tel. 0602 47048

NUNEATON, 15 Bridge Street, Tel. 0203 347522

OLDHAM, 25–26 Town Square Shopping Centre, Tel. 061-633 1817

ORPINGTON, 184 High Street, Tel. 0689 20544

OXFORD, 2–6 Market Street, Tel. 0865 241992

PETERBOROUGH, 55 Bridge Street, Tel. 0733 63722

PLYMOUTH, 20–24 Old Town Street, Tel. 0752 661423

POOLE, 37–38 Arndale Centre, Tel. 0202 675677

PORTSMOUTH, 113 Commercial Road, Tel. 0705 822521

PRESTON, 65–71 Friargate Walk, St. George's Shopping Centre, Tel. 0772 51080

RAMSGATE, 66 High Street, Tel. 0843 587787

READING, 99–100 Friar Street, Tel. 0734 590490

REDDITCH, 46–48 Evesham Walk, Tel. 0527 69376

ROCHDALE, 58 Yorkshire Street, Tel. 0706 47546

ROMFORD, 7–9 Lockwood Walk, Tel. 0708 46670

RUGBY, 5 Manning Walk, The Rugby Centre, Tel. 0788 76150

RUNCORN, 51 Central Square, Tel. 0928 718181

ST. ALBANS, 8 St. Peter's Street, Tel. 0727 58816

ST. HELENS, 6–8 St. Mary's Arcade, Tel. 0744 32995

SALISBURY, 41 New Canal, Tel. 0722 333196

SCUNTHORPE, 57–59 High Street, Tel. 0724 865783

SHEFFIELD, 65 The Moor, Tel. 0742 700981

SHREWSBURY, 12 Castle Street, Tel. 0743 62591

SLOUGH, 80 Queensmere, Tel. 0753 21009

SOLIHULL, 47–49 Mill Lane, Tel. 021-705 8825

SOUTHAMPTON, 52 Above Bar, Tel. 0703 334683

SOUTHEND, 107–109 High Street, Tel. 0702 346718

SOUTHPORT, 8 Eastbank Street, Tel. 0704 41739

SOUTH SHIELDS, 93–95 King Street, Tel. 0632 552459

STAFFORD, 20 Princes Street, Tel. 0785 42603

STAINES, 35–36 Elmsleigh Centre, Tel. 0784-62943

STEVENAGE, 78–80 Queensway, Tel. 0438 355474

STOCKPORT, 5–7 Adlington Walk, Merseyway, Tel. 061-480 6332

STOCKTON ON TEES, 47–48 High Street, Tel. 0642 672591

STRETFORD, Unit 9–10 Arndale Centre, Tel. 061-865 2752

SUNDERLAND, 70–71 High Street West, Tel. 0783 650432

SUTTON, 127–129 High Street, Tel. 01-642 9323

SUTTON COLDFIELD, 154 The Parade, Gracechurch Centre, Tel. 021-354 6171

SWANSEA, 58–60 Kingsway, Tel. 0792 52999

SWINDON, 49–51 The Parade, Tel. 0793 24856

TAUNTON, 56 North Street, Tel. 0823 70206
TELFORD, 39 Mall 4, Telford Shopping Centre, Tel. 0952 501065
TORQUAY, Union House, Union Street, Tel. 0803 211910
TUNBRIDGE WELLS, 26–28 Calverley Road, Tel. 0892 41241
UXBRIDGE, 6 Mercer Walk, Tel. 0895 55913
WAKEFIELD, 74 Bishopsgate Walk, The Riding Centre, Tel. 0924 371569
WALSALL, 43–47 Park Mall, Saddlers Centre, Tel. 0922 29770
WARRINGTON, 85–86 The Mall, Golden Square, Tel. 0925 59357
WASHINGTON, Unit 12–14 The Galleries, Town Centre, Tel. 091 4172580
WATFORD, 77–79 High Street, Tel. 0923 25410
WEST BROMWICH, 28–29 The Sandwell Centre, Tel. 021-553 5303
WEYMOUTH, 104F St. Mary's Street, Tel. 0305 789266
WINDSOR, 12–13 King Edward Court, Tel. 07535 55858
WOKING, 35–37 Commercial Way, Tel. 04862 70055
WOLVERHAMPTON, 11–12 Mander Square, Tel. 0902 26086
WORCESTER, 4–5 Broad Street, Tel. 0905 21124
WORKSHOP, 14 Bridge Place, Tel. 0909 474370
YORK, 2527 Coney Street, Tel. 0904 54200

SCOTLAND

ABERDEEN, 122 Union Street, Tel. 0224 646624
AYR, 149 High Street, Tel. 0292 61107
CLYDE, 65 Sylvania Way, Tel. 041-952 2729
CUMBERNAULD, 1–7 Teviot Square, Tel. 02367 27370
DUMFRIES, 70 High Street, Tel. 0387 68761
DUNDEE, 1–2 Wellgate Centre, Cowgate, Tel. 0382 28622
DUNFERMLINE, 19–23 Bridge Street, Tel. 0383 721775
EAST KILBRIDE, 9 The Plaza, Town Centre, Tel. 03552 20589
EDINBURGH, 84A Princes Street, Tel. 031-226 6503
FALKIRK, 16 High Street, Tel. 0324 29722
GLASGOW, 58–60 Union Street, Tel. 041-248 7663/3629
GLENROTHES, 17 Unicorn Way, Kingdom Centre, Tel. 0592 750030
GREENOCK, 51 Hamilton Way, Tel. 0475 84407
HAMILTON, 39 Regent Way, Tel. 0698 286554
INVERNESS, 15–16 Eastgate Shopping Centre, Tel. 0463 241910
KILMARNOCK, 121–123 King Street, Tel. 0563 26697

KIRKCALDY, 22–24 The Mercat, Tel. 0592 264832
PAISLEY, 24 Causeyside Street, Tel. 041-889 8535
PERTH, 174 High Street, Tel. 0738 29708
STIRLING, 39 Stirling Thistle Centre, Orchard Croft, Tel. 0786 70747

WALES

BRIDGEND, 9 Caroline Street, Tel. 0656 68306
CARDIFF, 20–22 Working Street, The St. David's Centre, Tel. 0222 42485
CWMBRAN, 24 The Mall, Tel. 063-335351
LLANDUDNO, 40 Mostyn Street, Tel. 0492 76906
LLANELLI, Bradford House, 15 Stepney Street, Tel. 05542 59163
MERTHYR TYDFIL, 8 Graham Way, St. Tydil's Square, Tel. 0685 5429
PONTYPRIDD, 103–104 Taff Street, Tel. 0443 404389
WREXHAM, 23–24 Hope Street, Tel. 0978 356198

PITLOCHRY KNITWEAR

This company has a large selection of sweaters, gloves, blouses, dresses, rugs, and other knitwear. For a description of these stores and their products, see the Spean Bridge Woollen Mill in SPEAN BRIDGE, Scotland.

ENGLAND

CAMBRIDGE	Scots Corner	Bridge Street
CANTERBURY	Stewarts Woolen Mill	St. Peter's Street
ELY	Stewarts Woolen Mill	Minster Place
KESWICK	Scottish Woollens	Main Street
LINCOLN	Stewarts Woolen Mill	Bailgate
LONDON	Scots Corner	Old Bond Street
OXFORD	Scots Corner	Turl Street
SALISBURY	Stewarts Woollen Mill	High Street
ST. ALBANS	Stewarts Woollen Mill	George Street
STRATFORD-UPON-AVON	Scots Corner	Chapel Street
TORQUAY	Scots Corner	Torwood Street
WELLS	Stewarts Woollen Mill	High Street
WINDERMERE	Scottish Woollens	New Road

WINDSOR, BERKS	Scots Corner	Thames Street
	Scots Corner	High Street
YORK	Scots Corner	Stonegate

SCOTLAND

ABERDEEN	Scott the Kiltmaker	160 Union Street
AVIEMORE	Spey Valley Woollens	By the Station
	Spey Valley Woollens	Grampian Road
BANCHORY	Banchory Woollen Co.	N. Deeside Road
BY CALLANDER	Trossachs Knitwear	Kilmahog
CLARKSTON	Pitlochry Knitwear	Busby Road
CRIEFF	Crieff Mill Shop	High Street
DUMFRIES	Pitlochry Knitwear	Church Place
EDINBURGH	Pitlochry Knitwear	North Bridge
GLASGOW	Pitlochry Knitwear	Argyll Arcade
INVERARAY	Inveraray Woollen Co.	The Anvil
INVERNESS	Spean Bridge Mill Shop	Bridge Street
	Inverness Woollen Co.	High Street
INVERNESS-SHIRE	Spean Bridge Woollen Mill	Spean Bridge
JOHN O'GROATS	John O'Groats Knitwear	
KIRKWALL	Pitlochry Knitwear	Albert Street
OBAN	Oban Woollen Co.	George Street
PITLOCHRY	Pitlochry Knitwear	Mill Lane
PITLOCHRY	Pitlochry Knitwear	Atholl Road
PORTREE	Portree Knitwear Co.	Wentworth Street
ST. ANDREWS	Pitlochry Knitwear	Bell Street
ULLAPOOL	West Highland Woollen Co.	Shore Street

THE EDINBURGH WOOLLEN MILL

Woolen sweaters, kilts, blazers, scarves, socks, and other items for men, women, and children. See the write-up for this chain of stores under EDINBURGH and LANGHOLM, Scotland.

ENGLAND

BATH, 41 Stall Street
BLACKPOOL, 22 Adelaide St.
BOURNEMOUTH, 64/66 Old Christchurch Rd.
BOURTON-ON-THE-WATER, High Street
BROADWAY, 26 High Street
CARLISLE, 81 English St.

CHELTENHAM, 16 The Promenade
KESWICK, 44/46 Main Street
LANCASTER, 30 Market Square
SALISBURY, 10 Queen St.
SCARBOROUGH, 122 Westborough
SOUTHPORT
    12/12a Chapel Street
    315 Lord Street
    21 The Square
STRATFORD-UPON-AVON
    15a Wood Street
    31 Bridge Street
WINDSOR, 10/11 Castle Hill
YORK
    15/19 The Shambles
    64/68 Low Petergate

SCOTLAND

ABERDEEN, 425 Union Street
AYR, 50 Newmarket St.
CALLANDER, 12/18 Main Street
CRIEFF, 29/31 James Square
DUMFRIES, 8 Church Place
EDINBURGH
    139 Princes Street
    9 Randolph Place
    51 High Street
    453/455 Lawnmarket
FORT WILLIAM, 13 High Street
GLASGOW, 75 St. George's Place
HAWICK, 14 Bridge Street
INVERNESS, 28/30 High Street
LANGHOLM, Mill Shop
OBAN, 42 George Street
PERTH, 17 St. John Street
ROSS-ON-WYE, 10 George Street

PRODUCT INDEX

E = England
S = Scotland
W = Wales

PRODUCT	CITY (COUNTRY)	COMPANY	PAGE
CLOGS			
Hebden Bridge (E)		F. Walkley Clogs Ltd.	136
CLOTHING, Children's			
Cockermouth (E)		The Sheepskin Warehouse Shop	107
Glasgow (S)		M & B Anson, Ltd.	338
Edinburgh (S)		Geoffrey (Tailor) Highland Crafts	321
Edinburgh (S)		Kinloch Anderson Ltd.	326
Edinburgh (S)		Laura Ashley Bargain Shop	328
Edinburgh (S)		The Edinburgh Woollen Mill	330
London (E)		Burberry's Ltd.	165
London (E)		C & A	166
London (E)		Harrods Ltd.	174
London (E)		Laura Ashley	179
London (E)		Mothercare Ltd.	183
London (E)		Selfridges Ltd.	189
Lerwick, Shetland Islands (S)		Anderson & Co.	373
Newton Stewart (S)		Glen Cree Ltd.	376
Penrith (E)		The Sheepskin Warehouse Shop	211
Spean Bridge (S)		Spean Bridge Woollen Mill	393
CLOTHING, Infant			
London (E)		Harrods Ltd.	174
London (E)		Mothercare Ltd.	183
CLOTHING, Maternity			
London (E)		Mothercare Ltd.	183
CLOTHING, Men's			
Aberdeen (S)		Clan Royal	292
Altrincham (E)		Lakeland Sheepskin Centre	54
Ambleside (E)		Lakeland Sheepskin Centre	60
Bath (E)		Lakeland Sheepskin Centre	67
Blackpool (E)		Lakeland Sheepskin Centre	75
Blairgowrie (S)		Moffat Weavers	299
Bowness-on-Windermere (E)		Lakeland Sheepskin Centre	83
Bridgend, Isle of Islay (S)		The Islay Woollen Mill	300
Brighton (E)		Lakeland Sheepskin Centre	90
Callander (S)		Kilmahog Woollen Mill	304
Chester (E)		Clan Royal	104
Chester (E)		Lakeland Sheepskin Centre	104
Chichester (E)		Lakeland Sheepskin Centre	106
Culloden (S)		Clan Royal	309
Dartington (E)		Dartington Hall Tweed Mill & Shop	111

PRODUCT	CITY (COUNTRY)	COMPANY	PAGE
London (E)		Laura Ashley	179
London (E)		Liberty & Co.	180
London (E)		Lillywhites Ltd.	181
London (E)		Selfridges	189
Marlow (E)		Scoops	198
Melrose (S)		The Abbey Mill	374
Milton Keynes (E)		Dickins & Jones	200
Milton Keynes (E)		Scoops	201
Minehead (E)		Celtic Crafts Ltd.	201
Moffat (S)		Moffat Woollens Ltd.	375
Newton-Stewart (S)		Glen Cree Ltd.	376
North Berwick (S)		Clan Royal	377
Oban (S)		MacDonald's Tweeds Ltd.	379
Peebles (S)		Clan Royal	381
Penmachno nr. Betws-Y-Coed (W)		Penmachno Woollen Mill	427
Perth (S)		Gleneagles of Scotland	385
Pitlochry (S)		Atholl Woollens	387
Portree, Isle of Skye (S)		Skye Woollen Mill, Ltd.	387
Richmond (E)		Dickins & Jones	215
Scarborough (E)		Clan Royal	217
Shipley (E)		The Llama Shop	220
Southport (E)		Lakeland Sheepskin Centre	223
Spean Bridge (S)		Spean Bridge Woollen Mill	393
St. Andrews (S)		Clan Royal	394
St. Davids (W)		Tregwynt Textiles	433
St. Johns, Isle of Man (E)		Tynwald Woollen Mills	225
St. Nicholas (W)		Tregwynt Woollen Mill	433
Stratford-Upon-Avon (E)		Scoops	253
Stratford-Upon-Avon (E)		The Mulberry Tree Craftware	256
Stroud (E)		West of England Woollen Mills	267
Trefriw (W)		Trefriw Woollen Mills	436
Troon (S)		Clan Royal	395
Trowbridge (E)		West of England Woollen Mills	270
Walkerburn (S)		Clan Royal of Scotland	396
Winchester (E)		Lakeland Sheepskin Centre	280
Woodstock (E)		Scoops	283
York (E)		Clan Royal	286

COATS, Sheepskin
See SHEEPSKIN COATS

COSMETICS

London (E)		Harrods Ltd.	174

PRODUCT	CITY (COUNTRY)	COMPANY	PAGE
EMBROIDERY KITS			
Bury St. Edmunds (E)		The Danish Embroidery Centre	95
ENAMEL BOXES			
Stoke-on-Trent (Longton) (E)		Staffordshire Enamels Ltd.	247
ENGRAVINGS			
Holt (E)		The Picturecraft Art Gallery	138
Kelling (E)		The Picturecraft Art Gallery	144
London (E)		Harrods Ltd.	174
London (E)		Henry Sotheran Ltd.	176
ETCHINGS			
London (E)		Christie's Contemporary Art	166
London (E)		Harrods Ltd.	174
FABRICS			
Bala (W)		Craftcentre Cymru	403
Barmouth (W)		Craftcentre Cymru	403
Betws-Y-Coed (W)		Craftcentre Cymru	404
Bridgend, Isle of Islay (S)		The Islay Woollen Mill Co.	300
Bridge of Marnoch nr. Huntly (S)		Coleman Chambers Weavers	300
Broadford, Isle of Skye (S)		Skye Crotal Knitwear Mill Shop	303
Caernarfon (W)		Craftcentre Cymru	405
Carlisle (E)		Linton Tweeds	99
Chirk (W)		Craftcentre Cymru	406
Conwy (W)		Craftcentre Cymru	406
Dartington (E)		Dartington Hall Tweed Mill & Shop	111
Fishguard (W)		Tregwynt Textiles	417
Galashiels (S)		Peter Anderson Ltd.	337
Glendale by Dunvegan, Isle of Skye (S)		Skye Venture Cottage Industry	341
Golan (W)		Brynkir Woollen Mill	417
Inverness (S)		Duncan Chisholm & Sons	352
Isleornsay, Isle of Skye (S)		Skye Crotal Knitwear Mill Shop	356
Kingston St. Mary nr. Taunton (E)		Church Farm Weavers	147
Laxey, Isle of Man (E)		St. Georges Woollen Mills	152
Llangurig (W)		Craftcentre Cymru	422
Llanwrtyd Wells (W)		The Cambrian Factory	423
London (E)		Dickins & Jones	167
London (E)		Harrods Ltd.	174
London (E)		Laura Ashley	179

PRODUCT	CITY (COUNTRY)	COMPANY	PAGE
FURNITURE, New			
	Crickhowell (W)	Grahame Amey Ltd.	413
	Grantown-on-Spey (S)	Robadina Woodworking	344
	London (E)	Harrods Ltd.	174
	London (E)	Mothercare Ltd.	183
	London (E)	Selfridges Ltd.	189
	London (E)	The General Trading Co.	191
	Stoke St. Gregory, Taunton (E)	P. H. Coate & Son	252
	Stroud (E)	Rooksmoor Mills	265
GARDEN ITEMS			
	London (E)	The General Trading Co.	191
GLASS, Engraved			
	Kirkcudbright (S)	David Gulland Engraved Glass	365
GLASSWARE			
	Ambleside (E)	Adrian Sankey Glass	58
	Bath (E)	Scoops	68
	Blackpool (E)	Venetian Glass Co.	76
	Bournemouth (E)	Scoops	79
	Broxbourne (E)	Nazeing Glass Works	91
	Cambridge (E)	Midsummer Glassmakers of Cambridge	98
	Cheltenham (E)	Scoops	102
	Freshwater, Isle of Wight (E)	Alum Bay Glass	122
	Great Torrington	Dartington Glass Ltd.	129
	London (E)	Harrods Ltd.	174
	London (E)	The General Trading Co.	191
	London (E)	The Glasshouse	192
	Marlow (E)	Scoops	198
	Milton Keynes (E)	Scoops	201
	Newent (E)	Cowdy Glass Workshop	203
	Oban (S)	Caithness Glass P.L.C.	378
	Old Amersham (E)	Scoops	208
	Oxford (E)	Scoops	210
	Palnackie (S)	North Glen Gallery	380
	Perth (S)	Caithness Glass P.L.C.	383
	Stoke-on-Trent (Barlaston) (E)	Josiah Wedgwood & Sons	230
	Stratford-Upon-Avon (E)	Scoops	253
	Stratford-Upon-Avon (E)	The Little Gallery	254
	Ventnor, Isle of Wight (E)	Isle of Wight Glass	275
	Wick (S)	Caithness Glass P.L.C.	396
	Woodstock (E)	Scoops	283

PRODUCT CITY (COUNTRY)	COMPANY	PAGE
Stoke-on-Trent (Fenton) (E)	Coalport and Crown Staffordshire	236
Wick (S)	Caithness Glass P.L.C.	396

KILTS

Aberdeen (S)	Clan Royal	292
Blairgowrie (S)	Moffat Weavers	299
Bowness-on-Windermere (E)	Windermere Woollens	84
Callander (S)	Kilmahog Woollen Mill	304
Chester (E)	Clan Royal	104
Culloden (S)	Clan Royal	309
Dinas Mawddwy (W)	Meirion Mill	414
Dunbar (S)	Clan Royal	312
Edinburgh (S)	Clan Royal	317
Edinburgh (S)	Geoffrey (Tailor) Highland Crafts	321
Edinburgh (S)	Gleneagles of Scotland	322
Edinburgh (S)	James Pringle Woollen Mill	323
Edinburgh (S)	John Morrison Ltd.	324
Edinburgh (S)	Kinloch Anderson Ltd.	326
Edinburgh (S)	The Edinburgh Woollen Mill	330
Elgin (S)	Clan Royal	332
Fort William (S)	Clan Royal	333
Fort William (S)	Moffat Weavers	334
Fort William (S)	Nevis Bridge Clanwear	334
Galashiels (S)	Clan Royal	336
Galashiels (S)	Peter Anderson Ltd.	337
Gretna Green (S)	Gretna Green Woollen Mill	345
Harrogate (E)	Clan Royal	134
Inverness (S)	Clan Royal	352
Inverness (S)	Duncan Chisholm & Sons	352
Langholm (S)	The Edinburgh Woollen Mill (mill shop)	372
Melrose (S)	The Abbey Mill	374
Moffat (S)	Moffat Woollens Ltd.	375
North Berwick (S)	Clan Royal	377
Oban (S)	MacDonald's Tweeds Ltd.	379
Peebles (S)	Clan Royal	381
Perth (S)	Gleneagles of Scotland	385
Pitlochry (S)	Atholl Woollens	387
Scarborough (E)	Clan Royal	217
St. Andrews (S)	Clan Royal	394
St. Johns, Isle of Man (E)	Tynwald Woollen Mills	225
Stratford-Upon-Avon (E)	The Mulberry Tree Craftware	256
Troon (S)	Clan Royal	395
Walkerburn (S)	Clan Royal of Scotland	396
York (E)	Clan Royal	286

PRODUCT	CITY (COUNTRY)	COMPANY	PAGE
KITCHENS			
Stroud (E)		Rooksmoor Mills	265
KITCHEN ITEMS			
Bath (E)		Scoops	68
Bournemouth (E)		Scoops	79
Cheltenham (E)		Scoops	102
London (E)		Harrods Ltd.	174
London (E)		The General Trading Co.	191
Marlow (E)		Scoops	198
Milton Keynes (E)		Scoops	201
Old Amersham (E)		Scoops	208
Oxford (E)		Scoops	210
Stratford-Upon-Avon (E)		Scoops	253
Woodstock (E)		Scoops	283
LAMPS, Miners			
Aberdare (W)		E. Thomas & Williams	402
LAMPBASES			
Bagborough (E)		Quantock Design Ltd.	61
Flitwick (E)		DEMA Glass Ltd.	121
Henley-in-Arden (E)		Torquil Pottery	138
Honiton (E)		Honiton Pottery	140
Rye (E)		Rye Pottery	215
LAVENDER PRODUCTS			
Heacham (E)		Norfolk Lavendar Ltd.	135
LEATHER CLOTHING			
Altrincham (E)		Lakeland Sheepskin Centre	54
Ambleside (E)		Lakeland Sheepskin Centre	60
Bath (E)		Lakeland Sheepskin Centre	67
Blackpool (E)		Lakeland Sheepskin Centre	75
Bowness-on-Windermere (E)		Lakeland Sheepskin Centre	83
Brighton (E)		Lakeland Sheepskin Centre	90
Chester (E)		Lakeland Sheepskin Center	104
Chichester (E)		Lakeland Sheepskin Center	106
Cockermouth (E)		The Sheepskin Warehouse Shop	107
Guildford (E)		Lakeland Sheepskin Centre	133
Kendal (E)		Lakeland Sheepskin Centre	145
Keswick (E)		Lakeland Sheepskin Centre	146
Kirkby Lonsdale (E)		The Sheepskin Warehouse Shop	149
London (E)		Harrods Ltd.	174
Southport (E)		Lakeland Sheepskin Centre	223

PRODUCT	CITY (COUNTRY)	COMPANY	PAGE
POTTERY			
Aller nr. Langport (E)		The Pottery	54
Arundel (E)		Duff Gallery	60
Bagborough (E)		Quantock Design Ltd.	61
Bala (W)		Craftcentre Cymru	403
Barmouth (W)		Craftcentre Cymru	403
Barnstaple (E)		C. H. Brannam Ltd.	64
Bath (E)		Reject China Shop	67
Blacktoft nr. Goole (E)		Jerry Harper Handthrown Pottery	77
Blaenau Ffestiniog (W)		Ffestiniog Pottery	404
Bourton-on-the-Water (E)		Bourton Pottery	79
Caernarfon (W)		Craftcentre Cymru	405
Caton nr. Lancaster (E)		The Lunesdale Pottery	101
Chessell nr. Yarmouth, Isle of Wight (E)		Chessell Pottery	103
Chirk (W)		Craftcentre Cymru	406
Clifton nr. Penrith (E)		Wetheriggs Country Pottery	106
Conwy (W)		Craftcentre Cymru	406
Corris (W)		Corris Pottery	408
Corris (W)		Glandwyryd Stores Ceramics	411
Cranham (E)		Prinknash Pottery	109
Crieff (S)		A. W. Buchan—Thistle Potteries	305
Denby (E)		Denby Tableware/Pottery	112
Ditchling (E)		The Craftsman Gallery	116
Fiddington nr. Bridgwater (E)		Whitnell Pottery	119
Haddington (S)		Margery Clinton Ceramics	346
Henley-in-Arden (E)		Torquil Pottery	138
Holtby nr. York (E)		The Studios	139
Honiton (E)		Honiton Pottery	140
Hornsea (E)		Hornsea Pottery	142
Kelso (S)		The Kelso Pottery	358
Kingussie (S)		Highland China Ltd.	362
Lancaster (E)		Hornsea Pottery	150
Llanarth (W)		Llanarth Pottery	421
Llangurig (W)		Craftcentre Cymru	422
London (E)		Harrods Ltd.	174
London (E)		Rawnsley Academy Ltd.	185
London (E)		The British Crafts Centre	189
London (E)		The Craftsmen Potters Assoc.	190
Low Bentham (E)		Bentham Pottery	195
Machynlleth (W)		Craftcentre Cymru	425
Newcastle-Under-Lyme (E)		Portmeirion Potteries	202
Norwich (E)		Le Dieu Pottery	206

PRODUCT	CITY (COUNTRY)	COMPANY	PAGE
Callander (S)		Kilmahog Woollen Mill	304
Chester (E)		Lakeland Sheepskin Centre	104
Chichester (E)		Lakeland Sheepskin Centre	106
Cockermouth (E)		The Sheepskin Warehouse Shop	107
Edinburgh (S)		Gleneagles of Scotland	322
Fort William (S)		Moffat Weavers	334
Fort William (S)		Nevis Bridge Clanwear	334
Glastonbury (E)		Avalon Basket & Sheepskin Shop	123
Glastonbury (E)		Baily's of Glastonbury	124
Glastonbury (E)		R. J. Draper & Co.	125
Guildford (E)		Lakeland Sheepskin Centre	133
Kendal (E)		Lakeland Sheepskin Centre	145
Keswick (E)		Lakeland Sheepskin Centre	146
Kirby Lonsdale (E)		The Sheepskin Warehouse Shop	149
London (E)		Harrods Ltd.	174
London (E)		R. J. Draper & Co.	187
Melrose (S)		The Abbey Mill	374
Moffat (S)		Moffat Woollens Ltd.	375
Oban (S)		MacDonald's Tweeds Ltd.	379
Old Cleeve (E)		John Wood & Son Ltd.	209
Penrith (E)		The Sheepskin Warehouse Shop	211
Perth (S)		Gleneagles of Scotland	385
Pitlochry (S)		Atholl Wollens	387
Southport (E)		Lakeland Sheepskin Centre	223
Stratford-Upon-Avon (E)		The Mulberry Tree Craftware	256
Street (E)		Avalon Sheepskin Shop	260
Street (E)		D. T. Bayliss & Son	260
Street (E)		STOP—Sheepskin Discount Centre	263
Taunton (E)		Tanns of Taunton Factory Shop	268
Winchester (E)		Lakeland Sheepskin Centre	280

SHEEPSKIN PRODUCTS

PRODUCT		COMPANY	PAGE
Barnstaple (E)		Messrs. S. Sanders & Son	65
Bungay (E)		Nursey & Son Ltd.	92
Cockermouth (E)		The Sheepskin Warehouse Shop	107
Dolgellau (W)		Enid Pierce	416
Glastonbury (E)		Avalon Basket & Sheepskin Shop	123
Glastonbury (E)		Baily's of Glastonbury	124

PRODUCT	CITY (COUNTRY)	COMPANY	PAGE
Porthmadog (W)		Craftcentre Cymru	430
Portree, Isle of Skye (S)		Skye Woollen Mill	387
Pwllheli (W)		Craftcentre Cymru	432
Scarborough (E)		Clan Royal	217
Shipley (E)		The Llama Shop	220
Southport (E)		Lakeland Sheepskin Centre	223
Spean Bridge (S)		Spean Bridge Woollen Mill	393
St. Johns, Isle of Man (E)		Tynwald Woollen Mills	225
St. Andrews (S)		Clan Royal	394
Stratford-Upon-Avon (E)		The Mulberry Tree Craftware	256
Street (E)		STOP—Sheepskin Discount Centre	263
Troon (S)		Clan Royal	395
Trowbridge (E)		West of England Woollen Mills	270
Walkerburn (S)		Clan Royal	396
Winchester (E)		Lakeland Sheepskin Centre	280
York (E)		Clan Royal	286

TAPES

London (E)		Harrods Ltd.	174
London (E)		H.M.V. Ltd.	177

TAPESTRY KITS

London (E)		Glorafilia	172

TEAS, Herb

Thornham Magna nr. Eye (E)		The Suffolk Spice & Herb Co.	269

TERRACOTTA

Barnstaple (E)		C. H. Brannam Ltd.	64
Llanarth (W)		Llanarth Pottery	421
London (E)		Harrods Ltd.	174
Wattisfield (E)		Henry Watson's Potteries	276

THEATER TICKETS

London (E)		Hotels Plus	178
London (E)		Theatre Tickets	189

THIMBLES

Williton (E)		The Paddingham Collection	278

TILES, Ceramic

London (E)		Rye Tiles Ceramics	188
Rye (E)		Rye Tiles Ceramics	216

PRODUCT	CITY (COUNTRY)	COMPANY	PAGE
TOYS, Children's			
Bridge of Weir (S)		Dormouse Designs	302
London (E)		Hamley's of Regent Street	173
London (E)		Harrods Ltd.	174
London (E)		Mothercare Ltd.	183
WALKING STICKS			
Bowness-on-Windermere (E)		The Horn Shop	84
Kendal (E)		The Horn Shop	146
London (E)		Harrods Ltd.	174
WALLPAPER			
London (E)		Laura Ashley	179
WATERCOLORS			
(See also CRAFT WORKSHOPS)			
(See also PAINTINGS)			
London (E)		Henry Sotheran Ltd.	176
WICKER			
London (E)		Harrods Ltd.	174
WILLOW, Baskets and Furniture			
London (E)		Harrods Ltd.	174
Stoke St. Gregory, Taunton (E)		P. H. Coate & Co.	252
WINES			
Brandeston (E)		Brandeston Priory Vineyards	86
Dorchester (E)		Dorchester Brewery	117
Felsted (E)		Felstar Estate Wines	118
Horam (E)		Merrydown Wine	140
London (E)		Harrods Ltd.	174
North Wootton nr. Shepton Mallet (E)		Wootton Vineyard	204
Stroud (E)		Raffles Wine Co.	264
Whippingham, Isle of Wight (E)		Barton Manor Vineyard & Gardens	277
WROUGHT IRON			
Cerne Abbas (E)		Cerne Valley Forge	101
YARN			
Carlisle (E)		Linton Tweeds	99
Kilwinning (S)		Busby Spinning Mill Shop	361
Lerwick, Shetland Island (S)		Anderson & Co.	373
Selkirk (S)		Gardiner of Selkirk Ltd.	391

COMPANY INDEX

COMPANY NAME	CITY	COUNTRY	NUMBER
Adams and Jones	Street	E	259
Adrian Sankey Glass	Ambleside	E	58
Alaven Designs	Newtown	W	426
Alison Morton	Corris	W	406
Alum Bay Glass Ltd. Glassmakers	Freshwater Isle of Wight	E	122
Anderson & Co.	Lerwick, Shetland Islands	S	373
Andrew Stewart Woollens and Crafts Shop	Galashiels	S	335
Aran Intern't. Knitwear	Ayr	S	295
Artista Designs Ltd.	Hawick	S	347
Atelier Fabrics	Selkirk	S	390
Atholl Woollens	Pitlochry	S	387
Austin Reed	London	E	164
Avalon Basket and Sheepskin Shop	Glastonbury	E	123
A. W. Buchan & Co. Ltd.	Crieff	S	305
Baily's of Glastonbury	Glastonbury	E	124
Barclaycraft Craft Gallery	Brighton	E	88
Barretts	Cambridge	E	97
Barton Manor Vineyard and Gardens	Whippingham, Isle of Wight	E	277
Bass Museum	Burton-on-Trent	E	93
Beckford Silk	Beckford	E	73
Ben Ghlas Workshops	Killin	S	360
Bentham Pottery	Low Bentham	E	195
Boehm of Malvern England, Ltd.	Malvern	E	196
Bookends, Ltd.	London	E	165
Border Fine Arts Company, Ltd.	Langholm	S	370

COMPANY NAME	CITY	COUNTRY	NUMBER
Bosham Walk Craft Centre	Bosham	E	78
Bourton Pottery	Bourton-on-the-Water	E	79
Braichgoch Slate Quarries	Corris Uchaf	W	412
Brandeston Priory Vineyards	Brandeston	E	86
Brynkir Woollen Mill	Golan	W	417
Bryn Melyn Studio	Dolgellau	W	416
Burberry's Ltd.	London	E	165
Busby Spinning Mill Shop	Kilwinning	S	361
C & A	London	E	166
Cairngorm Whiskey Centre	Aviemore	S	297
Caithness Candles	John O'Groats	S	357
Caithness Glass P.L.C.	Oban	S	378
Caithness Glass P.L.C.	Perth	S	383
Caithness Glass P.L.C.	Wick	S	396
Caithness Leather Products	Wick	S	398
Calderdale Piece Hall	Halifax	E	133
Canongate Jerseys	Edinburgh	S	316
Celtic Crafts Ltd.	Minehead	E	201
Cerne Valley Forge	Cerne Abbas	E	101
Chas. N. Whillans	Hawick	S	348
C. H. Brannam Ltd.	Barnstaple	E	64
Cheshire Candle Workshops	Burwardsley nr. Chester	E	94
Chessell Pottery	Chessell	E	103
Chewton Cheese Dairy	Chewton Mendip	E	104
Christie's Contemporary Art	London	E	166
Church Farm Weavers	Kingston St. Mary nr. Taunton	E	147
Clan Royal	Aberdeen	S	292
Clan Royal	Chester	E	104
Clan Royal	Culloden	S	309
Clan Royal	Dunbar	S	312
Clan Royal	Edinburgh	S	317
Clan Royal	Elgin	S	332
Clan Royal	Fort William	S	333
Clan Royal	Galashiels	S	336
Clan Royal	Harrogate	E	134
Clan Royal	Inverness	S	352
Clan Royal	North Berwick	S	377
Clan Royal	Peebles	S	381

COMPANY NAME	CITY	COUNTRY	NUMBER
Clan Royal	Scarborough	E	217
Clan Royal	St. Andrews	S	394
Clan Royal	Troon	S	395
Clan Royal	York	E	286
Clan Royal of Scotland	Walkerburn	S	396
Clifford House Craft Workshop	Brough	E	90
Close Second	Edinburgh	S	320
Coalport and Crown Staffordshire	Stoke-on-Trent (Fenton)	E	236
Coleman–Chambers Weavers	Bridge of Marnoch, nr. Huntly	S	300
Collection Craft Gallery	Ledbury	E	153
Coronation Rock Co.	Blackpool	E	74
Corris Craft Centre	Corris	W	409
Corris Pottery	Corris	W	408
Cowdy Glass Workshop	Newent	E	203
Craft at the Suffolk Barn	Great Barton nr. Bury St. Edmunds	E	129
Craftcentre Cymru	Bala	W	403
Craftcentre Cymru	Barmouth	W	403
Craftcentre Cymru	Betws-y-Coed	W	404
Craftcentre Cymru	Caernarfon	W	405
Craftcentre Cymru	Chirk	W	406
Craftcentre Cymru	Conwy	W	406
Craftcentre Cymru	Llangurig	W	422
Craftcentre Cymru	Machynlleth	W	425
Craftcentre Cymru	Porthmadog	W	430
Craftcentre Cymru	Pwllheli	W	432
Craft Design Centre of Wales	Tregaron	W	437
Craftsmen of Cumbria	Bowness-on-Windermere	E	82
Creetown Gold and Silversmith Workshop	Creetown	S	304
Crown Winsor Sylvac Ceramics	Stoke-on-Trent (Longton)	E	241
Cumbria Crystal Ltd.	Nottingham	E	208
Cumbria Crystal Ltd.	Ulverston	E	464
Cumbria Crystal Ltd.	York	E	286
Dartington Glass Ltd.	Great Torrington	E	129
Dartington Hall Tweed Mill & Shop	Dartington	E	111

COMPANY NAME	CITY	COUNTRY	NUMBER
David Gulland Engraved Glass	Kirkcudbright	S	365
DEMA Glass Ltd.	Flitwick	E	121
Denby Pottery	Denby	E	112
Denby Seconds Shop	Matlock Bath	E	198
Dent Crafts Centre	Dent	E	114
Derwent Crystal Ltd.	Derby	E	114
Dickins & Jones	London	E	167
Dickins & Jones	Milton Keynes	E	200
Dickins & Jones	Richmond	E	215
Dorchester Brewery	Dorchester	E	117
Dorraga Knitwear	Crieff	S	306
Dormouse Designs	Bridge of Weir	S	302
Drumohr Knitwear Millshop	Dumfries	S	312
D. T. Bayliss & Son	Street	E	260
Duff Gallery	Arundel	S	60
Duncan Chisholm & Sons, Ltd.	Inverness	S	352
Edinburgh Crystal	Penicuik	S	382
Englefields	London	E	168
Enid Pierce	Dolgellau	W	416
Enoch Griffiths Ltd.	Llanbedr	W	422
Eskvalley Knitwear Co. Ltd.	Langholm	S	372
Etcetera China Shops	Cambridge	E	98
E. Thomas & Williams Ltd.	Aberdare	W	402
Ehos Candles Ltd.	Mere	E	200
Ewe Nique Knitwear	Haddington	S	345
Felstar Estate Wines	Felsted	E	118
Ffestiniog Pottery	Blaenau Ffestiniog	W	404
Fine Shoes	Street	E	261
Fine Shoes	Wells	E	276
Fortnum & Mason	London	E	169
Foyles	London	E	170
F. Walkley Clogs, Ltd.	Hebden Bridge	E	136
Gardiner of Selkirk Ltd.	Selkirk	S	391
Geoffrey Tailor Highland Crafts Ltd.	Edinburgh	S	321
Georgian Crystal Ltd.	Tutbury	E	271
Gered	London	E	171
G. Heywood Hill	London	E	172
Glandwyryd Stores Ceramics	Corris	W	411

COMPANY NAME	CITY	COUNTRY	NUMBER
Glen Cree Limited	Newton-Stewart	S	376
Gleneagles of Scotland	Edinburgh	S	322
Gleneagles of Scotland	Perth	S	385
Glenturret Distillery	Crieff	S	307
Glorafilia	London	E	172
Gordon and MacPhail	Elgin	S	332
Grahame Amey Ltd. Furniture	Crickhowell	W	413
Grainger & Campbell Ltd.	East Kilbride	S	316
Gretna Green Woollen Mill	Gretna Green	S	345
Grewelthorpe Handweavers Ltd.	Grewelthorpe	E	131
Hamley's of Regent Street Ltd.	London	E	173
Harrods Ltd.	London	E	174
Hatchards	London	E	175
Hay-on-Wye	Hay-on-Wye	W	419
Healacraft China Ltd.	Stoke-on-Trent (Longton)	E	242
Hebridean Jewellery	Iochdar, South Uist Island	S	355
Henry Watson's Potteries, Ltd.	Wattisfield	E	276
Henry Sotheran Ltd.	London	E	176
Herald House	Langport	E	151
Highland Aromatics Ltd.	Drumchardine	S	310
Highland China Ltd.	Kingussie	S	362
H.M.V. Ltd.	London	E	177
Hobbs & Co.	London	E	177
Honiton Pottery Ltd.	Honiton	E	140
Hornsea Pottery Co. Ltd.	Hornsea	E	142
Hornsea Pottery Co. Ltd.	Lancaster	E	150
Hotels Plus	London	E	178
House of Nisbet, Ltd.	Winscombe	E	280
I. Gibson & Son Ltd.	Sheffield	E	217
Inderwood Pottery	Stroud	E	263
Ingasetter Ltd.	Banchory	S	298
Inigo Jones & Co. Ltd.	Groeslon	W	418
Isle of Wight Glass	Ventnor, Isle of Wight	E	275
James Pringle Ltd., Holm Woollen Mills	Inverness	S	354

COMPANY NAME	CITY	COUNTRY	NUMBER
James Pringle Woollen Mill and Clan Tartan Centre	Edinburgh	S	323
J. Bradbury & Co.	Uppermill nr. Saddleworth	E	274
Jedburgh Kiltmakers	Jedburgh	S	357
Jennie Ross Classic Knitwear	Macduff	S	374
Jeremy Law Ltd.	Dunkeld	S	313
Jerry Harper Handthrown Pottery	Blacktoft, nr. Goole	E	77
J. & G. Grant	Ballindalloch	S	297
John Beswick Ltd.	Stoke-on-Trent (Longton)	E	244
John Creed Antiques Ltd.	London (Islington)	E	179
John Dewar & Sons, Ltd.	Perth	S	385
John Morrison Ltd.	Edinburgh	S	324
John Walker & Sons Ltd.	Kilmarnock	S	360
John Wood & Son Ltd.	Old Cleeve	E	209
Johnson Brothers Works Shop	Stoke-on-Trent (Hanley)	E	239
Josiah Wedgwood and Sons, Ltd.	Stoke-on-Trent (Barlaston)	E	230
K.E.S. Mosaics Studio Gallery	Edinburgh	S	325
Kilmahog Woollen Mill	Callender	S	304
Kinloch Anderson Ltd.	Edinburgh	S	326
Lakeland Sheepskin Center	Altrincham	E	54
Lakeland Sheepskin Center	Ambleside	E	60
Lakeland Sheepskin Center	Bath	E	67
Lakeland Sheepskin Center	Blackpool	E	75
Lakeland Sheepskin Center	Bowness-on-Windermere	E	83
Lakeland Sheepskin Center	Brighton	E	90
Lakeland Sheepskin Center	Chester	E	104

COMPANY NAME	CITY	COUNTRY	NUMBER
Lakeland Sheepskin Center	Chichester	E	106
Lakeland Sheepskin Center	Guildford	E	133
Lakeland Sheepskin Center	Kendal	E	145
Lakeland Sheepskin Center	Keswick	E	146
Lakeland Sheepskin Center	Southport	E	223
Lakeland Sheepskin Center	Winchester	E	280
Langrigg Pottery	Winton	E	281
Laura Ashley	London	E	179
Laura Ashley Bargain Shop	Edinburgh	S	328
Le Dieu Pottery	Norwich	E	206
Liberty & Co. Ltd.	London	E	180
Lilian Forshaw	Battle	E	71
Lillywhites Ltd.	London	E	181
Linton Tweeds Ltd.	Carlisle	E	99
Llanarth Pottery	Llanarth	W	421
Lochleven Mill Shop	Kinross	S	363
Longdale Rural Craft Centre	Ravenshead	E	213
MacDonald's Tweeds Ltd.	Oban	S	379
Margery Clinton Ceramics	Haddington	S	346
Mason's Ironstone Factory Shop	Stoke-on-Trent (Hanley)	E	240
M & B Anson, Ltd.	Glasgow	S	338
Meirion Mill	Dianas Mawddwy	E	414
Merrydown Wine	Horam	E	140
Messrs. S. Sanders and Son, Ltd.	Barnstaple	E	65
Michael Gill	Kirkcudbright	S	366
Midsummer Glassmakers of Cambridge	Cambridge	E	98
Minerva Fine Arts of London, Ltd.	Grantham	E	127
Moffat Weavers	Blairgowrie	S	299
Moffat Weavers	Fort William	S	334
Moffat Woollens Ltd.	Moffat	S	375
Mothercare Ltd.	London	E	183
Moussie Designs Ltd.	London	E	184
Naturally British	London	E	184

COMPANY NAME	CITY	COUNTRY	NUMBER
Nazeing Glass Works Ltd.	Broxbourne	E	91
Neidpath Knitwear Ltd.	Innerleithen	S	351
Nevis Bridge Clanwear	Fort William	S	334
Norfolk Lavender Ltd.	Heacham	E	135
Norman Cherry	Kelso	S	358
North Glen Gallery	Palnackie	S	380
Nursey and Son Ltd.	Bungay	E	92
Orcadian Stone Company Ltd.	Golspie	S	343
Ortak Jewellery	Kirkwall, Orkney Islands	S	367
Penmachno Woollen Mill	Penmachno, nr. Betws-y-Coed	W	427
Perth Craft Centre	Perth	S	386
Perthshire Paperweights Ltd.	Crieff	S	308
Peter Anderson Ltd.	Galashiels	S	337
Peter Dingley Gallery	Stratford-upon-Avon	E	257
P. H. Coate & Son	Stoke St. Gregory, Taunton	E	252
Philip Laureston Designs	Torquay	E	270
Plas Robin Products	Montgomery	W	425
Poole Pottery Ltd.	Poole	E	212
Porthmadog Pottery	Porthmadog	W	431
Portmeirion Potteries, Ltd.	Newcastle-under-Lyme	E	202
Portmeirion Potteries, Ltd.	Stafford	E	224
Portmeirion Potteries, Ltd.	Stoke-on-Trent (Longton)	E	245
Presteigne Crafts	Presteigne	W	431
Prinknash Pottery	Cranham	E	109
Purbeck Pottery Ltd.	Poole	E	212
Quantock Design Ltd.	Bagborough	E	61
Quince Honey Farm	South Molton	E	222
Raffles Wine Co.	Stroud	E	264
Rawnsley Academy Ltd.	London	E	185
Raymond Hodgson and Co. Ltd.	Alva	S	292
Reawick Lamb Marketing Co. Ltd.	Reawick, Shetland Islands	S	389
Regency Crystal Limited	Cradley, nr. Halesowen	E	108
Reject China Shop	Bath	E	67

COMPANY NAME	CITY	COUNTRY	NUMBER
Reject China Shop	London	E	186
Reject China Shop	Oxford	E	210
Reject China Shop	Windsor	E	280
Renaissance International Ltd.	Stoke-on-Trent (Fenton)	E	238
Richard Martin	Litchborough	E	154
R. J. Draper & Co. Ltd.	Glastonbury	E	125
R. J. Draper & Co. Ltd.	London	E	187
R. J. Sheppy and Son	Bradford-on-Tone	E	85
Robadinia Woodworking	Grantown-on-Spey	S	344
Robert H. Towers	Kirkwall, Orkney Islands	S	368
Robert Noble	Peebles	S	381
Robin Watson Signs	Hunton, nr. Bedale	E	143
Rooksmoor Mills	Stroud	E	265
Royal Brierley Crystal	Brierley Hill	E	87
Royal Crown Derby	Derby	E	115
Royal Doulton	Stoke-on-Trent	E	227
Royal Doulton	Stoke-on-Trent (Burslem)	E	233
Royal Grafton	Stoke-on-Trent (Longton)	E	246
Russell Gurney Weavers	Turriff	S	395
Rye Pottery	Rye	E	215
Rye Tiles Ceramic	London	E	188
Rye Tiles Ceramic	Rye	E	216
Scarfskerry Pottery	Scarfskerry	S	389
Schofields of Sheffield Ltd.	Sheffield	E	218
Scoops	Bath	E	68
Scoops	Bournemouth	E	79
Scoops	Cheltenham	E	102
Scoops	Marlow	E	198
Scoops	Milton Keynes	E	201
Scoops	Old Amersham	E	208
Scoops	Oxford	E	210
Scoops	Stratford-upon-Avon	E	253
Scoops	Woodstock	E	283
Scottish Craft Centre	Edinburgh	S	329
Selfridges Ltd.	London	E	189
Sentre Arts	Stratford-upon-Avon	E	258
Shebeg Gallery	Ballasalla, Isle of Man	E	63

COMPANY NAME	CITY	COUNTRY	NUMBER
Sheffield Scene	Sheffield	E	219
Shetland Silvercraft	Soundside, Shetland Islands	S	393
Simon J. Gidden Engraving Studio	Kingswinford	E	148
Skye Crotal Knitwear Mill Shop	Broadford, Isle of Skye	S	303
Skye Crotal Knitwear Mill Shop	Isleornsay, Isle of Skye	S	356
Skye-Lytes Candlemaker	Arnisort, Isle of Skye	S	293
Skye Venture Cottage Industry	Glendale By Dunvegan, Isle of Skye	S	341
Skye Woollen Mill Ltd.	Portree, Isle of Skye	S	387
Slate Age Ltd.	Fence, nr. Burnley	E	119
Smallcombe Clocks	Grays	E	127
S. Moores, Dorset Biscuits	Morcombelake nr. Bridport	E	202
Spean Bridge Woollen Mill	Spean Bridge	S	393
Spode Limited	Stoke-on-Trent	E	228
Staffordshire Crystal Ltd.	Stoke-on-Trent (Longton)	E	249
Staffordshire Enamels Ltd.	Stoke-on-Trent (Longton)	E	247
Staffordshire Potteries Ltd.	Stoke-on-Trent (Meir Park)	E	251
St. Georges Woollen Mills Ltd.	Laxey, Isle of Man	E	152
St. Johns Crystal Ltd.	St. Johns, Isle of Man	E	224
Stockwell China Bazaar	Glasgow	S	339
STOP—Sheepskin Discount Centre	Street	E	263
Stuart Crystal	Wordsley, nr. Stourbridge	E	283
Stuart Strathearn Ltd.	Crieff	S	308
Tanns of Taunton Factory Shop	Taunton	E	268
Tenby Pottery	Tenby	W	435
The Abbey Mill	Melrose	S	374
The British Crafts Centre	London	E	189
The Cambrian Factory	Llanwrtyd Wells	W	423

COMPANY NAME	CITY	COUNTRY	NUMBER
The Sheepskin Warehouse Shop	Cockermouth	E	107
The Sheepskin Warehouse Shop	Kirby Lonsdale	E	149
The Sheepskin Warehouse Shop	Penrith	E	211
The Studios	Holtby nr. York	E	139
The Suffolk Spice and Herb Co.	Thornham Magna, nr. Eye	E	269
The Tappit Hen	Stratford-upon-Avon	E	256
Thomas Webb Crystal	Amblecote, nr. Stourbridge	E	56
Tommy Nutter	London	E	194
Torquil Pottery	Henley-in-Arden	E	138
Trefriw Woollen Mills Ltd.	Trefriw	W	436
Tregwynt Textiles	Fishguard	W	417
Tregwynt Textiles	St. Davids	W	433
Tregwynt Woollen Mills	St. Nicholas	W	433
Tudor Crystal Factory Shop	Wordsley, nr. Stourbridge	E	284
Tynllan Pottery	Penmorfa nr. Porthmadog	W	429
Tynwald Woollen Mills Ltd. and Craft Center	St. Johns, Isle of Man	E	225
Venetian Glass Co.	Blackpool	E	76
Viable Centre	Basingstoke	E	66
Waterford Aynsley China Reject Shop	Stoke-on-Trent	E	250
Webb Corbett Royal Doulton Crystal	Amblecote, nr. Stourbridge	E	57
Wedgwood Crystal Ltd.	King's Lynn	E	147
Wellow Crafts	Bath	E	69
Wendy Lawrence Ltd.	Knighton	W	420
West of England Woollen Mills	Stroud	E	267
West of England Woollen Mills	Trowbridge	E	270
Wetheriggs Country Pottery	Clifton, nr. Penrith	E	106
White of Hawick	Hawick	S	349
Whitnell Pottery	Fiddington, nr. Bridgwater	E	119

COMPANY NAME	CITY	COUNTRY	NUMBER
Windermere Woollens	Bowness-on-Windermere	E	84
Winter Flora	Beccles	E	72
W. Moorcroft Limited Limited Potters	Stoke-on-Trent (Burslem)	E	235
Wolf House Gallery	Silverdale	E	221
Wootton Vineyard	North Wootton, nr. Shepton Mallet	E	204
Workface	Glastonbury	E	126
Wrights of Trowmill Ltd.	Hawick	S	350

Maps

PURCHASES IN GREAT BRITAIN

DATE OF PURCHASE	STORE & PRODUCT	GIFT FOR	COST	DATE & PLACE MAILED	AIR OR SURFACE

PURCHASES IN GREAT BRITAIN

DATE OF PURCHASE	STORE & PRODUCT	GIFT FOR	COST	DATE & PLACE MAILED	AIR OR SURFACE

FROMMER/PASMANTIER PUBLISHERS   Date_____
1230 AVE. OF THE AMERICAS, NEW YORK, NY 10020

Friends, please send me the books checked below:

$-A-DAY GUIDES

(In-depth guides to low-cost tourist accommodations and facilities.)

☐ Europe on $25 a Day $11.95	☐ New Zealand on $25 a Day $10.95
☐ Australia on $25 a Day $10.95	☐ New York on $45 a Day............. $9.95
☐ England on $35 a Day.............. $10.95	☐ Scandinavia on $35 a Day........... $9.95
☐ Greece on $25 a Day............... $10.95	☐ Scotland and Wales on $35 a Day..... $10.95
☐ Hawaii on $35 a Day............... $10.95	☐ South America on $25 a Day $9.95
☐ India on $15 & $25 a Day........... $9.95	☐ Spain and Morocco (plus the Canary
☐ Ireland on $25 a Day............... $9.95	Is.) on $35 a Day $9.95
☐ Israel on $30 & $35 a Day $10.95	☐ Washington, D.C. on $40 a Day...... $10.95
☐ Mexico on $20 a Day $9.95	

DOLLARWISE GUIDES

(Guides to accommodations and facilities from budget to deluxe, with emphasis on the medium-priced.)

☐ Austria & Hungary $10.95	☐ Caribbean $12.95
☐ Egypt............................ $11.95	☐ Cruises (incl. Alaska. Carib, Mex,
☐ England & Scotland $10.95	Hawaii. Panama, Canada, & US) $10.95
☐ France........................... $10.95	☐ California & Las Vegas $9.95
☐ Germany $11.95	☐ Florida........................... $10.95
☐ Italy............................. $10.95	☐ New England..................... $11.95
☐ Japan & Hong Kong (avail. Apr. '86) . $11.95	☐ Northwest........................ $10.95
☐ Portugal (incl. Madeira & the Azores) . $11.95	☐ Skiing USA—East $10.95
☐ Switzerland & Liechtenstein $11.95	☐ Skiing USA—West $10.95
☐ Bermuda & The Bahamas........... $10.95	☐ Southeast & New Orleans........... $11.95
☐ Canada $12.95	☐ Southwest........................ $10.95

THE ARTHUR FROMMER GUIDES

(Pocket-size guides to tourist accommodations and facilities in all price ranges.)

☐ Amsterdam/Holland $4.95	☐ Mexico City/Acapulco $4.95
☐ Athens........................... $4.95	☐ Montreal/Quebec City $4.95
☐ Atlantic City/Cape May $4.95	☐ New Orleans $4.95
☐ Boston........................... $4.95	☐ New York......................... $4.95
☐ Dublin/Ireland $4.95	☐ Orlando/Disney World/EPCOT $4.95
☐ Hawaii $4.95	☐ Paris $4.95
☐ Las Vegas $4.95	☐ Philadelphia....................... $4.95
☐ Lisbon/Madrid/Costa del Sol......... $4.95	☐ Rome $4.95
☐ London $4.95	☐ San Francisco $4.95
☐ Los Angeles $4.95	☐ Washington, D.C. $4.95

SPECIAL EDITIONS

☐ Bed & Breakfast—N. America $7.95	☐ Museums in New York $8.95
☐ Fast 'n' Easy Phrase Book	☐ Shopper's Guide to England, Scotland
(Fr/Ger/Ital/Sp in *one* vol.) $6.95	& Wales........................... $10.95
☐ Guide for the Disabled Traveler....... $10.95	☐ Swap and Go (Home Exchanging) $10.95
☐ How to Beat the High Cost of Travel ... $4.95	☐ Travel Diary and Record Book........ $5.95
☐ Marilyn Wood's Wonderful Weekends	☐ Urban Athlete (NYC sports guide) $9.95
(NY, Conn. Mass. RI, Vt, NJ, Pa) $9.95	☐ Where to Stay USA (Lodging from $3
	to $25 a night) $9.95

In U.S. include $1 post. & hdlg. for 1st book; 25¢ ea. add'l. book. Outside U.S. $2 and 50¢ respectively.

Enclosed is my check or money order for $_____

NAME_____

ADDRESS_____

CITY_____ STATE_____ ZIP_____